THE
FUNDAMENTAL CONCEPTS
OF PUBLIC LAW

By
WESTEL W. WILLOUGHBY

Social Justice
Examination of the Nature
of the State

THE
FUNDAMENTAL CONCEPTS
OF PUBLIC LAW

BY

WESTEL W. WILLOUGHBY

PROFESSOR OF POLITICAL SCIENCE, JOHNS HOPKINS UNIVERSITY; TAGORE
PROFESSOR OF LAW, 1923, UNIVERSITY OF CALCUTTA.

New York
THE MACMILLAN COMPANY
1924

Copyright, 1924,
By THE MACMILLAN COMPANY.

———

Set up and electrotyped.
Published September, 1924.

Printed in the United States of America by
J. J. LITTLE AND IVES COMPANY, NEW YORK

PREFACE

POLITICAL PHILOSOPHY is concerned with the essential characteristics of political life. Its inquiries fall within two well defined categories. Upon the one hand it is juristic, having to deal with the State when regarded as an instrumentality for the creation and enforcement of law; upon the other hand it essays to establish upon firm ethical grounds the propriety of the coercion of individuals viewed as autonomous moral beings. In a volume which the author expects to publish in the near future the various questions relating to the ethical right of the State to exist and the legitimate extent of its authority will be discussed. In the present volume will be considered only those fundamental concepts which are employed by jurists in dealing with the State.

In Part One, the conclusions following from these fundamental concepts will be deductively determined. In Part Two the decisions of courts will be examined in order to ascertain the manner in which, and the extent to which, these primary assumptions and their logical consequences have been recognized and applied within the fields of constitutional and international law. By thus making more plain than has perhaps been previously done the processes of juristic thought within these fields it is hoped that the development of Public Law along consistent and coherent lines will be facilitated.

One point the author asks the reader to bear steadily in mind: that the doctrine of sovereignty that is developed in this study, is a purely juristic one, and, therefore, that the attribute of omnicompetence which is ascribed to the sovereign State in no way implies that the actual power of the State has no limits, or that those who influence or control the policies of the State may disregard the obligations which ethical justice and right impose. Care is taken in the body of the work to enter this caveat, but, because of its importance, it is also stated here.

Twenty-five years ago the author published a volume entitled *The Nature of the State*. From this essay a certain amount of material has been taken for use in the present volume. The substance of these pages was presented in 1923 to the students of the University of Calcutta in a course of lectures given by the author as Tagore Law Professor for that year.

CONTENTS

PART ONE

FUNDAMENTAL CONCEPTS

CHAPTER I.
THE PROVINCE OF POLITICAL PHILOSOPHY.

CHAPTER II.
JURISTIC POLITICAL PHILOSOPHY.

CHAPTER III.
THE VALUE OF JURISTIC POLITICAL PHILOSOPHY.

CHAPTER IV.
THE STATE AS A JURISTIC PERSON.

CHAPTER V.
STATE AND GOVERNMENT DISTINGUISHED.

CHAPTER VI.
THE TERMS NATION AND PEOPLE DEFINED.

CHAPTER VII.
TERRITORY AND PEOPLE AS CONSTITUTIVE ELEMENTS OF THE STATE.

CHAPTER VIII.
SOVEREIGNTY.

CHAPTER IX.
THE SITUS AND MODES OF EXERCISE OF SOVEREIGNTY; CONSTITUTIONAL AND PURE JURISTIC THEORY DISTINGUISHED.

CHAPTER XIV.

THE UNITED STATES OF AMERICA.

CHAPTER XV.

NON-SOVEREIGN BODIES-POLITIC.

CHAPTER XVI.

LAW AND SOVEREIGNTY AS ENVISAGED BY INTERNATIONAL LAW.

CHAPTER XVII.
THE CONCEPT OF THE STATE IN INTERNATIONAL LAW.

PART TWO.

FUNDAMENTAL CONCEPTS APPLIED

CHAPTER XVIII.
TERRITORIAL JURISDICTION.

CHAPTER XIX.
PERSONAL JURISDICTION.

CHAPTER XX.
DE FACTO AND DE JURE GOVERNMENTS.

TABLE OF CASES

PART ONE
FUNDAMENTAL CONCEPTS

CHAPTER I

The Province of Political Science. Political Science, using the term in its broadest sense, has for its purpose the ascertainment of political facts and the arrangement of them in systematic order as determined by the logical and causal relations which exist between them. These political facts, which include both objective phenomena and the subjective forces which create them or fix their functional activities, are those which relate to the State; and by a State is understood a group of human individuals viewed as an organized corporate community over which exists a ruling authority which is recognized as the source of commands legally and, in general, ethically, binding upon the individuals composing the community.[1] The qualifying adjective, political, may, therefore, be applied to all matters which relate to the origin and history of the State, to its governmental organization, its activities, its aims, its administrative methods, its legitimate sphere of authority, and to its very right to exist. Furthermore, inasmuch as the State may be viewed as comprehending within itself all types of organizations legally subordinate to itself, Political Science is concerned with political authority in all its forms of manifestation,—with inferior as well as with sovereign bodies politic, and with primitive and undeveloped types of public life as well as with those of the modern

[1] This, of course, is a merely provisional or general definition of a State. Its more precise definition will be the outcome of the discussions contained in this volume.

civilized world. These phenomena it deals with descriptively, historically and comparatively, and with regard to all the circumstances, objective and subjective, which condition their existence or activities.

State and Society Distinguished. An aggregate of human individuals, united by a mutuality of interests and by what has been termed a "consciousness of kind" is termed a Society. Such a group thus has a certain psychological unity, and possesses, in a measure at least, to use Rousseau's terminology, a *volonté générale* as distinguished from a *volonté de tous*. When, for the realization of its common interests through the united efforts of its members, this group comes to have a more or less definitely organized existence, and possesses definite organs for the expression of its corporate will, and when there is a recognition by the individual members of the group of a general obligation upon their part, moral and legal, to obey the expressions of this will as thus disclosed, and, therefore, an admission of the right of the ruling authority to enforce its commands by physical or other sanctions, the group takes on a political character. The social body becomes a body-politic and, as such, is brought within the purview of Political Science.

Whether or not the term "State" should be employed only as designating political entities possessing supreme legal authority or sovereignty is a question later to be discussed. For the present it is sufficient to say that a political group is one which is itself a State, an integral part of a State, or a group the members of which are united by some common purpose which directly relates to the conduct or administration of a State. Integral parts of a State include all corporate groups of individuals or instrumentalities created by a State for the government or administration of its territorial divisions, such as colonies and dependencies, member commonwealths of a federation, and the less autonomous administrative or local government units. Associations or leagues of sovereign States constitute, of course, political groups. Under the third class of bodies-politic as enumerated above may be grouped political parties and insurrectionary and revolutionary organizations. In so far as a group of individuals place themselves in armed opposition to the laws of the land in which they are, they become, as such, subjects of distinctively political interest, since their actions are directed against the integrity and administrative efficiency of the existing ruling political organization. Such groups are not, however, political groups when that which unites their individual members is merely resistance to existing law without the effort or desire upon their part to nullify the law in its general application. It is only when it is their aim to overthrow the existing political authority and to establish a new one in its place, or to bring to a standstill the operation of the existing government with reference to certain of its policies, that the group takes on, strictly speaking, a political character. Thus a band of brigands, although well organized, is not a political group, while a body of individuals seeking by their concerted efforts to bring about the overthrow of the existing government or to transfer their fealty and allegiance to another State, is to be so termed.

The distinction between a political group and a non-political group is, therefore, that, in the one, a public, and in the other, a private end is sought. At times it may be difficult to determine whether individuals who are refusing obedience to existing law are to be treated simply as a body of law-breakers, or as a revolutionary and therefore political group. Though this fact may not be one that is easy of determination, the distinction between the two is sufficiently clear, and is one which is substantially similar to that which the courts have some-times to draw between acts which constitute treason as defined in the United States Constitution and those which do not.[2]

Organized political parties which are formed in States whose governments are more or less subject to popular control play an important part in the determination and execution of the policies of those States. Strictly or legally speaking, these party machineries are not parts of the States' governments. In certain respects they may be subject to legal regulation, but, from their very nature, as determined by the functions which they exercise, they are organizations voluntarily established and maintained by their adherents. Though thus not a part of the gov-ernment, their aim is to obtain control of the government in order that the public policies which their respective members support may be carried into effect. Their pur-pose is thus primarily political, and the study of their forms of organization, their activities and their modes of operation is an important and legitimate branch of Political Science.

The Science, the Art, and the Philosophy of Politics Dis-tinguished. In the preceding paragraphs the term Science as contained in the title "Political Science" has been used in a general sense as carrying with it no other meaning than that of systematic and logical treatment of matters of a political character. Within the field of inquiry thus comprehensively marked out there is room

---

[2] In the case of *United States v. Mitchell* (2 Dallas 343), it was held by the federal Supreme Court that a gathering of armed men, the object of which was to suppress the excise offices and to prevent by force and intimidation the execution of an act of Congress, was a levying of war, that is, an attack upon the integrity of the government itself and, as such, constituted a treasonable organization. Upon the other hand, it was held, in the case of *United States v. Hoxie* (Paine, 265), that if the resistance to the law had no public purpose in view, treason was not committed however great might be the amount of force employed. *Cf.* Willoughby, *Constitutional Law of the United States*, vol. I, p. 443.

for a Science, in the narrower sense of the word, as well
as for an Art and for a Philosophy of Politics.

In this narrower sense of the word, that is, as contrasted with an Art or Philosophy, the Science of Politics
seeks an accurate description and classification of political
institutions, and the precise determination of the forces
which create and control them. It thus satisfies the
definition of Science as "knowledge gained and verified
by exact observation and correct thinking, especially as
methodically formulated and arranged in a rational
system."[3]

The Art of Politics. The Art of Politics, as distinguished from its Science, has for its aim the determination of the principles or rules of conduct which it is necessary to observe if political institutions are to be efficiently
operated. How precisely and specifically these rules can
be laid down as regards the precepts contained in them,
or how general their applicability as regards time, place
and people, can be declared to be, is a question that must
be answered in each individual case. Certainly, because
of the extraordinary variety of conditioning circumstances
that may exist, it is not possible to create an Art of
Statesmanship as complete and specific as is possible in
the case of arts founded upon data collected in the fields
of the so-called exact or experimental sciences. But
that the Political Scientist can furnish the information
upon which sound advice can be based with regard to
the organization and operation of governments so that
they may efficiently realize the purposes for which they
are established and maintained, there can be no doubt.
Human thought would indeed be bankrupt if it were to
confess itself unable to raise the conduct of public affairs
above the plane of mere chance or of specific judgments
uncontrolled or uninfluenced by the conclusions reached

[3] *Standard Dictionary. verb.* "Science."

by the systematic study of political phenomena and forces.

Political Philosophy. When a Political Philosophy is spoken of, the word philosophy is not used in its metaphysical or epistemological sense, nor as indicating a synthesis of political conclusions in a sense analogous to that employed by Herbert Spencer when he designated his system of thought a Synthetic Philosophy—a *Scientia Scientiarium*. The only meaning attached to the word is that which it has when one speaks of the discussion of the essential characteristics of the material and phenomena of any particular branch of knowledge as its "philosophy." Political Philosophy, as thus understood, is abstract, but not hypothetical or visionary. It deals with generalizations rather than with particulars, and seeks to determine essential and fundamental qualities as distinguished from accidental or unessential characteristics. Though abstract and theoretical, its results are precise, and, indeed, furnish the basis for exact political thinking.

Juristic and Ethical Political Philosophy Distinguished. Surveying the general domain of Political Theory or Philosophy, it is found that the field is divisible into two areas sharply distinguishable from each other. In the one area the aim is to determine the nature of the State as the creator and enforcer of positive law, that is, as regarded by Public Law. As thus viewed, the inquiries are wholly juristic, and, as will later appear, formalistic in character. In the other department of political speculation, the nature and sphere of authority of the State is sought to be ascertained in the light of the purposes for the realization of which it exists. This branch of political theory may therefore be termed Ethical or Final Political Philosophy. It defines the State in terms of its ends and essays to determine what its activities and organization should be in the light of those ends.

In the present volume, as stated in the Preface, the State will be juristically considered, that is, as a concept of Public Law. In a companion volume shortly to be issued the principles of Ethical Political Philosophy will be examined.

CHAPTER II

THE State which, in its manifold activities and forms of organization, furnishes the material for Political Science may be regarded from a number of viewpoints. It may be studied sociologically as one of the factors, as well as one of the results, of communal life; it may be examined historically for the purpose of ascertaining the part which it has played in the life of humanity, its varying phases of development being traced and their several causes and results determined; it may be considered as an entity to the existence and activities of which are to be applied the ethical criteria which the moralist and philosopher establishes; it may be psychologically surveyed in order to make plain the manifestations of will, emotion and judgment which support and characterize its life; it may be regarded from the purely practical standpoint to determine how it may be most efficiently organized and operated; and, finally, it may be envisaged and studied by the analytical jurist simply as an instrumentality for the creation and enforcement of law.

Aim of Analytical or Juristic Political Philosophy. Juristic political philosophy, then, has for its purpose the determination of the nature of the State as an organization for the creation and enforcement of law. As thus limited, the inquiry is not concerned with political policies, whether from the ethical or the practical point of view. The practical phases of political rule do not fall,

10

except incidentally, within the sphere of its theory, and ethical aspects, as has been said, will receive discussion in another volume.

Considered negatively, it will be found that analytical political theory is not curious regarding the historical origin of political authority among men, nor of the historical circumstances surrounding the birth of any particular sovereignty. It does not inquire as to the ethical right of the State to exist, nor as to its ethically legitimate sphere of authority, nor concerning the purposes which political government may be made to subserve, nor as to the elements which go to increase or diminish the strength and importance of a given State. It is indifferent to all questions as to the relative merits of different forms of government or of different administrative systems. It takes political institutions as it finds them, and views them in a single aspect, namely, as legal institutions, and, as thus viewed, seeks to ascertain the essential qualities exhibited by them.

The point of departure of the analytical jurist is, that, in all communities which have reached any degree of definite political organization, public affairs, whether domestic or international, are not carried on in a haphazard manner, without system or fixed principles, but are governed by bodies of rules logically related to one another, and all depending, as deductive conclusions, upon certain assumptions regarding the juristic nature of the State, of its sovereignty, of its law, and of the relations which it bears towards other bodies-politic similarly viewed.

It is thus seen that juristic political theory is a purely formalistic inquiry. Its task is not to seek substantive truth, but to provide conceptions, and to furnish an apparatus of thought, by the employment of which public law thinking may be systematized and its various propositions brought, if possible, into logical harmony with one another. By the methods which it employs, a given constitutional system may be analyzed and the fundamental conceptions, upon which it is based, revealed. Or, working in the other direction, these fundamental conceptions being given, the constitutional doctrines which are logically deducible from them may be stated.

Constitutional Theory. The relation of such an abstract or generalized body of juristic concepts or doctrines,—of a system of *Allgemeine Staatslehre,* to use a German term,—to particular systems of constitutional jurisprudence of individual States, needs a word of discussion.

Every constitutionally developed State, through accepting and employing the concepts which this *Allgemeine Staatslehre* supplies, adds to them special premises of its own, especially as regards the source whence the right of rulership is conceived to be derived: And, of course, each constitutional system has its own special doctrines as regards the organs of government that are to exist, and the legal powers that are to be severally allotted to them.

Viewed in the abstract, the constitutional theory in accordance with which a given government is operated cannot be said to be either true or false. Such an inquiry is meaningless, for, being purely formalistic, a constitutional theory may start with any premises which it is deemed useful to assume. The logical consistency with which these premises are applied, or their applicability to given facts for purposes of interpretation, may be put in issue, but, viewed simply as creations of analytical jurisprudence, an attempt to examine their abstract validity would be as devoid of meaning as it would be to question whether it is correct to use "X" or "Y" to indicate the unknown quantity in an algebraic expression.

In short the application of a constitutional theory may be analytically or juristically questioned, but not the abstract validity of the theory itself. Thus, to illustrate, Prussian constitutional law, until 1918, was founded upon the premise that all legal authority is derived directly or indirectly from the King as its *fons et origo,* and, from this juristic premise, important principles of constitutional practice were deduced. Other constitutional systems, the American, French, or Belgian, for example, are founded upon the doctrine that all political right and all legal legitimacy may be traced back to a delegation of authority by the governed, or by a substantial portion of them, and from this premise also important practical deductions are made. These deductions it would be impossible to justify upon the basis of the older German constitutional theory, as it would be to explain former German public law by assuming the fundamental theory of the French, the Belgians, or the Americans; but it would be meaningless to assert that the one premise is juristically correct and the other one false.

Back of these conceptions of analytical jurisprudence there exist doctrines regarding the ethical or utilitarian right of the State to exist, the relation of its commands to the precepts of morality, and convictions as to the wisdom of centralizing or decentralizing political authority. The validity of these conceptions may be open to question. But, it is to be again emphasized, so long as we are dealing merely with the concepts of analytical jurisprudence, we are in a field where only formalistic criteria apply.

International Jurisprudence. What has been said in the preceding paragraph with reference to constitutional concepts, applies with equal force in the field of international jurisprudence. Here, too, an analytical examination of the generally accepted principles of the relations of one State to another shows that they are founded upon certain primary conceptions as to the juristic nature of States viewed as the "subjects" of international law— certain conceptions, that is, as to their equality of status and the rights and powers connoted by their existence as severally independent political entities. Thus, for example, there was adopted, on January 6, 1916, at the first session of the American Institute of International Law, a Declaration of the Rights and Duties of Nations. This declaration claimed to state the premises upon which an enlightened and beneficent system of international jurisprudence might be erected. The propriety of such a declaration cannot be questioned. Whether or not the statements of fact contained in the preamble prefixed to the Declaration are correct, or the rights and duties defined by the Declaration are such as conform to present usage, or, if not, whether they are such as it is desirable to have generally recognized, are questions that may properly furnish subjects for discussion. Also, of course, it is proper that the logical inter-consistency of these propositions should be examined. But it would be a fruitless inquiry to attempt to determine whether or not, as purely abstract propositions, they are true or false.

Summary. To state once again the fundamental character of juristic or analytical political philosophy, it is seen that it does not attempt the statement of metaphysically correct propositions. The essential juristic qualities which it predicates of the State, whether viewed from the standpoint of constitutional or of international law, are not supposed to correspond to substantive qualities which, ontologically speaking, inhere in the State and in Law. This does not mean, however, that the original postulates of the analytical political philosopher should be arbitrarily selected. As a mere matter of deductive achievement it might be possible to start with certain wholly arbitrary assumptions regarding the juristic nature of the State, of Law, and of political institutions generally, and, upon them, by a rigorous application of the deductive method, to elaborate a complete system of public law, constitutional and international, which, while logically perfect, would have little relation to, or consonance with, the principles actually recognized at the present time by States in their domestic or international affairs. But, as does not need to be pointed out, if analytical political philosophy is to have any practical value, and is not to remain a mere exercise of speculative subtlety, it must explain and reduce to logical order the propositions of international and constitutional jurisprudence that are found in existing systems of public law. The task of analytical political philosophy, thus, though a deductive one, is one that, in a measure, may most profitably be worked back from conclusions to premises. What has to be done is to fix upon those primary legal conceptions of the State, of law and of sovereignty (if such can be found), which will serve to give unity and logical support to systems of constitutional and international jurisprudence as we now find them.

This task might be thought an impossible one for the reason that the specific principles of public law which now prevail have been adopted from time to time in order to meet current political needs, and, therefore, cannot be expected to be logically inter-consistent and uniformly in harmony with fixed underlying principles. In fact, however, as it is hoped Part Two of this volume will show, there has been an acceptance of fundamental ideas which have been applied with remarkable consistency. The terminology, however, has frequently been faulty and loosely used, and some confusion has been caused by the failure to distinguish with sufficient sharpness the conception of the State as employed in constitutional law, from its conception as implicit in international law, with the result that certain technical terms, such as "law" and "sovereignty" have been made to do service in both fields, whereas the ideas which they have connoted in the two domains have been by no means the same. It is the fact that there has been this confusion of ideas and misuse of terms that has led the author, in the present treatise, to endeavor to give to the concepts of public law a greater precision than, in the past, they have ordinarily received. In order to do this, it will be found that it has been necessary to give to certain terms commonly employed by the political scientist meanings somewhat more restricted than those that are usually attached to them. But, in order that accurate thinking may be had, this could not be avoided.

Idea and Concept of the State. It is to be observed that the abstract juristic conception which will be given to the State, being one of purely legal significance, is not that notion which is sometimes termed by German writers the *Staatsidee.* Thus, for example, Brie, in his *Theorie der Staatenverbindungen* uses the term to express the ideally perfect State, that is, one possessing and itself directly exercising all the powers that properly belong to a State, rather than the general or universal idea of the State as we have above described it. He says: "Concrete States are ever more or less incomplete pictures of the *Staatsidee,* in that they do not themselves possess and exercise all the powers that logically belong to them."[1]

Professor Burgess likewise makes a distinction between what he calls the "Idea" and the "Concept" of the State. He says: "The idea of the State is the State perfect and complete. The concept of the State is the State developing and approaching perfection. From the standpoint

[1] *Op. cit.,* p. 6.

of the idea, the State is mankind viewed as an organized unit . . . From the standpoint of the concept, it is a particular portion of mankind viewed as an organized unit. From the standpoint of the idea the territorial basis of the State is the world, and the principle of unity is humanity. From the standpoint of the concept, again, the territorial basis of the State is a particular portion of the earth's surface, and the principle of unity is that particular phase of human nature and of human need, which, at any particular stage in the development of that nature, is predominant and commanding. The former is the real state of the perfect future. The latter is the real State of the past, the present, and the imperfect future." [2]

Bluntschli, also, says: "The conception (*Begriff*) of the State has to do with the nature and essential characteristics of actual States. The idea (*Idee*) of the State presents a picture, in the splendor of imaginary perfection, of the State as not yet realized, but to be striven for."[3] Continuing, Bluntschli goes on to declare that the *Idee* of the State is the World State.

Whatever difference of meaning there may be to the Germans between *Begriff* and *Idee*, the terms *conception* and *idea* do not, in English, mark the distinction between the actual and the ideal. Whether or not one be a product of the understanding and the other of reason, neither, in our tongue, is synonymous with the ideal. Furthermore, both Bluntschli and Burgess assume, without attempt at proof, that a universal State is the ideal to be striven for. As a matter of fact this may be denied, and even these writers would, it is imagined, admit that universality, desirable though they may think it to be, is but one of the many qualities that would be required

---

[2] *Political Science and Comparative Constitutional Law,* vol. I, p. 49.
[3] *The Theory of the State* (Eng. transl.), p. 15.

in a perfectly organized and administered State. Surely
they would not consider ideal a universal State whose
rulers are unenlightened, corrupt, and oppressive to those
whom they govern.

CHAPTER III

Complexity of Modern Political Conditions. The description which has been given of the sphere and aim of analytical political philosophy has been sufficient to indicate, in general, the value of the results which may be obtained from its pursuit. It but remains to refer to the peculiar need which political scientists have for this analytical inquiry as a preparation for scientific discussion because of the unfortunate fact that political science lacks a characteristic nomenclature. Instead of employing terms which are peculiar to itself, and, therefore without other connotations, political science is obliged to rely in very large measure upon terms which are in popular, and therefore unscientific, use. For this reason it is indispensable to precise political thinking that, when these terms are used, a clear understanding should be had as to the exact meanings attached to them. This need is one which, rather than decreasing, is constantly increasing by reason of the growing complexity of political relations whether regarded from the national or international point of view. With the development of constitutional forms of government operating under written instruments of government, with the growth of more or less autonomous local administrative or governmental organs, with the recognition of spheres of private rights of life, liberty, and property which are not open to legislative or executive control, and with the growth of the activities of government, the complexity of con-

19

stitutional jurisprudence is increased, with a resulting necessity for clearly and finely drawn distinctions, which, under more autocratic forms, such as absolute monarchy, do not need to be made.

So, similarly, in the field of international politics, modern times have witnessed the development of complex relations, which, for their juristic analysis demand the utmost exactness in the use of terms, and the most accurate employment of the processes of deductive reasoning.

At the same time that the principles of international law, through the practice of nations and the efforts of commentators, have been rendered fairly definite and systematized, and the formal rights and duties of sovereign States toward one another have thus, in the main, been made evident, the application of these principles and the determination in concrete cases of these rights and duties, have been made more difficult than before by the great increase in the complexity of constitutional and international relations which has marked the last century, and, especially, the last quarter of it. Instead of a family of nations composed of members completely autonomous in fact, as well as in name, we find nations, severally sovereign in name and theory, in some instances associated in the closest of constitutional bonds, and, in others, surrendering up the enjoyment of their international rights in whole or in part to alien powers. In some cases, indeed, this surrender has extended to the exercise of domestic powers as well. In the middle ages, the feudal state was the prevailing type, and, in the early modern age, the absolute monarchy. At the present time, however, we find many instances of the composite or federated form. In Europe we have the federal states of Germany and Switzerland, and, until 1918, the dual empire-kingdom of Austria-Hungary. Australia and

Canada are federated bodies, and, in the Americas, we have the federal states of the United States, Mexico, Brazil, Argentine and Venezuela. Each of the greater powers of the world has, within comparatively recent years, established political interests over the less developed peoples of Asia, Africa and the Pacific Islands. Where these political interests have taken the definite colonial form international conditions have not been greatly complicated; but where, as has been the case in so many instances, these interests have arisen, not out of the formal subjection of the territories in question to the sovereignty of the powers claiming the interest, but from treaties providing for the establishment of a protectoral relation, or for the lease for a number of years of a particular tract of land, or, still more definitely, the setting up of simply a "sphere of interest," or, most extreme of all, the lease of a sphere of interest,—a host of novel international problems have been born for the solution of which, in most cases, only purely political theory is competent.

Juristic Complexities of the League of Nations. The establishment of a League of Nations carrying with it a system of mandatories, raises still other intricate questions of public jurisprudence. In his recent address before the American Bar Association, Ex-Secretary of State Lansing, referring especially to the proposed system of mandatories, pointed out that, while simple in principle and application, it is a novelty in political authority which, the more it is studied from the legal standpoint, the greater the number of problems it presents. Continuing, he said:

"The determination of the possession of the sovereignty over territory is essential to the determination of international rights and obligations. In the case of territory subject to a mandatory the question therefore arises as to who possesses the sovereignty of such territory. Certainly not the mandatory which derives its authority solely from an agreement conferring upon it a limited exercise of sovereign rights. Is it, then, the League of Nations which possesses the full sovereignty, the exercise of which is delivered in part only to an agent or trustee? That would seem to be the logical answer, and yet consider the questions which that answer raises. Does the League of Nations possess the attributes of an independent State so that it can function as the possessor of sovereignty over territory? Is the League then a supernational World-State clothed with world sovereignty? If the League possesses the sovereignty can it avoid responsibility for the misconduct of its agent, the mandatory? If the League is not capable of possessing sovereignty, then who does possess it, who is responsible for the acts of the mandatory; and upon what ultimate authority does the League base the issuance of a mandate? I might present a score of other questions of a similar nature which with those propounded will have to be definitely answered sometime if the mandatory system comes into operation. Today these questions are academic and may be considered technical and no doubt by many are so considered, but it may not be long before they become concrete and very practical. It is not an overstatement to say that nine-tenths of all international controversies arise over questions pertaining to the possession of sovereignty and the conflict of sovereign rights. I do not think that mandatories and the source of their authority can escape from the test of the legality of their exercise of sovereign rights. The system must be philosophically and logically worked out from the legal point of view or it will result in confusion."[1]

In this same address, Secretary Lansing went on to

---

[1] *Reports of the American Bar Association*, vol. XLIV (1919), p. 247.

observe that modern conceptions of national needs and corresponding rights would make it necessary to work out new fundamental principles upon which to base doctrines of international servitudes,—not the older recognized servitudes on land based upon expediency and mutual advantage, but upon the principle that a nation ought not, against its will, to be barred from access to the sea, "the common property and highway of mankind."

Still further, Secretary Lansing adverted to the difficulties inherent in bringing the German Emperor to trial for his personal responsibility in bringing about the Great War and for the acts of cruelty committed by the German armies in its prosecution—that is, difficulties involved in the creation of a competent tribunal, the determination of the law to be applied by it, and the enforcement of its judgment, without doing violence to accepted principles of international and municipal jurisprudence.

Aviation. Another new field of public law that has recently been created is that of jurisdiction of the air. The fundamental principles which are to govern the exercise of sovereign rights in the air by territorial Powers remain yet to be determined. They can be satisfactorily determined only by employing the methods of analytical political philosophy.

Enough has been said to show that present political conditions, international as well as constitutional, make it imperative that the connotations of such terms as sovereignty, suzerainty, half-sovereignty, protection, vassalage, allegiance, will have to be examined with a carefulness never before required. Among other problems it will be necessary to determine anew what powers and attributes are incidental to the possession of sovereignty; whether its existence is an infallible and necessary test of statehood; to what extent the exercise of its powers may be delegated without parting with its possession; the distinction between governments *de facto* and governments *de jure;* whether states may be created by international compact; whether the origin of political authority in general is susceptible of a juristic determination; and to what extent so-called international law is binding or is law at all *in sensu strictiore.*

Fallacies of Phrases. A collateral advantage which attends the pursuit of analytical philosophy is that it provides not only the intellectual training which enables, but the mental disposition which inclines, one to seek for the real meanings that lie back of current phrases and conceptions. Such training and disposition are especially valuable to those who live under a popular form of government. It is a fact upon which all political observers are agreed that a democracy is particularly prone to be influenced by broad generalizations and high-sounding words and phrases. The democratic Leviathan is a being whose actions are controlled as often by sentiment as by sense, and it eagerly seizes upon catchwords and aphoristic phrases with but slight reflection as to the meaning embodied in them. No one, for example, can doubt that Stephen A. Douglas obtained much support for his doctrine regarding slavery in the territories by endowing it with the seductive title "popular sovereignty." So, too, it is not unreasonable to believe that in the phrase "free silver" the word "free" had an influence other than that which its real meaning, as used in such connection, would legitimately give it. It was the pride of every republican Frenchman of that time that when he looked in his glass he could see reflected a portion of a king, forgetting, as some cynic has said, that he was at the same time the whole of a slave. Nor does the danger of being misled by mere words and expressions into false analogies and conclusions threaten the populace alone. It is one to which all of us are exposed, and it is only by the use of the philosophical method, which looks to essential nature rather than to mere appearance or name, that we are able to keep ourselves aright.

Thus it is one of the very first canons of analytical political philosophy that names are not conclusive of facts. Of a given political body the analytical political philosopher does not ask the name by which it is called: he seeks the extent of its powers and the legal sources of its authority. Nor does he look to prior historical facts for the determination of political essence. To him, sovereignty is a matter of fact, but not a fact that may be demonstrated by the historical conditions precedent to its establishment. It is a fact which has to be determined wholly by existing powers and competences, irrespective of the conditions out of which such powers and competences may have sprung. In the analysis of the federal state he does not feel himself precluded from further inquiry by the fact that the constitution expressly declares this or that organ or body to be sovereign; he determines where the supreme control is placed by the actual distribution of powers that is provided for. Mr. Bryce, in his "Impressions of South America," tells the story of a white man, who, when driven by urgent need to hire himself to a native chief, preserved his *amour propre* by stipulating in the contract that he should be called "boss" by his employer. In scientific political thought the fact that a thing is called by a certain name is not more conclusive as to actual legal character than was the title "boss" of the real status of the white man of Bryce's story. Yet it is a most common occurrence to find names used as conclusive arguments in political discussions.

Juristic Analysis Needed to Interpret History. It seems

scarcely necessary to call attention to the fact that, as
an interpreter of the past, analytical political philosophy
is of especial interest to students of American history.
The theories which have centered around the nature of
the Union established in 1789 have all of them depended
upon presuppositions as to the nature of sovereignty;
whether it could be alienated or divided, the tests by
which its existence might be determined, and the consequences logically deducible from the definitions given
to it. Much of this discussion was inconclusive because
of a failure to agree upon the juristic significance of the
facts regarding which there was no dispute. Had the
framers of the Constitution had a clear conception of
sovereignty as indivisible and as connoting supreme legal
omnipotence, the essential distinction between a national
state federally organized and a confederation of States
severally sovereign would have appeared, and, as a consequence, it may be presumed, an instrument of government would have drawn that would not have contained
in it the seeds of future secession and civil strife. But
whether this be so or not, it is certain that the acceptance
of the illogical and unworkable theory of a divided sovereignty unduly complicated the working of our federal
system and hindered the harmonious development of our
constitutional jurisprudence. That, despite the formal
acceptance of this theory, our national sovereignty has
been realized in the law and in fact was in very large
measure due to the fortunate chance that for more than
a generation we had at the head of our supreme judicial
tribunal a chief justice who had an adequate conception
of the requirements of our national life, and an appreciation of the corresponding spirit in which our fundamental
instrument of government should be interpreted. I refer,
of course, to Marshall, who exhibited his transcendent
abilities rather as a political philosopher than as a tech-

nical jurist. All of his chief opinions are almost wholly essays in political theory. This is evident from the fact that in them very rarely is a legal authority or precedent cited to sustain the reasoning employed or the conclusions reached.

Since Marshall's time, though references to previously decided cases abound in its written opinions, the *ratio decidendi* of the decisions of the United States Supreme Court has, in many of the more important cases been derived from principles established by pure political theory. Thus, to cite but two instances, in *United States v. Lee*[2] the right of a private citizen to recover possession of property held by a federal officer under authority of an unconstitutional executive order was sustained by basing it upon the principle, declared to be essential to the idea of a free and constitutional government, that no authority can be so high that an act by it, unauthorized by a valid law, can operate to divest the private citizen of a legal right. So also in *Texas v. White.*[3] the distinction between a State and its Government, a distinction emphasized by political theory, was seized upon by the court to enable it to assert the continuation of a State in the Union at the same time that the legitimacy of its government was denied. Finally, in the recent cases dealing with the constitutional rights of the inhabitants of our insular possessions, the decisions were based upon the purest of political theorizing regarding the nature of the rights enumerated in the first eight articles of amendment to the Constitution, and the essential character of the American federal system.

During the period of the Civil War and of the "Reconstruction" which followed, the necessity for clear analytical thinking in the field of constitutional jurisprudence

[2] 106 U. S. 196.
[3] 7 Wallace 700.

was especially evident. Starting with the theory upon which the war was waged by the Northern party, the validity of the ordinances of secession and the status of the seceding States, as well as of that of the Confederacy which they formed, had to be determined. The character of the governments of the Southern States and the validity of their acts, in both public and private law, had to be considered. The respective rights and liabilities of the loyal as well as of the disloyal inhabitants of those districts which were in rebellion demanded determination in the civil and criminal courts. The status of Southern property and the powers of confiscation by our congress had to be fixed. In addition, a host of international problems arose for settlement. Aside from these, there were the questions which arose out of the so-called war powers—questions as to their actual scope, and as to the extent to which their exercise lay, respectively, with Congress or with the President. After the close of the war the necessity of reconstructing the governments of the States lately in rebellion involved problems still more perplexing. Was their rehabilitation as members of the federal union to be based upon the "conquered territory" theory of Stevens, upon the "state suicide" theory of Sumner, the "forfeited rights" or the "full rights" theory? The confusion of thought which reigned supreme during these years bears eloquent testimony to the absence of true principles of juristic political philosophy.

CHAPTER IV

THE STATE AS A JURISTIC PERSON

THE State appears as the central concept in two distinct spheres of juristic thought: in International Law, which is concerned with the relations of States to one another; and in Municipal Law, which has to deal with the relations between the State and its own citizens or subjects. It will be found that the State, as a concept of International Jurisprudence, has a connotation different from that which it has as a concept of Municipal Law. By most writers this has not been sufficiently recognized, and not a little confusion in political thinking can be traced to this fact. Especial effort has been made in the present volume to avoid this error.

The science of Municipal Law is divisible into two main parts; the one, known as Private Law, which has to deal with the juristic relations which the State establishes or enforces for regulating the relations of individuals to one another; the other, known as Constitutional Law, which is concerned with the political organization of the State and the allotment of powers to its several governmental organs, and, therefore, with the direct relations of the State to its own citizens or subjects.[1]

In the chapter entitled "Positive Law," the conceptual relation of the State to Private Law will be considered. In the present and immediately following chapters we

[1] In what sense a corpus of Administrative Law, as distinct from Constitutional Law upon the one side and from Private Law upon the other side, may be said to exist is a matter which requires special discussion, which, however, will not be attempted in this volume.

shall be exclusively concerned with the State as a concept of Constitutional Law. In this inquiry the task will be to obtain that juristic idea of the State which will best serve to give logical consistency to the bodies of principles which, in all politically developed communities, determine the form and define the power of their several governments.

For this inquiry two starting points are conceptually possible. The State may be viewed as an agency for the interpretation and enforcement of rules of human conduct which, in whole or in part, are not created by itself, but which are regarded as brought into being by some other agency,—by custom, by popular approval, or by divine establishment, or as binding by reason of some inherent virtue or force ascribed to the principles or rules of conduct which they declare; or the State may be conceived of as itself the sole source of legality, the *fons et origo* of all those laws which condition its own actions and determine the legal relations of those subject to its authority. This second concept is the one adopted in this treatise, not because it is not logically possible to construct a system of jurisprudence upon the other conception as a basis, but because the author is convinced that what has come to be known as the "positive" conception of law and of the State is the one which can be most consistently applied, and which, in fact, most readily interprets the various systems of constitutional jurisprudence that now exist in the world. It will be found, however, that in thus ascribing to it exclusive and omnipotent legal competence, the State, as a juristic entity, is sharply distinguished from its Government as well as from those who have control of the Government, and also from the *civitas* or body of persons subject to its legal authority.

A political body has already been defined as a group

of individuals possessing a definite organization in the nature of a governing authority which is recognized as having the authority to issue commands which are legally binding upon individuals, and, presumably, enforceable when necessary by the collective strength of the group. What special characteristics, whether of sovereignty or of less autonomous and inherent powers, must be possessed in order that, in the strictest sense of the word, a political body may be termed a State, will receive later consideration. But, for the purpose of this chapter, we shall deal with the legally supreme, or sovereign, state.

An organized group of individuals, thus viewed as a political unit, may be regarded from several standpoints, and, as viewed from each of them, be termed a State. Thus, considered collectively, the individuals who constitute the group may be said to form or to be the State. In this sense the *civitas,* or citizen body, or body-politic, is said to constitute the State, concretely or substantially viewed. Or, still regarded as a concrete or substantive being, the State is said to be the people and their government, together with the territory over which their primary and paramount political jurisdiction extends. Or, finally, the State may be regarded from an abstract point of view as an entity or concept of juristic thought. As thus viewed the State is spoken of as a Person. This envisagement of the State as a legal person is perhaps the central concept of juristic political thinking and it will therefore be necessary to examine with some degree of care the exact sense in which this idea is employed. And, in order to do this, we shall have first to consider the meaning attached by the jurist, in general, to the term Person.

Legal Personality. It is unfortunate that the word Person as a technical term, should have found lodgement in jurisprudence, for the idea connoted by it is quite distinct from the meaning attached to it by the moralist or psychologist, and, this difference not being steadily kept in mind, much confusion of thought has resulted.

To the moralist or psychologist a person is a living being, with reflective powers, capable of self-consciousness, that is, of conceiving of itself as an entity with interests and desires of its own, and with a continuous individuality distinct from that of other similar beings, of being able to exercise a will, and, therefore, to determine its conduct according to deliberate judgments, to appreciate distinctions between good and evil, and, as a result, to feel, or have imputed to it, a moral responsibility for all such acts as are within its own control.

This psychological and moralistic conception of a person as a being capable of reflection, judgment and volition, and to whom moral responsibility may be imputed, is of course of significance to the jurist in so far as he attempts to measure legal by moral rights and duties. This, however, relates to the substance of the law and not to its essential juristic character. To the jurist a law states a rule of conduct which, as made compulsory upon individuals, imposes upon them legal obligations, and, as guaranteeing to them conduct upon the part of other individuals or of the State itself, which the State, through its political power, will enforce, endows them with legal rights. Those beings or entities which the law recognizes as capable of possessing rights and obligations of this kind are termed Persons, and, when they make use of their legal powers, they are spoken of as exercising their legal will.

Things. Thus the jurist makes a fundamental distinction between a Person and a Thing. "A Thing is, in law, some possible matter of rights and duties conceived of as a whole and apart from all others, just as, in the world of common experience, whatever can be separately perceived is a thing."[2] It may be corporeal or incorporeal, tangible or intangible, but it is always, in the eyes of the law, something which can be brought into relation with Persons, that is, of interest to them in some way, and these interests, as defined and protected by the law, provide the substantial basis for the rights and duties which these persons possess or have laid upon them. Thus, the human individual who is a person in the psychological or ethical sense, and who, in other respects, may also be treated by the law as a legal person, may, at the same time, be treated as a thing when brought into relation to other legal persons. For example, a slave so far as he is treated as the property of his master, or a serf, so far as he is bound to serve his superior, is viewed as a thing. So also in a legal action to recover damages for injuries to a wife or child or apprentice, or to obtain possession of them if they are detained by someone else, the wife or child or apprentice is, *quoad hoc,* viewed as a thing. That is, the suit is instituted not in pursuance of a right of the wife or child or apprentice, but of the right of the husband, father, parent, or master.[3]

Persons. It is thus seen how technical is the use in jurisprudence of the term Thing. Similarly technical and formalistic is the legal conception of Person. Beings who in all other realms of thought, are spoken of as Persons may not be such in the eyes of the law, as, for example, in the case of a slave over whom his owner has full proprietary rights, and who has no rights which the law recognizes and which, at his instance, the State will enforce; and also, as we have just seen, beings who for many purposes are treated by the law as persons, may, in other

---

[2] Pollock, *First Book of Jurisprudence,* chap. VI.

[3] Sheldon Amos, *The Science of Law,* chap. VI. Holland (*Jurisprudence,* p. 83) defines a Thing as "the object of a right, that is, whatever is treated by the law as the object over which one person exercises a right, and with reference to which another person lies under a duty."

respects, be regarded as things. But, more than this
(and here we approach the sense in which the State is
spoken of as a person), what is ordinarily spoken of as a
thing, is often viewed by the law as a person, and rights
and duties attributed to it. Furthermore, this is done
not only with regard solely to tangible but also to intangible things, and to groups of individuals and things
regarded, for the purpose in view, as unities. Thus, all the
pieces of property of an estate may, as a matter of legal
convenience, be treated as a person, that is, be regarded as
possessing legal rights and as resting under legal obligations which can be determined and enforced by actions in
law brought by or against it as such. The same may be
done in the case of a particular fund of money.

When a legal personality is ascribed to a human being
he is spoken of as a natural person, which, it may be supposed, is a recognition of the fact that the individual is
also a person in a moral, or psychological sense. When
legal personality is attributed to what, in other than legal
respects is known as a thing, or when this personality
is held to attach to a group regarded as a unity or entity
distinct from its constituent members, and with legal
rights and duties distinct from those of these members,
the resulting legal person is spoken of as an artificial
person. In truth, however, the legal personality of the
so-called natural person is as artificial as is that of the
thing or group which is personified. In both cases the
character or attribute of personality is but a creation of
the jurist's mind,—a mere conception which he finds it
useful to employ in order to give logical coherence to his
thought.[4]

---

[4] One of the best discussions of the juristic conception of component
personality is that of Michoud. The word "person" as he properly says,
in juristic literature indicates an entity capable of possessing or having
imputed to it legal rights and obligations—"Le mot signifie simplement

Corporate Persons. The most important of the legal persons which are not also natural persons are what are known as Corporations. These, as is well known, are regarded by law as deriving their existence and legal rights and duties from the State which charters or incorporates them. Regarded as such entities, they may sue or be sued, hold property and enter into contractual relations in their own names, and maintain a continued existence independently of who may happen to own their shares or stock. Furthermore, for the most part, though not always, the law does not hold these shareholders individually responsible for its acts, nor upon the other hand, are their acts, as individuals, though joined in by them all, ordinarily held to be acts of the corporation. In these and other ways the personality of the corporation, as distinct from that of the individuals constituting it, is asserted and maintained. Thus we find the term Corporation defined by Black in his *Law Dictionary*, as follows:

"An artificial person or legal entity created by or under the authority of the laws of a state or nation, composed, in some rare instances, of a single person and his successors, being the incumbents of a particular office [the "corporation sole"], but ordinarily consisting of an association of numerous individuals who subsist as a body politic under a special denomination, which is regarded

un sujet de droit, un être capable d'avoir des droits subjectifs lui appartenant en propre,—rien de plus, rien de moins. Pour savoir si certains êtres répondent à cette définition, il ne faut donc pas examiner si ces êtres constituent des personnes au sens philosophique du mot. Il faut se demander seulement s'ils sont de telle nature que des droits subjectifs doivent leur être attribués. Indirectement sans doute, la notion de personnalité philosophique pourra influer sur celle de personnalité juridique. Nous montrerons plus loin que le législateur peut y trouver un motif pour donner à tout être humain la qualité de sujet de droit. Mais rien ne prouve a priori que les deux notions coïncident, et que cette qualité de sujet de droit ne puisse être appliquée à d'autres qu'à des hommes." (*La theorie de la personnalité morale*, vol. I, p. 7.)

in law as having a personality and existence distinct from that of its several members, and which is, by the same authority, vested with the capacity of continuous succession, irrespective of changes in its membership, either in perpetuity or for a limited term of years, and of acting as a unit or single individual in matters relating to the common purpose of the association, within the scope of the powers and authorities conferred upon such bodies of law."

The legal nature of the ordinary corporation has been dwelt upon because it is in exactly the same sense in which legal personality is attributed to it that the State, its creator, is conceived of by the analytical jurist as a person. Both are collectivities, both are regarded as the subjects of legal powers, that is, entities which possess and have the legal right to exercise these powers. In fundamental conception they are, as persons, identical in character. They differ only in respect to the extent of their powers and the legal source whence their powers are deemed to be derived. To the State as a person is imputed a legal omnicompetence and a will that is supreme. As thus legally omnicompetent and supreme the State's authority is regarded as an inherent one, that is, as underived from the legal will of any other legal person. The corporation,[5] upon the contrary, draws its legal life and powers from the State which charters or otherwise recognizes it as a body corporate. It is therefore neither supreme nor of unlimited legal competence. But, *in conceptu,* its personality is the same as that of the State. Hence it follows that by clearing up the idea of the corporation's personality we obtain at the same time an

[5] One of the classifications of legal corporations is that which groups them into public and private, the former being those which act as governmental agencies of the State. In the text, however, the term corporation has been employed to indicate all those bodies which owe their existence as legal persons to the State which charters or otherwise recognizes them as incorporated bodies.

understanding of the sense in which the State may properly be spoken of as a person.

It has been seen that, in the eyes of the jurist, a person is viewed as the subject, that is, the possessor of legal rights and duties. The fact that the State is viewed as itself the creator of its own legal rights and duties does not make this conception an illogical one. Especially will this appear when the nature of constitutional law is discussed, and the distinction between the State and its Government pointed out. It will also appear that all States permit themselves to be sued in the courts with reference to certain matters, that is, they are *quoad hoc* treated as persons who are obligated to satisfy legal claims in favor of the plaintiffs who are asserting their respective legal rights. Also, of course, all States appear as plaintiffs in civil as well as criminal causes against other juristic persons. When the State appears as the owner of property or as the directing head in industrial, commercial, or other economic enterprises its legal personality becomes, in most cases, and for nearly all practical purposes, the same as that of the juristic persons which it itself creates.

The legal personality of the State is, however, specially evident in its Public as distinguished from its Private Law. In so far as the rules of conduct that authoritatively obtain in a political community are devoted to the regulation of interests between individuals as such, they create only private rights and obligations, and the State appears only as their enunciator, and, if need be, their enforcer. Such law is therefore termed Private Law. Distinguished from this class of rules are those that concern either the organization of the State and the allocation and delimitation of the powers of government, or the direct relations between the State and the individual. These are termed Public Laws. In Private Laws, as

Holland points out, "the parties concerned are private individuals, above and between whom stands the State as an impartial arbiter. In Public Law also the State is present as arbiter, although it is at the same time one of the parties interested." [6]

The Juristic Person as Volitional. It has already been pointed out that when a juristic person exercises a legal right it is spoken of as expressing its will. In the case of a legal person who is also a natural person, that is, an individual human being, this expression of legal will is usually, though not always, also an expression of the person's will in a psychological sense. Sometimes, however, with regard to such persons, their legal wills are expressible only through other persons, as, for example, is the case when a guardian acts as the legal representative of his ward, or when the parent acts for his child, or in fact, in all those cases in which the natural person, though recognized as a juristic person, is not deemed by the law to be fully *sui juris*. In such cases, by a veritable fiction, the will of the representative is imputed to, or treated as though it were the will of the person whose legal rights are involved, just as, in cases of agency, in which no element of legal disability enters, the acts of the agent, when acting within the general sphere of his agency, are deemed to be the acts of his principal and to have been willed by him although they may in fact not have been in accordance with his psychological will. [7]

In all cases in which groups of individuals are treated as legal persons it is unavoidable that their respective legal wills should be expressed,—their legal rights exercised,—through agents, such as, for example, the boards of directors and other officers of corporations. In the case

---

[6] *Elements of Jurisprudence*, 6th ed., p. 117.

[7] There are many other instances, in all systems of law, in which a legal willing is imputed to one who, in an actual or psychological sense, has not willed at all.

of States there is the same necessity. Their legal wills are
expressed through their legislative or other policy-forming organs of government, and these legal volitions or
laws are carried into effect by their administrative and
judicial officials. When thus acting, the acts of these officials are deemed to be the acts of the State. Thus, as a
psychological proposition, the policies of a State are determined by the judgments of those particular individuals
who are recognized to have the legal right to speak the
will of the State. In those States in which the principle
is accepted that public policies should conform to the
will of the governed, the judgments of the persons who
actually determine the policies of the States are, by an
imputation which in all cases is, to a considerable extent,
and in some cases almost wholly, a fiction, deemed to
express the will of the whole citizen body. But, in any
and all cases, the substantive content of the will of the
State is necessarily determined by the judgment of
particular human beings. These individuals thus have, in
the eyes of the law, two distinct legal personalities. In
their private relations they are legal persons in the sense
that they possess legal rights and rest under legal obligations; in their public or official capacities they are mouth-
pieces or agents of the State, giving expression to its will,
and, within the limits of their official authority, enforcing
its commands. In all States enjoying what is termed constitutional government, the instant public officials exceed
the powers granted them by existing law, they no longer
speak or act for the State, and become legally responsible,
as private legal persons, for what they do. Only in the
case of the completely autocratic ruler is his official will
so discretionary that it is possible for him to maintain an
actual, if not a technical, identity between the substance
of his personal or psychological will and that of the legal
will of the State which he governs.

The State as a "Real" Person. In mediæval Canon Law the corporation was spoken of as a *persona ficta,* and this description, developed especially by Savigny in the first half of the nineteenth century, has been very generally followed by modern jurists. However, during recent years, there has arisen a school of writers, represented especially by Gierke in Germany and Maitland in England, who have insisted that this is an incorrect statement of fact, and that, instead, the corporation, and, indeed, all other groups of individuals which have a unity of purpose and interest, whether incorporated by the State or not, should be viewed as "real" persons.[8]

Maitland, in his introduction to his translation of a portion of Gierke's *Genossenschaftsrecht,* stating his conception of the "reality" of the personality of the corporation, says: "It is no fiction, no symbol, no piece of the State's machinery, no collective name for individuals, but a living organism and a real person, with body and members and a will of its own. Itself can will, itself can act; it wills and acts by the men who are its organs as a man wills and acts by brain, mouth and a hand. It is not a fictitious person; it is a *Gesammtperson,* and its will is a *Gesammtwille;* it is a group-person, and its will is a group-will."[9]

This theory of Gierke, as Maitland properly points out, and which he unreservedly accepts, is indissolubly connected with the ascription of a similar real personality to the State, and, he declares, the failure of mediæval theorists to grasp this idea of the State's personality was their central defect, and one which, if not now corrected, is likely to lead to evil consequences.

[8] The literature upon the nature of corporate personality is voluminous, but especial reference may be made to Varseilles-Sommières, *Les personnes morales;* Michoud, *La théorie de la personnalité morale;* and J. T. Carter, *The Nature of the Corporation as a Legal Entity.*
[9] *Political Theories of the Middle Ages,* p. xxvi.

Maitland predicts that English jurists will be compelled to accept this new doctrine thus introduced from Germany, but it would appear that this forecast is not likely to be verified. However, if the jurists have not followed his lead, other thinkers have to some extent done so. Thus we find Dr. Figgis eagerly urging the doctrine in order to give greater autonomy and dignity to associations within the State, and especially to the churches; and so-called "Guild Socialists" making use of the idea to reinforce their contention that "functional" groups of industrial workers should be permitted to determine for themselves the manner in which their respective occupations should be carried on.

Dr. Figgis' views are best set forth in his volume, *Churches in the Modern State,* published in 1913, in which he says:

"What really concerns us is not so much whether or no a religious body be in the technical sense established, but whether or no it be conceived as possessing any living power of self-development or whether it is conceived either as a creature of the State, or, if allowed a private title, is to be held rigidly under the trust-deeds of her foundation, thereby enslaved to the dead. . . . Does the Church exist by some inward living force, with powers of self-development like a person; or is she a mere aggregate, a fortuitous concourse of ecclesiastical atoms, treated it may be as one for purposes of convenience, but with no real claim to a mind or will of her own except so far as the civil power sees good to invest her for the nonce with a fiction of unity?"

This question, he properly points out, is not one with which the Church or the State is alone concerned. "Since, as a fact, religious bodies are only one class of a number of other societies, all having claim to this inherent life, it is clear that the question concerns not merely ecclesiastical privilege, but the whole complex structure of civil society and the nature of political union. . . . Are corporate societies to be conceived as real personalities or as fictitious ones, that is, is their union to be throughout of such a nature that it has a life greater than the mere sum of the individuals composing the body; that it is not merely a matter of contract; that in action it has the marks of mind and will which we attribute to personality; that this corporate life and personality grows up naturally and inevitably out of any union of men for permanent ends, and is not withheld or granted at the pleasure of the State. . . . It is, in a word, a real life and personality which those bodies are forced to claim, which we believe that they possess by the nature of the case, and not by arbitrary grant of the sovereign. To deny this real life is to be false to the facts of social existence, and is of the same nature as that denial of human personality which we call slavery, and is always in its nature unjust and tyrannical." [10]

Again, he says: "The State did not create the family nor did it create the Churches; nor even in any real sense can it be said to have created the club or the trades union; nor in the Middle Ages the guild or the religious order, hardly even the universities or the colleges within the universities; they have all arisen out of the natural associative instincts of mankind, and should all be treated by the supreme authority as having a life original and guaranteed, to be controlled and directed like persons, but not regarded in their corporate capacity as mere names, which for juristic purposes and for these purposes only are entitled persons. As a matter of fact, in England at least, it is these smaller associations which have always counted for most in the life of the individual. His school or college, his parish or county, his union or regiment, his wife

[10] *Op. cit.*, pp. 40-42.

or family is the most vitally formative part in the life of most men; and in so far as England has anything worthy in civic life to show to the world, it is this spectacle of individuals bred up or living within these small associations which mould the life of men more ultimately than does the great collectivity we call the State." [11]

It will be seen that the argument of Dr. Figgis and of those who agree with him is not to break down the legal supremacy of the State but to emphasize the point that, just as the State is a real person with its own independent life to lead and its own general ends to realize, so the other and smaller groups or associations within the body-politic have their independent lives to live and ends to realize, and that, therefore, this fact should be recognized by the State with the result that these other corporate personalities should be left to live and function within the respective spheres, thus marked out for them, free from the controlling direction of state law. "Of course," says Dr. Figgis, "the State may and must require certain marks, such as proofs of registration, permanence, constitution, before it recognizes the personality of societies, just as it does, though in a less degree, in the case of individuals; and the complex nature of the body may necessitate a more complex procedure. Also the State will have to regulate and control the relations of corporate individuals to one another and to natural persons. But all this does not and need not imply that corporate personality is the gift of the sovereign, a mere name to be granted or withheld at its pleasure; and that permanent societies can come into being and go on acting without it." [12]

Other writers, however, among whom may be especially mentioned Harold J. Laski, are not thus considerate towards the State. They would deny the legal supremacy

[11] *Idem,* p. 47.
[12] *Op. cit.,* p. 41.

of the State, and place all real *Gesammtpersonen* upon a plane of complete juristic equality, and thus introduce a veritable régime of political pluralism.

It is not convenient in the present work to examine in detail the views of Laski regarding the nature of the State's sovereignty, and it will be sufficient to say here that, for some reason or other, he persistently adds to the jurist's conception of sovereignty qualities which the jurist expressly excludes, and that it is upon the basis of this false definition that he denies to sovereignty that omnicompetence which jurists ascribe to it. Having as he thinks, thus stripped sovereignty of its absoluteness, he claims to show that the State is not the only group of individuals which can be said to be sovereign in character, but that, upon the contrary, it shares this quality, as well as that of real personality, with an indefinite number of other organized associations of men.

Criticism of the Doctrine of "Real" Personality. As has been the case in so many other long continued disputes, and as was indeed the case in the dispute between the mediæval nominalists and realists whose roots ran back to the differences between the metaphysics of Plato and Aristotle, the real trouble in the matter of group or state personality has been that the disputants have had different ideas in mind and, therefore, have not squarely met each other's contentions. Thus, those who have urged that a politically organized or otherwise united group of individuals should be viewed as real rather than as merely fictitious persons have had in mind the fact that, irrespective of their recognition by law as bodies corporate, they constitute real unities, something more than arithmetical sums of the individual human beings constituting them, the constitutive or creative principle or force producing this unity being the fact that the group, as such, has ends to be realized which are distinct from the ends of its individual members, distributively considered, as well as from the sum of those ends, and, furthermore, that there is a common consciousness upon the part of their members that they are integral members of the collectivity to which they belong, and that, only through the activity of this whole, can they secure the ends which they all desire. That, in this sense, group entities are real, and come into being irrespective of state action, and that incorporation by law is but a recognition by the political authority of conditions of fact which the State has had no part in creating, may be at once admitted. As one of the earlier, but still authoritative, American writers upon the law of corporations, Victor Morawetz, has said:

"The conception of a number of individuals as a corporate or collective entity occurs in the earliest stages of human development, and is essential to many of the most ordinary processes of thought. Thus, the existence of tribes, village communities, families, clans, and nations implies a conception of these several bodies of individuals as entities having corporate rights and attributes. An ordinary copartnership or firm is constantly treated as a united or corporate body in the actual transaction of business, though it is not recognized in that light in the procedure of the courts of law. So, in numberless other instances, associations which are not legally incorporated are considered as personified entities, acting as a unit and in one name; for example, political parties, societies, committees, courts." [13]

Quoting this paragraph another leading American jurist says: "All that the law can do is to recognize, or refuse to recognize the existence of this entity. The law can no more create such an entity than it can create a house out of a collection of loose bricks. If the bricks are put together so as to form a house, the law can refuse to

---

[13] *Private Corporations*, 2d ed., sec. 1.

recognize the existence of the house—can act as if it did not exist; but the law has nothing whatever to do with putting the bricks together in such a way that, if the law is not to shut its eyes to facts, it must recognize that a house exists and not merely a number of bricks. Hence, it follows that in recognizing the existence of a corporation as an entity, the law is merely recognizing an objective fact." [14]

However, recognizing to the full this group "reality" which comes into being independently of state action, and which may operate without recognition by the State's law, no admission is made which prevents the jurist from holding that, as a legal entity or person, no group can exist save as created or recognized by the State, that is, by its laws. Nor can anything but confusion of thought arise from failing to distinguish between this unity of psychological or social or economic fact and that legal unity or personality which the jurist ascribes to the State, and which the State, in turn, through its law, imposes upon, or ascribes to, individuals, groups of individuals, or even to things, such as a fund or an estate. In other words, this unity, or personality if one so wishes to call it of which writers like Gierke, Maitland, Figgis and Laski speak, is not a juristic attribute, and, therefore, its "reality," granting it to exist, cannot be attached to, or pasted upon, as it were, the juristic conception of personality. The two ideas do not fall within the same realm of thought. They are irrelevant to each other.

The question, then, whether or not groups of individuals which are united by common sentiments or material interests possess, by that very fact, a *real* personality in other than a juristic sense, is one that may be left to metaphysicians. We cannot, however, resist the temptation

[14] Arthur W. Machen, Jr., "Corporate Personality" in the *Harvard Law Review*, vol. XXIV, p. 253 (February, 1911). Mr. Machen is the author of a standard treatise on the law of private corporations.

to quote the point so well made by Professor Cohen, that, because a number of individuals find themselves united by the closest of common interests or opinions, there is no warrant for saying that a *thing,* much less a thing that has a life and will of its own and therefore entitled to be termed a *person,* has been brought into existence. However strong or intensive the unity that exists, it is, after all, a *relationship* and not a new entity or real thing that has been created. Professor Cohen continues: "The tendency to think of relations and operations as *things* is one of the most common sources of philosophic error. All are agreed that groups are characterized by some kind of unity, and the fundamental issue is whether this unity shall be viewed as an entity additional to the entities unified and of the same kind, or whether it shall be viewed for what it is, as just the unifying relation. The tendency to personify groups, ships, storms, debates, and everything else, is as old as human thought, and is in some measure unavoidable. For we must always depend on analogies, and personal analogies give our language a vividness without which our hearers may be entirely unmoved. But modern mathematical logic has taught us to avoid the old form of the issue between nominalism and (the older) realism by recognizing the relational character of unity, or at any rate to recognize the different types of unity. When any one oracularly informs us that the whole is more than the sum of its parts, we reply that that depends upon the meaning of the word *sum.* Of the things that can in any definable sense be added, the whole *is* just the *sum* of its parts and nothing else. . . . The history of philosophy from Aristotle to Bradley has fully shown the vicious infinite regress which follows when our substance becomes an additional quality, or when our unifying reality becomes an additional thing. When two persons are united in the marriage relation the unity is not in itself an additional person, though such unity makes possible many things which could not otherwise happen." [15]

[15] "Communal Ghosts and Other Perils in Social Philosophy," in the *Journal of Philosophy*, vol. XVI (1919), p. 673.

CHAPTER V

By the term "Government" is designated the organization through which the will of the State is formulated, uttered and executed. The distinction between the State and its Government is thus analogous to that between a given human individual, as a moral and intellectual person, and his material physical body. By the term State is understood the political person or entity which possesses the lawmaking right. By the term Government is understood the agency through which the will of the State is formulated, expressed and executed. The Government thus acts as the machinery of the State, and those who operate this machinery—the Magistracy—act as the agents of the State. They exercise, but do not possess, sovereignty; and the extent of their several legal powers is determined by the will of the State as expressed in its laws.

This distinction between the possession of sovereignty and its exercise is of fundamental importance as will later appear when the juristic nature of the Federal State, of the Confederacy and of other composite forms of State life is considered.

The State Wholly Organized in its Government. At all times the State is wholly organized in its Government. That is to say, the only way in which the State can operate is in and through its Government. This is true whether the State is expressing or executing its will with reference to a minor routine administrative matter, or

49

declaring its will with reference to questions of fundamental constitutional concern. Thus it may be that, as in the United States, certain organs of Government, such as constitutional conventions, are but seldom employed. But when they do function for the creation either of State or Federal Constitutional Law, they are as much parts of the Government as are any other of the permanent portions of the State's governmental system.

The only respect in which it may be said that a State acts outside of its Government is when it is conceived of as establishing that Government. As will later appear when the juristic origin of the State is examined, the State, though the source of law, is not, and cannot be conceived of as founded upon a pre-existing law. That is, every sovereign State starts *de novo,* and not by way of emanation from, or a creation of, another sovereignty. Therefore, it necessarily follows that its Government must also come into being as a spontaneous act of the State or of its People. When a Government is established by legal means, that is, by a process of constitutional amendment in accordance with the forms provided by existing constitutional law for its own amendment, the Government is, of course, not a new one, but the old one merely altered. If, however, a change in the form of Government is brought about by illegal or revolutionary means, however peaceably, a new Government régime is instituted which finds its basis in the original, spontaneous or directly sovereign act of the State or its People.

As comprehensively used, the Government of a State includes every political agency of the State down to the most minor local administrative organ. And, in a State such as the United States, which is conceded to possess the sovereignty, its Government may be said to embrace not only the federal governmental organs, but those of the individual member States including, of course, all of their local governmental agencies.

State and Government Distinguished by the United State Supreme Court. The distinction between State and Government, as well as that between the citizen body of a State and the State itself, frequently needs to be drawn in the courts as a matter of concern to municipal law, and it is constantly employed in international relations. This latter necessity will appear in later chapters in which the juristic concepts of international law are examined. As illustrating the need for making the distinction in national or constitutional law, may be quoted the language of the United States Supreme Court in two of its most important decisions.

In *Poindexter v. Greenhow*,[1] one of the Legal Tender Cases, the Court said:—

"In the discussion of such questions the distinction between Government of a State and the State itself is important and should be observed.

"In common speech and common apprehension they are usually regarded as identical; and as, ordinarily, the acts of the Government are the acts of the State (because within the limits of its delegation of power), the Government of the State is generally confounded with the State itself, and often the former is meant when the latter is mentioned. The State itself is an ideal person, intangible, invisible, immutable. The Government is an agent, and within the sphere of the agency, a perfect representative; but, outside of that it is a lawless usurpation. The Constitution of the State is the limit of the authority of its Government, and both Government and State are subject to the supremacy of the Constitution of the United States and of the laws made in pursuance thereof.

[1] 114 U. S. 270.

So that, while it is true, in respect to the Government of a State, as was said in *Langford v. U. S.* (101 U. S. 341) that the maxim that the King can do no wrong has no place in our system of Government, yet it is also true, in respect to the State itself, that whatever wrong is attempted in its name is imputable to its Government and not to the State. For, as it can speak and act only by law, whatever it does say and do must be lawful. That which, therefore, is unlawful because made so by the Supreme Law, the Constitution of the United States, is not the word or deed of the State but is the mere wrong and trespass of those persons who falsely speak and act in its name. It was upon the ground of this important distinction that this court preceeded in the case of *Texas v. White,* 7 Wall 700, when it adjudged that the acts of secession which constituted the Civil War of 1861 were the unlawful acts of usurping state governments and not of the States themselves, inasmuch as the Constitution, in all its provisions, looks to an indestructible union, composed of indestructible States, and that, consequently the war itself was not a war between States, nor a war of the United States against unlawful and usurping governments representing, not the States, but a rebellion against the United States. This is, in substance, what was said by Chief Justice Chase, delivering the opinion of the Court in *Thorington v. Smith,* 8 Wall, 1, 9, when he declared, speaking of the Confederate Government, that 'it was regarded as simply the military representative of the insurrection against the authority of the United States.' The same distinction was declared and enforced in *Williams v. Bruffy,* 96 U. S., 176, 192, and in *Horn v. Lockhart,* 17 Wall, 570, both of which were referred to and approved in *Keith v. Clark,* 97 U. S., 454, 465."

In *Texas v. White* [2], the leading case in which was

[2] 7 Wall 700.

considered the status of the Southern States during and immediately after the Civil War, the Supreme Court, speaking of the word "State," declared as follows:

"It describes sometimes a people or a community of individuals, united more or less closely in political relations, inhabiting temporarily or permanently the same country; often it denotes only the country or territorial region, inhabited by such a community; not infrequently it is applied to the Government under which the people live, at other times it represents the combined idea of people, territory and Government.

"It is not difficult to see that in all these senses the primary conception is that of a people or community. The people, in whatever territory, dwelling, either temporarily or permanently, and whether organized under a regular Government or united by looser or less definite relations, constitute the State. . . .

"In the Constitution the term 'State' most frequently expresses the combined idea just noticed of people, territory and Government. A State, in the ordinary sense of the Constitution, is a political community of free citizens, occupying a territory of defined boundaries, and organized under a Government sanctioned and limited by a written constitution, and established by the consent of the governed. It is the union of such States, under a common constitution, which forms the distinct and greater political unit, which that Constitution designates as the United States and makes of the people and States which compose it one people and one country.

"The use of the word in this sense hardly requires further remark. In the clauses which impose prohibitions upon the States in respect to the making of treaties, emitting of bills of credit and laying duties on tonnage, and which guarantee to the States representation in the House of Representatives and in the Senate, are found some instances of this use in the Constitution. Others will occur to every mind.

"But it is also used in the geographical sense, as in the clauses which require that a representative in Congress shall be an inhabitant of the State in which he shall be chosen, and that the trial of crimes shall be held within the State where committed.

"And there are instances in which the principal sense of the words seem to be that primary one to which we have adverted, of a people or political community as distinguished from a Government. In this latter sense the word seems to be used in the clause which provides that the United States shall guarantee to every State in the Union a republican form of Government, and shall protect each of them against invasion. In this clause a plain distinction is made between a State and the Government of a State. . . . Our conclusion, therefore, is that Texas continued to be a State and a State of the Union, notwithstanding the transactions to which we have referred.

"When the war closed there was no Government in the State except that which had been organized for the purpose of waging war against the United States. That Government immediately disappeared. . . . The new freemen necessarily became part of the people, and the people still constituted the State; for States, like individuals, retain their identity, though changed to some extent in their constituent elements. And it was the State, thus constituted, which was now entitled to the benefit of the constitutional guaranty. There being, then, no government in Texas in constitutional relation with the Union, it became the duty of the United States to provide for the restoration of such a Government."

Other Uses of the Word Government. A use of the word Government, which is a common one but which is quite aside from the analytical conception is that according to which the ruling executive chiefs, in whose hands for the time being the direction of the larger public policies of the State is placed, are termed the Government. Thus, in England, one speaks of the Liberal or Conservative Government. In Germany, "Regierung" is employed to designate the Chief Executive and his advisers who have in their hands the general guidance of the Ship of State. So also, in the United States, one describes as a "government measure," a legislative proposal which has the active support of the President and his advisers. The word "Administration," it may be added, is often used almost synonymously with "Government" as thus employed. Thus a government measure is also often spoken of as an "administration measure."

Burgess Criticized. A distinction between the concepts of State and Government which is quite different from the one accepted in this treatise, is that which is employed by Professor John W. Burgess in his various publications. In the writer's opinion, the distinction which Professor Burgess makes is a very confusing one, and one that cannot consistently be employed in the interpretation of the principles of constitutional law as they actually exist. Inasmuch, however, as this doctrine has, through the influence of Professor Burgess, obtained considerable currency in America, space must be spared to consider it.[3]

Professor Burgess defines the State as "a particular portion of mankind viewed as a political unit." Further examining this definition, he declares the State to be, as to the people over whom it rules, all-comprehensive,— that "its organization embraces all persons, natural or legal, and all associations of persons," within its territory; that it is exclusive in the sense that there cannot

[3] The author first made the criticism which follows in an article entitled "The Political Theories of Professor John W. Burgess," published in the *Yale Review* for May, 1908.

be an *imperium in imperio;* that the State is permanent;
and finally, that it is sovereign. This sovereignty he defines as "original, absolute, unlimited universal power
over the individuals subject and over all associations of
subjects."

In the foregoing definition and description of the State,
we find little to criticize, unless, indeed, it is to observe
that the possession of sovereignty by the State necessarily implies the other features which he has particu-
larized as distinct characteristics. But when we turn to
the paragraphs in which he distinguishes between the
"State" and "Government" we find, in fact, the terms
State no longer used in the sense in which he has thus
formally defined it. The term Government, he nowhere
defines, but from his use of the term it is apparent that
by it he understands the machinery or organization of
the State with the exception of that organ or portion of
it which possesses constituent functions, *i.e.,* which has
to do with the creation or the amendment of existing constitutional law. Thus, when the same organs and the
same processes are used for the creation of ordinary
statute law and for constitutional amendment, as, for
example, in England, he speaks of the State as being
organized in the Government. When, on the other
hand, a different organ, as, for example, in the United
States and in France, or a different process, as, for example, in the German Empire, is provided for constitutive acts from that used or followed in ordinary
legislative measures, he describes the State as being
organized outside of the Government. Thus, in distinguishing between "immediate" and "representative"
Government, he says: "Immediate government is that
form in which the State exercises directly the functions of government . . . Representative government is
. . . that form in which the State vests the power of

government in an organization or in organizations more or less distinct from its own organization." [4]

In the chapter entitled "The Forms of State," speaking of their transformations, he says: "A close scrutiny of this process will disclose the following significant facts, *viz.*, that in the transition from one form of State to another, the point of sovereignty moves from one body to another, and the old sovereign body, *i.e.*, the old State, becomes in the new system only the Government, or a part of the Government. Take the example of English history after 1066 to make this clearer. First, the King was the State as well as the Government. Then the nobles became the State, and the King became the government only. Then the commons became the State, and both King and lords became but part of the government."

From the foregoing, taken in connection with the author's earlier definition of State, it is impossible to trace a clear and consistent theory. The State has been defined as "a particular portion of mankind viewed as a political unit," and sovereignty predicated of it as its most important and essential characteristic; yet in the sentences which have just been quoted, the State appears not as the political person or entity which possesses this absolute, supreme authority, but as identical with that organ which exercises constitutive functions. This plainly appears when the King of England is spoken of as having been at one time the State as well as the government, and at another time the nobles as having been the State and the King the government only. How can the King or the nobles have been the State and yet the State be defined as "a particular portion of mankind viewed as a political unit?" Again, Professor Burgess speaks of the State as being in some instances organized outside of the

[4] *Political Science and Comparative Constitutional Law,* vol. II, pp. 1, 2.

government. If this be so, the government must be considered as not a part of the organization of the State, that is, of the political entity which possesses the sovereignty. But if this be so, what is the status of the government? Of what is it the organization? Whence does it derive its powers? Whose will does it execute? When defining Representative Government, he describes it, as we have seen, as one in which the State vests the power of government in an organization, or in organizations more or less distinct from its own organization. But if it is the State which creates the representative government and endows it with powers, how can that government be anything but a part of the State's Organization? [5]

It will have been observed that the distinction which Professor Burgess makes between State and Government depends upon the distinction between constitutional and ordinary law. But this distinction, as will later be made clear, is one which cannot be so easily made as Professor Burgess seems to imagine.

The alternative to Professor Burgess's use of the terms "State" and "Government" is that which has been earlier referred to; namely, according to which the word "State" is applied to that entity, that abstract political person, which possesses the sovereignty and is thus the ultimate source of all legitimate control over the individuals subject to its authority; and the word "Government" employed to designate the machinery through which the will of this sovereign political person is expressed and executed. As thus used the Government of a State includes the constitutive as well as the ordinary legislative, executive, and judicial organs.

[5] Professor Burgess's reasoning becomes still more confused when he attempts to apply his theories and definitions to an interpretation of the historical events preceding and attending the drafting and adoption of the present Constitution of the United States. As to this see *post*, pp. 227ff.

CHAPTER VI

THE TERMS NATION AND PEOPLE DEFINED

IT has been seen that the term State, when employed by the jurist, is an abstract one, and indicates that a given group of individuals is viewed as an entity or person endowed with certain specific juristic attributes. This same group of persons, when viewed concretely, constitutes the body-politic of the State, and is then spoken of, sometimes as a People and sometimes as a Nation. These two terms are, unfortunately, also used to designate groups of individuals which, whether politically united or not, are drawn together by the bonds of race, language, culture, common historical experiences, common economic interests, or similar institutions. It would, of course, increase the precision of political terminology if the publicists and political scientists of the world could agree that one of these two terms should be reserved exclusively to designate the citizen body or body-politic of a State, and the other employed exclusively with reference to aggregates of individuals, which, whether under a common political rule or not, may be viewed as constituting distinct units because of the homogeneity of their race, history, institutions, culture or economic interests. However, so inveterate and widespread is the confusion of the two terms, as well as of the adjectives drawn from them, that it is not possible for the writer to do more than indicate his own usage of them, a usage to which he himself is unable, without pedantry, absolutely to conform.

In general, then, in this volume, the term People will

be employed to denote the body-politic, or aggregate of citizens or subjects of a given State; and the term Nation will be used to designate a group of individuals which may be regarded as unified by race, language, culture or common interests or aspirations, but which may or may not be so politically united as to constitute a People. In other words, when the word People is employed the factor of political unity is implied. When the term Nation is used, the unifying sentimental or psychological factor is implied. When it has not been feasible to adhere strictly to this usage care is taken to have the thought shown by the context. However it may be well at once to point out two important respects in which it has been necessary frankly to abandon the usage of the terms that have been indicated.

In International Relations, the terms State and Nation are used synonymously to designate the entities or persons which possess the rights and rest under the obligations which International Law creates; and, in both Constitutional and International Law, there is a growing tendency to employ the term "Nationals" to include not only those who are deemed citizens in a narrow constitutional sense of the word, but also those who, though not so recognized, are deemed to owe their primary allegiance to the State in question, and, as such, entitled to its protection in international matters. Thus, in the United States, Indians and the natives of unincorporated Territories have been held not to be citizens of the United States within a narrow constitutional sense of the term, but are, nevertheless, held to be its "Nationals."

Nation Defined. Returning now to the non-juristic concept of Nation, it is to be pointed out that when it is said that the influences of race, custom, language and history create a Nation, it is meant that from these sources springs the feeling or sentiment that binds to-

.gether a community of people and constitutes from them a single unit. Each of these factors invites the formation of a Nation, but no one of them compels it. The essential element is the feeling which is the result of one or more of these factors. Thus, as says Renan: "A Nation is a spiritual principle, resulting from the profound complications of history; a spiritual family, not a group determined by the configuration of the soil. . . . A Nation is, then, a great solidarity constituted by the sentiment of the sacrifices that have been made, and by those which the people are disposed to make. It supposes a past; it is, however, summed up in the present by a tangible fact: the consent, the clearly expressed desire of continuing the common life. The existence of the Nation is (if the metaphor is permissible) a continued Plebiscitum, as the existence of the individual is a perpetual affirmation of life." [1]

According to Mill: "a portion of mankind may be said to constitute a nationality if they are united among themselves by common sympathies which do not exist between them and others—which make them coöperate with each other more willingly than with other people, desire to be under the same government, and desire that it should be government by themselves or a portion of themselves exclusively." [2]

The tendency of course is, as indicated in Mill's definition, for Nations to constitute themselves as individual States, and this demand for political unity constitutes the surest index to the existence of a national feeling. Hence, most publicists see in the national State the most perfect type of political development thus far attained.

The advancing enlightenment of the masses has been instrumental in creating the true feeling of nationality,

[1] Article "Nation" in Lalor's *Cyclopedia of Political Science.*
[2] *"Representative Government,"* chap. XVI.

that is to say, a demand for unity based upon some other
ground than mere coercive political control; and the last
hundred years has seen the enormous influence that this
principle has had in reforming the political map of
Europe. At the same time it is not too much to hope
that this same spirit of enlightenment that has given rise
to a demand for a re-demarcation of political boundaries
will, in turn, as civilization continues to advance, make
this demand less imperative. And for this reason; While
at first the enlightenment of the masses creates in them a
consciousness of their own individuality and solidarity,
and thus a national feeling, as the culture of the people
increases, their sympathies may become more cosmopolitan, and their appreciation of the true unity of all humanity more real. Ethnic, linguistic and even political unity
may thus exercise comparatively less and less influence as
Nations find themselves drawn into a higher and more intellectual union. At the same time, also, economic interests tend more and more to cross national and political
boundaries, and thus to unite with increasing closeness
the material interests of different Peoples. It may thus
be entirely possible that the spirit of nationality at present so active in politics will prove to be a phase of civilization rather than a permanent product; and that while
the realization of a true World-State may never be possible, we may yet look forward to a growth of inter-
nationality that will largely deprive the feeling of nationality of its present force.

CHAPTER VII

TERRITORY AND PEOPLE AS CONSTITUTIVE ELEMENTS OF THE STATE

Territory. According to the definitions of many political scientists the existence of a State implies the exercise by it of authority over a definite portion of the earth's area. Thus the German jurist Seydel says: "A State comes into existence whenever a number of persons who have taken possession of a part of the Earth's surface unite themselves together under a higher will." [1]

So also Bluntschli declares a State to be "the politically organized national person (*Volkperson*) of a definite territory." [2] In like manner Rivier says: "A State is an independent community organized in a permanent manner in a definite territory." [3] And a definition substantially similar to this is found in the treatises of almost all writers on international law.

Some writers, among whom the present author was formerly included, incline to the view that a State may conceivably exist without a territory of its own, and, therefore, assert that the foregoing and similar definitions which included territory as an essential element of the State are incorrect. The author is now convinced, however, that, although the political jurisdiction of a State is not, in some aspects of its exercise, exclusively territorial in character, the existence of sovereignty itself, and

---

[1] *Grundzüge einer allgemeinen Staatslehre*, p. 1. See Garner, *Introduction to Political Science*, for a large number of definitions of the State.
[2] *Theory of the State*, p. 23.
[3] *Principes du droit des gens*, I, sec. 45.

63

therefore of a State, is dependent upon the claim upon the part of the State to a territory of its own.

In a later chapter we shall have occasion to show in considerable detail that, in many respects, the political jurisdiction of a State is personal as well as territorial in character; in other words, that sovereignty is recognized by the public law of all constitutionally developed States to imply the legal right upon the part of its possessor to attach legal significance to acts committed, or occurrences taking place outside of its own territorial limits. This legal significance, however, is one which the State cannot enforce outside its own territorial limits except with the express or implied consent of the other States within whose limits the enforcement is to take place. It is, then, not an adequate description of sovereignty to speak of it simply as territorial in character, unless, from the context, it is plain that reference is had to the enforcement, and not to the assertion, of the State's legal right of control.

There is, indeed, some justification for holding that, the essential quality of sovereignty consisting in a predicated right to issue commands legally binding upon individuals, the enforcement of these commands is a secondary matter which may or may not be actually effected, and which, in fact, in no State is always effected; and that, therefore, it is possible to conceive of a State without any territory of its own. Those who argue thus say that, so long as there is an aggregate of individuals who regard themselves as politically united under a ruler or Government which they regard as entitled to determine for them their legal rights and obligations, a State may be fairly said to exist. For example, they would say that during the period, while the World War was in progress, when the territories of Serbia and Montenegro were wholly occupied by Central Powers, these Kingdoms, though then without any territories upon which they could exercise their rights of sovereignty, were nevertheless States.

Of such a view it may be said that, while a possible one, and of value in so far as it emphasizes the personal element in the conception of sovereignty, it is inadequate as an analysis of present conditions of fact. In the world as we now know it, all, or substantially all, of the land surface is claimed by one State or another as its own territory over which it asserts exclusive political jurisdiction. This being so, no opportunity is presented for the existence of an independent politically organized people which has no land area within which to exercise its sovereignty. Wherever such a hypothetical landless body politic might be—unless it remained aboard ship upon the high seas—its members would be subject to the legal jurisdiction of the State within whose borders it was, and, therefore, it would not be a sovereign body.

As for the status of the Serbians and Montenegrins during the Great War, when their territories were in hostile military possession, it may be said that, regarded from their own legal point of view, the military governments of the Central Powers had no more than a *de facto* character. In other words, that, though for the time being dispossessed of them, their legal claim to these territories persisted. This point will appear more clearly in the chapter in which the distinction between government *de facto* and governments *de jure* will be discussed.

In result, then, it becomes necessary that territory be regarded as an essential constituent element of a State, and must therefore appear in its definition.

By some writers the jurisdiction which a State exercises over its territory is spoken of as a special right of sovereignty, and distinguished from the authority which it exercises over its citizens or subjects. This, however, is not a satisfactory view since it tends to regard sovereignty as an aggregate of rights or competences—a view which, as will later appear, is not an accurate one. As Malberg says: "La territorialité n'est pas une partie spéciale du contenu de la puissance étatique, mais uniquement une condition et une qualité de cette puissance." [4]

As one of the products of revolutionary thought, French writers and statesmen developed a special doctrine of the State's territory according to which a sort of sacred or transcendental character was ascribed to it, and from that ascription the deduction drawn that, as regarded the French State at least, the territory claimed by it as its own was so interwoven with or bound up in its own life, that no portion of it might rightfully, under any circumstances, be withdrawn from under its sovereignty. By article 1, title 2, of the Constitution of 1791 it was declared that *"Le royaume est un et indivisible"*; and the same declaration in substance was declared by the republican constitutions of 1792, of 1793, of the year III, of the year VIII, and that of 1848. The National Convention, indeed, by a unanimous vote of December 16, 1792, declared that whoever should propose or attempt to break the unity of the French Republic or to detach from it any of its integral parts in order to unite them to the territory of a foreign power, should be punished by death.[5] And a similar decree was passed on April 13, 1793.[6]

[4] *Contribution à la Théorie Générale de l'État,* vol. I, p. 4. Malberg, in a footnote, adds: "A vrai dire, le rapport entre l'État et son territoire ne doit aucunement être considéré comme un rapport de sujet à objet. Le territoire n'est point un objet situé en dehors de la personne juridique État, et sur lequel cette personne posséderait un pouvoir plus ou moins comparable aux droits qui peuvent appartenir à une personne privée sur les biens dépendant de son patrimoine; mais il est un élément constitutif de l'État, c'est-à-dire un élément de son être et non point de sa avoir, un élément par conséquent de sa personnalité même, et en ce sens il apparait comme partie composante et intégrante de la personne État, qui sans lui ne pourrait même pas se concevoir."

[5] *Arch. parl. ser. I,* vol. IV, p. 79.

[6] *Arch. parl. ser. I,* vol. LXII, p. 3.

It would seem from these declarations that the doctrine was asserted not merely that territory was a constituent and essential element in the life of the French State, but that that life was so bound up in the exact national territory which existed at the time the declarations were made, a mortal wound would be inflicted upon the State should any portion of its territory be taken from it, whether forcibly or otherwise. It will be remembered that Thiers, at the conclusion of the Franco-Prussian War of 1870, arguing in the courts of the neutral nations that they should aid France in resisting the cession of Alsace-Lorraine to Germany, urged that this principle of the inherent inviolability of French soil should be recognized. Gladstone at this time wrote to Bright: "My opinion certainly is the transfer of territory and inhabitants by mere force calls for the reprobation of Europe, and that Europe is entitled to utter it, and can utter it with good effect." Nevertheless, as reported by Morley, Gladstone "could not understand how the French protests turned more upon the inviolability of French soil, than on the attachment of the people of Alsace and North Lorraine to their country. The abstract principle he thought peculiarly awkward in a nation that had made recent annexations of her own." [7]

To the writer, except upon mystical or transcendental grounds, it is difficult to follow the argument of the French writers or statesmen who have advanced the foregoing argument as to the inviolability of a State's territory. That the life of a State, regarded juristically or from any other point of view, is dependent upon the maintenance of its authority over a specific extent of territory which may not be altered, at least by way of diminution, has been repeatedly disproved in historical fact; and there would seem to be no logical or theoretical

[7] Morley, *Life of Gladstone* (3 vol. ed.), vol. II, p. 346.

reason why the juristic proposition that a territory of some extent is essential to the existence of a State should imply the enjoyment by the State of sovereign authority over a territory of specific and unalterable boundaries. Upon the contrary it may be said that the juristic conception of the State places no limits, maximal or minimal, upon the extent of its territory. The nature and extent of the jurisdiction which a State claims the right to exercise over the territory claimed as its own will be discussed in a later chapter.[8]

The Citizen Body of the State. In the same sense in which its territory is to be deemed an integral and constitutive element of a State, its citizens, subjects, or nationals are to be so regarded. It is of course clearly impossible to conceive of a State as existing when there are no persons upon whom its authority is to be enforced, or by whom it is to be formulated and declared. And yet it is necessary to distinguish the abstract juristic concept or idea of the State from the corpus or collectivity of its citizens. As has been already several times emphasized, the State juristically viewed is but a political personality, an abstract idea, which the jurist, for his own convenience of thought, forms of the national or substantive State which requires for its existence a territory and body-politic. Thus, while it is necessary that there should be a territory and a citizen body in order that there may exist an object to which the juristic conception of statehood may attach or be applied, this abstract idea is not to be confused with the concrete State composed of its territory and citizens, any more than the qualities of a thing are to be identified with the thing itself.

As in the case of territory so with regard to the number of persons included within a politically organized group,

[8] Chap. XVIII.

the juristic conception would seem to impose upon the State no maximum or minimum which cannot be over-stepped.[9]

Citizenship. Allegiance, as its etymology implies, is the name for the tie which binds the citizen to his State —the obligation of obedience and support which he owes to it. To use feudal phraseology, the State is the political person to whom liege fealty is due. Nominally, according to the English law of today, English subjects owe their allegiance to the English monarch. They are *ad fidem regis.* Essentially, however, their allegiance is due to the English State viewed as a person, and the Crown is but the outward symbol and representative of that abstract political personality. Thus, analytically and juristically viewed, citizenship imports a personal relationship of the subject to his State. Sovereignty, as will later appear, being essentially the legally supreme power of willing, it lies wholly within the discretion of a State, or of those who direct its policies, to determine the persons over whom it will extend its authority. In a legal, constitutional sense, therefore, the citizens or subjects (the terms are juristically interchangeable) [10] of a State are those persons wherever they may be, and whatever their nationality, over whom authority has been asserted by those departments of its Government which are authorized to express its will. Thus, in very many cases, States claim and enforce their authority over individuals who owe allegiance to other sovereignties. For example, this is done whenever control is exercised by a State over aliens temporarily residing or travelling, or permanently

[9] There must of course be a group, which means a union between a plurality of individuals. See *post*, p. 164.

[10] These two terms are synonymous, although it is usual to use the former with reference to those States whose governments are more or less popularly founded, and the latter with reference to those whose governments are of a monarchical or autocratic character.

domiciled within its territory, or where naturalization is granted to citizens of other States which do not recognize the right of expatriation.

Souveraineté Nationale. French publicists, since the Revolution, have developed a doctrine known as *Souveraineté Nationale,* according to which the entire citizen body of the French State is viewed as, in itself, the political entity or person in which the right to rule inheres. The French Nation or People is thus confused, if not identified, with the French State, instead of being regarded as but one of its constituent elements. In a later chapter dealing with the location of sovereignty in the State we shall have occasion to consider in how far this doctrine of *Souveraineté Nationale* is of significance simply within the special field of French constitutional law.

CHAPTER VIII

In the pages which have preceded it has been frequently necessary to use the term "sovereignty." In this chapter the signification of this term will be more specifically considered.

Starting with that juristic conception of the State which views it as the sole source of positive law—a conception which will, in turn, receive particular consideration in the chapter dealing with the nature of Law— sovereignty is the name given to the supreme will of the State which finds expression in legally binding commands. As thus conceived, sovereignty is an abstract term. It implies the conception of the State as a volitional entity or political person, and designates that faculty which this political person possesses of determining, by its fiat, what are to be the legal rights and legal duties which it will recognize and, if necessary, enforce; what persons it will consider subject to its authority; and over what territory it will claim exclusive jurisdiction.

It is, of course, to be understood that when we speak of the State as willing this or that, and describe laws as being the formulated expressions of these volitions of the State, this is but a juristic mode of speaking. The State, not being a person in a biological sense, cannot possess or exercise a will of its own in the sense that a human individual is able to do. The substance of what is actually willed is determined by those individual persons who have control of the government and these, of course, are

71

more or less influenced in their determination by the wishes of the people generally. Juristically viewed, then, though regarded as expression of the will of the State, laws, in their substantive provisions, declare the will of human individuals.

Sovereignty a Unity. Viewed as a quality or faculty of Statehood, and as connoting legal omnipotence rather than physical power, sovereignty is, by its very nature, a unity. It is the name ascribed to the will of a legally supreme political person. It is the plenary faculty which that entity is assumed to possess to express its will in the form of commands legally binding upon all persons over whom it sees fit to claim jurisdiction and with respect to any matters which it may select. As thus conceived it is clear that sovereignty is not regarded as a bundle or aggregate of jurisdictional powers. In other words, it cannot be summed up by adding together such legal powers as those of taxation, of eminent domain, of police authority, etc. These powers are sometimes spoken of as peculiarly sovereign in character, that is, as inherent in the very nature of sovereignty. This characterization, however, is correct only in the sense that, as a practical proposition, it is difficult to conceive of a State which does not need constantly to exercise them. But, strictly speaking, all legal or jurisdictional powers involve the exercise of sovereignty inasmuch as they find their ultimate source in the sovereign will of the State.

Legislative, Executive and Judicial Functions. It is not proper, therefore, to view the sovereignty of the State as composed of a number of functions so generically distinct from one another that, in their exercise, they may be kept apart or treated as co-ordinate in authority.

It is true that there is a very real distinction between the creation of law, its interpretation, and its enforcement, and, for reasons of expediency, and especially in order to minimize the possibility of a tyrannical use of political power by those to whom its exercise is entrusted, it may be desirable to create and maintain a complexus of governmental organs, and, so far as possible, to vest law-making, law-interpreting, and law-enforcing in different hands, yet it is practically impossible to push this so-called principle of the "separation of powers" to its extreme limit; and, even as a theoretical proposition, it is found that many kinds of State action partake of the qualities of two or more of these functions, and cannot by any process of analysis be reduced to simpler terms. Certainly, at any rate, no State, however elaborate its constitutional jurisprudence, has been able to devise or operate a form of government under which legislative, executive, and judicial powers have, as regards their exercise, been kept wholly distinct and vested in different hands.

However, the fact remains that there is a distinction between law-making, law-interpreting and law-enforcing, and that, to some extent, it is possible to vest the exercise of these functions in different governmental organs. But the important point to the political theorist is that this does not imply that sovereignty is fascicular in character. It remains a unity, although the realization of its commands involves a process in which judicial and executive as well as legislative characteristics are involved. In other words, whatever the governmental authority that is exercised, whether legislative, executive or judicial in character, sovereignty of the State is manifested. As to this we may quote with full approval the statement of Malberg:

"Il n'y a pas, dans l'état trois pouvoirs, mais bien une puissance unique, qui est sa puissance de domination. Cette puissance se manifeste sous des formes multiples: son exercice passe par des phases diverses, initiative,

délibération, décision, exécution; les divers modes
d'activité qu'elle comporte, peuvent nécessiter l'intervention d'organes pluraux et distincts. Mais, au fond, tous
ces modes, formes ou phases, concourent à une fin unique:
assurer dans l'état la suprématie d'une volonté domi-
nante, laquelle ne peut être qu'une volonté unique et
indivisible. Le mot même de nomination exclut la pos-
sibilité d'une pluralité de pouvoirs proprement dits: car
si la puissance d'état se divisait en plusieurs pouvoirs
juxtaposés et égaux, aucun d'eux ne pourrait posséder le
caractère dominateur, et, par suite, la puissance totale
dont ils sont les éléments constitutifs et partiels,
demeurerait elle-même dépourvue de ce caractère." [1]

The Exercise of Sovereignty May Be Delegated. It has
already been seen that the exercise of sovereignty is conceived of as delegated by a State to the various organs
which, collectively, constitute the Government. For
practical political reasons which can be easily appreciated,
it is desirable that the public policies of a State should
be formulated and executed by governmental agencies of
its own creation and which are not subject to the control of other States. There is, however, nothing in the
nature of sovereignty or of State life which prevents one
State from entrusting the exercise of certain powers to
the governmental agencies of another State. Theoretically, indeed, a sovereign State may go to any extent in
the delegation of the exercise of its powers to the governmental agencies of other States, those governmental
agencies thus becoming *quoad hoc* parts of the governmental machinery of the State whose sovereignty is exercised. At the same time these agencies do not cease to be
instrumentalities for the expression of the will of the
State by which they were originally created.

[1] *Contribution à la théorie générale de l'état,* vol. II, p. 24. The
chapter of Malberg's work from which this paragraph is taken presents
an acute analysis of Montesquieu's doctrine of the separation of powers.

By this delegation the agent State is authorized to express the will of the delegating State, and the legal hypothesis is that this State possesses the legal competence again to draw to itself the exercise, through organs of its own creation, of the powers it has granted. Thus, States may concede to colonies almost complete autonomy of government and reserve to themselves a right of control of so slight and so negative a character as to make its exercise a rare and improbable occurrence; yet, so long as such right of control is recognized to exist, and the autonomy of the colonies is conceded to be founded upon a grant and continuing consent of the mother countries the sovereignty of those mother countries over them is complete and they are to be considered as possessing only administrative autonomy and not political independence. Again, as will be more fully discussed in a later chapter, in the so-called Confederate or Composite State, the co-operating States may yield to the central Government the exercise of almost all of their powers of Government and yet retain their several sovereignties. Or, on the other hand, a State may, without parting with its sovereignty or lessening its territorial application, yield to the governing organs of particular areas such an amplitude of powers as to create of them bodies-politic endowed with almost all of the characteristics of independent States. In all States, indeed, when of any considerable size, efficiency of administration demands that certain autonomous powers of local self-government be granted to particular districts.

The Determination of the Existence of Sovereignty. In all those cases in which, owing to the manner in which the governmental powers have been distributed, there is doubt as to the political entity or person in which the sovereignty rests, the test to be applied is the question as to which political entity or person, in the last instance, has the legal power to determine its own competency as well as that of others. For the essential criterion of the sovereign State is that it is supreme, not only as giving the ultimate validity to all law, but as itself determining the scope of its own powers, and itself deciding what interests shall be subject to its regulation. It sets to itself its own rights and establishes the limits of its own authority. As Jellinek puts it in his *Gesetz und Verordnung:* "The rights and duties of individuals receive their potency and authority from grounds set forth in objective law. The State finds the grounds for its own rights and duties in itself." [2] Or, as he expresses it in another work: "Obligation through *its own will* is the legal characteristic of the State." [3]

Sovereignty Cannot Be Limited. Sovereignty as a State attribute is not only a unity, but one that, by its very nature and definition, connotes absolute legal authority. To place a legal limit upon it is, therefore, to destroy it. As Austin says in his *Province of Jurisprudence Determined:* "Supreme power limited by positive law is a flat contradiction of terms." And he continues: "Nor would a political society escape from legal despotism, although the power of the sovereign were bound by legal restraints. The power of the superior sovereign imposing the restraints, as the power of some other sovereign superior, would still be absolutely free from the fetters of positive law. For, unless the imagined restraints were ultimately imposed by a sovereign not in a state of subjection to a higher or superior sovereign, a series of sovereigns, descending to infinity, would govern the imagined community, which is impossible and absurd."

If, then, we have the case in which one State is recognized to have the legal authority to place a legal restraint

[2] *Op. cit.,* p. 196.
[3] *Die Lehre von den Staatenverbindungen,* p. 34. There will later be occasion to criticize Jellinek's conception of "own will."

Science of union of States

of any sort upon the legal will of another political body, that political body cannot be said to possess sovereignty.

A Sovereign State Cannot Impair Its Own Sovereignty. Equally true is it that no State is able to impair its own sovereignty. Since, *ex hypothesi,* its own sovereignty is the source of all law for itself, it cannot by a law (except formally) limit itself, for, by an exercise of the same will that creates the limitation, the limitation may be removed. To this point we shall later return.

The State not a Subject of Legal Rights and Obligations. There is some dispute among jurists as to whether or not a sovereign State may be regarded as itself a "subject" of legal rights and duties.[4]

If, however, the viewpoint of the analytical jurist is rigidly adhered to, there would seem to be no difficulty in asserting the negative upon this point. The State, being regarded as itself the source of a law, cannot be regarded as bound by the obligations which that law creates; and, even as to rights, the ascription of them to the State is meaningless, since their continuance as well as their creation, their character and their content, are wholly subject to the State's will. In other words, there would seem to be no more value in attaching legal rights and duties to the sovereign State than there is in predicating the attributes of goodness and justice of a Divine Being who is regarded as Himself the creator, by His own unrestrained will, of all distinctions between goodness and badness.

It scarcely need be said that this denial of legal rights and duties has reference only to the State and not to its various governmental organs or officials. These, as has been earlier pointed out, have their competences determined by law, and, therefore, they must, at least in every constitutionally organized State, be regarded as the

[4] See especially, Brown's, *The Austinian Theory of Law,* pp. 191-193: Gray's *Nature and Source of Law,* paras. 184-190. *Cf.* also Holland's *Jurisprudence;* Markby's *Elements of Law.*

possessors of legal rights and as the subjects of legal obligations. This will presently be made more evident when the nature of constitutional law and of constitutional government is discussed.

Hobbes in whose writings are to be found so many of the fundamental principles which Bentham and Austin were later to develop into a system of Analytical Jurisprudence, fails to make this distinction between the monarch or other instruments of government and the sovereign political entity or person, the State, but, in the following passage the logic of his argument as to the impropriety of ascribing legal rights and duties to the person or organ that creates them cannot be successfully attacked. He says: "The sovereign of a commonwealth, be it an assembly or one man, is not subject to the civil law. For, having power to make and repeal laws, he may when he pleaseth, free himself from that subjection, by repealing those laws that trouble him and making of new; and consequently he was free before. For he is free, that can be free when he will: nor is it possible for any person to be bound to himself, because he that can bind, can release; and therefore he that is bound to himself only, is not bound." [5]

Austin who subjected juristic ideas and terminology to meticulous, although not always successful, analysis, first, after Hobbes, emphasized the doctrine that a sovereign law-making power cannot be held to be itself a subject of legal rights any more than it can of legal obligations. To hold that the sovereign State can be legally obligated, he declares, would be contrary to the very definition of sovereignty. Thus, in Lecture VI of his *Province of Jurisprudence Determined,*[6] he says:

"Every legal right is the creature of positive law; and

---

[5] *Leviathan,* chap. XXVI, sec. 2.
[6] Edition of 1875, New York, ed. by Campbell, p. 166.

it answers to a relative duty imposed by that positive law, and incumbent on a person or persons other than the person or persons in whom the right resides. To every legal right, there are therefore, three several parties: namely, a party bearing the right; a party burdened with the relative duty; and a sovereign government setting the law through which the right and the duty are respectively conferred and imposed. A sovereign government cannot acquire rights through laws set by itself to its own subjects. A man is no more able to confer a right on himself than he is able to impose on himself a law or duty. Consequently, if a sovereign government had legal rights against its own subjects, those rights would be the creatures of positive law set to its own subjects by a third person or body, who must, therefore, be sovereign over them. The community would therefore be subject to two different sovereigns, which is contrary to the definition of sovereignty."

Therefore, says Austin, when a sovereign State appears in a court as a plaintiff, or, with its own consent, as a defendant, the rights and duties that appear to attach to it, are only quasi legal rights and duties,—analogous to, but not identical in character with the rights and duties predicated of non-sovereign persons or bodies.

Markby in his *Elements of Law* [7] takes practically the same position as Austin upon this point. So, also, does Sheldon Amos in his *Science of Law*.[8]

Holland in his *Elements of Jurdisprudence* [9], and Gray in his *Nature and Sources of Law* [10], take emphatically the position that legal rights and duties may be predicated of the sovereign State, but it is clear that, in doing so, insofar as they assert more than Austin admits under

[7] Sections 154 *et seq.*
[8] Ed. 1874, p. 99.
[9] Chap. IX.
[10] Sections 186-190.

the term quasi or analogical legal rights, they confuse the ideas of State and Government, and, as a result, apply to the former entity an amenability to law that can properly be imputed only to the latter. Thus Gray says: "It is for the interest of the State that robbery should be prevented. It protects this interest by issuing a command and imposing a duty; it creates for itself a legal right. . . . The State has an indefinite power to create legal rights for itself, but the only legal rights which the State has at any moment are those interests which are then protected by the Law,—that is, by the rules in accordance with which the judicial organs of the State are then acting."

Here there is a double error. In the first place there is the incorrect assumption that interests can be predicated of the State as distinguished from its citizens. The truth is that it is because of the citizen's interest that robbery is sought to be prevented. As an abstract legal entity, considered apart from its own citizens, a State cannot possibly have substantive interests to be protected or advanced. Secondly, the law as it exists at any given time operates not as a limitation upon the State, or to endow it with legal rights or powers, but solely, in these respects, upon individuals whether as private citizens or as public officials.

A similar failure to distinguish between the State as the creator of law, and as operating through law, but as not itself subject to the control of law, and its governmental agencies which have only such legal rights and obligations as are given to them by law, is seen in the energetic protest made by Mr. John M. Zane to the statement made by Mr. Justice Holmes in his opinion in the case of *Kawananakoa v. Polyblank* [1] that "there can be

¹ 205 U. S. 349.

no legal right as against the authority that makes the law on which the right depends.[12]   Mr. Zane starts out with the erroneous impression that Mr. Justice Holmes had asserted the principle "that no law can create a legal right against the government." If this be true, says Zane, "we may as well apologize to Germany at once for daring to question the divine right of government to override every law, contritely confess *nostram culpam, nostram maximam culpam,* and start anew on a truly Hegelian basis; for the divine right of government is simply the divine right of Kings writ large." In a historically learned essay Zane then traces from Roman times the doctrine iterated and reiterated by moralists, jurists, and courts that public officials should be, and, under constitutional systems of government, are subject to the operations of law. It must, however, be clear from what has gone before in the present treatise, as well as from the long line of decisions of the Supreme Court of the United States from which no departure was suggested in the Kawananakoa case, that Justice Holmes did not intend to assert, or the court to hold, that no law could create a legal right against the Government of a sovereign State. Mr. Zane's argument thus exhibited an *ignoratio elenchi.*

Sovereignty Not Impaired by International Obligations. The legal omnipotence of the sovereign State, constitutionally viewed, is not impaired by the obligations assumed by it in its agreements with other sovereign Powers, or by the existence of constitutional legal provisions, written or unwritten. The nature of the limitations imposed upon States by treaties or by International Law will be discussed in a later chapter of this volume in which the nature of the State as internationally viewed is examined. Here it is sufficient to state the result of

[12] "A Legal Heresy," in the *Illinois Law Review,* XIII, p. 431.

the inquiry there pursued, namely, that, *in sensu stric-tiore,* these limitations are not legal in the sense in which that term is employed in positive or analytical juris-prudence. In order to determine the nature of the limitations placed upon state action by Constitutional Laws, it will be necessary to examine with some degree of care the essential character of these laws.

Laws Do Not Constitute a Limitation upon the State's Sovereignty. It has been seen that when sovereignty is predicated of a State, there is asserted the doctrine that the State is the creator of all the laws in accordance with which its own activities are conducted. In other words, it sets to itself, that is, to its own governmental organs and officials their legal powers. This legally unlimited competency—*Kompetenz Kompetenz,* as the Germans term it—distinguishes the sovereign State from all other human associations of a political or juristic character. The State is supreme, not only as giving the ultimate validity to all the laws which are to fix the rights and obligations of those over whom it chooses to claim juris-diction, but as itself determining the scope of the legal powers of its own governmental agencies and the manner of their exercise. Thus, at any one time, the domain of the legal and political liberties of the individual is simply that field of interests which the State has willed shall be protected from violation, whether by private persons or by public officials. From the possible control of the State itself, however,—from the very source of all law—there can be no possible legal guarantee of immunity, except in the formal sense that, from its very nature, a State must express and execute its will in the form of law. Private individuals and those who are in possession of public authority may, indeed, as a matter of fact, invade the rights of the individual and destroy those interests which existing law defines and establishes and which the

State professes to defend, but such action, because illegal, cannot be said to be the act of the State itself, even if committed by its highest governmental officials.

Constitutional Law Defined. The distinction between constitutional and ordinary statute laws cannot as a general proposition be based upon the fact that the former are embodied in formal written instruments of government for the reason that some States, Great Britain for example, do not possess written constitutions.

Equally unsatisfactory are the criteria that the constitutional laws may not be amended or repealed in the same manner as other laws, or that they are applied by the courts in preference to other laws which may be in conflict with them. This is shown not only by the fact that in such countries as England there is no formal distinction, either as to creation or repeal, between constitutional and other laws, but also by the fact that, in most of those countries which have adopted written constitutions, the courts do not assume the authority to refuse recognition to statutory enactments which contravene the provisions of those constitutions. And, in truth, in some of those constitutions, the formal provision which is made for constitutional amendments makes the process only slightly more difficult than that of ordinary legislation. In countries like the United States which possess written instruments of government it is of course possible to limit the application of the term constitutional to those provisions which find statement in these instruments. This gives to these laws a very distinct character for the reason that the amendment of these instruments is made more formal and more difficult than is the process of ordinary legislation, and because, in the United States at least, the doctrine is fully established that, in case of conflict, other laws or attempts at legislation must yield to the provisions of these written constitutions. But, when this defi-

nition of constitutional law is accepted, the distinction as
to substantive content between constitutional and other
laws is wholly abandoned, since American constitutions
contain many provisions which have no direct relation
to the form and powers of government but concern matters of private law.

In order, then, to have a definition of Constitutional
Law which is susceptible of general application and which
also has the merit of going to the substantive content
rather than to the form of the laws that are defined, we
are led to denominate as constitutional those laws which
relate directly to the form of government that is to exist,
and to the allotment of powers to, and the imposition of
limitations upon, the several governmental organs and
functionaries.[13]

**Constitutional Law Limits the Government But Not the
State.**   Constitutional provisions do not purport to control the State but only its Government.   These laws are
the creation of the State itself for its own purposes, and
the limitations upon public action which they impose are
not designed for, and do not operate as, a limitation upon
the State that comes from a source outside itself and
thus restrains the free exercise of its legally omnipotent
will.   This is so even in those cases in which, as in the
United States, the courts hold null and void all laws the
provisions of which are inconsistent with constitutional
mandates, and where the amendment or repeal of these
mandates is made extremely difficult.   The limitation

---

[13] It will of course be recognized that even this definition does not draw
a clear line of distinction between constitutional and other municipal
laws so as to make it always easy to draw the line of distinction.   Constitutional provisions defined according to their substantive content
shade off into administrative laws and regulations and executive or administrative decrees.   This difficulty in classifying laws in clear-cut
categories is one that runs through the entire field of jurisprudence.
But, after all, the only purposes of such classifications is to obtain a
convenient working apparatus of juristic thought, and this, these general, though not absolutely definite, classifications secure.

upon the exercise of the State's sovereignty is still a purely formal one.

It is common to speak of constitutional laws as of a legal force higher than that of ordinary legal statutes. Not only is this not true of the constitutional laws of many foreign States, but, even in the United States, it is not a correct way in which to describe the distinction.[14] Because our constitutions set limits to the legal

[14] As evidencing the extent to which constitutional and ordinary law are assimilated in Germany, we may quote the following from Laband's standard work, *Das Staatsrecht des Deutschen Reiches* (2d ed., I, 546). "There is no will in the State," he says, "superior to that of the sovereign, and it is from this will that both the constitution and laws draw their binding force. The constitution is not a mystical power hovering above the State; but, like every other law, it is an act of its will, subject accordingly to the consequences of changes in the latter. A document may, it is true, prescribe that the constitution may not be altered indirectly (that is to say, by laws affecting its content), that it may be altered only directly, by laws modifying the text itself. But when such a restriction is not established by positive rule, it cannot be derived by implication from the legal character of the constitution and form an essential difference between the constitution and ordinary laws. The doctrine that individual laws ought always to be in harmony with the constitution, and that they must not be incompatible with it, is simply a postulate of legislative practice. It is not a legal axiom. Although it appears desirable that the system of public and private laws established by statute shall not be in contradiction with the text of the constitution, the existence of such a contradiction is possible in fact and admissible in law, just as a divergence between the penal, commercial, or civil code, and a subsequent special law is possible." (*Cf.* Borgeaud, *Adoption and Amendment of Constitutions in Europe and America*, trans. p. 69 *et. seq.,* where this passage is quoted and adversely commented upon.)   Such a condition as above described by Laband would, of course, be impossible in the United States, where the decision as to the conformity of a given statute with the constitution is vested in an independent judiciary. But, in the German Empire, though it was provided that no amendment of the constitution should be made, if there were fourteen votes opposing in the Federal Council (*Bundesrath*); yet, since it lay only with the legislature or the Emperor to decide when a given statute did operate as an amendment of the constitution, it was possible to change that instrument in any way desired by ordinary legislative enactment, so long as that body or the Emperor did not see fit to declare such acts to be unconstitutional in character. Thus, as a matter of fact, the German constitution was several times modified, as Laband says it properly might be done, by special laws in which more than fourteen opposing votes were registered in the Upper Chamber. What has been here said in reference to the Empire held true as well in Prussia. In France, likewise, there is no provision guarding against a modification of its constitution by ordinary laws, which, without nominally changing its text, do in fact violate its principles. Thus Dicey, in enumerating the various senses in which the term "unconstitutional

powers of our legislatures, laws enacted by them transcending such limits are not recognized by the courts as valid. But, when so doing, the courts do not thereby declare that there has been a conflict between two laws of differing degrees of legal force, the lower having to give way to the higher. That which they do is simply to say that the statutes in question, though enacted in the usual form, are not laws at all, and never were laws, because their subject matter did not lie within the legal competence of the legislature enacting them. As Cooley says in his *Principles of Constitutional Law,* "Such enactment is in strictness no law, because it establishes no rule; it is merely a futile attempt to establish a law." Strictly speaking, then, the term "unconstitutional law" is a *contradictio in abjecto*: if it is unconstitutional it is not law; if it is law, it is not unconstitutional.

Carrying this point still further, it will be seen that this distinction as to degree of validity is not to be drawn between laws and ordinance or decrees. As ordinarily understood an ordinance signifies a command of limited application, not necessarily permanent, and usually issued

law" is used says: "The expression, as applied to a law passed by a French Parliament, means that the law, *e. g.,* extending the length of the President's tenure of office, is opposed to the articles of the constitution. The expression does not necessarily mean that the law in question is void, for it is by no means certain that any French court will refuse to enforce a law because it is unconstitutional. The word would probably, though not of necessity, be, when employed by a Frenchman, a term of censure," (*Law of the Constitution,* 4th ed., Appendix, Note VI.) In a recent very able analysis of the present status of constitutional law in France, the writer says: "The first point to be emphasized is the tendency which now leads the French legislator to render the transformation of the constitutional laws easier by transferring to the domain of ordinary legislation, that is to say, placing within the normal competence of Parliament, matters belonging to the domain of constitutional law." As examples of this tendency are cited the amendment of June 21, 1879, which strikes out from the constitution the provisions relating to the seat of government, and that of Aug. 14, 1884, Article 3, which deprives of their constitutional force Articles 1 to 7 of the Constitutional Laws of February, 1875. (*The Development of the Present Constitution of France,* by Professor R. Saleilles, in the *Annals of the Am. Acad.,* VI, 227-257, article by G. Arangio Ruiz.)

as an administrative direction by a department of government. If legally issued, however, that is, if within the legal competence of the authority uttering it, these ordinances are of equal juristic validity with the more general and formal mandates of the State.

In another work [15] the author has discussed this point and from that treatise the following two paragraphs are taken:

"There are not and cannot be degrees of legal validity. Any given rule of conduct or definition of a right either is or is not law. When, therefore, we describe any particular measure as an unconstitutional law, and therefore, of course void, we are in fact, strictly speaking, guilty of a contradiction of terms, for if it is unconstitutional, it is not law at all; or, if it is law, it cannot be unconstitutional. Thus, when any particular so-called law is declared unconstitutional by a competent court of last resort, the measure in question is not 'vetoed' or 'annulled,' but simply declared never to have been law at all, never to have been, in fact, anything more than a futile attempt at legislation on the part of the legislature enacting it. This is a very important point, for did the decision of the court operate as a veto the effect would be simply to hold that the law should cease to be valid from and after the time such decision was rendered, whereas, in fact, the effect is to declare that the law never having had any legal force, no legal rights or liabilities can be founded upon it. In *Norton v. Shelby County*.[16] Mr. Justice Field said: 'An unconstitutional act is not a law, it confers no rights, it imposes no duties, it affords no protection, it creates no office; it is, in legal contemplation, as inoperative as though it had never been passed."

[15] *United States Constitutional Law,* vol. I, p. 9.
[16] 118 U. S. 425.

"In declaring unconstitutional, and therefore void, the enactment of a legislative body, it has sometimes been argued that a court defeats the will of the people as whose law-making organ and mouthpiece the legislature acts. In truth, however, what is done is this: The people, acting solemnly and deliberately in their sovereign capacity, declare that certain matters shall be determined in a certain way, and these matters, because of their great and fundamental importance, they reduce to definite written form, and declare that they shall not be changed except in a particular manner. In addition to this, they go on to say, in substance, that, so decided is their will, and so maturely formed their judgment, upon these matters, any act of their own representatives in legislature inconsistent therewith, is not to be taken as expressing their deliberate will. Therefore, when the courts declare void legislative acts inconsistent with constitutional provisions, the judges are giving effect to the will of the people as they have previously solemnly declared it. Thus, 'In exercising this high office the judges claim no judicial supremacy; they are only the administrators of the public will. If an act of the legislature is held void, it is not because the judges have any control over the legislative power, but because the act is forbidden by the Constitution, and because the will of the people, which is therein declared, is paramount to that of their representatives expressed in any law.' "[17]

Correct as is the statement of this doctrine, its application with respect to acts of those holding office under an unconstitutional statute is not without practical as well as logical difficulties. Some courts have held that, there being no *de jure* office, there can be no *de facto* officer. Other courts, however, have held that, until a law purporting to create an office has been declared unconstitu-

[17] *Lindsay v. Commissioners,* 2 Ray 38.

tional by the courts, one holding an office has a color of title thereto, and is, therefore, a *de facto* officer whose authority may be questioned only by direct proceedings as, for example, in the nature of *quo warranto*. In other words, though not legally an officer, because of the unconstitutionality of the law creating the office, or providing the conditions under which he has qualified, the acts of such a person may not be questioned in collateral proceedings by persons affected by them.[17a]

As is well known, John Austin refused to recognize that constitutional law (designating by that term the rules that define the organization of the State, and the extent and manner of exercise of governmental powers) has a "positive" legal character. That which gives to them force, he said, is public opinion regarding their expediency and morality,—in fine, that they belong to the class of moral rather than of legal rules. In so holding he was clearly wrong, and his error is traceable to his failure to distinguish between the State and its Government. He was controlled by the view that constitutional laws purport to control the State itself, which, according to his conception of sovereignty, as well as according to the one accepted in the present treatise, is a logical impossibility. He did not appreciate that constitutional laws operate only as a limitation upon the organs of Government.[18]

The fact is, that Austin's conception of the nature of constitutional law was largely determined by the particular conditions under which the powers of his own government were exercised. As is well known, a very

[17a] See especially State v. Carroll, 38 Conn. 449, and State v. Gardner, 54 Ohio 24. See also *Cyclopedia of Law and Procedure*, vol. 29, pp. 1390 et seq., under title "Officers."

[18] Austin was also influenced in this matter by the belief that it was necessary to find in every government some definite or determinate person or organ which could be viewed as the supreme or sovereign mouthpiece of the State.

large portion of the rules according to which the English Government is, and was at Austin's time, habitually exercised, are truly to be considered, as he maintains, not laws at all but customary rules of morality and political expediency. They are, as Dicey says, "conventions, understandings, habits or practices, which, though they may regulate the conduct of the several members of the sovereign power of the Ministry, or of other officials, are not in reality laws at all since they are not enforced by the courts."[19] Examples of these conventions are the maxims that the King must consent to any bill passed by the two Houses of Parliament; that the House of Lords may not originate a money bill; that the Ministers must resign office when they cease to command the confidence of the House of Commons.

That which distinguishes these conventions or customs of the constitution from positive law is not so much their lack of actual binding power (for their actual obligatory force is great enough to make the open contravention of many of them as unlikely as if they were actually established in a fundamental instrument of government), but the fact that, should they be violated, no greater consequence would be entailed upon the officers so doing than popular blame and unpopularity. There would be no legal action that could be sustained either to enforce the recognition of such violated maxims or to punish their contravention.[20] Insofar as Austin limited the exclusion of constitutional regulations from the domain of law to principles of this class he was logically correct. But he did more than this. He erroneously applied

---

[19] *Law of the Constitution*, 4th ed., p. 23.

[20] As shown, however, by Dicey, though these constitutional conventions are not capable of legal enforcement, so intimately are they connected with those operations of the English government which are backed by legal sanctions, it would be practically impossible for a ministry to carry on the administration of public affairs in opposition to them, without bringing its members into almost immediate conflict with positive law. *Op. cit.*, chap. XV.

the exclusion without reservation to all provisions that purport to regulate the manner of exercise of the State's power.

In result, then, we arrive at the proposition that all law, whether public or private, is, while it remains in being, a substantive limitation upon the Government of a State, but not upon the State itself. Through the laws are fixed the rights and duties of individuals, and the manner in which such rights are to be exercised and enforced. As such, they are all of the same validity, and are as binding upon the Government as are constitutional provisions. A public official will be as readily checked by the courts for the exercise of a power that contravenes an ordinary statute as for an action that transgresses a rule of constitutional law. All law thus constitutes a limitation upon the State's legal power in the sense that, only by a change in that law can the rights which it protects be legally infringed, and this change in the law, whether by way of amendment or annulment, if it is to be the act of the State, must be made in the manner which has been provided for its alteration or repeal; or, at any rate, the change must be made in the same manner and through the same agencies as the original law itself was created. As a logical proposition, an irrepealable or unalterable law is an impossibility, for the same legislative competency which is adequate to enact must be conceded the power to repeal. But what, then, it may be asked, is the value of formal provisions of laws with reference to the manner in which they may be amended or repealed? None whatever, legally speaking, when we have to deal with a law-making body of unlimited competence, such, for example, as the English Parliament, and this is proved by the fact that upon more than one occasion that body has repealed laws which, when enacted, were declared irrepealable. If, instead of being declared irrepealable, the law embraces a clause providing that it may be repealed only in a certain manner, here, too, this limitation may be disregarded by the law-making body if it be one of unlimited legislative competence. When, however, we have to deal with the enactments of a law-making body whose legislative powers are themselves defined by law, a different proposition is, of course, presented.

That a State is legally supreme and the source of all the law which it enforces, and that, therefore, it is logically impossible to conceive of the State as legally unable to change or abolish any existing law, applies to constitutional as well as to private law, for constitutional law is, equally with private law, the creation of the State. In other words, unless we would sacrifice the sovereignty of the State, we must hold that no constitution or constitutional provision, however formally adopted and declared unalterable, can, in legal contemplation, be held to be such.

Thus, in the case of written constitutions, of which there have been a considerable number, which have had no amending clauses, it must be held either that they may be amended by ordinary legislative act, or that they may be changed by the same authority which originally promulgated them. Where public pressure has wrung written instruments of government from former autocratic rulers, it is but natural that, in the absence of specific provisions for amendment, they should have been held subject to alteration only with the consent of the electorate or by the organ of government, if there is any such, which is deemed to represent the governed. This, for example, has been the doctrine held by Italian jurists regarding the instrument which serves as the constitution of the Kingdom of Italy. But, from the legal point of view, it would, perhaps, have been more logical, if not more politic, to have held that the amending power is in the Crown, inasmuch as the constitution owed its establishment as law to a royal fiat.

It is not uncommon to hear the written constitutions of Europe which have been promulgated by monarchs in response to overwhelming popular demand spoken of as compacts between the governed and their respective rulers. This is juristically incorrect. However expressed, and whatever may have been the actual conditions that necessitated the establishment of these instruments, they do not have, legally speaking, a contractual character. Their legal life was breathed into them by the ruler, who, before their establishment, was the sole depository of law-making power, and who, indeed, after their promulgation, retains the legal right to speak the will of the State according to his own judgment except as otherwise provided in the constitution, and, even as to them, only so long as he may see fit to maintain in force the constitution which he had granted. This, of course, is only the juristic point of view, and has no reference to the fact that, as a practical political matter, he would not be able to disregard, in this respect, the wishes of his subjects, or that, if he could, it would be a breach of a moral obligation for him to do so.

Legal theory asserts that so long as an autocratically conceded or "octroyed" constitution remains in force the monarch is legally bound by its provisions. If he wishes to depart from its provisions, and would clothe his acts in legal form, he must first change the constitution so as to give to himself the desired legal authority. It has thus been commonly argued that if, in the constitution which he has granted, a formerly autocratic monarch has declared that it shall be changed only in a special manner, that is, only when a certain procedure has been gone through with, as for example, the acceptance of the proposed changes by the elected representatives of the people, he cannot legally change the constitution except when such specified conditions have been met. It is, however, somewhat questionable whether this conclusion is a necessary result of juristic logic. It might be maintained that, inasmuch as the constitution in question derived its sole claim to legality from the will of the monarch, that monarch would have the legal right to alter or amend its provisions, including its clauses providing for its amendment, in virtue of that same legal competency which empowered him to establish the constitution in the first place. Similar reasoning applies in the case of constitutions created by constitutional conventions or the votes of electorates or other organs for expressing the popular will; namely, that, irrespective of their provisions, they may be amended by an exercise of that same constitutive power which originally stamped upon them the quality of law. To substantially this conclusion American constitutional jurists have been frequently, though not uniformly, led.

This deduction has been so closely related to, as to be practically a corollary of, the characteristic doctrine of American constitutional jurisprudence that the Constitutional Convention is, *par excellence,* the organ through which the citizen body of a State exercises that sovereign power which it is assumed to possess by virtue of the very fact that it is a body-politic. Hence, it has been held by American courts that, when a written constitution contains no provisions for its own amendment, it may nevertheless be amended or replaced by a new instrument drafted by a Constitutional Convention and either promulgated by that body or submitted by it to the vote of the electorate.

In some instances this doctrine has been applied even in the cases of constitutions which have specified other modes of amendment; and, still more extreme, in instances in which the constitutions have declared that the modes of amendment specified in them should be the only modes in which they may be amended or replaced by new instruments of Government. Hoar, in his *Constitutional Convention: Their Nature, Power and Limitations,* Chapter XIII, asserts broadly this constituent power of conventions called by the legislatures without authority given by the existing constitution, and criticizes the narrower view of Dodd in his *Revision and Amendment of State Constitutions.* Hoar says: "The whole people in their sovereign capacity, acting through the forms of law at a regular election, may do what they will with their own frame of government, even though that frame of government does not expressly permit such action, and even though the frame of government attempts to prohibit such action."[21] To the substantiation of the statement as a principle that has been applied in American constitutional practice, he denotes Chapter IV of his work. Again he says, after a summary of historical examples: "Thus we come back to the fact that all conventions are valid if called by the people speaking through the electorate at a regular election. This is true, regardless of whether the constitution attempts to prohibit or authorize them, or is merely silent on the subject. Their validity rests not upon constitutional provisions, nor upon legislative act, but upon the fundamental sovereignty of the people themselves."[22]

As to this point this much may be said: the position has been quite consistently taken that constitutional amendments or new constitutions adopted in modes not provided for by the existing constitutions cannot be rec-

[21] *Op. cit.,* p. 115.
[22] P. 52. For a further discussion of the theoretical questions involved in this proposition, see, *post,* the discussion of Popular Sovereignty and the Juristic Origin of the State.

ognized as legally valid unless they have received the formal approval of the old existing government. Thus, in the case of the State of Rhode Island, the old constitution of which contained no provision for its own amendment, the President of the United States refused to recognize as *de jure* a government established under a new constitution which, without the approval of the old government, had been drawn up and adopted by a majority of the adult male citizens of that State.[23] But when, somewhat later, a new constitution was adopted in accordance with provisions which the old government laid down and approved, it was, and has since been, held a valid instrument both by the people of the State and by the National Government of the United States.

Whether or not a constitutional amendment has been constitutionally adopted, and is therefore to be recognized as law, is a matter for the courts to determine unless the constitutions in question have made specific provision for this determination by some other body. When, however, the question is as to the *de jure* character of an entirely new constitution, or of an amendment so radically changing the structure of the old government as practically to create a new one, the matter is deemed a political one, the determination of which by what are called the political departments of the government being held by courts as conclusive upon themselves. And it need scarcely be said that the courts established under a given constitution will not question the legal validity of that constitution, for, of course, it is only upon the basis of its validity that the courts themselves could claim any rights whatever of jurisdiction.

[23] The Supreme Court of the United States, in the case of *Luther v. Borden*, 7 Wallace, p. 1, held itself concluded by this executive decision, the question as to when a government is to be deemed to be *de jure* in character being declared to be a political one, and, as such, to be decided by the political department of the government. The same doctrine has been repeatedly declared by the courts of the States of the Union. See the authorities cited by *Corpus Juris*, vol. XII, p. 880, note 35.

Corpus Juris, summing up the general doctrine of American jurisprudence upon the matter of adoption and amendment of written constitutions, says: "Whether or not a new constitution has been adopted is a question to be decided by the political departments of the government. But whether an amendment to the existing constitution has been duly proposed, adopted, and ratified in the manner required by the constitution, so as to become a part thereof, is a question for the courts to determine, except where the matter has been committed by the constitution to a special tribunal with power to make a conclusive determination, as where the governor is vested with the sole right and duty of ascertaining and declaring the result, in which case the courts have no jurisdiction to revise his decision."[24]

The State Though not Limited by, Must Operate Through, Law. In only one sense can it be said that the sovereign State, as conceived of by the Analytical Jurist, is controlled by Law. Being itself, when viewed as a legally omnicompetent person, wholly a product of juristic reason, it is, by its very nature, a legal entity, that is, one that necessarily operates exclusively through legal processes. Law, in other words, constitutes the medium or space, if a dimensional term may for the purpose of illustration be employed, in which it lives and moves and has its being. No act of a Sovereign State can, therefore, be illegal; and no illegal act can be an act of a State. Its governmental agents may act illegally, but, when they do, they do not represent the State. Thus,

[24] Vol. XII, p. 880. See also *idem,* p. 682, and authorities cited in note 78. The federal courts in the United States have declared that they will not question the validity of the processes by which constitutions of the States have been adopted or amended, if these constitutions or amendments have been recognized as valid by the political departments and judiciaries of the States concerned.

Corpus Juris (vol. XII, p. 682, sec. 18) refers to a Georgia case in which it was held that it was not essential to the validity of a constitutional amendment which in effect modified a constitutional limitation that the limitation should first be changed, since the amendment itself was to be construed as working the change.

though the State, as juristically conceived, is not, and cannot be controlled by law, and, therefore, cannot logically be regarded as the subject of legal rights and duties, it at all times is compelled, by its very juristic nature, to operate through law.

The fact that the State is above, if not outside of law, does not, of course, prevent it from permitting itself, as to particular matters, to be treated as though it were a private or non-sovereign person, and as such, to hold itself amenable to law. This is a practice which practically all modern States follow to some extent, and the principles of public law that relate to this practice will later be considered when the subject of the jurisdiction of the State is discussed.[25]

Sovereignty as a Title. A very common usage is that which describes as sovereign that organ of government which plays the more important or decisive part in the determination of what the State shall will, that is, which controls in fact the policies of the State. Thus, in an absolute monarchy, or in a limited monarchy in which the Crown retains a dominant influence in government, the King is often spoken of as the possessor of sovereignty. So, similarly, in States organized upon the democratic or representative basis, the people are spoken of as constituting collectively the entity in which the sovereignty inheres. This is an inaccurate statement, whatever may be the extent of the political authority of the absolute monarch, of the constitutional ruler, or of the citizen body. It is, indeed, of very great importance to determine in the case of any constitutional system whether all public powers shall be deemed to find their legal origin in an assumed *plenitudo potestatis* of a monarch, or in the body-politic from which, by specific delegation, the competences of other governmental officials are considered to derive their existence. But, it is to be

[25] *Post,* chap XXIV.

repeated, in all cases, the sovereignty inheres in, and is possessed by, that political entity or person which we term the State. A government or any of its organs never does more than exercise sovereignty in behalf of, and as an agency of, the State.

As a mere matter of titular distinction it is common to speak of the ruler of a monarchically organized State as the Sovereign of the State. This usage, which prevails especially in international relations, has no relation to the constitutional powers or status of the King, Czar, Emperor, Sultan, or whatever he may be termed. The ruler whose actual influence and authority is insignificant is as universally termed the Sovereign in this honorific sense as is the most powerful autocratic Prince.

Sovereignty of Law. The phrase "the Law is Sovereign," which is not infrequently met with, has no other juristic significance than that the State is able to speak its legal will only in the form of law and in accordance with the constitutional provisions that, at the given time, are in existence. Stated negatively, it means that every governmental official must be able to justify every exercise of public power upon his part by a reference to a constitutional or other valid statutory delegation to him of legal authority. Purely personal and arbitrary discretionary power is thus excluded. The doctrine is thus that stated by Mr. Justice Matthews, when he says that "the law is the definition and limitation of power."[26] The same principle is enounced in the Massachusetts Constitution when it declares that the government is to be one of laws and not of men.

Popular Sovereignty. The terms then, "sovereignty of the people," "popular sovereignty," and "national sovereignty," as will be more fully explained, cannot accurately be held to mean that, under an established government, the sovereignty remains in the people. It may

[26] *Yick Wo v. Hopkins,* 118 U. S. 356.

mean, however, that the constitutional jurisprudence of
the State to which it is applied is predicated upon the
principle that no political or individual or organ of government is to be regarded as the source whence, by delegation, all other public powers are derived, but that, upon
the contrary, all legal authority finds its original source
in the whole citizen body or in an electorate representing
the governed.

CHAPTER IX

THE SITUS AND MODES OF EXERCISE OF SOVEREIGNTY:
CONSTITUTIONAL AND PURE JURISTIC THEORY DIS-
TINGUISHED

As has been earlier suggested, a clear line of distinction
divides a doctrine of constitutional law from one of pure
jurisprudential theory. The first is special in its application and relates to a particular system of constitutional
law; the second relates to the very nature of public law,
and is, therefore, general in character, and applies to the
State, whatever may be its particular type of governmental organization or its special system of constitutional
jurisprudence. Sovereignty we have found to be an essential attribute of the State. Its nature and qualities
are determined by pure political or jurisprudential theory.
Its modes of exercise in any given State are, however, determined by the system of government and of constitutional law which that State has established for itself.
The determination in each particular case of these modes
is, therefore, a matter of constitutional law, the discussion of which might be omitted in such a treatise as the
present one. However, it seems proper that a certain
amount of space should be devoted to this matter if only
for the purpose of making more plain the distinction
between sovereignty as a purely juristic concept, and the
same term when employed to indicate the ultimate source
whence the ethical right of a given government to exist
is drawn, or the actual forces which, in fact, determine
the policies of that government, or, finally, the organ or

organs which, under the given system of constitutional law, may be said to have the final or supreme legal right to express the will of the State.

Constitutional Theory of Pure Monarchy. As a matter of pure political or juristic theory, the State remains the same whatever may be its form of government or constitutional jurisprudence. That jurisprudence may start with the premise that the original and continuing fountain of all legal authority is the Crown. Deductions from this premise are: that by the will of the ruling monarch all other organs of government have been created and continue to exist; that from that will such legal powers as they possess have been derived; and that by that will they may, at any time, be curtailed or wholly withdrawn; and that, if a written constitution exists, its legal force is dependent upon that will. These are the constitutional doctrines upon which a system of pure monarchy is founded.[1]

[1] Commentators upon the constitutional law of the German Empire, and of Prussia as it existed prior to 1918, agreed in holding that the essential element in legislation is not the action of the legislative chambers at all, but the approval of the King of Prussia and of the Federal Council in the Empire. The Chambers simply draft the contents of the proposed law. Its legal character is wholly due to the approval of the executive. Thus says Schulze (*Preussisches Staatsrecht,* 2d ed. I., p. 158): "Everything which is decided or carried out in the State takes place in the name of the King. He is the personified power of the State." And again: "The chambers have no co-ordinate sovereignty, and no *co-imperium.* As individual members and as a whole, they are *subjects* of the King." (*Op. cit.,* pp. 567-568.) "In the acceptance or rejection by the King lies the really decisive act. Only the approval of the King converts a will into a law. . . . It does not correspond with the theory of German constitutional law to speak of the various factors of legislation, still less to designate the positive law-creating power of the King as simply a negative veto. The King is not only one of the factors in legislation, *he is the law giver himself.*" (*Op. cit.,* II, pp. 21-22. *Cf. The Constitution of Prussia,* Translated and Supplied with an Introduction and Notes by J. H. Robinson, published as supplement to the *Annals of the Am. Acad.,* vol. V, No. 2, in which the above citations from Schulze are quoted.) Likewise says Laband in reference to imperial law: "The sovereignty of the State does not enter into the determination of the content of law, but only into the sanction which gives to the law its value. The sanction alone is an act of legislation in the legal sense of the word." (*Das Staatsrecht des Deutschen Reiches,* 2d ed., vol. I, p. 517), quoted by Borgeaud, *op. cit.,* p. 70. To much the

Secondly, the constitutional jurisprudence of a State may take as its logical basis or starting point, the principle that certain organs of government other than the Crown, such as elected legislative chambers or an electorate having referendal legislative powers, shall divide with the Crown, upon a basis of full legal or constitutional equality, the various or certain powers of government, that is, in such a way that these several organs may act independently of each other as to the specific powers constitutionally vested in them, or that they may be legally obliged to co-operate with one another.

In such a constitutional system it is obvious that all its provisions derive their legal force from some single source. If these provisions are to be found in a written Constitution or fundamental instrument of government, the original and continuing fountain of all legality, corresponding to the legal autocracy of the absolute monarch,

same effect as the above is the view of the Austrian publicist, Jellinek. "Nicht die Kammern im Vereine mit dem Monarchen, sondern der Monarch allein nimmt die entscheidende legislatorische Thätigkeit vor," says he. "Die Zustimmung der Kammern zum Gesetzesbefehle ist Bedingung, nicht Ursache desselben." (*Gesetz und Verordnung*, p. 317.)

In the Japanese Constitution it is declared (Article IV) that "The Emperor is the head of the Empire, combining in Himself the rights of sovereignty, and exercises them according to the provisions of the present Constitution."

Commenting upon this Article, Prince Ito says: "The sovereign power of reigning over and of governing the State, is inherited by the Emperor from His Ancestor, and by him bequeathed to His posterity. All legislative as well as executive powers of State, by means of which He reigns over the country and governs the people, are united in this Most Exalted Personage. . . . His Imperial Majesty has Himself determined a Constitution, and has made it a fundamental law to be observed both by the Sovereign and by the people." Commenting also on Articles V and VI of the Constitution which provide that the Emperor shall exercise his legislative power with the consent of the Diet or Parliament, and that he shall give sanction to laws and order their promulgation and enforcement, Ito expressly denies that laws are contracts between the governing and the governed, and that, in their enactment, the Sovereign and the people have equal share. Ito says: "Such a theory arises out of a misconception of the principle of the unity of sovereignty. From the nature of the original polity of this country, it follows that there ought to be one and only one source of sovereign power of State. . . . The legislative power is ultimately under the control of the Emperor, while the duty of the Diet is to give

is the particular organ or complexus of organs of government, or electorate or determinate group of individuals acting *ad hoc* as an organ of government, which is recognized to have the legal right to change the terms of the written Constitution, which Constitution, therefore, however it may have been originally adopted, is to be regarded as continuing to have force of law only because the constitutional organ or complexus of organs so wills it. This is the constitutional situation which now exists in practically all of the States of the world.

A third constitutional or governmental possibility is that exhibited by Great Britain which has a King, and does not possess a formal written Constitution or instrument of government, but has, nevertheless, built for itself a complicated and yet definite system of government and a body of constitutional principles according

advice and consent. Thus between the Emperor and the Diet, a distinction is to be strictly maintained as to their relative positions." Distinguishing the right of veto which chief executives may have under other constitutional systems, from the Emperor's right in Japan to refuse to sanction measures that have been approved by the Diet, Ito says: "The so-called veto power is, in its principle, negative. The legislature enacts laws, while the Sovereign only vetoes the same. It will thus be seen that this is an offshoot of principles which aim at confining the sovereign power of a Ruler within the executive power only, or at least at allowing him only a part of the legislative power. In our Constitution, a positive principle is adopted, that is to say, the laws must necessarily emanate at the command of the Emperor. Hence it is His sanction that makes a law. As the laws must necessarily emanate at the command of the Emperor, it naturally follows that he has power to withhold sanction to the same. Thus, although there may be some semblance of similarity between our system and the veto system above alluded to, the one is as far separated from the other as the heavens are from the earth."

In conformity with the general philosophy of the Japanese polity, it is expressly provided that amendments to the Constitution shall not be attempted except as initiated by the Emperor.

Reasoning the same as above is possibly applicable to English law, notwithstanding the apparent weakness of the Crown in that country and the actual overwhelming power of the "Commons." Professor Hearn, in his work on *The Government of England,* is perhaps the one among English writers who most strongly emphasizes this point. "We hear constantly of the royal veto," says he, "of its absolute character, and of the danger that its revival might produce. It is assumed that the power of legislation resides in the council; and that the sovereign has merely a negative control on its deliberation, which power, how-to which that plenitude of constitutional power, which, in a pure monarchy, is vested in the Crown, is vested in the Crown and a Parliament, the members of one House of which sit, for the most part, by hereditary right, and the members of the other House by selection by an electorate which has been broadened from time to time until now it includes nearly all adult citizens.[2]

Consent of the Governed. A fourth constitutional doctrine, often asserted, but never actually put into force, and, in fact, practically impossible of operation, is that which declares that all governmental powers are validated by the consent of all the governed. Regarded as an ethical proposition, this assertion will be examined in the

ever, he is bound not to exercise. Such a doctrine is altogether inconsistent with a right understanding of our constitution. The very use of the term 'Veto' suggests a false analogy. There is nothing in common between the refusal of our King to add to or alter the law, and the power of a Roman tribune to prevent in a particular instance the application of an existing law. Every act of Parliament bears in its very front the work of its original. It is 'enacted by the Queen's Most Excellent Majesty.' It is in the Crown, and not in the body which law assigns as the assistants and advisers of the Crown, that our constitution places this right. It is the King, as the old Year Book asserts, that 'makes the law by the assent of the peers, etc., and not the peers and the commune.' The power of legislation resides in Queen Victoria no less than it resided in William the Norman; but the conditions under which that power is exercised are indeed very different." (P. 51. *Cf.* Jellinek, *Gesetz und Verordnung,* pt. I, chap. I.) *Law + Decree*

As regards legislation in the United States, it need scarcely be said that all of the departments of its government trace their origin to the same source; and, in so far as they divide among them the law-making power, are co-ordinate organs for the exercise of the sovereign power. Thus the final approval affixed by the President to the acts of Congress is essentially a legislative act, but is not a more vital element in the law-creating process than is the approval of the Chambers. That is to say, the law, as finally established, embodies the joint will of the President and Congress, and not that of one alone. As regards his function of approving or disapproving of acts of Congress, the President is to that extent as much a part of the legislative organ as is any Representative or Senator. The case is not changed even in those cases in which laws are passed over the presidential veto. His will is overcome, but not excluded from the legislative act any more than the will of any member of the legislative body itself may be said to be so treated, when his vote is with that of the minority.

[2] It is barely possible, as suggested in the preceding note, though only at the risk of being charged with constitutional pedantry, and by divorcing oneself wholly from realities, to assert that the ultimate source of all constitutional power in Great Britain is still in the Crown.

volume on Ethical Political Philosophy, referred to in the preface. Regarded as a legal or constitutional principle it is easy enough to show that it has never been adopted by any State, and that, as a practical proposition, it cannot be.

The statement of the American Declaration of Independence that "Governments derive their just powers from the consent of the governed," considered as an absolute one that applies to all States is, of course, an ethical proposition, the validity of which is not of concern to the analytical jurist. If it be advanced as a constitutional principle the term "governed" becomes synonymous with the People or citizen body of the State, and it then becomes necessary to ask if this aggregate of individuals is to be viewed distributively, or collectively as a corporate unit. If in former sense, all valid legal or political authority is at once rendered impossible and the State destroyed. By this doctrine, as Bluntschli says, "the State is resolved into its atoms, and supreme power ascribed to the unorganized mass or to the majority of these individuals. This extreme radical opinion contradicts the very essence of the State, which is the basis of sovereignty."[3] If the latter view is taken, and the governed regarded as a corporate unit, it is necessary to determine who are to be regarded as the constituent members of this composite political body, and the modes in which it can make its legal will authentically manifest.

As regards this matter of membership, but two alternatives are possible: either the People, thus viewed as the sole source of positive law, as the legally supreme organs of the Government, must be conceived of as including every citizen or subject of the State, children and infants of the tenderest years as well as adults, the wholly uneducated as well as the educated, the feeble-

---

[3] *Theory of the State,* trans. 2d ed., p. 497.

minded as well as those of sane intelligence, and each of them given a right to participate in determining the laws and policies of the State,—a result so obviously absurd, from a practical point of view, that no politically organized body of individuals has ever attempted it; or the other alternative accepted that the "active citizens," to use Rousseau's phrase, are to be limited to certain classes of individuals who are to participate directly in the operation of the government, or, indirectly, as an electorate either for the purpose of selecting representatives who will act for them, or, by way of the initiative to propose laws, or the referendum to pass final judgment upon laws which their elected representatives draft, or which they themselves have initiated.

If, then, we take this second view as to the constitutional meaning of "consent of the governed," the way is at once opened to all forms of government, except possibly that of autocratic or pure monarchy as described above. If the step is once taken of conceding that a portion of the governed, less than the whole, may arrogate to itself the legal right to act for the whole People and to claim obedience to its commands upon the part of those citizens who are excluded from this "active citizenship," there is no logical limit to the process. Such a small portion of the whole citizen body may claim the right to act for the whole that, instead of being what is ordinarily known as democratic or popular in character, the Government becomes highly aristocratic or oligarchic. It may even assume a monarchic form with extensive discretionary powers vested in the ruler, provided only that it is understood that this monarch rules not by reason of any inherent personal right of his own but as an agent of the body of active citizens, small or large as that body may chance to be. Furthermore, this electorate, in every constitutionally organized State, can act legally only according to predetermined forms, in conventions or assemblies, or by registering their will at prescribed times and in the modes already fixed by law. And, even when so acting, it is necessary that there should be definite laws as to what proportion of the votes cast shall be deemed to express the will of the entire electorate, and, as such, to bind the entire citizen body.

It is plain, then, that, as a constitutional proposition, the doctrine of popular sovereignty, or sovereignty of the people, carries with it little more than the negation of the doctrine that supports absolute or pure monarchy. Indeed, it is barely possible to hold that it does not do even this,—that, in other words, the autocratic monarch can declare himself to be the agent or representative of his entire people in exactly, and in as logical, a sense as that in which a portion of the entire People arrogates to itself the legal right to speak and act for the whole.

The value, then, of constitutional government is not that it places Sovereignty in the hands of the people, but that it prescribes definite ways in which this sovereign power shall be exercised by the State. The value of popular government is that it provides the means through which the wishes of the people may be known and felt, and that thus the conduct of a State may be brought into conformity thereto. Constitutional government thus protects the citizen from arbitrary action on the part of the State: popular government secures to him the probability that his wishes and interests will be considered.

Public Opinion. Sharply distinguishable from the doctrine of popular sovereignty according to which, as an ethical proposition, the just powers of government are declared to be necessarily based upon the consent of the governed, as well as from the constitutional doctrine that the legal powers of all the organs of government are to be traced back, in the last resort, to grants from an electorate or other constituent body which is assumed to represent and speak for the entire body of citizens, is the doctrine, or rather the assertion of fact, that, in all States, whether autocratically or democratically organized, the actual dominance of power lies with the governed, and that, therefore, their will may not be opposed, except to a limited extent, by those who occupy the official or legal seats of power.

The fact is, as must be apparent to all, that there are limits to the endurance of any people, however patient, unenlightened, and submissive, and, that, when oppressed beyond this limit, they will prefer the evils of open resistance to those of submission; and, if this oppression be carried so far as to excite the opposition of the entire people or a large portion of them, the ruling powers will be overthrown. These are facts that are necessarily recognized by every ruler. As Hume well says, "As force is always on the side of the governed, the governors have nothing to support them but opinion. It is therefore on opinion only that government is founded, and this maxim extends to the most despotic military governments as well as to the most free and most popular."[4]

In fact, Austin himself expressly and repeatedly affirms that the legal sovereign is actually controlled in the exercise of power by the wishes of the community. In this very definition he says, "If a determinate human superior not in a habit of obedience to a like superior receive *habitual* obedience," etc., the word "habitual" thus indicating the possibility of the sovereign will being opposed. Again he says, "If perfect or complete independence be of the essence of sovereign power, there is not in fact the human power to which it will apply. Every government, let it be ever so powerful, renders occasional obedi-

[4] *Collected Essays*, pt. I, No. 4.

ence to the commands of other governments. And every government defers habitually to the opinions and sentiments of its sovereign subjects."[5] And, also, "To an indefinite though limited extent, the monarch is superior to the governed, his power being commonly sufficient to secure compliance with his will. But the governed, collectively or in mass, are also the superior of the monarch, who is checked in the abuse of his might by fear of exciting their anger and of arousing to active resistance the might which slumbers in the multitude."[6]

It is plain that, when dealing with this popular ultimately conditioning force, which exists in all political societies, we are not dealing with a legal factor. It may be, as Lieber describes it, the sense and sentiment of the community which gives meaning to the letter and life to the law, and without which the written law is a mere husk,[7] but it is, nevertheless, not a legal force, but, as Woodrow Wilson has defined it, "a catalogue of influences."[8]

As has been already several times said, sovereignty as a legal force or element can be exercised only through the organs of the constitutionally established Government.[9]

Those doctrinaires who emphasize this factor of "popular sovereignty," and make it include a right of revolution, are not always careful to explain that this "right," so far as it is anything more than mere might, is ethical rather than legal in character. By the mere fact of a

[5] *Lectures on Jurisprudence,* ed. 1867, vol. I, p. 242.
[6] *The Province of Jurisprudence Determined,* p. 14 (ed. 1861). See also, *idem,* note to p. 192, and p. 272; Professor Dewey, in the *Political Science Quarterly* for March, 1894, shows the tendency of Maine and others to treat Austin's system as if it ignored this ultimate conditioning power of popular approval.
[7] *Political Ethics,* sec. 65.
[8] *An Old Master and Other Essays,* p. 78.
[9] *Cf.* the argument of Daniel Webster in the case of *Luther v. Borden,* 7 How. 1.

people putting themselves in a revolutionary attitude toward their government, that is, by attempting the enforcement of their demands in ways other than those provided by law, they are placed outside of the State so far as such acts are concerned. However proper their conduct from a moral standpoint, from a legal standpoint they are then acting not as a body politic, but as a mob. They have, in fact, expressly repudiated State agencies. This, then, cannot be an act of Sovereignty, for Sovereignty, as expressly defined and conceded by all, is of the State and is possessed by a political community, and not by an uncivic aggregate of men. Until a people become politically organized there is no Sovereignty.[10]

[10] Thus says Bluntschli in his *Staatswörterbuch*: "Es giebt keine Souveränetät der Gesellschaft. Keine Souveränetät vor oder über dem Staate. Die Souveränetät als ein staatlicher zunächst ein staatrechtlicher Begriff ist durch die Existenz und durch die Verfassung des Staates bedingt."

To the same effect says Cooley (*Constitutional Limitations*, 3d ed., p. 598): "The voice of the people in their sovereign capacity can only be of legal force when expressed at the times and under the conditions which they themselves have prescribed and pointed out by the constitution, . . . and if by any portion of the people, however large, an attempt should be made to interfere with the regular working of the agencies of government at any other time, or on any other mode than as allowed by existing law, either constitutional or statutory, it would be revolutionary."

According to Judge Jameson, sovereignty resides in a society only as a body politic; "in the corporate unit resulting from the organization of many into one, and not in the individuals constituting such unit, nor in any number of them as such, nor even in all of them, except as organized into a body politic and *acting as such*." (*The Constitutional Convention*, p. 21.) However, though assuming this correct position, he proceeds to declare that Sovereignty may be exercised in an extra-governmental or revolutionary manner. Its characteristic as a *legal* power is thus explicitly abandoned. "Sovereignty," says he, "manifests itself in two ways: first, *indirectly* through individuals acting as agents or representatives of the sovereign, and constituting the civil government; and, secondly, *directly* by organic movements of the political society itself, without the ministry of agents; the movements referred to exhibiting themselves either in those social agitations, of which the resultant is known as *public opinion*, that *vis a tergo* in all free commonwealths, by which the machinery of government is put and kept in orderly motion; or in manifestations of *original power* by which political or social changes are achieved irregularly, under the operation of forces wielded by the body politic itself immediately." (*Idem*, p. 23 Citation is made of Lieber's *Political Ethics*, vol. I, p. 256.) But what the tests are by which "organic movements" of society are to be dis-

If it be necessary to make this point still more conclusive, the circumstance may be pointed out that in all cases the actions of States are, as a matter of fact, largely determined and limited by the claims of other States, and thus their independence is practically governed by influences identical in character with those exercised by the public opinion of their own citizens. The legal, or rather non-legal, nature of both are the same. No greater validity can be predicated of the one than of the other, yet even Lieber and Jameson would not hold that Sovereignty rests, not with the individual States, but in a Community of States.

"Political" Sovereignty. Professor Ritchie, in an article upon this subject[11] distinguishes between this power of the people exercised by public opinion, which he terms "the ultimate *political Sovereignty*," and the highest political power of the State as exercised through its legally established organs, which he designates as "legal Sovereignty." It is undoubtedly correct thus to make this distinction, but, to the writer, it seems unfortunate that the same term, "Sovereignty," should be applied to two forces so radically different, even though distinguishing adjectives be prefixed. Is it not better to term such extra-legal force simply "Public Opinion" or "General Will," and to limit the word "Sovereignty" to its purely legal application?

In thus distinguishing between Sovereignty and General Will or Public Opinion, between legal absolutism

tinguished; how Sovereignty, as necessarily inhering in a social body only as a political body, and exercised *as such,* can likewise be discovered in mere opinion or in "irregular" acts for the achievement of social as well as political changes; what valuable distinction there is between revolutionary and legal conduct—a distinction emphasized throughout the work;—these are questions that Judge Jameson does not attempt to answer. (*Cf.* his article entitled "National Sovereignty," in the *Pol. Sci. Quar.,* vol. V, p. 193.)

[11] "On the Conception of Sovereignty," *Annals of the Amer. Acad. of Pol. and Soc. Science,* January, 1891.

of the State and its powers as absolutely limited by
political exigencies, we are, in fact, but stating a result
that correlates with the position which we shall assume
in regard to the relation of custom to law.[12]   That is to
say, we shall deny to the people a capacity for legislation
except through State organs.   It is the essential office of
representative or public government to make an approximately correct formulation of Public Opinion, and
to secure political action in conformity thereto,[13] but
this is not to place the exercise of Sovereignty in the unorganized community.

In conclusion, then, of this point, it may be said that,
though legally absolute, Sovereignty is to be considered
in reference to the institutions, the character of the
people governed, and other objective conditions.   While
force is and always must be an incident of Sovereignty,
the highest ideal of statesmanship is to render the actual
exercise of such force as seldom necessary as possible,
and the extent to which this aim is attained will depend
largely upon the degree in which State action corresponds
with the desires of Public Opinion or the General Will.
As T. H. Green says, "If once the coercive power which
must always be an incident of Sovereignty becomes the
characteristic thing about it in its relation to the people
governed, this must indicate one of two things; either
that the general interest in the maintenance of equal
rights has lost its hold upon the people, or that the Sovereignty no longer adequately fulfils the function of maintaining such rights, and thus has lost the support derived from the general sense of interest in supporting it

[12] See chapter, "The Nature of Positive Law."
[13] See the remarks of Dicey (*Law of the Constitution,* pp. 73-76), according to which the function of representative government is to produce a coincidence between what he terms the "external limits" to
Sovereignty, arising from the possibility of resistance on the part of the
people, and the "internal limits," depending upon the wishes of those
who wield the sovereign power.

. . . It is certain that when the idea of coercive force is that predominantly associated with the law-imposing or law-enforcing power, either a disruption of the State or a change in the sources of Sovereignty must sooner or later take place."[14]

Souveraineté Nationale. A constitutional doctrine superficially resembling and often confused with that of "popular sovereignty" is that known as "Souveraineté Nationale," which the French, since the time of the Revolution, have, except for a single exception—the Charter of 1814—adopted as the fundamental principle of their constitutional jurisprudence. Article 3 of the Declaration of the Rights of Man and the Citizen of 1789 declared that "all sovereignty resides essentially in the Nation. No body, no individual may exercise any authority which has not expressly emanated from it." The Constitution of 1791 declared that "The sovereignty is one, indivisible, inalienable and imprescriptible. It belongs to the Nation." A similar declaration occurred in the Constitution of the Year III. It was impliedly affirmed by plebiscites under the Constitution of the Year VIII, and the Empire. It was again explicitly declared in the Constitutions of 1848 and 1852, in the Resolution of February 17, 1871, and in the Preamble of the Constitutional Law of August 31, 1871.

This principle, as Malberg so well shows in his analysis of it[15] is best interpreted in the light of the historical conditions under which it was first enunciated, and, as thus interpreted, is shown to have the negative purpose of denying, once for all, the fundamental constitutional principle of the former French Monarchy that all con-

---

[14] Green, *Philosophical Works,* vol. II, p. 410. To many persons it will seem that these remarks of Green have a pertinency to present conditions in the United States with reference to the enforcement of the Eighteenth Amendment to the Federal Constitution.

[15] *Contribution à la Théorie Générale de l'État,* vol. II, pp. 167-187.

stitutional power found its source in the King, and that
he had an inherent divine or patrimonial right of rulership. As opposed to this royal doctrine, the doctrine of
Souveraineté Nationale asserts that no person has such
a personal or inherent right to exercise political power.
Such a right can only be a delegated or constitutional one
—one that has been created and sanctioned by the French
Nation.

This constitutional premise that the ultimate constituent power is vested in the Nation has meant that sovereignty, as a legal concept, resides, not distributively in
each of the individuals that compose the Nation, but in
the citizen body as an individual and indivisible whole.
In the Constitution of 1791 sovereignty is expressly declared to be one and indivisible. It is thus clear that,
from the beginning, the doctrine was essentially different
from the popular sovereignty of Rousseau. Indeed, the
first constitution, that of 1791, made no attempt to provide a legislative body the members of which would be
elected by a direct and universal suffrage. And later
constitutions, without abandoning the doctrine of Souveraineté Nationale, limited the suffrage to holders of
landed property, and, in the Charter of 1830, established
even a monarchy—of course a constitutionally limited
one.

In result, then, according to this doctrine, the Nation
is declared to have that exclusive right to exercise the
sovereign or constitutional powers, which, prior to 1789,
had been claimed by the King.

It might at first be thought that this investment of
sovereignty in the Nation, conceived of as an indivisible
political whole or corporate unit, amounts to practically
the same thing as the ascription of sovereignty to the
State, as assumed in the present treatise. The two doctrines are not, however, the same. Souveraineté Na-

tionale is a special constitutional doctrine. It permits, indeed, the establishment and maintenance of a great variety of governments, its only requirement being that they and their several organs and officials shall be deemed to have only such legal powers of rulership as they may have obtained by way of delegation by the Nation, that is, by those constituent bodies that are assumed to speak for the Nation. The doctrine therefore renders constitutionally impossible all forms of government which are founded upon, or which involve, the recognition of a right of rulership inhering as a personal underived right, in particular persons or groups of individuals. The doctrine of the sovereignty of the State, upon the other hand, as developed in the present treatise, is one of pure political or juristic theory. It is wholly indifferent to, and, therefore, is compatible with, any form of government, whether autocratic or democratic.[16]   In other words, the concepts of Nation (or People) and the State are not to be confused. The vesting of sovereignty in the Nation or people is, as has been said, a constitutional doctrine and not one of pure political theory.

Austin's Theory as to the Determinateness of the Situs of Sovereignty in the Body-Politic.   As is well known, in his definitions of law and of the State Austin emphasized the idea that a law is a command that emanates from a

[16] Malberg is, therefore, not quite correct when, contrasting the constitutional doctrine of the pure monarchy with that of Souveraineté Nationale, he says: "Dans le premier, l'État ne personnifie que lui même, la nation n'étant que l'un des facteurs dont la réunion a pour effet de former l'établissement public État; dans le second, la nation n'est pas seulement l'un des éléments qui concourent à constituer l'État, mais elle s'identifie avec lui et il ne personnifie qu'elle. Dans le premier système encore, l'État devient une personne par le fait qu'il a un organe propre, le monarque; dans le second, la personne État, étant identique avec la personne nation, existe par le fait que la nation elle-même se trouve organisée. Enfin et par suite de ses différences initiales, dans le premier système, le monarque a puissance sur la nation considérée comme élément subalterne de l'État; dans le second c'est, au contraire, la nation qui a puissance sur le monarque envisagé comme organe national." *Op. cit.*, II, p. 189.

determinate source, and that, as a prerequisite to the existence of a State, there must exist a determinate individual or a determinate group of individuals who possess the sovereign right of declaring law, and who, in addition, are able to secure, if not the uniform, at the least the habitual, obedience to this law upon the part of the bulk of the community to which it is addressed.

Austin says: "If a determinate human superior, not in a habit of obedience to a like superior, receive habitual obedience from the bulk of a given society, that determinate superior is sovereign in that society, and that society (including the superior) is a society political and independent."[17]   This determinate human superior, Austin elsewhere says, may be a single individual definitely marked out, or a body of individuals the members of which may be determined by some definite ascertainable quality or characteristic.

It is especially to be observed in this definition that Austin vests the sovereignty, not in the State, but in this determinate individual or body of individuals. There is no question as to this for he goes on to say: "It is only through an ellipsis that the society is termed independent. The part truly independent (independent, that is to say, of a determinate human superior) is not the society, but the sovereign portion of that society." And again he says: "An independent political society is divisible into two portions, namely, the portion of its members which is sovereign and superior, and the portion of its members which is merely subject . . . When the sovereign portion consists of a single member, the supreme government is properly termed a monarchy, or the sovereign is properly termed a monarch."

At this point the doctrines developed in the present treatise depart from those of Austin. Austin, it is clear,

[17] *Province of Jurisprudence Determined,* chap. VI.

does not make that distinction between the State and its Government, between pure political theory and constitutional doctrine, which the author has continued to emphasize. It may be granted to Austin that a command or positive law must issue from a determinate source, but, in political theory, that determinate source is always the particular State that is under examination.

Legislative Power. Bearing in mind what has gone before, it is evident that the search for the determinate sovereign governmental organ of a State is an inquiry that has to be separately performed for each State, and the answer obtained from the special system of constitutional jurisprudence which such State possesses. This much, however, may be declared in general terms: that sovereignty being the omnicompetent legal will of the State, its operation is especially manifested when the policies of the State are declared. These policies are for the most part embodied in the laws of the State, but may also, as, for example, in international affairs, be decided upon or made known either in the form of treaties or by other executive declarations or action. In a very true sense, however, every act of every organ of government, if justified by existing constitutional and statute law, is an act of sovereignty. In a more special sense, however, the State's sovereignty is manifested in the enactment of the laws which determine what the various organs of government shall be legally competent to do. There is thus some force in the statement of Locke that, "In all cases whilst the Government subsists the legislative is the supreme power. For what can give laws to another must needs be superior to him, and since the legislative is no otherwise legislative of the society but by the right it has to make laws for all parts, and every member of the society prescribing rules to their actions, and giving power of execution where they are transgressed, the legislative must needs be supreme, and all other powers in any members of parts of the society derived from and subordinate to it." [18]

It has already been pointed out that the electorate of a State is to be distinguished from the People or entire citizen body. There are instances in which the electorate acts as a legislative organ. This happens whenever there exists a constitutional provision or practice according to which law may be created by a *referendum* or other plebiscital method. When so called upon for its vote, the electorate is to be considered *ad hoc* a legislative body. Of course, in those cases where a vote of the people is had merely for the purpose of discovering what the public sentiment is upon a given proposal, and without the power of such a vote itself to give a legal validity or non-validity to the proposal, we do not have the electorate exercising the law-making power.

Understanding now by Sovereignty a power which is capable of exercise only through existing governmental agencies, it necessarily follows that this supreme power is exhibited whenever the will of the State is expressed. In fact, it is almost correct to say that the sovereign will is the State, that the State exists only as a supreme controlling will, and that its life is only displayed in the declaration of binding commands, the enforcement of which is left to mere executive agents. These executive agents, while acting as such, have no will of their own, and are but implements for the performance of that will which gives to them a political and legal authority.

This, then, locates the exercise of Sovereignty in the law-making bodies. By whomsoever, or whatsoever body, therefore, the will of the State is expressed, and the law created, there we have Sovereignty exercised. If we distinguish between executive, judicial and legislative departments of the State, it is in this last-named department that the exercise of Sovereignty rests. The only

[18] *Two Treatises of Government*, bk. II, chap. 13.

point that we must remember is that the term "legislative" must not be so narrowly construed as to limit its application to those bodies by which formal statutory enactments are made. Insofar as the chief executive of the State has the ordinance power, he may express the sovereign will and therefore exercise Sovereignty. As we know, this power was, in former times, very extensive in England, and still persists to a considerable degree in all modern States. The entire constitutional history of England is in fact but little more than a record of the manner in which this royal power of law-making has been curtailed, and the legislative power of Parliament taken its place. Again, constitutional conventions, insofar as they have the direct power of creating constitutional law, exercise this sovereign power. Finally, insofar as courts are the organs of the State for the creation of law, they express the will of the State and hence exercise Sovereignty.

It may be said that courts are able to legislate only by the acquiescence of the legislative body which may negative by statute the principles which they have declared; and hence that they act but as agents of the legislature proper. In the same way, it may also be said that, in many States, the ordinary legislature exercises its powers only by right of constitutional law, and therefore that it, in turn, but voices the will of those who establish this fundamental law. This is certainly true, and therefore, in any given State, it may be said, in one sense, that that organ possesses the final sovereign power which creates those laws that organize the Government, and distribute powers among its several governmental agents. In a measure we have already discussed this point in our consideration of the nature of constitutional provisions as compared with that of other forms of law. In a country like England, such a supreme body is the Parliament, but in those countries where government rests upon written constitutions, it is the organs that have the legal right to modify the terms of such instruments.

By some jurists it is asserted that courts create law not merely by reason of the fact that they establish and apply rules that have previously had no legal—or even customary—existence, but because in them lies the authority to determine the meaning to be given to the laws as enacted by the formal legislative organs of the government. Thus Gray, after defining the law of a State as "composed of the rules which the courts, that is the judicial organs of that body, lay down for the determination of legal rights and duties," [19] in a later section [20] says:

"The true view, as I submit, is that the Law is what the judges declare; that statutes, precedents, the opinions of experts, customs, and morality are the sources of the Law; that back of everything lie the opinions of the ruling spirits of the community; who have the power to close any of the sources; but that so long as they do not interfere, the judges, in establishing Law, have recourse to these sources."

Earlier in his volume, Professor Gray had made his position upon this point still more emphatic in the following words: "It has been sometimes said that the Law is composed of two parts,—legislative law and judge-made law, but, in truth, all law is judge-made law. The shape in which a statute is imposed on the community as a guide for conduct is that statute as interpreted by the courts. The courts put life into the dead words of the statute." [21]

It cannot be denied that there is considerable force in

---

[19] *The Nature and Sources of Law,* sec. 191.
[20] *Idem,* sec. 602.
[21] *Op. cit.,* sec. 276. Professor Gray quotes with approval the words of Bishop Hoadly: "Nay, whoever hath an absolute authority to interpret

the foregoing views; and to the extent that it is accepted it increases the part played by the courts as the legislative or will-expressing organs of the State. But so long as the courts, in fact, make no claim of right and in fact exercise no right to construe statutes in a wholly arbitrary manner, according to their own opinions as to the justice or expediency of the rules of conduct embodied in the enactments of the legislature, but limit their function to the interpretation or construction of the language of these statutes, the doctrine which denies a real law-making function to the legislature seems a forced one. In any case, however, the will that is declared and enforced is that of the Sovereign State.

Austin's Error. It might have been thought that Austin, in his search for the determinate superior in a given politically organized society, would have been satisfied when he had found the supreme law-making organ of government. But this he was not content to do, and, by continuing his search, overstepped the bounds of the jurisprudence for the determination of the limits of which his lectures were denoted, and wandered confusedly in the realms of political or social forces.

Thus, Austin located sovereignty in Great Britain in the Kings, Lords, and Commons. But by Commons he was not content to mean the lower branch of Parliament, but designated thereby the electors of the lower house. "Speaking accurately," he says, "the members of the commons' house are merely trustees for the body by which they are elected and appointed; and consequently the Sovereignty always resides in the Kings and the peers, with the electoral body of the commons." [22]   Here, as

any written or spoken laws, it is He who is truly the law-giver, to all intents and purposes, and not the person who first wrote and spoke them."

[22] *The Province of Jurisprudence Determined*, ed. 1861, p. 201.

Professor Ritchie has pointed out, he no longer speaks as
a lawyer. "For a lawyer *qua* lawyer a law is good law
though it were passed by a Parliament which had abol-
ished the Septennial Act and had gone on sitting as long
as the Long Parliament, quite as much as if the law were
passed by a newly summoned Parliament of the elected
part of which, an overwhelming majority, had been returned expressly pledged to vote for this very law. With
the wishes or feelings of the electors the lawyer as lawyer
has nothing whatever to do, however much they may
affect him as a politician or as a reasonable man." [23] To
the same effect is the dictum of Professor Dicey, that
nothing is more certain than that no English judge ever
conceded, or under the present constitution can concede
that Parliament is in any legal sense a trustee for the electors: a dictum that is conclusively verified by the power
of parliament, several times exercised, to lengthen its
own existence without any reference to the voters by
whom its members had been elected for a shorter
period.[24]

[23] *Annals of the Am. Acad. of Pol. and Soc. Science,* January, 1891,
p. 392.
[24] *Law of the Constitution,* 4th ed., pp. 69-71. We may profitably
quote the following paragraphs as not only showing this point, but as
illustrating the distinction that we have emphasized between Sovereignty
as a purely legal conception, and as the ultimate conditioning force of
public opinion: "It should, however, be carefully noted," says Dicey,
"that the term 'Sovereignty,' as long as it is accurately employed in the
sense in which Austin sometimes uses it, is a merely legal conception,
and means simply the power of law-making, unrestricted by any legal
limit. If the term 'Sovereignty' be thus used, the sovereign power under
the English constitution is clearly 'Parliament.' But the word 'Sovereignty' is sometimes employed in a political, rather than in a strictly
legal sense. That body is 'politically' sovereign or supreme in a State
the will of which is ultimately obeyed by the citizens of the State. In
this sense of the word, the electors of Great Britain may be said to be,
together with the Crown and the Lords, or perhaps, in strict accuracy,
independently of the King and the Peers, the body in which sovereign
power is vested. . . . But this is a political and not a legal fact.
The electors can in the long run always enforce their will. But the
courts will take no notice of the will of the electors. The judges know

In like manner, in the case of the United States, Austin does not discover legal Sovereignty in the legislative bodies of the individual Commonwealths, or in the federal Congress, or in both combined. He sees the legal competence of these bodies apparently limited by written constitutions, and therefore places Sovereignty in the electorates that select the bodies by which these written instruments may be amended. "I believe," says he, "that the Sovereignty of each of the States, and also of the larger State arising from the federal union, resides in the State's government, not its ordinary legislature, but the body of its citizens which appoint its ordinary legislature, and which, the union apart, is properly sovereign therein." [25]

The same criticism is here valid that was applied to Austin's location of Sovereignty in the English electorate. His doctrines are unsatisfactory, not only to the jurist, but to those who, when they speak of sovereignty, refer to the ultimate force of Public Opinion, for those who take this latter view make the electorate but an organ of the whole body of citizens, by whom it is influenced and in many ways controlled.

Professor John Dewey makes also the criticism that this electorate is not even determinate. His argument is as follows: If the electorate be the sovereign, then each voter is a sharer in the Sovereignty. But what of the voters who prove to be in the minority? "If we say he (*i.e.*, one of the minority) did share in Sovereignty because he had a right to vote, we say Sovereignty may be exercised apart from the utterance of commands, indeed, even in opposing the fundamental command. But if we say that, since not participating in the expression of the

nothing about any will of the people except in so far as that will is expressed by an Act of Parliament, and would never suffer the validity of a statute to be questioned on the ground of its being passed or kept alive in opposition to the wishes of the electors."
[25] *The Province of Jurisprudence Determined,* ed. 1861, p. 222.

supreme command, he is not sovereign, the question arises by what right he voted at all." [26]

This reasoning of Professor Dewey is unsatisfactory. It is just as applicable to a legislative body as to a popular gathering. What of the members of the minority in the English Parliament? The fact is, that when Austin or any other writer refers to an electorate as exercising Sovereignty, he, or they, refer to such an electorate as a collective body of which each member possesses an indivisible portion of the Sovereignty of the whole. That is, that the citizen shares in the Sovereignty not as an individual but as a member of the whole. Each citizen holds, as lawyers say, *per tout* only, and not *per my,* as Professor Dewey would seem to think. Rousseau makes this distinction very plain by expressly distinguishing between the "will of all" and the "General Will." [27] The distinction between Sovereignty as a juristic conception and the ultimate conditioning power of popular opinion, was, however, one that was never reached by Rousseau, who completely identifies Sovereignty with the "General Will." It is in consequence of this assumption, that, in searching for the manner in which this sovereign power may be legally exercised, he was forced to hold that "laws being but authentic acts of the General Will, the sovereign cannot act except when the People is assembled." [28] And again, that "Sovereignty cannot be represented for the same reason that it cannot be alienated; it consists essentially of the General Will, and the will cannot be represented; it is the same or it is different; there is no mean. The deputies of the people then are not, and cannot be its representatives, they are only its commissioners; they can conclude nothing definitely. Any law which the people in

[26] "Austin's Theory of Sovereignty," *Pol. Sci. Quar.,* March 1894.
[27] *The Social Contract,* bk. II, chap. III.
[28] *Idem,* bk. III, chap. XII.

person has not ratified is null; it is not a law." [29]   Thus the position is taken that all authority exercised other than by warrant of the general assembly of the people is illegal, and a government thus acting has only a *de facto* and not a *de jure* existence—a position according to which there was not at the time of Rousseau's writing, nor has there been since, a State in Europe in which rebellion would have been an illegal act.

Comparing these views with those held by Hobbes and Locke, we find that, according to the former of these writers, a sovereign organ, be it a monarch or a popular assembly, is made practically identical with the sovereign State itself, and, as such, incapable of legal limitation. Thus, in all truthfulness, the absolute ruler might say that *l'état, c'est moi*. The agent is identified with the principal, government is confused with the State, the machine absorbs the power that moves it. Apart, however, from this confusion between State and Government Hobbes developed a substantially correct theory of law and Sovereignty, though he needlessly based it upon an illogical fiction.

Locke, though founding his system on the same fictional contract, came much nearer the comprehension of the true nature of government in his declaration of its limited delegated character, and the essentially representative capacity, of all political agents. It would also seem that at times he perceived the distinction between the actual ultimate power of the people to condition political action, and the legal or sovereign action of the State. Thus he declares "the community may be said in this respect to be always the supreme power but not as considered under any form of government, because this power of the people can never take place till the

[29] *Two Treatises of Government*, bk. III, chap. XV.

government be dissolved." [30]   But his preconceived ideas
of natural rights and of sovereignty as resting upon a
contract make him speak in general of this ultimate
right of the people as something more than a mere moral
right, or as a power founded upon mere might.   For the
same reason he does not always sufficiently recognize
that the State may be so organized as to permit sovereign
action greatly opposed to public will and to public interest, and yet strictly constitutional and legal.   Thus,
in considering what is to be done in case an executive,
to whom has been entrusted the power of calling together
the legislative branch, should refuse to exercise such
power, to the detriment of the people, he describes such
action as "contrary to the trust put in him that does
so," and as "a state of war with the people who have a
right to reinstate their legislative in the exercise of their
power." [31]

Here the theory of a contract between governed and
governing again crops out.   The juristic fact is, however,
that governmental agents exercise a power delegated or
granted to them by the State, and not one created by a
joining of their wills with those of the subjects.   The only
will concerned is that of the State.   Public officials are,
in other words, agents of the State, not of the People.
They have no legal relation to the People as such, and,
therefore, there can be no breach of contract with them
in whatever manner they may exercise their power.   If
they exceed their legal competence, or are in any way
guilty of non-feasance or malfeasance of office, they are
punishable only by the State.   Therefore, any action of
theirs, however oppressive, does not, as Locke would say,
ipso facto deprive them of political power, and place them

[30] *Two Treatises of Government,* bk. II, p. 149.
[31] *Two Treatises of Government,* bk. II, p. 155.

in a state of war with their former subjects. Such action is not even illegal if within their competence, and is as fully valid as would be the most beneficent measure. If *ultra vires*, however, the action is of course illegal and not an act of the State, but of the official as a private individual, and one for which he is personally responsible. But such illegality extends only to the particular act itself. It has no influence over the general public or sovereign *status* of such official. Rousseau is thus perfectly correct in denying that a Government is established by a contract.

CHAPTER X

THE ascription of Sovereignty to the State, and the definition of Sovereignty as legal omnicompetence have made it necessary to view the State as the sole source of law in a positive or strictly juristic sense. This is a proposition which many have found the most difficult to accept of all the assertions of analytical jurisprudence and it will therefore be necessary to consider it with some degree of care, and especially is this so because of the varying meanings which are commonly attached to the word "Law."

As opposed to the description of Law as the sequences of events in the physical universe—sequences that occur without reference to and beyond the control of men's wills —the jurist uses the word as declaring a rule or principle for the governance of human action. Its characteristic in this sense is that it is capable of being expressed as a distinct proposition to rational beings in the form and character of a command. As thus conceived, a law implies that he who issues it has, or claims to have some sort of legal authority over the persons whose actions are to be controlled; that, in other words, as between him and them there is a relation of jural superiority and inferiority. Out of this relation also arises the idea of legal obligation upon the part of those to whom the commands are directed, and of legal right upon the part of those who will be beneficially interested in having these obligations fulfilled.

Laws, as Austin says, are rules laid down for the guidance of intelligent beings by intelligent beings having authority over them. As thus defined, they include commands set by God to men, and those set by men to men. With the former, jurisprudence is not concerned. But, even with regard to the laws set by men to men, the analytical jurist is concerned only with those which are issued by men who claim a political superiority over those men whose actions are to be controlled by them. Laws, thus set, are spoken of as positive in character.

Rules of conduct not in the form of commands from a superior to an inferior, Austin continues, are rules of morality, and, though often spoken of as laws, are not properly so-called, or at least, are not properly so-called if the term law be used in its sense of a command emanating from a determinate political source. Such are the so-called laws of honor or of fashion, and other rules of conduct supported by public opinion. These become "positive" rules, though still not positive laws, when they assume the form of commands from determinate human beings but not as based upon a claim of political superiority. They become positive laws, or laws properly so-called only when there is this relationship of political superiority and political inferiority.

Thus, with reference to the recognized rules of conduct regulating the relations between States, Austin says: "These are not laws properly so-called. But one supreme government may doubtless command another to forbear from a kind of conduct which the [so-called] law of nations condemns. And, though it is fashioned on law which is law improperly so-called, this command is a law in the proper sense of the term [but not a 'positive' law]. Speaking precisely, the command is a rule of positive morality set by a determinate author. For, as no supreme government is in a state of subjection to another, the command, though fashioned on the law of nations, would not amount to a positive law. Nor does the government which gives the command act as the executor of a command proceeding from the uncertain body—the collective family or aggregate of nations. That government may, however, act as the executor of a command proceeding from a definite number of sovereign States allied under a treaty. In that case there would be a command issuing from the allied States collectively, and enforced by the one government as their minister. This would be still a rule of positive morality and not positive law, because the government or State which is to be coerced would not (on the hypothesis) be in a state of subjection either to the allied governments collectively, or to the government which has for the occasion acted as their minister." [1]

Austin, as we have seen, classifies also constitutional laws as rules of positive morality rather than as positive laws properly so-called. His error in this respect has already been examined.[2]

We are thus prepared for the statement of Austin that: "Every positive law or every law simply and strictly so called, is set by a sovereign person, or a sovereign body of persons, to a member or members of the independent political society wherein that person or body is sovereign or supreme." [3]

In another place Austin somewhat expands the statement which we have quoted by saying that every positive law is set directly or circuitously by the sovereign, and, therefore, that laws may be declared by private persons in pursuance of legal rights.

The foregoing are declarations of fact, and the question is whether they may be squared with other well known facts, and especially with the fact that the judicial

---

[1] *Province of Jurisprudence Determined*, sec. 150.
[2] Chap. VIII.
[3] *Province of Jurisprudence Determined*, sec. 189.

tribunals of all governments, in the settlement of controversies coming before them, apply principles or rules of conduct which have not found previous explicit and definite statement as commands of the State of which these tribunals are the governmental agents.

If, in a given State, one wishes to determine concretely what are the laws of that State, it is certainly correct to say that they are the rules or principles which the judicial tribunals of the State will apply in the cases adjudicated by them. Thus says Salmond: "Law consists of the rules recognized and acted on in courts of justice" [4]; or, as Gray declares: "The Law of the State or of any organized body of men is composed of the rules which the courts, that is, the judicial organs of that body, lay down for the determination of legal rights and duties." [5]

It was of course obvious to Austin, as it has been to all those who have accepted his proposition that the State's will is to be viewed as the creative source of all positive law, that the rules or substantive principles of conduct embodied in the decisions of courts have been, in considerable measure, the product of popular custom or of the practice of the courts themselves. Hence it has been contended by many that the Austinian doctrine is not in accordance with obvious and incontestable facts. In other words, it is argued that the large body of legal principles, commonly called customary law, which the courts apply and the State enforces, arises independently of State enactment. Especially has this criticism of the orthodox analytical jurist been advanced by writers of what is termed the Historical School of Jurisprudence, and by those who still cling to doctrines of Natural Law.

The contention of Natural Law adherents that the State is not to be viewed as the sole creator of law, is suf-

[4] *Jurisprudence.*
[5] *The Nature and Sources of Law,* sec. 191.

ficiently disposed of by pointing out that, granting all that is claimed, the only result is to show that, as an ethical proposition, those in possession of political power should be guided by certain fundamental and absolute principles of justice and moral right when determining the positive laws which they will cause to be enforced by political power. The argument of the Historical School of Jurists requires, however, a more detailed examination. In England this school is headed by the name of Sir Henry Maine, and, upon the Continent by Savigny and Puchta. In general American writers are also of this school.

"Positive Law," says Savigny, "springs from that general spirit which animates all the members of the Nation, and the unity of the law is revealed necessarily to their consciences and is by no means the effect of chance." [6] The growth of custom he compares to that of language, and continues: "Law which lives in the common consciousness of the people is not composed of abstract rules. It exists rather in the actual perception of a legal institute in its organic connection, and the rule appears in its logical form so soon as the need for it is felt; it is then singled out from this connection, and is translated in an artificial manner." [7] In other words, according to Savigny, law exists as law independently of the State. It is the creation of the national consciousness or spirit of a people and is evidenced by their customary habits. Even formal statutory enactments, according to this view, are able to secure recognition and enforcement only insofar as they conform in their provisions to the "Spirit" of the people. When, therefore, they are formally enunciated by the courts or legislatures, the function of the State is rather that of realizing and enforcing the law than of creating it.

[6] *System des heutigen römischen Rechts*, sec. **7.**
[7] *Idem*, sec. **7.**

While the above quotations from Savigny serve to show
what has undoubtedly been the dominant attitude of
German jurists during the last century, certain of their
number show a tendency to turn to a position more
similar to that of the analytical jurists of England.
Especially is this apparent in Ihering's *Zweck im Recht,*
and Lasson's *System der Rechtsphilosophie.*

In England, on the other hand, the high authority of
the Austinian School has been considered as greatly
shaken by the historical method introduced into the study
of law by Sir Henry Maine. This writer is supposed to
have pointed out that, throughout the greater portion of
the world's history, law was created otherwise than according to the Austinian theory, and, therefore, that, if
his conception of the source of law be applicable at all,
it is applicable only to highly developed States. The following quotation from Maine sufficiently indicates his
position. Referring to an Indian despot, he says: "At
first sight there could be no more perfect embodiment
than Runjett Singh of sovereignty as conceived by
Austin. He was absolutely despotic. Except occasionally
on his wild frontier he kept the most perfect order. He
could have commanded anything: the smallest disobedience to his commands would have been followed by death
or mutilation, and this was perfectly well known to the
enormous majority of his subjects. Yet I doubt whether
once in all his life he issued a command which Austin
would call a law. . . . . He had all material of power
and he exercised it in various ways. But he never made
law." [8]

It is to be observed that Maine admits the verbal
truth of Austin's theory, for he adds: "I do not for a
moment assert that the existence of such a state of
political society falsifies Austin's theory. The maxim by

[8] *Early History of Institutions,* p. 380.

which objections to it are disposed of is, as I have so often said before, that what the sovereign permits, he commands." The position which is taken, however, in the present work is that there is more than a verbal truth in the thesis that all law, as law, emanates from the sovereign; and that when a customary rule is declared by a court of justice to be one which the State will enforce, such rule becomes specifically distinct from what it had before been.

A characteristic American argument against the Austinian view is that contained in the opening chapters of Wharton's *Commentaries on American Law*. This author writes as follows: "By whom were existing English statutes winnowed in the colonies of Massachusetts and Pennsylvania, for instance, so as to retain such as suited the temper and met the wants of the people, and to set aside all others? This was not done by the colonial assemblies; had such a process of radical revision been attempted by these assemblies it would have been promptly vetoed by the king in Council. It was not done by the British Parliament, though the British Parliament assumed to be the sole supreme legislature by whose laws these colonies were controlled. It was done by popular assent produced by national conscience and national need. It is true that when the colonies became independent sovereigns they passed laws by which the process of selection and rejection thus carried out was approved. But it was never pretended that the process of selection and rejection derived its authority from such legislation. On the contrary, when the colonies became sovereigns, what their court said was, 'the law of the land, in this respect, was not imposed by the sovereign on the people, but was adopted by the people and afterwards accepted by the sovereign.' The same may be said of the rulings of our courts as to international and interstate law, and the law regulating Indian tribes." [9]   And again he says: "That custom makes the law and not law custom, is shown by the fact just noticed, that when a custom is recognized by the courts as existing, the recognition operates retrospectively, the custom being regarded as law before it was judicially recognized." [10]

In considering now these criticisms that are made upon the Austinian position as to the nature of law, it is to be observed that much the greater part of these objections are in fact examples of *ignoratio elenchi,* the confusion arising, as Holland correctly points out, from the ambiguous sense in which the term "source of law" may be used.[11]   This expression may be used either to denote the mode in which, or the person through whom, have been formulated those rules which have acquired the force of law; or, to denote the authority which gives them that force.

Now, so far as it is used in the first sense, there is no denial made by the Analytical School that custom is, in very large measure, the source of law; that is, that, through this medium, have arisen the principles of social conduct that have been subsequently embodied in law. Furthermore, it is not asserted that, as an actual fact, the exigencies of public life have not at all times demanded that the sovereign power should found the expression of its will upon these rules. What the analytical jurist does maintain is, that these customary rules do not become law in a strictly legal or positive sense, until they are accepted by the political power. As Austin says, "There can be no law without a judicial sanction, and until custom has been adopted as law by courts of justice it is always uncertain whether it will be sustained by that sanc-

[9] *Commentaries on American Law,* sec. 2.
[10] *Idem,* sec. 15, note.
[11] *Elements of Jurisprudence,* 6th ed., p. 49.

tion or not." [12] And, again, "The description, completion, and correction of positive morality are as much an end for which political government is wanted, as the obtaining by its establishment of a more cogent sanction. But the sovereign makes it law, not by the mere description, but by the sanction with which he clothes it." [13]

It is obvious that the objections that have been founded on the historical evidences quoted by Wharton and Maine are applicable solely to the question of the origination of the principles embodied in the law,—a question with which the Austinians are not concerned. Thus, when Maine says that the Indian despot never made a law, he can only mean that he never arbitrarily established a general rule of conduct. What he did do, however, was to accept such rules of conduct as rules of the State, and thereby, as the Analytical School claims, elevate such principles into legal rules. It is no answer to say that, in the case of many of the earlier monarchies, they were simply tax-collecting empires, and that there was no attempt, or even desire, on the part of their rulers to interfere with the domestic rules that obtained in the various portions of their kingdoms. The point is, that the very least important of the customary rules that obtained acceptance in those countries by the lowest courts or judicial officers, thereby obtained a sanction that was ultimately supported by the entire strength of the sovereign political authority.

Again, it is no answer to the assertion that the State is the sole creator of law to show that no State can maintain its control that does not in general accept as its will those principles of justice and utility that are evolved by the customary habit of its people; that, in other words, the attempt on its part to establish arbitrary

[12] *Lectures on Jurisprudence*, sec. II, p. 564.
[13] *Idem*, sec. II, p. 567.

rules of conduct not based on the needs and capacities of the people, as evidenced by their customary habits of life, would lead inevitably to revolt and revolution. This would only show that, as a principle of political expediency, (*i.e.,* of caution and prudence), a general acceptance of customary rules is necessary. The fact that legislative commands or judicially declared principles of conduct are not enforced, or, possibly, cannot be enforced because of the active or passive resistance upon the part of the people that an attempt to put them into effect would arouse, does not deprive these state-sanctioned orders of their right to be entitled laws; for it is not the actual enforcement of a rule by the State which transmutes it into a positive law, but the authentic manifestation by the State that it accepts or declares that rule to be an expression of its sovereign will.

Finally, it is not a refutation of the position which is here defended, to point to the fact that a court of justice, in accepting a custom as law, does not declare that henceforth such principle shall obtain as law, but holds it to have been the law at the time of the accruing of the cause of action whose merits are then decided.

The position of Holland, who is possibly the best exponent of Austin's system today, differs from that of Austin upon this point, and is an attempt, it would seem, to avoid the objection rather than to answer it. Holland says: "The Courts have, therefore, long ago established as a fundamental principle of law, subject of course in each case to many restrictions and qualifications, that, in the absence of a specific rule of written law, regard is to be had in looking for the rule which governs a given set of circumstances, not only to equity and to previous decision, but also to custom. Binding authority has thus been conceded to custom, provided it fulfils certain requirements, the nature of which has also long since been settled, and provided it is not superseded by law of a higher authority. When, therefore, a given set of circumstances is brought into Court, and the Court decides upon them by bringing them within the operation of a custom, the Court appeals to that custom as it might to any other pre-existent law. It does not *proprio motu* then for the first time make that custom a law; it merely decides as a fact that there exists a legal custom, about which there might up to that moment have been some question, as there might about the interpretation of an Act of Parliament. It then applies the custom to the circumstances just as it might have applied an Act of Parliament to them. A good custom or an intelligible Act of Parliament either exists or does not exist objectively, before the case comes into Court; although it is from the decision of the Court in the particular case that a subjective knowledge is first possible for the people of the existence or non-existence of the alleged custom, or that this or that is the meaning of the Act of Parliament." [14]

It would certainly seem that Holland admits the very point against which he contends, when he says that the court does not for the first time make a custom a law by its adjudication, but "merely decides as a fact that there exists a legal custom about which there might up to that moment have been some question, as there might about the interpretation of an Act of Parliament." This certainly limits the action of the court to one of interpretation. And, as one of his critics has properly said, "To say that customs are regarded as laws by virtue of a tacit law to that effect, is simply to beg the whole question. It is to say that custom is law in virtue of custom." [15]

The proper position upon this point would seem to be to admit frankly that judicial legislation is *ex post facto*

[14] *Elements of Jurisprudence*, 6th ed., pp. 54, 55.
[15] Prof. John Dewey in *Pol. Sci. Quar.*, March, 1894, p. 47.

legislation. But what has this to do with the question as to the effect of such decisions of the courts upon custom? It is, to be sure, a general principle of legislation that laws should not be retroactive in their effect, but this is a principle dictated by general considerations of justice, and not of necessity. There is no more inherent difficulty in the State establishing retroactive law than there is in its creating law that shall be of only prospective application. That this is the case, is seen in the necessity of explicitly providing in our own written constitutions that neither Congress nor the State legislatures shall pass *ex post facto* enactments. In the case of legislatures not thus arbitrarily limited, as, for example, the British Parliament, no court would hold a retroactive act invalid if passed according to due forms and procedure. Laws established by means of formal statutory enactments, are, as a rule, created without reference to particular cases, and therefore injustice would necessarily result had such enactments a retroactive character. When, however, we come to judicial legislation, we come to a field where this *ex post facto* principle is not recognized,—not recognized because from the very nature of the case no necessity of justice demands it. By the recognition of a custom as law, no arbitrary or novel doctrines of right are established by the court. Principles only are declared as enforcible that already obtain in practice among the people. Hence, no possible injustice is done by declaring such customs then and there to be laws, and at the same time applying them to the causes of action that have previously accrued. There is no need to predicate a tacit law to the effect that such customs shall be law, but simply to admit that judicial legislation is *ex post facto* legislation, and to defend it as such; in fine, to make the action of the court not simply interpretative, but actually creative of law.

We may, then, accept as valid the reasoning of Austin when he says: [16]

"At its origin, a custom is a rule of conduct which the governed observe spontaneously or not in pursuance of a law set by a political superior. The custom is transmuted into positive law when it is adopted as such, either by being expressly embodied in statutes promulgated by the sovereign authority, or implicitly by decisions of the courts of justice which are enforced by the power of the State.

"For a legal rule introduced by a judicial decision (whether suggested by custom or not) is in effect legislation by the sovereign. A subordinate or subject judge is merely a minister. The rules which he makes derive their legal force from authority given by the State; an authority which the State may confer expressly, but which it commonly imparts by way of acquiescence. For, since the State may reverse the rules which he makes, and yet permits him to enforce them by the power of the political community, its sovereign will that the rules shall obtain as law, is clearly evinced by its conduct though not by its express declaration. . . . . Like other significations of desire, a command is express or tacit. If the desire be signified by words (written or spoken) the command is express. If the desire is signified by conduct (or by any signs of desire which are not words) the command is tacit. Now when customs are turned into legal rules by decisions of subject judges, the legal rules which emerge from the customs are tacit commands of the sovereign legislature. The State which is able to abolish, permits its members to express them; and it therefore signifies its pleasure by its voluntary acquiescence, that they shall serve as a law to the governed."

[16] *Province of Jurisprudence Determined*, Lecture I.

A little reflection shows how indefinite would be the term "law" if applied to custom and civil rules alike. So long as customary rules retain their purely customary form, that which gives to them force and efficiency for regulation is not the threat of coercion, or the imposition of penalties by a superior power in case of their violation. Their force is solely derived from the pressure of public opinion, of religious sanction, of individual sense of right, or the possibility of personal retaliation on the part of those persons injured by such violation. Such influences as these are of the most variable character, and personal in the highest degree. Their force depends almost wholly upon the subjective condition of the individual, upon his own peculiar temperament of mind, his sense of justice, his religious reverence, his regard for the traditional, his power of self-restraint, and his sensitiveness to the good-will of the community. Such principles, then, possess no force of their own, no compelling power; obedience to them is secured only by the voluntary consent of the individual, such consent being based upon the dictates of reason, expediency, and right that dwell within his own breast.

When, therefore, it is asked so to broaden the connotation of the term "law" as to include such elements as these, it may be answered that logical exactness and scientific accuracy demand that a more definite meaning be given to this word. Definitions are valuable only insofar as they give a precision of meaning to words and expressions. Their sole utility consists in the demarcation of a definite field within which the word or phrase is applicable, and it will be apparent that to include within the meaning of law elements that differ so widely as the purely customary principles of which we have been speaking, and the rigid rules of conduct, formally enunciated by the State and enforcible by its sovereign right, is to create a signification for the word that cannot be sufficiently definite to serve as a basis upon which to found a formal science of jurisprudence and politics. What decisive and universally applicable definition shall we give to law, if custom is to share with the State the power of its creation? When shall we know at any one time what is and what is not the law? What but confusion must necessarily result from conceiving two co-ordinate law-making authorities, each having the right to create law independently of the other, or to abrogate and overrule each other's creations?

In result, then, we are justified in defining law, in the strict positive or juristic sense, as those rules of conduct that courts of justice apply in the exercise of their jurisdictions. As distinguished from all other rules of conduct that obtain more or less general recognition in a community of men, they are such as have for their validity the sanction of the State. The scientific value of such a definite connotation of the term "law" is obviously great. By it alone is rendered possible a definite and exact knowledge of the facts to which this department of knowledge relates, and a sound basis afforded upon which to rest the conception of the Sovereignty of the State.[17]

The sense in which the courts rather than the formal law-making or legislative branches of a government may be said to be organs through which the State creates its law has been examined in the preceding chapter in which the location of sovereignty in the body-politic was considered. The matter of the recognition and application of

[17] Regarding the value of Austin's conception of law and Sovereignty, Mr. Justice Markby (*Elements of Law*, 2d ed., p. 4) speaks as follows: "Austin, by establishing the distinction between law and morals, not only laid the foundation for a science of law, but cleared the conception of law and of sovereignty of a number of pernicious consequences to which, in the hands of his predecessors, it had been supposed to lead. Laws, as Austin has shown, must be legally binding; and yet a law may be unjust. Resistance to authority cannot be a legal right, and yet it may be a virtue."

international law principles by municipal courts is discussed in the chapter entitled "International Law." [18]
The argument there stated applies as well to the recognition and enforcement by one State of the municipal law
of another State.

Permissive Laws. The objection to viewing laws as
"commands" of the State, based upon the fact that many
laws are permissive rather than mandatory or declaratory
in character, is sufficiently answered by pointing out that
in all cases where this is so there are created or recognized rights which have a legal force and which are protected by laws which are mandatory in character. Of
permissive and merely declaratory laws, it can always be
claimed that they are to be considered not as complete
legal provisions but as integral parts of the mandatory
laws which support them.

Considerable discussion has centered around the point
whether the term law, in a positive or any other sense,
should be limited in its application to those expressions of
the States' will which state a general rule. To the writer,
however, it seems clear that any order, or decree, or administrative ordinance, even though it relate to the performance of but a single act by a particular individual, is
a law; that is, it expresses the sovereign will of the State
if it is one which has the support of some more general
law or is declared in pursuance of a legally delegated governmental power.[19]

**Actual Enforcement Not an Essential Element in the
Concept of Positive Law.** A more difficult question is
whether it is necessary that a rule should be actually en-

[18] See chap. XVI.
[19] A by-law of a corporation, or a rule established by any other society
or body which has not a public character, that is, which is not a part
of the governmental organization of the State, is a *fact* rather than a
law—a fact to which, as in the case of other facts, the courts will attach significance in determining the law to be applied in controversies
involving such fact or facts.

forced in order that it may properly be termed a law in a strictly positive sense.

It is the opinion of the writer that this is not necessary. In discussing the nature of the State's sovereignty it was pointed out that the ascription to the State of legal omni-competence carries with it no implication that the States, or rather those who control their governmental agencies, have the actual power to carry into effect any policies that they may desire or see fit to adopt. So, in determining what is positive law, the only criterion is whether the rules or act commanded by it is an authentic expression of the State's will as determined by existing constitutional law,—is, in other words, a rule of conduct or a command which the constituted courts will, if resorted to, order obeyed.

Such a court order may, in fact, be not obeyed either because the executive branch of the government refuses to lend its assistance, or because there is such popular resistance that the executive, though willing, finds itself unable to enforce it, or deems it inexpedient to do so. In such cases all that can be said is that there has been a violation of law which, however, no more destroys the law, as law, than is the criminal law destroyed when crime is committed.[20]

[20] *Cf.* Gray, *Nature and Sources of Law,* sec. 234 ff. Gray, discussing the situation presented when juries fail to convict persons violating an established law, as for example, a law forbidding the sale of wine, says: "This statute, being followed by the courts is an element of the law in the State, but it is not the whole law. It is also doubtless law in the State that no one shall be punished for crime except after being found guilty by a jury. The whole law must be taken together. We say the law is that a man selling wine shall be punished, but in truth the law is, that a man selling wine and convicted thereof by a jury shall be punished. If there has been no conviction by a jury, one of the elements which the law declares necessary for the infliction of punishment does not exist."

In a later section (§260) Gray discusses the situation presented when two or more courts of coördinate power render divergent decisions as to what is the law, and says that it must then be said that, as to the matter involved, there is no established law. This conclusion is not wholly satisfactory. For the judgments or decrees of the courts in each case con-

Sanction. Austin and those who follow him emphasize in the concept of law, the element of sanction, by which they mean the penalty or evil threatened to be inflicted upon those legal inferiors who fail to obey the commands of their legal superiors. Thus, in his *Province of Jurisprudence Determined*,[21] Austin says, "A command is distinguished from other significations of desire, not by the style in which the desire is signified, but by the power and the purpose of the party commanding to inflict an evil or pain in case the desire is disregarded. If you cannot or will not harm me in case I comply not with your wish, the expression of your wish is not a command, although you utter your wish in imperative phrase."

Austin does not go to the extent of declaring that an unenforced command ceases to be a command, and is not, therefore, a law. He is content to assert that, in order that an expressed desire may be classified as a command, there should be some likelihood, however small, that some sort of evil or pain, however slight, will be inflicted by the one expressing the desire upon those to whom it is addressed who do not conform to it. Thus he says: "The magnitude of the eventual evil, and the magnitude of the chance of incurring it, are foreign to the matter in question. The greater the evil, and the greater the chance of incurring it, the greater is the efficiency of the command, and the greater is the strength of the obligation. But when there is the smallest chance of incurring the smallest evil the expression of a wish amounts to a command, and, therefore imposes a duty."

Austin here attenuates his own distinction between a

stitute the law for the parties to such cases. They are legally bound by them. The result is, not that there is no law upon the subject involved, but that—unfortunate though it may be—it is a different one in the different jurisdictions of the courts which have passed upon it, and that, as a result, there is probably uncertainty as to what the law will be declared to be in still other jurisdictions of the State.

[21] Lecture I.

command and a wish to an extent that makes it a worthless one. In place of the idea thus rejected, the writer would emphasize the circumstance that a positive law, as distinguished from either a wish or a command has the official imprimatur of the State, and that this should be the essential fact connoted by the term Sanction. A law thus becomes an order or command issued by some one who claims a right upon his own part to the obedience of those whom he addresses, and, therefore, of a genuine obligation upon their part to obey. In the case of a divine law or command, this right and correlative obligation is based upon the fatherhood or other conceived status of superiority which the Divine Being has as compared with that of the individuals whose conduct is sought to be regulated and controlled. In the case of a positive law, such as we are concerned with in the present treatise, the superiority of the law-giver is a political or legal one. This plainly appears when we have to deal with the distinction between *de jure* and *de facto* governments. When a person is directed to do a certain thing by a government which he does not recognize as having a legal right to control his actions, he cannot deny that the direction amounts to a command, for he may know that serious evil or pain will almost surely be inflicted upon him in case he does not conform, in his conduct, to the direction he has received. But, even if he obeys, he does not admit that he has fulfilled a legal obligation. Upon the contrary, as to him, the matter has been nothing more than one of illegal force or power. Of course, if the Government that issues the order does so in pursuance of a claim upon its part that it has a legal right to require the obedience of those to whom the order is addressed, the order is a positive law when regarded from the point of view of that Government.

The true sanction of a positive law consists, then, in

the fact that the authority issuing it claims to be politically superior to the persons to whom it is directed; or, looking at the law from the point of view of the ones commanded, that they recognize the law-issuing authority as having a legal right to regulate their conduct in the premises.[22]

[22] Austin's emphasis upon the idea of force or compulsion, that is, upon the matter of obtaining, in fact, obedience to the directions contained in laws, appears also in his definition of sovereignty and of sovereign bodies-politic. There he says, "If a determinate human superior, not in a habit of obedience to a like superior, receive habitual obedience from the bulk of a given society, that determinate superior is sovereign in that society and that society (including the superior) is a society political and independent." *The Province of Jurisprudence Determined,* chap. IV.

CHAPTER XI

THE ORIGIN OF THE STATE HISTORICALLY AND PSYCHOLOGICALLY CONSIDERED

ANALYTICAL jurisprudence is concerned not so much with the evolution of political institutions as with the juristic analysis of these institutions as they exist at any given time. Nevertheless, the determination of the historical processes by which distinctively political life has grown out of non-political, social life is not without importance since light is thus thrown upon the nature of political as distinguished from other types or kinds of communal existence of men. Furthermore, as to any given legally sovereign organization, it is important to determine the manner in which its juristic birth may be interpreted, and, if possible, to fix the moment in time of that birth. So, similarly, as will be discussed in the chapter which is to follow, it is important to determine the modes in which the juristic life of a State may be terminated and the juristic consequences which flow from such a dissolution. First, then, we will speak, in general terms, of the historical origin of political life among men.[1]

Historical Origins. The study of origins is always an attractive one, and the work of many anthropologists has thrown a vast amount of light upon the early history of social and political institutions. The parts played by consanguinity, by religion (especially by the worship of ancestors), by the communal ownership of land and other

[1] In the paragraphs which immediately follow, the author has drawn liberally from the first chapter of his *Political Theories of the Ancient World*, a work published in 1903.

economic interests, and, above all, by the influence of the family upon the development of social and political life, have all been carefully considered. The significance of totem worship, of endogamy and exogamy, of polygamy of polyandry, and of patriarchal life has been discussed in the light of the facts presented by the earliest literary and archæological records, and interpreted by analogy with the present customs of races now in the lowest stages of civilization. All of these facts have been compared and exhaustively studied, but the absolute origin of civic life has not been historically determined. The fact is that the first subjection of man to public authority of some sort or other must have been practically coæval with the beginning of his social life, and this carries us back to periods of human development anterior to those that furnish historical records.

Furthermore, even after we reach periods regarding which we have authentic historical information, we are often without exact knowledge as to the manner in which the men of those times viewed their own institutions. However, reasoning back from such later records as we have, and judging from analogy with the thoughts and customs of peoples of whose primitive institutions we have knowledge, we can, after all, form a fairly confident opinion as to the character of the ideas held concerning social and political institutions during their very early stages of development, if not at the time of their original institution.

One thing we know with practical certainty, and this is that, from the time when any sense whatever of social or political obligation came to be recognized by men, the ideas of religious sanction, of customary obligation, and of legal authority, were so intermixed that they were not distinguished even in thought. Law, in a juristic sense, was not distinguished from what Austin would term "positive morality," and this morality was deemed to derive its obligatory force from super-human sources. A divine sanction or prohibition was attached to nearly every act of which the social group took any direct cognizance. The family group had its gods and its divinely ordered rules of conduct, as did the larger social groups of which the families were the constituent units. A "consciousness of kind" and common material interests may, in reality, have furnished the cement that kept the groups together, but all the historical evidence that we have indicates that, to the individuals themselves, the uniting bond was conceived to be a religious one, and community of worship the one objective evidence of their unity. Thus, whatever may have been the actual origin or utilitarian basis of any recognized rule of conduct or principle of authority, the source was conceived to be in the will of the gods, and its compelling force derived from the evil which it was believed the gods would inflict upon those who should fail to conform to it.

Regarding the probable historical steps by which political as distinguished from merely social institutions arose among men, and by which a corresponding distinction in thought between a political, a social or religious sense of obligation was created, varying theories or conclusions have been reached by anthropologists and other scholars.

The Patriarchal Theory. According to the so-called Patriarchal theory, to which Sir Henry Maine and Herbert Spencer have given the support of their names, the primitive type of society among all early peoples, or at any rate, among the Aryans and Semites, was one in which all individuals were grouped into families or households, united by bonds of kinship (real or fictitious), marriage, or domestic service, and ruled over in a practically absolute manner by the chief male or patriarch.

As long as this stage persisted, the family, according to this theory, remained the sole social unit and the *patria potestas* the only political authority. By a natural process of growth, as this theory goes on to hold, these families or households grew into clans, the clans into tribes, and the tribes, by conquests and alliances, into nations. At the same time, corresponding to this increase in communal life, the political powers of the heads of the families developed into those of the chiefs of the clans, and these, in turn, into the authority of the King of the tribe or of the nation.

The simplicity and apparent reasonableness of this explanation of early social and political development immediately secured for it a wide acceptance. Later years, however, witnessed a destructive criticism of it, especially by such writers as L. H. Morgan [2], and J. F. McClennan [3]. According to these critics, social life in its earliest forms, exhibited a horde condition in which there was an almost complete promiscuity in sexual relations, and out of which, only as a later historical development, did patriarchal or family life, headed by the male, emerge.

Whether or not the patriarchal type of family life was the original form of social organization, either generally or for particular races, is, after all, not a matter of considerable importance to the political scientist. But what is of importance to him is the fact that a better reading of history shows that the patriarch's authority was not the germ out of which developed, by a natural process of growth, first the powers of the chiefs of the clans and tribes, and then those of the State. In addition, and what is of still more significance to the political scientist, is the fact that a careful analysis of patriarchal power shows that it is so different, in its very nature, from

[2] *Ancient Society,* 1907.
[3] *Studies in Ancient History,* 1874; second series 1896.

political authority, that, as an *a priori* proposition, it is difficult to see how it could have developed into that authority.

The Tribe. Viewed historically, it is probably true that, founded as it is upon the physical facts of parentage, there existed among all races of men some sort of family life before any other social units were formed. But it is equally probable, that, before the family grew into patriarchal form, a grouping into tribes had taken place. In truth, aside from the temporary association of mother and child, which the helpless condition of the latter necessitates, the tribal form of association is the simplest conceivable type of social and political organization. For its establishment and maintenance nothing more is needed than a slight feeling of friendship between its constituent members, and a recognition of its offensive or defensive value in war—a recognition which stern experience must, at a very early time, have almost universally brought about. For the maintenance of tribal authority, no more elaborate form of government is needed than a chieftain whose right to direct and command is founded upon a personal prowess, and whose sphere of authority, in war, is that of a military commander, and, in peace, that of an arbitrator of private disputes. As savagery gave way by degrees to civilization, a double development undoubtedly went on. Upon the one hand, the authority of the tribe increased and its sphere of authority over its individual members widened; while, upon the other hand, within the tribe, family life increased in its integrity and control until it assumed, in many communities at least, the patriarchal form. Thus, instead of the family developing into the tribe, the likelihood is that there was a synchronous or parallel development of both social units.

The Clan. The historical relation of the clan, gens, or

sept to the family upon the one side, and to the tribe or nation upon the other side, has been a point even more disputed than that of the family to the tribe. As stated above, a once generally accepted theory was that the clans were originally formed from families,—that several families united to form a clan, or that single families ultimately became so large as, in themselves, to constitute clans. Modern scholars, however, are now disposed to deny that this was the probable course of development. Morgan bases this denial upon the view that, in primitive societies, exogamy is the general rule.

It is not necessary, however, to rest the denial of a genetic relationship between the clan and the family upon the more or less uncertain matter of exogamy. A better proof is that which proceeds from the fact that the aims, functions, and basis of membership of the clan are different from those of the family. The family is founded upon kinship, actual or assumed, and, in it, the degree of relationship is fundamental. Its head is, as a rule, determined by birth and not by voluntary selection on the part of its members, and he rules rather as owner of the persons subject to his authority than as a leader or judge over them. In the clan, upon the other hand, although a certain degree of community of blood is usually present or assumed, degrees of relationship are not recognized, or, if recognized, are not deemed important. The real bond of union is a religious one. The clan possesses a certain amount of common property, it exercises certain important functions in the way of settlement of disputes between its members, and in furnishing mutual aid and protection; but its one essential, avowed end is the maintenance of a common worship.

In membership the clan resembles the tribe. That is to say, its constituent units are the individuals themselves and not groups of them. Its members are, of course, grouped into families, just as are the citizens of the modern State, but the elementary cells are individuals, and whatever authority the clan possesses is exercised directly upon them.[4]

As to the historical relationship of the clan to the tribe, there is a dispute among scholars, some maintaining that the tribe results from a union of clans, others asserting that the tribe comes first in point of time, and later exhibits a differentiation into clans. It is not unlikely that, in some instances, clans united to form a tribe; in other cases, that the tribal relationship was first established, and the clans a later development.[5]

The question as to which came first in point of time, the clan or the tribe, is of importance to the historian. To the political scientist the significant point is that these two types of human groupings were generally alike as regards both their form of organization and their units of membership. Both were associations of individuals having common interests, and were ruled over by chiefs whose rights or rulership were based upon their personal qualifications. The tribe thus differed from the clan rather in size and scope of functions than in essential nature. There were, however, the following differences: the fact of a general kinship was more emphasized in the clan than in the tribe, and the maintenance of a common worship was deemed more essential. The tribe had its gods and spiritual religious rites, just as had the clan, but community of religion was rather one of the outward symbols

[4] F. Hearn, *The Aryan Household*, p. 138. Speaking of the Roman gentes Hearn says: "There were many *familiæ* of the Claudii and of the Cornelii, but there were Claudii and Cornelii before any of the *familiæ* came into existence. On the other hand there were *gentes* such as the Mantii and the Marii who never seemed to have branched into any *familiæ*." However, Fustel de Coulange (*Ancient City,* book II, chap. X, p. 3) says: "The Gens was not an association of families . . . it was a family itself. It might comprise only a single line, or produce several branches, it was always but one family."

[5] Jenks, *History of Politics,* p. 19.

of tribal unity than the basis upon which it was founded. Primarily the tribe existed for the purpose of offence and defence against other tribes, and assistance in the performance of this duty was supposed to be obtained from the gods of the tribe. Upon the other hand, in the clan the maintenance of a particular worship was the chief aim sought, the elements of mutual help and common ownership of property being secondary.

Origin of Political Authority. As regards the genesis of political as distinct from social authority over men, it would seem to be clear that its beginning is to be traced to the tribe, or to the clan in those cases in which the tribe was a product of the growth of a clan or of the union of two or more clans. In other words, political authority cannot be properly regarded as having developed out of the patriarchal authority as found in the early family. Even if it be held that some sort of family life must have existed before the formation of gentile or tribal associations, the groups of such individuals thus formed cannot be said to have exhibited distinctively political characteristics: they were purely social units founded upon the facts of parentage. Their members were limited to specific determinate individuals. The bond of union was a temporary one, and the status of the members was that of virtual slaves or chattels of the family's head, and not that of citizens. It is true that, in early times, the control of many matters, now regulated by the commands of the State, was in the hands of the head of the family, but its interests and authority were essentially private in character. It never was, and never became a subject of public law.[6]

As contrasted with that of the family, the authority of the tribe must have been, from the beginning, purely political in character. Its chief derived his right to rule

[6] Cf. Bentham, *A Fragment on Government*, sec. XIII, note C.

from the actual agreement or acquiescence of his subjects. No absolute limits were fixed to the membership of the tribe, nor to the duration of its existence; no degrees of citizenship were recognized; and, so far as its sphere of control extended, it was sovereign and self-sufficient. It was not one of a number of groups of equal status and co-ordinate power which composed a larger social unit.

It is of course true that, in the earliest times, the form of governmental organization that obtained was simple in the extreme, and that the extent to which the attempt was made to control the acts of its individual members, was comparatively slight, but, once established, the tribe and its authority furnished a beginning out of which the modern political State could develop by a mere process of elaborating its governmental organization and extending its control over additional human interests and activities. Thus, once established, an event which must have occurred very early in the history of every people, the tribe was able to grow, by conquest or natural increase, into the nation, its government into that of the modern State, and the authentic expressions of its will into the great systems of jurisprudence which the complicated character of present day life makes necessary. Beginning with a jurisdiction that extended little beyond that of direction in times of war, and judgment in a comparatively few matters in times of peace, the tribe had but to stretch out gradually its control, first by way of increase of its executive and judicial functions, and then, finally, by the exercise of direct legislative authority, in order to develop into the sovereign body-politic of today which practically monopolizes the legal right to employ physical coercion.

In this process of development, political authority has not changed its essential character, whatever may have been the varying importance of the family or other social groupings within the body-politic. From the very beginning, as Hearn correctly says, "the State is not composed of other social organisms. Its members may be members of other social organisms, and the activities of these other social organisms may or may not clash, or tend to clash, with the activities of the State. But the organization of the State is complete within itself, and its power, within its own sphere and over its own members, is supreme. It has its own worship, its own property, its own functions, its own claim upon its members, its own duties towards them. It respects the rights and duties of the other associations which it includes, and does not, at least in its earlier stages, seek to interfere with the relations of its members to any of those other associations." [7]

Psychological Origin of Political Authority. Just as it is an idea or sentiment that transmutes an aggregate of individuals into a Nation, so it is a desire for political unity that provides a psychological basis for the State. As the eminent Austrian publicist, Jellinek, has put it, "The inner ground of the origin of the State is the fact that an aggregate of persons has a conscious feeling of its unity, and gives expression to this unity by organizing itself as a volitional and active subject." [8]

It may be correct to say this desire for political union is, in many cases at least, the moving force that brings about the establishment of the State, but the mere existence of this psychological condition, granting, in a particular instance, that it exists, is not sufficient ground for asserting that a body-politic has been created. A State is not born until this subjective condition leads to the existence, in objective fact, of a ruling political or-

[7] *The Aryan Household,* p. 318. For an excellent popular discussion of the development of the modern State from its primitive form see Edward Jenks, *The State and the Nation,* published in 1919.
[8] *Die Lehre von den Staatenverbindungen,* p. 157.

ganization. Other conditions favoring, or at least not hindering, this objective realization will result from the subjective inclination. But, except in rare cases, there is not this absence of hindrance. The political *status quo ante* has always to be considered. Existing political institutions and methods have the support of tradition, backed by the natural indisposition of men to change their habits and manner of life, especially when they cannot foresee with absolute precision the results that will follow from a change. And, most of all, an existing political authority is always supported by an enormous weight of selfish interest. To the desire to rule, which is almost universal in the human breast, are added the material and social interests and honors that are bound up in an existing political régime, thus making those in power reluctant to consent to even a change in administration, much less to the establishment of a new body-politic. It thus frequently happens that there exists in the minds of a community of people a desire for a political unity of a particular sort, and that this desire would be of sufficient strength to maintain the unity of a State, were it once established and organized, but that objective conditions prevent for many years the realization of such an end. It is only when this pent-up flood of feeling rises to sufficient height and strength to burst the existing political barriers that hold it in, that a new State is created.

As has been said, the natural tendency of the feeling of ethnic or cultural unity is to find expression in political unity. The two sentiments, then, that lie at the basis of the Nation and of the State are largely similar. The same conditions that tend to create the feeling of Nationality tend also, in most cases, to demand the establishment of the State. Absolute identity of these two sentiments, however, cannot be affirmed. It is possible, in other words, for a well developed feeling of Nationality to exist with but slight desire for political unity. On the other hand, we find instances in which the establishment of political unity is clearly demanded by a People, among whom there is no other claim of Nationality. The factors that create the feeling of Nationality are community of race, language, historical tradition, mutuality of economic interests, and like degree of civilization. That which calls for the establishment of political control over a definite territory and community may be nothing more than political expediency,—the necessity for self-defensive or offensive strength. Certainly the feelings of American and British Nationality were very strong at the time of the severance of the American colonies from their mother country, yet independent political organization was nevertheless demanded and obtained by the Americans. Strong feelings of common Nationality were frequently displayed by the Greeks, especially when combating a common foe, yet at no time during the height of Grecian posperity was political unity called for. At the present day we see three distinct Nationalities organized under the Swiss Government with no demand for separate political existence.

To those who would say that a national feeling does not truly exist unless there be a demand for political unity,—that, in other words, the desire for such unity is a necessary consequence of the feeling of Nationality, it is to be replied, that this gives a more intensive and exacting definition to the sentiment of Nationality than is usually ascribed to it. It is an obvious fact that we often have instances of political unions in which there is an absence of such elements as community of race, language, custom, and historical tradition. It is, therefore, impossible to identify the desire for political unity, even before it obtains realization, with the sentiment of

Nationality, unless we assume the position that only political expediency is able to create the feeling of Nationality. But to do this is not only to go counter to all accepted usage of terms, but, in fact, entirely to destroy the very idea of Nationality, which is supposed to rest upon other than political foundations. Though intimately connected, it seems best, then, to distinguish from each other the feelings of National and Political unity; in fine, to recognize that though the desire for political unity does, as a rule, arise from and out of a sentiment of Nationality, it may arise independently of it.

An attempt to argue the existence of a State and of political sovereignty from the mere fact of a condition of mind which has not found outward objective expression is seen in the argument of Professor Burgess in support of his contention that a National State existed in America during the period from the time of the outbreak of the Revolution of the American colonies against their mother country, that is, before the adoption, in 1789, of the Federal Constitution. During the years when the former colonies were associated under the Articles of Confederation—from 1781 to 1789—he is forced to admit that the thirteen former colonies were severally sovereign, for the Articles incontestably constituted only a League and not a constitutional Union, but this sovereignty, thus enjoyed by the States he speaks of as "usurped."[9] In thus speaking, however, it is clear that he is led to take positions that are logically absurd, for it must appear that, if there had been a real will upon the part of the people during those years to create a National State, one would have come into being. And equally we must hold that the existence of the Thirteen States as several sovereign bodies must have been due

[9] *Pol. Sci. Quar.*, vol. I, p. 9, "The American Commonwealth."

to a will to that effect upon the part of those who constituted their citizen bodies.

There has been inclination on the part of many publicists to refuse the designation of State to the earlier types of political life, especially to those undeveloped groups which have not obtained for themselves a settled abode. Those taking this ground must be considered as governed by a special conception of the State. According to the conception adopted in the present work designation of State cannot be refused to any independent society of men that is politically organized.[10] In other words, low order of development does not deprive an institution of its generic name. A society is politically organized if it have established within it and over it a public authority for the control of those interests that are connected with its orderly existence, and the enforcement of its jural ideal, however crude and limited that ideal may be. Thus organized, a society of men is properly embraced within the scope of the *Staatsidee* and is as truly a State as when in its more developed form.

To make this point clear, we can, for this particular purpose, liken the term "State" as used in Political Science to the term "living being" as employed in Biological Science. The biologist does not refuse to recognize as living beings the lowest orders of life, even though they be but mere splotches of protoplasm, so structureless and homogeneous in composition that different individuals can be scarcely distinguished, and in each of which the

---

[10] "That moment of the organization of every society," says Pulszky, "in which it presents itself as independent, dominant, and capable of asserting its own conditions of life *by force,* forms always a distinct phase in the process of association; and whenever any particular society assumes this form it appears as the State. The State is properly a law-creating and law-maintaining society which proclaims and asserts the conditions of its existence in connection with its own conduct and that of its subjects, through commanding, permissive, and prohibitory rules." *Theory of Law and Civil Society,* p. 216.

most powerful microscope is barely able to discover differentiation of parts. The point that is conclusive to him is that such beings have crossed the line from the inorganic to the organic, from the inert to the living, and that within them is contained a possible growth, a potential development. Likewise, for purposes of illustration, we may compare, though not identify, the growth of the living being toward a higher life, with the development of political institutions. In both there appear an increasing differentiation of parts, and growth in variety of their needs. As the higher forms are assumed, the organism becomes more definitely and delicately constructed; its activities become increasingly self-directive, until finally the self-conscious individual appears. At the same time that this elaboration of structure has proceeded, varying influences and conditions of life have caused individuals to differ from one another until the number of classes, genera, and species becomes almost beyond estimate.

The development of political society is characterized by these same features. With the advance of civilization come augmented social needs and activities. The governmental organization of the State becomes a more complex structure, and is endowed with wider, and, at the same time, more definite power, and the exercise of these powers becomes more intelligently controlled, and in a sense self-directed, that is, dictated rather by the interests of the governed than by the personal interests of the individuals in whom the exercise of the State's powers happens to be entrusted. Likewise, from substantial similarity of governmental organization, in the early stages, States, in the course of their development, assume diverging forms. Geographic, ethnic, economic, and moral conditions, all have their influence in determining the direction in which the development of political forms proceeds. Distinctions arise as to the number of interests to be regulated by the State, as to the extent to which the people generally shall participate, either actively or by way of popular control, in the administration of their public affairs, and as to the manner in which the powers of the State shall be distributed among its several departments. Thus arise all those varieties of governments running from the despotic Oriental State to the democracy of the Swiss communes. Later arise such forms as the feudal State, and the so-called national State. Within each of these classes are also to be found the members distinguished from each other by the greatest variety of internal organizations. The manner and order in which these various forms have historically appeared, belong, however, rather to historical and descriptive Political Science, than to Political Philosophy.

There has been some speculation upon the part of political theorists as to the minimum number of individuals required in order to constitute a State. It would seem that no such minimum can be logically fixed. As our argument proceeds, it will appear that all of the essential juristic elements of the State are such as can be predicated as well of a small as of a large body of individuals. Aristotle fixes a limit below which the number of citizens should not go, but this is based not so much upon logical grounds as upon the non-juristic principle that when a community is so small that there is not the possibility of a varied life the true ethical aim of the State cannot be attained. Austin denies the possibility of a State being constituted from a single family upon the ground of its absurdity, and quotes Montesquieu as taking the same position.[11] After admitting that a single family living in total estrangement from every

[11] *Spirit of Laws,* book I, chap. III.

other community might exhibit all the traits of an independent political society, Austin, however, says: "But, since the number of its members is extremely minute, it would, I believe, be esteemed a society in a state of nature; that is, a society consisting of persons not in a state of subjection. Without an application of the terms, which would somewhat smack of the ridiculous, we could hardly style the society a society *political* and independent, the imperative father and chief a *monarch* or *sovereign*, or the obedient mother and children *subjects.*"[12] As to this Clark says:[13] "In this *dominion* so-called (ownership) of the original patriarch, *law* is *possible*. He *may*, that is, govern by *general rules*. It is not, however, *probable*, because he would have little interest in setting, or at least in adhering to, such rules. He would be more likely to govern by means of *occasional commands.*" In other words, though it is entirely improbable that a single, isolated family should ever become *politically* organized, it is not logically impossible. It is not the size but the lack of that element of possible perpetuity of dominion that prevents the family from becoming, *as such*, a State.[14]

[12] *Province of Jurisprudence Determined*, 2d ed. 1861, Lect. VI, p. 183.
[13] *Practical Jurisprudence*, p. 147.
[14] Italics in the original. For a comment upon the logical value of the argument based upon the ridiculous see Maine, *Early History of Institutions*, p. 379.

CHAPTER XII

THE juristic birth of a particular State occurs when
the political organization that is involved first assumes,
or becomes endowed with, the attribute of sovereignty.
In order, then, that this genesis may be determined, if it
has occurred within a period concerning which authentic historical records exist, it is first necessary that
some conclusions be reached as to the tests by which
the existence of the quality of sovereignty in a given
body-politic may be certainly recognised, and some agreement be reached as to the processes by which this juristic
attribute may be created. It will conduce to clearness
of thought if we separate the discussion of the tests by
which the existence of sovereignty may be determined,
from the juristic processes by which sovereignty may be
brought into being. And first as to the processes.

One Sovereignty Cannot Create Another Sovereignty. It
would seem to be a necessary logical conclusion from the
nature of sovereignty that legal authority cannot, by its
own will or act, create another authority legally superior
or even equal to itself. The created cannot be the equal
and much less the superior of its creator: it necessarily
remains but the agent for the exercise of the authority of
the political being that brings it into being. When,
therefore, this juristically created entity functions voli-
tionally, it can do no more than express what, in the last
analysis, is the legal will of its legal progenitor.

Sovereignty Cannot Be Created by a Union of Sovereign-

ties. The same reasoning applies to the attempt of a number of severally sovereign political entities to create, by a joint action or common agreement among themselves, an authority legally superior to themselves. A general or public will, in other words, cannot be created by a mere union of individual or private wills. Thus, a number of severally sovereign States may create for themselves organs of government which each of them will severally regard as their own governmental organs for the purposes specified, and through which they will be able to maintain concerted and unified action. But they cannot create above and over themselves a sovereign body-public. As a result, sovereign States may enter into agreements or compacts with one another by which they or their peoples become morally or politically or internationally obligated, but they cannot conceivably be legally bound by the terms of the treaty or compact into which they have entered or, by that treaty or compact, create a legal superior which, for the future, can legally control them by its commands.

John C. Calhoun, in his *Discourse on the Constitution and Government of the United States,* expounded the logic of this proposition in a manner that has since permitted no successful denial. His argument is so cogent that it may profitably be quoted at length. Starting with the premise that the Constitution of the United States of America was, in its essential character, a product of the concurring wills of the original thirteen severally sovereign American Commonwealths, he says of its National instrument of government:

"They (the States) stand (to it) in the relation of superior to subordinate—the creator to the created. The people of the several States called it into existence, and conferred by it on the Government, whatever power or authority it possesses. Regarded simply as a constitution, it is as subordinate to them as are their respective State Constitutions, and it imposes no more restrictions on the exercise of any of their sovereign rights than they do."

Such, says Calhoun, remains the relation of the States to their common agent, the National Government. As between themselves, the States having ratified and adopted the constitution, "they stand to it in the relation of parties to a constitutional compact, and of course, it is binding between them as a *compact,* and not on or over them as a *Constitution.* But, as solemn and sacred as it is, and as high as the obligations may be which it imposes, still it is but a *compact* and not a *Constitution,* regarded in reference to the people of the several States in their sovereign capacity . . . Hence, a State, acting in the same manner in which it ratified and adopted the constitution, may be guilty of violating it *as a compact,* but cannot be guilty of violating it as a *law.* The case is the reverse as to the action of its citizens, regarding them in their individual capacity. To them it is a law,—the supreme law within its sphere. They may be guilty of violating it *as a law,* or of violating the laws and treaties made in pursuance of, or under its authority, regarded as laws or treaties, but cannot be guilty of violating it as a *compact.* The constitution was established *over them* by their respective States, to whom they owed allegiance, and they are under the same obligation to respect and obey its authority, within its respective sphere, as they are to respect and obey their respective State constitutions; and for the same reasons, namely: that the State to which they owe allegiance, commanded it in both cases."[1]

Sovereignty Cannot Be Transferred. It follows from what has been already determined, that one sovereign

---

[1] *Works of Calhoun,* vol. I, p. 275. The italics are in the original.

State can no more obtain its sovereignty by a transfer from another sovereign State already in being, than it can create *de novo,* a sovereignty over and above itself.

As a matter of fact, of course, it often happens that one State extends its jurisdiction over the citizen body and lands of another State, and, not infrequently, this extension is marked and evidenced by the formal consent of the governing authorities of the State whose lands and citizens are thus absorbed. But, juristically viewed, the change is due to a unilateral act upon the part of the annexing State, which, exercising its sovereign authority, asserts its legal control over the annexed lands and their inhabitants. In other words, the political jurisdiction thus obtained owes its juristic validity in no wise to any consenting act of the State previously having jurisdiction over the lands and peoples that have come under the new sovereignty. This is true even when the transfer of sovereignty is provided for by a treaty between the two States concerned. In such a case the treaty acknowledges rather than accomplishes the transfer."[2]

[2] Upon this point may be quoted the following from Brownson's *The American Republic,* chap. IX: "An independent State, a nation, may, with or without its consent, lose its sovereignty, but only by being merged in, or subjected to, another. Independent sovereign States cannot, by convention or mutual agreement, form themselves into a single sovereign State or nation. The compact or agreement is made by the sovereign States, and binds by virtue of the sovereign power of each of the contracting parties. To destroy that sovereign power would be to annul the compact, and render void the agreement. The agreement can be valid and binding only on condition that each of the contracting parties retains the sovereignty that rendered it competent to enter into the compact; and States that retain severally their sovereignty do not form a single State or Nation. The States in convention cannot become a new and single sovereign State unless they lose their several sovereignty and merge it in the new sovereignty; but this they cannot do by agreement, because the moment the parties to the agreement cease to be sovereign, the agreement on which alone depends the new sovereign State is vacated in like manner as a contract is vacated by the death of the parties. The convention either of sovereign States or of sovereign individuals, with the best will in the world, can form only a

Juristically viewed the same result is obtained when we have to deal with the recognition by a State of the independence of a colony or province which has withdrawn from beneath the sovereignty under which it has formerly lived. In such a case the existence of the new State dates from the time of the withdrawal, and not from the time when its independence is conceded by the parent State; and the existence of its sovereignty is founded upon the fact that it no longer recognizes allegiance or renders obedience to the old sovereignty, and not upon the fact that the old sovereignty has by a treaty or other form of declaration indicated that it no longer claims its allegiance. So, similarly, the sovereignty of any new State which is recognized by other States as such and admitted into the "Family of Nations" is not created by or founded upon, such international recognition. That recognition is extended by each State when it sees fit, and, when accorded, is nothing more than an acknowledgment of an accomplished fact. There is no claim that the recognition is a creative act; and this fact is shown, if indeed any demonstration is needed, that it frequently happens that recognition of a new sovereignty is denied by one or more States for years after its existence has been conceded by the other States. If, then, a creative character were assigned to "Recognition" the absurd result would be reached that the new State both existed and did not exist, its status being determined not by any real fact of independent existence, but, in each case, by what might fortuitously happen to be the state of mind of other bodies-politic.

Applying the foregoing reasoning, by way of illustration, to the United States of America, it is seen that the colonies formerly in allegiance to Great Britain acquired

compact, whatever its terms or conditions—is only an alliance, a league or a confederation, which no one can pretend is a sovereign State or republic."

their sovereignties when they organized themselves as independent communities. Their autonomous condition did not date from the promulgation of the treaty of peace with the mother country, but, if any precise date can be assigned to it, from the signing of the Declaration of Independence. This doctrine was accepted by the Supreme Court of the United States in the case of *McIlvaine v. Coxe's Lessee*[3] in the opinion in which case it is said: "The several States which compose this Union, so far at least as regards their municipal regulations, became entitled, from the time when they declared themselves independent, to all the rights and powers of sovereign States, and they did not derive them from concessions made by the British King. The treaty of peace contains a recognition of their independence, not a grant of it."

A somewhat different proposition is presented when a new State emerges from the Union of two or more sovereign States. The juristic interpretation of this political transaction will receive full consideration in the chapter dealing with the so-called Composite State. It is sufficient here to say that where there is such a merger of formerly sovereign States and the creation of a single new sovereign body, the original States must be conceived to have gone out of existence, and the bodies-politic which continue to bear their name and apparently continue their existence, must be regarded as new bodies-politic of an essentially different nature. They are non-sovereign bodies,[4] which, in contemplation of constitutional law, are the creations of the new sovereignty, and have a status only insofar as they are conceived of as products of its will. The original sovereignties cease to exist; and the new sovereignty rests upon its own basis

[3] 2 Cranch 280.

[4] Whether or not they may properly be termed States will be later considered.

and is not the product of their union. Their agreement to unite, as evidenced in a treaty or other instrument, is thus of no juristic significance. Its importance is purely political, marking, as it does, merely the acquiescence of the peoples of the original States, or, at least, of their governing bodies, in their dissolution as independent bodies-politic, and their willingness to live under the new sovereignty which is to come into being.

Where a portion of the lands and the citizens of one State are transferred from beneath one sovereignty and brought under the jurisdiction of another sovereignty, there is clearly no transfer of its sovereignty by the one State to the other. Both States remain in existence with their several sovereignties unimpaired.[5]

To the historian it may be convenient to date the origin of a new State from the adoption of a constitution, as, for example, to date the birth of the United States from 1789; but, to the jurist, the Constitution must be viewed as a Law,—as the product of the legislative will of a State already in existence, and as providing an outline for its governmental machinery. The State itself must be conceived of as the product of the desire and will of a people to maintain a political existence as a group, as a sovereign legal person, acknowledging no legal control arising outside of its own will. Synchronously with the establishment of this political unity is the estab-

---

[5] It is, of course, possible for a State to relinquish and consent to the incorporation into another State, of a portion of its own territory without at the same time surrendering, or the annexing State claiming, the primary allegiance of the inhabitants of the territories which are concerned. Where such allegiance is not altered, these inhabitants, by the transfer of the territory which they occupy, become resident aliens in their relation to the annexing State. It may, indeed, be said that it is now the practice of civilized States, when territories are transferred from one to another sovereignty, to provide that their inhabitants may have the option whether or not they will become citizens of the annexing State. See, for example, the treaty by which the jurisdiction of Spain over the Philippines and Porto Rico was surrendered and the jurisdiction of the United States over these islands asserted.

lishment, more or less spontaneously and informally, of new instrumentalities for the expression of the State's will or the adoption as its own for the same purpose of old governmental organs already in existence. Thus, if we conceive that a sovereign national state existed in 1789, we must view that State as accepting *ad hoc,* as its own organs the conventions in the several States which ratified the Constitution.

Non-Juristic Origin of Sovereignty. In result, then, we may say that, strictly speaking, a juristic origin cannot be ascribed to sovereignty. Legally, each sovereign State starts, as it were, *de novo,* and cannot have any legal bonds that unite it to any previously existing political body. Juristically a new State can take its origin only by the entire withdrawal of the people organized under it from the civic bonds under which they may have been living, and the establishment by them of a new body-politic. Not until the old State has been destroyed, either peaceably or by force, can the new State take its rise. It cannot derive its vitality from the old, for, as we have seen, the transference of sovereignty is a legal impossibility.

A State Cannot Commit Juristic Felo de Se. It has been earlier pointed out that the sovereign State may, through its constitutional law, fix the manner in which and the governmental organs through which, its sovereignty is to be exercised, but that these self-set constitutional limitations are necessarily repealable by the State, acting in pursuance of that same sovereign authority which enabled it to establish them in the first place, and that thus the State's sovereignty is neither destroyed nor impaired. It has also been shown that a change in form of the governmental organization of a State does not mean that the existence of the State has been destroyed and a new sovereignty created.

Dicey in his *Law of the Constitution*[6] says: "The impossibility of placing a limit on the exercise of sovereignty, does not in any way prohibit either logically or as a matter of fact, the abdication of sovereignty. This is worth observation because a strange dogma is sometimes put forth that a sovereign power, such as the Parliament of the United Kingdom, can never by its own act divest itself of sovereignty. The position, however, is clearly untenable. An autocrat, such as the Russian Czar, can undoubtedly abdicate; but sovereignty, or the possession of a supreme power in a State, whether it be in the hands of a Czar or of a Parliament, is always one and the same quality. If the Czar can abdicate, so can Parliament. To argue or imply that because sovereignty is not limitable (which is true) it cannot be surrendered (which is palpably untrue) involves the confusion of two distinct ideas. It is like arguing that because no man can, while he lives, give up, do what he will, his freedom of volition, so no man can commit suicide. A sovereign power can divest itself of authority in two ways, and (it is submitted) in two ways only. It may simply put an end to its own existence. Parliament could extinguish itself by legally dissolving itself and leaving no means whereby a subsequent Parliament could be legally summoned. A sovereign, again, may transfer sovereign authority to another person or body of persons."

Here it is clear that Dicey is confusing the existence of the sovereign State with the continuance of the governmental machinery through which its sovereignty is exercised. The abdication of an absolute monarch or the surrender of power by a legally omnipotent legislative body does not operate to destroy the State which stands back of those governmental agencies.[7]

[6] Fourth ed., p. 65.
[7] Westlake in his *International Law,* p. 63, is thus correct when he says: "It is impossible that the extinction of a State, or even its union with

The Annexation of the Hawaiian Islands by the United States Juristically Analyzed. Instances have occurred, however, in which one State, by its own official act, has consented to its own absorption into another State and thus to a cessation of its own independent existence. An illustration of this was exhibited in 1897-1898, when the Hawaiian Islands were incorporated into and became an integral part of the territory of the United States. Article XXXII of the Constitution of the Republic of Hawaii, adopted in 1894, expressly authorized the President, with the approval of his Cabinet and ratification of the Senate, to make a treaty of political union between the Republic and the United States of America. The power thus granted was exercised in 1897, a treaty providing for union with the United States being negotiated by the President with the approval of his Cabinet and ratified by the Hawaiian Senate. This treaty was not, however, ratified by the treaty-making organ of the United States—the President and Senate. Instead, a Joint Resolution was adopted on July 7, 1898, by the two Houses of the American Congress, which read, in part, as follows:

"Whereas, the Government of the Republic of Hawaii having in due form signified its consent, in the manner provided by its Constitution, to cede absolutely and without reserve to the United States the absolute fee and ownership of all public Government or crown lands, public buildings or edifices, ports, harbors, military equipment, and all other public property of every kind and description belonging to the Government of the

another State on terms involving the loss of its separate existence as a State of International Law, can ever be effected by voluntary arrangement in a constitutional manner. This is so, even when the extinction or union is voted by a parliament which, for all purposes comprised in carrying on the State as it exists, is regarded as omnipotent."

Hawaiian Islands together with every right and appurtenance thereto appertaining; therefore be it

"Resolved, that said cession is accepted, ratified and confirmed and that the said Hawaiian Islands and their dependencies be, and they are hereby annexed as a part of the territory of the United States, and are subject to the sovereign dominion thereof, and that all and singular the property and rights hereinbefore mentioned are vested in the United States of America."

Later, on August 12, 1898, upon the occasion of the formal raising of the American flag over the Hawaiian Islands, Mr. Dole, who until then had been the President of the Hawaiian Republic, addressing the American representative, said:

"A treaty of political union having been made, and the cession formally consented to by the Republic of Hawaii having been accepted by the United States of America, I now in the interest of the Hawaiian body-politic, and with full confidence in the honor, justice and friendship of the American people, yield up to you as the representative of the Government of the United States, the sovereignty and public property of the Hawaiian Islands."

Analyzing the foregoing steps by means of which the absorption of Hawaii into the United States, and its consequent disappearance as a sovereign entity was effected, it is clear that, so far as the United States was concerned, no more than a moral or political significance was attached to the fact that the Hawaiian Government, presumably voicing the wishes of the Hawaiian people, had given its assent to the annexation. As a legal proposition, the extension of American sovereignty over the Islands resulted from the act of the American Government as manifested in the Joint Resolution. As to the legal effect, if any, which the action of the Hawaiian

Government had as towards the Hawaiian people or State, it can be said that it was not an illegal act since it was one authorized by the Hawaiian constitution; and yet it cannot be said to have operated, *ipso facto,* to terminate the juristic life of the Hawaiian State. That did not occur until the American sovereignty was extended over the Islands and their inhabitants. It is correct, therefore, to say that, even in this case, in which express constitutional authority was given to the Government to agree to union with the United States, the annihilating stroke to the Hawaiian sovereignty was the act of the American State.

Summary. In result then, we are justified in saying that, as regards the termination of sovereignty, the situation is the reverse of that of its birth or creation. In other words, every State derives its sovereignty from itself. Sovereignty is a spontaneous or self-generated status and is never derived from an outside source. Upon the other hand, the juristic death of a sovereign State necessarily results from the act of another State, except perhaps in the conceivable case of the disappearance of every vestige of political authority over a people brought about by the acts of that people and without acceptance by them of the sovereignty of or the assertion of such sovereignty by another State.

As contrasted with the birth of a sovereign body-politic, the creation of a non-sovereign body is always due to the juristic act of some other sovereign State. But sovereign and non-sovereign entities are alike as regards their death or destruction. In both cases this is brought about by the act of another State.

Tests for the Determination of the Existence of Sovereignty. As has been above pointed out, the question as to the manner in which, from a juristic point of view, a sovereignty may be created or terminated, is distinct from the enquiry as to the tests by which the existence of a sovereign body-politic may be determined.

The conclusion that we have reached that each sovereignty begins *de novo,* and is not the juristic product of another sovereign will, leads necessarily to the proposition that the existence or non-existence of sovereignty is, strictly speaking, a matter of fact rather than of law. This fact is whether or not the political organization in question is regarded as having complete juristic competence to determine its own legal powers.

The phrase "recognized as having" is used advisedly since it points to the fact that if sovereignty, in its strict juristic sense, be divorced from the ideas of physical power, of ethical rights, or of political expediency, the question whether or not a given political organization is an agency of a legal sovereignty depends upon the point of view from which it is regarded. It is not only conceivable, but often the actual case, that a given government is regarded by certain of the individuals of a community as legally entitled to declare and enforce the will of the sovereign State, whereas other persons of that same community assert that the Government in question has no legal basis and therefore that it is not qualified, in their opinion, to express and enforce the sovereign will to which they conceive themselves to be subject, and, consequently, that such actual powers of coercion over them as it is able to exercise are matters of mere superiority of might and not of legal right. Thus arises the important distinction between Governments *de facto* merely, and those which are *de jure.*

De Facto and De Jure Governments Distinguished. As an abstract or detached proposition, it cannot be said that any given government is *de jure* or *de facto,* for the application of the terms necessarily depends upon the points of view of those who employ them. Thus a government is *de jure* as well as *de facto* when it is recognized as such by the individuals over whom its control is extended. It is *de facto* but not *de jure* as to any particular individual when, though actually in existence and able to exercise a certain amount of power, its legal character is denied by him. Thus, in the case of an attempted revolution, from the standpoint of those who have repudiated their allegiance to the old State, who refuse obedience to its government, and have organized for themselves a new political machinery, the old government has only an actual and not a legal existence, the new government being the only one which, in their eyes, possesses a legal basis. Upon the other hand, from the point of view of those who still support the old State, the newly established government has but a *de facto* existence, the old government being regarded as the only legal organization. Thus, during the American Civil War, the existence of the Southern Confederacy as a State, though regarded as *de jure* by its adherents, was never recognized by the United States nor by Foreign Powers. The existence of a *de facto* Confederate Government was, however, recognized by the United States for belligerent purposes. The continued allegiance of its supporters to the United States was, however, always asserted by the United States, and no legal force of any sort was ever ascribed, then, or after the end of the war, to any of the acts of the Southern Confederacy. No formal treaty of peace was entered into between the United States and the Southern Confederacy, the surrender of its armies being received simply as military acts, and its Government permitted to go out of actual existence without any formal action to mark its demise.

Thus, also, in 1660, when the Stuarts were restored to rule in England, the beginning of the reign of King Charles II was dated from the death of his father, Charles

I, in 1649, for, from the standpoint of the Stuarts, the Commonwealth Government, though in actual control for more than a decade, had never had more than a *de facto* existence. So, also, when the Bourbons again ascended the French throne, the first ruler took the title of Louis the Eighteenth, although the legitimate successor of Louis the Sixteenth never, in fact, for a moment held the reins of government. If he had done so, however, he would have been styled Louis the Seventeenth. During the time that the Commonwealth Government was in existence in England and the period of revolutionary rule in France, the governments that existed were, of course, *de jure,* regarded from the points of view of their supporters.

No government which is regarded as *de facto* can be said to evolve by mere effluxion of time into a *de jure* government. Therefore Bryce is not correct when he says: "Sovereignty *de facto,* when it has lasted for a certain time and shown itself stable, ripens into sovereignty *de jure.*"[8] What really happens in such a case is that the persons who at first deny a legal character to the *de facto* government abandon this point of view, accept the situation of fact, and give their allegiance to the existing government.

Final Test of Sovereignty. In the chapter which follows, dealing with the Federal State, we shall have occasion to apply, in the case of the United States, the distinction that has been made between governments *de facto* merely, and those which are *de jure,* and also to examine the juristic tests by means of which it is possible to determine whether, in the American Union, the sovereignty resides in the National body or is retained by each of the constituent States. The general proposi-

[8] *Studies in History and Jurisprudence;* chapter: "The Nature of Sovereignty."

tion may here be laid down, however, that the presence or absence of sovereignty in a given political entity depends upon whether or not that entity has such complete control over its own legal competence that it cannot, against its own legal will, be legally bound in any way whatsoever by the legal will of another political body. This is the one and final test of sovereignty. The sovereign state may, in other words, bind itself to any extent by its own will, in the form of constitutional limitations laid upon the powers of its own governmental agencies, or, by treaties it may give its undertaking to other States not to exercise certain of its powers, or to exercise them only in certain ways, but these self-set limitations it may legally—if not morally—escape from by an exercise of that same sovereign will in pursuance of which they were created. Its sovereignty is not, therefore, impaired. If, then, we find a political entity so united to, or so associated with, another political entity that it cannot escape from that union or association without a breach of law, as distinguished from a violation of international or moral obligation, it is not a sovereign State. If, upon the other hand, it can escape without its secession being an illegal act, it remains sovereign. Having this right, it may, while still retaining its sovereignty, enter into comprehensive agreements as to conforming its actions to those of other States with which it may associate itself, or as to accepting as its own the acts of a common governing agency which it, or those other States, may have agreed to establish and maintain.

The foregoing reasoning applies to cases in which a new sovereignty is created in derogation of one or more pre-existing sovereignties. When this is not the case, whatever political changes may occur relate only to alterations in governmental structure. No new State is created and no State goes out of existence. This is true,

as has been earlier adverted to in the chapter dealing
with Government, even when the changes in political
organization have been brought about by means not
sanctioned by pre-existing constitutional law. In this
latter case it is perhaps possible to conceive of the State,
as organized in its older Government, as going out of
existence and a new State as being born with a new
Government. But such an interpretation hardly seems
necessitated by juristic logic. It would mean that, with
the demise of the older sovereignty, all the existing legal
rights and duties, public and private, would have to be
regarded as destroyed, because the legal basis upon which
they had rested would have been removed, and they
would then have to be conceived of as impliedly recreated by the new sovereignty. It seems simpler and
sufficiently logical to regard the original State as maintaining a continued existence and as having merely given
to itself, by an original and direct constitutive act, a new
governmental organization.

CHAPTER XIII

THE FEDERAL STATE

THE facts that seem to make especially difficult the application of the principles that have been evolved with reference to the subject of Sovereignty, are those presented by the various types of so-called Composite or Federal States.[1] To many publicists, these political forms exhibit examples of States with divided or limited sovereignty, of non-sovereign political bodies but yet entitled to be termed States, and of sovereign States juristically created by the joint action of other States.

Associations of States. The problem of properly classifying and designating the various associations into which the States of the world have at different times entered, is one that has especially attracted the attention of German publicists. The most important work in this field is, perhaps, that of Jellinek, entitled *"Die Lehre von den Staatenverbindungen,"* which we have already had occasion to cite. Other works are those of Brie,[2] Westerkamp,[3] and Waitz.[4] This subject is also, of course, con-

---

[1] Strictly speaking, this term should perhaps be "Federally Organized State," for all States are, juristically regarded, alike in character. A State may have a federal form of government, but it is not itself federal. However, the term is so commonly employed, especially as a technical one in distinction to a Confederacy or Confederation of States, that it would be pedantic to attempt to avoid its use. Care will, however, be taken to use the term Federal State when the State which is federally organized is referred to; and Federal or National Government when its Government is distinguished from those of its constituent commonwealths. In the United States of America the terms "Union" or simply "the United States" are frequently employed to designate the National or Federal State.

[2] *Theorie der Staatenverbindungen.*

[3] *Staatenbund und Bundesstaat.*

[4] *Das Wesen des Bundesstaats* contained in his *Grundzüge der Politik.*

sidered by all writers dealing particularly with the public law of the German Empire. The work of Laband[5] is especially valuable in this respect. Those American writers who have dealt with the constitutional character of their own States, have generally limited themselves to a consideration of the differences between a "Federal State" and a "Confederacy."[6]

Jellinek, in his classification of associations, makes the first division into *Unorganized* and *Organized Unions*.[7] These names serve to indicate the distinction that is made between the two classes. In the first class are included instances in which more or less permanent relations between States have been entered into for the regulation of certain mutual interests, but in which no central organization has been created. Such common action as is necessary in these unions is had through one or more of the governmental organs of the individual States. Of course there is not created in any of such cases what would be called a Composite State even by those publicists who use the term "non-sovereign State." Within this category fall such types as "Alliances" for offence or defence, and for the guarantee of particular rights or status, as, for example, the perpetual neutrality of particular territories.

Within this class Jellinek also places that type which he terms the *Staatenstaat,* or that form of union in which there is a superior and an inferior State or States, the latter receiving the orders from the former as from a

[5] *Das Staatsrecht des Deutschen Reiches.*

[6] Professor A. B. Hart is the author of a monograph entitled, "An Introduction to the Study of Federal Government" (*Harvard Univ. Historical Monographs,* No. 2), which is rich in bibliographical matter. The work is, however, descriptive and comparative, rather than theoretical. The work of the English historian Freeman, entitled *Federal Government,* is limited to an historical examination of the Grecian types.

[7] Here, again, it is more accurate to speak of associations rather than of unions of States, for, as has been earlier pointed out, States cannot form juristic unions. It is believed, however, that no confusion of thought will be caused by conforming to the general usage of terms.

Foreign Power, and the citizens of the inferior States owing allegiance only to their own States. The most conspicuous historical examples of this type have been the feudal States of the Middle Ages, and the mediæval German Empire. Of this nature, also, have been the relations between the Ottoman Porte and some of its Christian Provinces, as well as the relation between the United States and some of the Indian tribes. Of this order was the relation of Egypt and Turkey, and of Nicaragua and the Mosquito Indians.[8]

All of the above unions Jellinek designates as (unorganized unions of a juristic character) (*Nichtorganisirte Verbindungen mit juristischem Charakter*). We may properly ask ourselves, however, whether these "Alliances" constitute in any proper sense of the word "unions" of States. Every international treaty provides for the regulation of certain interests in common, and according to conditions mutually agreed upon. In the above-mentioned instances there is not the first beginning made or step taken toward the fusion of the con-

[8] The utility of this term *"Staatenstaat"* in the vocabulary of political science is very doubtful. There is not an agreement as to its meaning between publicists, and those who use it, as, for example, Jellinek, are not able to give to it a precise definition. Jellinek, in his *Allgemeine Staatslehre* (Dritte Auflage, 1922), p. 748, can give no more precise description of this form of association of States than the following: "Ein souveräner Staat übt seine Herrschaft über ihm unterworfene Staaten aus, die sich innerhalb der von dem oberherrlichen Staatswesen gezogenen Rechtsschranken frei organisieren nach innen weitgehende Selbständigkeit besitzen, nach aussen jedoch Kraft ihrer Abhängigkeit grosse Einschränkungen erfahren und dem Oberstaate zur Heerfolge oder doch ökonomischen Leistungen (Tribut) verpflichtet sind. Innerhalb dieses Typus sind zahlreiche Spielarten vorhanden. . . . Das Characteristische dieser Verbindungsform liegt darin, dass kein notwendiger Zusammenhang zwischen dem politischen Leben des Ober—und Unterstaates besteht, in der Regel auch keine Institutionen vorhanden sind, in denen eine derartige Gemeinsamkeit zum Ausdrucke kommen könnte. Der Staatenstaat gehört daher ganz oder doch überwiegend zum Typus der nicht organisierten Verbindungen. Die Unterordnung von Gebiet und Angehörigen des Unterstaates unter die Gewalt des oberherrlichen ist in der Regel indirekt, sie sind durch das Medium der Unterstaatsgewalt dem Oberstaate unterworfen." See also Jellinek's *Lehre von den Staatenverbindungen,* p. 137 *et seq.*

tracting States. Certainly, at any rate, they cannot be designated as unions of a juristic character, for, as analysis will later show, treaty relations are not of this character.[9]

Coming now to "Organized Unions" we find in them, as their name imports, permanent central organs. They admit of segregation into the four following classes: (1) International Administrative Unions, (2) The Realunion and Personalunion, (3) The Staatenbund (Confederacy), and (4) The Bundesstaat (Federal State).

Examples of the first sub-class are combinations of States for the common regulation of particular interests wherein permanent administrative authorities are created. Of this kind are the commissions for the regulation of navigation upon the rivers Po and Danube, and the international Postal and Telegraph Unions. There is the same objection to considering these types of unions of States that we have made to the whole of the class of unorganized unions above considered.

By the term *"Realunion"* is indicated by German publicists that composite type of State life in which there is an intimate and lasting union entered into between two or more sovereign States, according to which there is a common ruler, but a preservation of the territorial divisions, and a recognition and protection of the constitutional rights of each of the uniting States. Thus, it is "that form which arises when two or more independent States unite for common protection, according to which one and the same physical person appears as the representative of the States' authority and according to which the extending of this union to other functions is not forbidden."[10] In other words, the essential element of the Realunion is that it is provided by the constitution of

---

[9] Upon this point, compare Gareis, *Allgemeines Staatsrecht*, pp. 103-105.
[10] Jellinek, *Die Lehre von den Staatenverbindungen*, p. 215.

each member State that the representative of its Sovereignty (*Repräsentationshoheit*) shall be in one and the same physical person, and that this connection shall obtain irrespective of who the prescribed qualifications happen to determine this common ruler shall be. The most conspicuous example of this form of union is that formerly exhibited by Austria and Hungary, and Norway and Sweden. And, it may be added, the relation between Great Britain and its "Dominions" is tending toward, if it has not already reached, this type of political association.

It will be seen that that which distinguishes a Realunion from a simple sovereign State whose organization provides for distinct governmental agencies in different portions of its domain is that the members of the union are true sovereign States and that though the powers of the Crown of all of them are vested in the same individual, that individual is constitutionally viewed as having as many distinct official or public personalities as there are States over which he rules. Thus it is possible that, as to one of the States he may be constitutionally regarded as the original and subsisting source of all legal authority, while, as to another of the States he may be viewed as possessing only such powers as have been delegated to him by the citizen body from whose will it is assumed that all legal legitimacy is derived.

A type of union much resembling the Realunion, and, in fact, juristically of the same class, is the so-called Personalunion. The distinction between the two consists merely in the fact that the associated States come to have the same ruler only by reason of the casual circumstance that their rules of royal descent, as fixed by their several systems of constitutional law, happen to call to their thrones the same person. In such cases the union of course lasts only during the reigns of such monarchs. Of this character were the relations for a time between England and Hanover, Denmark and Schleswig-Holstein, Prussia and Neuenburg; and such was the relation that once existed between Holland and Luxemburg. In these cases the ruler is to be considered as possessing as many political personalities as there are States under his rule. It is thus proper to consider each of the members of a Personalunion as well of the Realunion as having its own ruling head. The Sovereignty of each of the individual States is preserved.[11]

Federal States (Bundesstaaten) and Confederacies (Staatenbunden). The two main types of the composite State are the Confederacy (*Staatenbund*) and the Federal State (*Bundesstaat*), and a critical examination of the nature of these two forms will serve to bring out the general principles that are applicable in determining the juristic form of all kinds of political unions. The necessity of this examination is amply testified to by the great diversity that exists in the views held by different publicists upon the various points involved. Thus, Waitz, Bluntschli, Ruttiman, de Tocqueville, and many American writers, maintain the doctrine of divided sovereignty in a Federal State. As regards the nature of our own union, Wheaton and Halleck and other international law writers declare that the international sovereignty of the

[11] Thus says Jellinek (*op. cit.*, p. 212), "Die Personalunion ensteht durch Momente, welche keine Willenseinigung der Staaten voraussetzen und zur Folge haben, die Realunion hingegen beruht auf dem übereinstimmenden, geeinigten Willen der Staaten, welche die Fülle der Staatsgewalt, die Entscheidung über die wichtigsten Angelegenheiten der Staaten Einer natürlichen Persönlichkeit zuweisen." In his latest work, *Allgemeine Staatslehre,* Dritte Auflage, p. 751, Jellinek, as to the distinction between Personalunion and Realunion, says, "Die ursprüngliche Unterscheidung beider Typen, je nachdem bloss die Person des Monarchen oder überdies staatliche Angelegenheiten den einzelnen Staaten gemeinsam seien, die noch in der ausserdeutschen Literatur und in der Sprache der Tagespresse angetroffen wird, ist auf rein äusserlichen Merkmalen basiert und rechtlich belanglos."

individual State is destroyed, but domestic sovereignty retained, though it is apparent that in taking this view a conception of sovereignty is taken that makes of it a mere collection of powers so loosely related that they may be separated without loss of real sovereignty to the possessor of any part. According to Twiss, the members of our union though not "independent" are yet "all sovereign States."[12] According to Calhoun and his school, they are completely sovereign; while by the opponents of that school they are held as entirely devoid of this character. As opposed to complete sovereignty, either of the individual States or of the national government, Brownson holds that, "while the sovereignty is and must be in the States, it is in the States united and not in the States severally." "The organic American people do not exist as a consolidated people or State, they exist only as organized into distinct but inseparable States."[13]

Treitschke did not attempt a rigorous juristic analysis of the Federal State, but he evidently had a conception of it peculiar to himself, for he maintained that, in the German Empire, Prussia remained sovereign, although the sovereignties of all the other member States had been swallowed up in that of the Empire.[14]

LeFur says that the peculiar characteristic of the Federal State is the joint participation of the several subordinate states collectively, and their citizens individually, in the formation of the sovereign will: "Un seul caractère peut être considéré comme appartenant en propre à l'Etat fédéral, c'est l'existence dans cette forme d'Etats, entre l'Etat lui-même et les citoyens, d'un nouveau facteur coopérant comme les derniers à la forma-

---

[12] *The Law of Nations Considered as Independent Political Communities*, vol. I, p. 23.
[13] *The American Republic*, pp. 221, 245.
[14] *Politics*, chapter XXII.

tion de la volonté souveraine. Ce nouveau facteur, ce sont les Etats particuliers, qui participent à la souveraineté sous une double forme, tantôt indirectement par l'intermédiaire de leur representants, tantôt directement, surtout en matière de révision constitutionnelle, grâce à l'existence d'un véritable referendum d'Etats, semblable à celui qui existe au profit des citoyens dans les républiques démocratiques. Cette participation de certaines collectivités publiques à la formation de la volonté souveraine existe, on l'a vu, dans tout Etat fédéral; et à l'inverse elle n'existe que là."[15]

Von Mohl declares that the sovereignty is divided between the collective state and its members: "Als Bundesstaat bezeichnet man aber bekanntlich die jenige Vereinigung von Staaten, über welcher eine gemeinschaftliche Regierung mit allen dazu nothwendigen Rechten und Organen besteht, so dass die Selbständigkeit und namentlich die völkerrechtliche Souveränität der einzelnen theilnehemenden Staaten sehr geschmälert ist, und eine durchgehende Theilung der Regierungsrechte zwischen ihnen und der oberen Gesammtgewalt staatfindet."[16]

Borel, who has given us one of the best discussions of the subject, defines a Federal State as: "un Etat souverain, dont les membres ne sont pas souverains . . . L'Etat fédératif est donc l'Etat dans lequel une certaine participation à l'exercice du pouvoir souverain est accordée à des collectivitiés inférieures, soit qu'on les adjoigne à l'organe souverain pour la formation de la volonté nationale, soit que, prises dans leur totalité elles forment elles-même cet organe souverain." [17]

This diversity of opinions could be further multiplied

[15] *État fédéral et confédération d'États,* p. 673.
[16] *Staatswissenschaften,* vol. I, p. 560.   (Ed. 1855.)
[17] *La Souveraineté et l'État Fédératif,* pp. 74, 172.

if it would serve any good purpose. The point has, however, been made sufficiently plain that, upon this most important topic of public law, an almost chaos of thought reigns. The explanation for this must be that there has not been a proper analysis of the problem as a purely juristic one. We shall therefore be justified if we consider this question with some degree of particularity.

Preliminary Propositions. As an introduction to this examination it will be well to repeat certain of the propositions which have been already established and which will furnish the premises of our argument. These are:

1. That sovereignty signifies the legal competence of the State to determine its own legal rights and obligations as well as those of all persons, natural and artificial, over whom it claims jurisdiction.

2. That sovereignty, thus denoting the legally omnipotent will of the State, is indivisible and inalienable.

3. That two or more States, each possessing this sovereignty or legal omnipotence, cannot enter into relations with one another which are of a strictly legal character. This is a topic which will be more fully discussed in a later chapter, but it is sufficient here to say that inasmuch as a law, *in sensu strictiore,* imports a command from a legal superior to a legal inferior, it cannot apply to relations between two or more sovereign states which stand towards one another as equals. They can enter into agreements that create moral or political but not legal obligations.

4. From this third proposition it follows, as has been shown in an earlier chapter, that a sovereign State cannot be created through the joint action of two or more previously existing sovereign States. In other words, sovereignty cannot be the product of a treaty.

These principles being established, it is clear that, when dealing with political groups composed of two or more bodies-politic terming themselves States,[18] but two possible juristic alternatives are presented. Either the central or so-called federal body possesses the sovereignty, in which case the federated units are wholly without sovereignty; or these federated units are severally sovereign, in which case the central body is wholly without this attribute. If, then, we give the name Federation or Federal Union or Federal State (*Bundesstaat*) to the first of these forms, and to the second the name Confederation or Confederacy (*Staatenbund*), we find that these two political types stand almost poles apart from one another. They are not different species of the same genus, but are juristically antithetical to each other.

Confederacies. In a Confederation the member States retain their full sovereignty and legal independence and, strictly speaking, no central State is created. There is a common or central government but no central sovereignty. The central government is thus nothing more than the common organ or complexus of organs which the severally sovereign States establish and maintain for the carrying out of purposes with reference to which these States have agreed to act as a unit. This central government may thus be viewed as, in effect, a branch of the government of each of the associated States, and all the authority that it exercises as obtained by delegation from these States. The instrument which defines the powers of the central government and the corresponding obligations of the States may be known as a Constitution, but, accurately speaking, it is nothing more than a treaty or compact between the States, and derives its validity from their consent to it.

This being the juristic nature of a confederacy, any member State may withdraw from it without being

---

[18] Whether or not properly so terming themselves will be later considered.

chargeable with the commission of an illegal act, and this is so even though the articles of confederation may provide for a perpetual union. Such a withdrawal by one or more States may be a violation of international good faith and furnish serious grounds for complaint upon the part of the States remaining within the confederation, but it cannot be properly asserted by them that the secession is an illegal or unconstitutional act.

Distinct from the right of secession is the claim sometimes put forth that, in a confederacy, each member State retains the right to determine whether or not it will permit the enforcement within its limits of those orders of the central government which, in the opinion of such State, are not authorized by the constitution or articles of union. This is known as the doctrine of Nullification. Here again it may be said that, inasmuch as each State is admitted to be legally sovereign, it cannot be held to act illegally if it refuse obedience to orders of which it disapproves. But such a disobedience, unless expressly recognized by the articles of union, is necessarily a breach of those articles; and, furthermore, the assertion of the right is, in itself, an unreasonable one, for, if exercised, the effect is to allow a State to remain in the confederation and obtain all the advantages flowing from it while at the same time refusing to abide by such special commands as happen to be onerous or otherwise objectionable to itself. The claim of a right of nullification is thus, in some ways, a more extreme claim than is the assertion of a right of secession from the Union.[19]

Among the more important examples of confederacies may be mentioned the old German Union which lasted

[19] In 1861, at the time of the secession of the Southern States from the American Union, a number of their leading spokesmen took pains to say that they repudiated the doctrine that the States, while remaining in the Union, might "nullify" for their own citizens such acts of the Union as they might disapprove.

from 1815 to 1866, the Swiss Confederacy under the Pact of 1815 (1815 to 1840), and the Union of the former American Colonies from 1781 to 1789 under the Articles of Confederation.

Federal States. As distinguished from a confederacy, a federal State (Bundesstaat) connotes the existence of a true central sovereign State, composed of constituent States which are not themselves severally sovereign. There are some jurists who deny that these constituent bodies-politic may be properly termed States, but in common speech they are usually spoken of as such, and the question whether or not this is technically correct, from a juristic standpoint, will, for the present, be postponed.

The central government of a federal State, being conceived of as the organ of a true central State, is not to be regarded as the common organ through which the member States of the Union realize certain of their individual ends. Rather, the reverse is the case, for the central State, being admittedly sovereign, and the member States not sovereign, their governments may properly be regarded as organs through which the central State exercises its sovereign will in the several areas of the non-sovereign member States.

The federal State is thus to be viewed as deriving its authority from its own inherent sovereignty and not by way of delegation from the member States. It may, indeed, be the historical fact that the Union was established at the common desire and by the joint cooperation of these States, but, if it be conceded that a national sovereignty exists, it is irrelevant, legally speaking, how this was brought about. The constitutional result is that the member States may no longer be viewed as themselves sovereign and upon a constitutional level with the National State.

Federal States and Confederacies Distinguished. In the Federal State, then, a true central State is created, its several units are legally and constitutionally united, and sovereignty—the power of ultimately determining one's own legal competence—resides in the federal body. In the Confederacy, on the other hand, the individual States retain their character as States, and their relations to each other are of an international or treaty character. Consequently no central State is created, and sovereignty lies wholly within such individual political units. What union there is in the Confederacy is the creation of the wills of the individual States. In a Federal State, on the other hand, its foundation rests in itself. It is created by the people as a whole, and the individual States are creations of its will. In the case of a Federal State, historically founded upon a union of previously existing sovereign States, one is to consider the citizens of the Federal State as first divesting themselves of their old State Sovereignties, and then, as a People, establishing a national Federal State. These two volitional acts may be synchronous and made apparent by a single outward act, *viz.,* the establishment of a federal control, but they are distinct acts from a political standpoint. The apparent continued existence in the Federal States of what were formerly independent political bodies, is not real. Those bodies-politic are destroyed when their citizens transfer their allegiance to the central power. They are recreated as bodies-politic by the federal constitution. They are thus creations of the Federal State, and, as Lincoln said in his first message to Congress, "The States have their status in the Union and they have no other legal status. The Union is older than any of the States, and in fact created them as States." [20]

[20] Bearing upon this point, as well as upon the comparison which we have before made of our individual Commonwealths with their own

Thus, if we take the position that a national State was created by the American people in 1789, we must consider them to have become a psychologically united People before that time and to have destroyed their former individual States when they established the present Federal States. This being so, the fact that the constitution was adopted by conventions convened in what had formerly been the several States, must be interpreted as meaning merely that a united People saw fit, for the sake of convenience and expediency, to utilize existing governmental machinery and territorial divisions for the formal adoption of its new constitution. And that therefore such conventions were, in fact, Federal and not State organs.

Austin states so concisely the distinctions between federal States and Confederacies, his words deserve quotation. He says:

"A composite (federal) state, and a system of confederated states, are broadly distinguished by the following differences. In the case of a composite state, the several united societies are one independent society, or are severally subject to one sovereign body; which, through its minister, the general government, and through

subdivisions, may be cited the following quotation from an address by Lincoln to the Legislature at Indianapolis, February 12, 1861. "In what consists the special sacredness of a State? I speak not of the position assigned to a State in the Union by the Constitutions; for that, by the bond, we all recognize. That position, however, a State cannot carry out of the Union with it. I speak of that assumed primary right of a State to rule all which is *less* than itself, and ruin all which is larger than itself. If a State and a county in a given case should be equal in extent and territory, and equal in number of inhabitants, in what, as a matter of principle, is the State better than the county? Would an exchange of *names* be an exchange of *rights* upon principle? On what rightful principle may a State, being no more than one-fiftieth part of the nation in soil and population, break up the nation, and then coerce a proportionately larger subdivision of itself in the most arbitrary way? What mysterious right to play tyrant is conferred on a district or county, with its people, by merely calling it a State?" From what has been said in this chapter it would follow that ascription of "limited sovereignty" to the members of our Union by American courts and Congress is, strictly speaking, incorrect. A more proper phrase would be that of "limited legal competence."

its members and ministers the several united governments, is habitually and generally obeyed in each of the
united societies, and also in the larger society arising from
the union of all. In the case of a system of confederate
states, the several compacted societies are not one society,
and are not subject to a common sovereign; or (changing
the phrase) each of the several societies is an independent
and political society, and each of their several governments is properly sovereign or supreme. Though the
aggregate of the several governments was the framer of
the federal compact, and may subsequently pass resolutions concerning the entire confederacy, neither the terms
of that compact, nor such subsequent resolutions, are
enforced in any of the societies by the authority of that
aggregate body. To each of the confederated governments, these terms and resolutions are merely articles of
agreement which it spontaneously adopts; and they owe
their legal effect, in its own political society, to laws and
other commands which it makes or fashions upon them,
and which, of its own authority, it addressed to its own
subjects. In short, a system of confederated states is not
essentially different from a number of independent governments connected by an ordinary alliance. And where
independent governments are connected by an ordinary
alliance, none of the allied governments is subject to the
allied governments considered as an aggregate body;
though each of the allied governments adopts the terms
of the alliance, and commonly enforces those terms, by
laws and commands of its own, in its own independent
community. Indeed, a system of confederated states,
and a number of independent governments connected by
an ordinary alliance, cannot be distinguished precisely
through general or abstract expressions. So long as we
abide in general expressions, we can only affirm, generally
and vaguely, that the compact of the former is intended

to be temporary; and that the ends or purposes which are embraced by the compact are commonly more numerous, and are commonly more complicated, than those which the alliance contemplates." [21]

Distinctions Improperly Made. The analysis of the Federal State as thus far conducted enables us, by way of negative criticism, to point out the invalidity of the following *criteria* that have at times been applied in distinguishing the *Staatenbund* and *Bundesstaat*.

First, the distinction does not lie in the amount of powers actually vested in the central government as compared with those retained by the individual States. As long as the governments of the individual members of the union are considered as parts of the central government, no essential distinction can arise regarding the distribution and actual exercise of its powers. Sovereignty consists not so much in the actual and immediate exercise of functions as in the power potentially possessed to draw to oneself those particular powers that may be seen fit. Federal States may be conceived in which but very few functions are centrally exercised; and, on the other hand, Confederacies imagined, in which the powers of the central government are most ample. But in neither case is the political character of the union thus determined.

Secondly, the distinction between these two political types does not consist in the fact that in the Federal State the operation of federal law is in all cases, directly upon individuals, while, in the Confederacy, the acts of the central power apply to the States as such and through them to their citizens. It is true that the Federal State must not be dependent upon the acquiescence of the individual States for the execution of its laws, but it is entirely possible that the Federal State may, in some

[21] *The Province of Jurisprudence Determined*, ed. 1861, pp. 223-224.

instances at least, operate through the individual States as such.

Also, vice versa, in the Confederation law may operate in some instances directly upon the individual. Thus, while Americans have been accustomed to distinguish the present Union from that maintained under the Articles of Confederation upon this ground, as a matter of fact this rule does not hold good in all cases. As Madison points out in the Federalist:[22] "In some instances, as has been shown, the powers of the new government will act on the States in their collective characters. In some instances also, those of the existing government act immediately on individuals. In cases of capture; of piracy; of the postoffice; or coins; weights, and measures; or trade with the Indians; of claims under grants of land, by different States; and above all, in the case of trials by courts-martial in the army and navy, by which death may be inflicted without the intervention of a jury, or even of a civil magistrate; in all these cases the powers of the confederation operate immediately on the persons and interests of individual citizens."

In fact, then, provided the Federal State has the direct or primary allegiance of the governed, the exact means through which laws are executed is not juristically significant. The essential point is as to whose will is embodied in them. Political expediency demands that the greater and more important functions of the Federal State should be performed through its own central organs rather than through those political bodies in which there rest historical traditions of complete Sovereignty and national autonomy, and a jealousy of over control by the central power. If the Federal State trusts too much to such particular organs there is the danger of its commands being less faithfully performed than they would be by its

[22] *No. 40.* See also Westerkamp, *Staatenbund und Bundesstaat.*

own agents. This has been the consideration that has caused the United States to create its own courts and marshals and other officers for the determination and execution of matters of federal or interstate interest. In cases where there is even a remote danger of rebellion on the part of the States, the necessity that the central power should keep well within its own hands not only the formulation but the execution of its own orders is proportionately enhanced. The same principles require that, in Confederacies, where there is danger that the central power may usurp the Sovereignty, the States should limit to the smallest amount the functions actually exercised by their common and central organs.

Thirdly, the absence of a requirement for unanimous consent of the States for purposes of amendment of the instrument of union is not decisive as to the non-confederate character of such union. For example, the constitution of the Confederate States of 1861-65, though avowedly creating but a *Staatenbund,* did not require such unanimity. In this case the express provision that each State was to continue individually sovereign, and with the right at any time to withdraw from the union, saved the union from being a federal one. Without this express sovereign provision, the power of a fraction of the individual States to amend the constitution, against the will of the remaining fraction, would necessarily have resulted in creating a *Bundesstaat.* For, under such a condition, it would have been theoretically possible at any time for any particular State to be subjected to a legal control against its own will,—a condition incompatible with its Sovereignty.[23]

[23] "Granting the correctness of the theory that the several States were once political sovereignties, and that each surrendered a portion of its inherent powers to the general government, such surrender would go no further than the express provisions of the constitution; as to all other matters not reached by that instrument, their sovereignty would remain intact. By this theory, then, it is entirely impossible that three-

On the other hand, where there is this requirement of unanimity of vote for purposes of constitutional amendment, a Confederacy is not necessarily created, any more than the absence of such a provision denotes the existence of a Federal State. To be sure, under such a condition, no individual State can be further deprived of any of its powers without its own consent, yet, on the other hand, it may not legally escape from the obligations already imposed upon it by the constitution, or withdraw from the union. Where there is not this power on the part of a State of avoiding obligations already created, the Sovereignty must be held to rest with the central authority. The fact that the unanimous vote of the federated States is necessary means only that the federal State has made the act of altering its actual competence extremely difficult. In other words, no one individual State has the legal power to alter its actual legal competence, and hence is not sovereign. The central State alone has the power of constitutional amendment, though it is a power subject to extreme formal limitation. But the fact that it is so formally limited does not mean that the power does not exist, any more than it can be claimed that the old Polish assembly did not have legislative power because of the existence of the *liberum veto*. Practically, of course, in any State of developing civilization, such a condition as this in which the individual State has not the power of secession, and, at the same time, the central power cannot change its governmental powers except under conditions that in the great majority of cases could not be obtained, would soon prove unworkable and would precipitate a revolution either by way of secession on the part of the individual States, or by an unconstitutional enlargement of central powers.

fourths of the States can compel the remaining one-fourth to give up a further portion of their attributes contrary to their will." Pomeroy, *Constitutional Law*, p. 111.

Fourthly, and finally, the distinction between a Federal and a Confederate State is not one of enumerated or unenumerated powers. It is not a question, as has been already said, of the amount of powers actually exercised at any one time by the central government. Even Westerkamp, who holds the distinction between these two types of union to be a quantitative rather than a qualitative one, does not place any weight upon this feature.[24]

The True Test. The final test in all cases is, as has been so many times said, the power or lack of power of the individual State to determine the extent of its own obligations under the articles of union, and, in the last resort, if their view be not acquiesced in by the general government, to withdraw from the union. Where it is constitutionally provided that, in case of alleged conflict between federal and state law, such conflict shall be considered by a federal tribunal whose decrees are enforceable by the federal executive, then, in such case, a *Bundesstaat* certainly exists. If, on the other hand, it be held that a dissatisfied State has the right of secession, there is only a provisional right of federal enforcement, namely, provisional upon the consent of the State to remain in the union.

Nullification. The doctrine of nullification which grants to the individual members of the union the right to refuse obedience to any general law that it deems inconsistent with the articles of union is of course applicable only to a Confederacy. But even there it cannot be termed a legal "right" of nullification. Each member of the union, being completely sovereign, may govern its action by its own will, and no other member may legally say nay. But, as a practical proposition, it is inconceivable that the assertion of such a power on the part of a particular State would not lead to disruption of the union.

[24] *Staatenbund und Bundesstaat,* p. 45.

For it can scarcely be imagined that the other members would consent to the avoidance by such State of the execution of a part of the general law while they held themselves bound to it. Such a condition of affairs would, in fact, result, *ipso facto,* in a destruction of the union to that extent, its sole purpose being to secure a concert of action in matters of general interest. It would, indeed, be a just *casus belli* against the State so refusing obedience to the agreement in which it bound itself to common action. Jefferson, the author of the Kentucky Resolutions, himself asserted the propriety of even a confederate government coercing a State when he wrote to Cartwright advising the Congress of the old Confederacy to send a frigate and compel a State to pay its quota of taxes.

American and German Federations Contrasted. The foregoing has had reference to the essential juristic distinction between Confederacies and Federal States. It has been seen that the difference is not a quantitative one as to the number or importance of the powers which are exercised by the central government. With reference to most of the functions of government it is a matter of policy rather than of constitutional or juristic necessity as to which of them shall be exercised by organs and agencies of the central government or by the member States through their several governmental organizations. Thus the United States and the German Republic are both types of Federal States, but they differ widely in this respect. The United States is legislatively decentralized; that is, the great body of the private law is furnished by each State of the union for its own citizens. The subjects of legislation that are placed within the control of the national congress, though very important, are not many in number. From the governmental point of view, however, the United States is a highly developed

Federal Union, for there exists a complete central governmental machinery—executive and judicial as well as legislative—through which all the federal powers are exercised. Only in a very few instances are federal laws enforced through the agencies of the individual State.

As contrasted with the United States, the German Republic is legislatively highly centralized. The entire body of the private law and judicial procedure, civil and criminal, is within the control of the national Parliament, the States retaining legislative powers only with reference to their own public law and local police. When, however, it comes to the interpretation and execution of the law thus federally determined, the governments of the States are relied upon. Thus the executive branch of the national government includes only those bureaus or departments which have to deal with certain national matters the execution of which it is impossible to concede to the States, and there is no complete judicial system such as is found in the United States.

It does not need to be pointed out that it is an element of weakness for the Federal State to be obliged to resort to the authorities of the member States for the enforcement of its commands. In Germany, however, this weakness under the Empire was rendered negligible by reason of the fact that one State—Prussia—had a prestige and military power that made futile any attempt upon the part of the other States to resist its will, and that the King of this State was *ex officio* Emperor of the Union and constitutionally vested with the duty of bringing back into obedience to federal authority such States as might be declared by the *Bundesrath* to be derelict in the performance of their imperial duties. In such cases the imperial coercion was to be applied directly to the States concerned.

In the United States the existence of complete executive and judicial departments makes possible the vindication of national supremacy by applying compulsion to the individuals who resist the national authority. If, in justification of this resistance, these individuals appeal to laws or executive orders which their respective States have issued, the reply is that, insofar as those laws or orders are in violation of the Federal Constitution or laws, they are without legal force and therefore furnish no legal defence for any actions taken in pursuance of them. Thus, in constitutional theory, the American Civil War of 1861-1865 was a contest carried on by the United States against the citizens of the eleven Southern States which had sought to withdraw from the union, rather than against those States themselves.

Citizenship in Federal States. In all federally organized States the aim is to harmonize the continued existence of the member States with the maintainance of national unity and strength. Thus we find alongside of national citizenship the recognition of a State citizenship which has no real analogue in the most autonomous local government areas of unitary States.

In the United States there was for many years a dispute as to the constitutional nexus or relation between federal and state citizenship—whether the former depended upon or arose out of the latter or vice versa—and this controversy was not finally settled until the adoption, in 1868, of the Fourteenth Amendment to the Federal Constitution. This made it certain that federal citizenship was to be held paramount to State citizenship, for, upon the one hand, the States were permitted to play no part in determining who should be deemed citizens of the United States, and, upon the other hand, they were not henceforth to be able to control their own citizenship since it was provided that any person enjoying national citizenship should, by mere residence within a State (which that State could not constitutionally prevent), become one of its own citizens. As regards both federal and State citizenship the Fourteenth Amendment declared in absolute terms that "All persons born or naturalized in the United States, and subject to the jurisdiction thereof, are citizens of the United States and of the State wherein they reside."

Though thus placed upon a subordinate plane, the effect of this amendment was not in any way to destroy or to merge State citizenship in the national citizenship. To each citizenship are still attached distinctive and important appurtenant rights, the enumeration or specific description of which would, however, carry us too far into the special constitutional jurisprudence of the United States.

Under the German Imperial Constitution prior to 1918 every citizen of a constituent State was, *ipso facto*, a citizen of the Empire, but there could also be an imperial citizenship without state citizenship, as for example, of one living in a German colony (*Schutzgebiete*) or accepting an Imperial office.[25] The constitution of the recently established German Republic gives to the National Government exclusive jurisdiction to determine all matters of citizenship (Article 6) and declares (Article 110) that citizenship in the Republic and in the States shall be acquired or lost in accordance with the provisions of national laws passed in pursuance of this national authority. It is, however, specifically declared that every citizen of a State shall be at the same time a citizen of the Republic.

In the constitution of the Swiss Republic it is declared that "every citizen of a canton is a Swiss citizen."

Territories and Dependencies of a Federal State. There is nothing in the nature and form of a federally organized

[25] See the Imperial Law of June 1, 1879.

State to make impossible the extension of its sovereignty over areas which are not included within the limits of the member States. Thus, since the beginnings of its existence, the United States has possessed what are called "Territories" which are not States, which occupy a different constitutional status, and have only such autonomous powers and rights of self government as Congress sees fit to grant to them. Some of these areas, known as "Unorganized Territories," have had almost no self-government, while to others, known as "Organized Territories," Congress has given complete governmental structures, including locally elected legislatures. The governors and judges of these organized Territories have, however, been appointed by the President of the United States and the acts of the legislatures have been subject to annulment by Congress,—a right which Congress has, however, very seldom exercised. Since the Spanish-American War the United States has possessed the Philippine and Hawaiian Islands, Porto Rico and other less important islands, which are termed Insular Dependencies but which are, in all but name, colonies pure and simple. In a number of decisions defining the constitutional status of these islands the federal Supreme Court has introduced what is practically a new classification of Territories, dividing them into two groups according to whether or not they have been "incorporated" into the United States. By these decisions it is held that certain constitutional guarantees do not apply to those Territories which have not been "incorporated" but do apply to those which have been accorded this status. Thus, for example, the constitutional provision that all indirect taxes shall be "uniform throughout the United States," has been held not necessarily applicable to "unincorporated" areas. It lies within the discretion of Congress to determine when incorporation shall take place; but, whether incorporated or not, the form of government which a Territory is to enjoy is a matter with regard to which Congress can act as it sees fit.

Constitutional provision is made for the admission of new States into the American Union and thirty-five have been admitted, all of them, with the exception of Texas, being created out of areas previously under the sovereignty of the United States. Texas seceded from Mexico, its independence was recognized by the United States, and it was then admitted to the Union as a State without passing through the Territorial status.

The German Empire, from 1871 to 1919, possessed the Imperial Territories of Alsace and Lorraine. These two provinces, taken from France were, step by step, accorded greater rights of self-government, and a higher constitutional status until, shortly before the outbreak of the Great War, they enjoyed most of the rights possessed by the States of the Empire. In the Dominion of Canada and in the Commonwealth of Australia considerable areas exist which are not accorded the full rights of federal membership. To New Zealand and Australia have been given by the League of Nations "mandates" over certain of the South Pacific islands formerly belonging to Germany.

Equality of States. It is not essential to the federal form of government that the member States should all stand in exactly the same relation to the federal government as regards their respective autonomous powers or of their citizens to participate in the control and management of the general government.

In the United States, however, the doctrine of State equality prevails. It is true that different States have a different voting power in the election of the President and Vice-President, and send different quotas of representatives to the lower house of Congress. But these differences arise out of differences of population and are determined by a rule which is uniform in its application to all of the States, so that, even here, it cannot be said that the States are constitutionally unequal.

In Canada the Provinces, and in Australia the States, have equal constitutional rights, and the same is substantially true in Switzerland, where, however, certain of the cantons are known as "half-cantons," which send only one member to the Council of States, whereas the other cantons send two, and have but half a vote when constitutional amendments are being passed upon.

In the old German Empire, however, there were substantial differences in constitutional powers of the different States. These are too numerous to enumerate but, as illustrations of them it may be mentioned that Prussia's King was *ex officio* the German Emperor, and that to Bavaria, Würtemburg and Baden special rights were accorded with reference to the control of the posts and telegraphs and taxes upon brandy and beer.

Residual Powers. In the United States the federal government possesses only those powers specifically given to it by the constitution and such as are "necessary and proper" for the carrying into effect of these specifically granted powers. The State governments, are thus the residual claimants to all powers not granted to the federal government or specifically denied to them by the National Constitution. In the Canadian Federation a greater attempt is made to enumerate just what powers shall be possessed by the Provinces as well as by the Dominion Government, but, from the nature of the case, such enumeration could not be exhaustive and, though the language of the British North American Act of 1867 which serves as the Canadian Constitution is not very plain, it has been established by judicial interpretation that the residual or unenumerated powers belong to the Central

Government. In the Australian Commonwealth, in Switzerland, and in Germany the General Government possesses only those powers specifically, or by necessary implication, granted to it. The fact, however, that in Switzerland and Germany the constitutionality of a federal statute may not be questioned in the courts, makes it, of course, possible for the federal legislature to construe its own powers as liberally as it may please.

Federal Supervision of the States. In all federally organized states the general government is given certain rights of supervision over the States in order to see that they faithfully execute their constitutional duties. This supervision extends not only to seeing that the national supremacy is maintained and the free and efficient exercise of its powers in no way interfered with, but to making it certain that the member States do not violate certain personal and property rights which are specially recognized and guaranteed in the Federal Constitution. It may, however, be remarked that in the United States, until the adoption in 1868 of the Fourteenth Amendment to the Federal Constitution, this federal guarantee of protection to the individual against oppressive action upon the part of his own individual State extended only to a few specific matters such as the impairment of the obligation of contracts and protection against penal laws of an *ex post facto* character. Since the adoption of the Fourteenth Amendment, however, the private rights of the individual have to a considerable extent been brought under the protecting power of the National Government by the operation of the provision of that Amendment that no State "shall deprive any person of life, liberty or property, without due process of law; nor deny to any person within its jurisdiction the equal protection of the laws." The requirement of "due process of law" has been given a very broad construction so that it includes not only

matters of procedure but substantive rights, irrespective
of the procedure by which they may be affected. Thus,
in all their dealings with their own citizens or with those
who happen to be within their borders, including corporations, the Federal Government sees to it that private
rights of life, liberty and property shall not be abridged
except upon good grounds, and that, in every case, the
procedure by which they are affected shall be such as
furnishes the individual affected an opportunity to present before an impartial tribunal such arguments or evidence as he may have, showing why he or his rights
should not be brought within the control of a given State
law.

**Coercion of its Member Commonwealths by a Federal
State.** In a Confederacy which is, as we have seen, a
league of sovereign States, it is quite appropriate that
where one or more of these States may refuse obedience
to the commands of the central government coercion
should be applied directly upon these States as such.
When this becomes necessary a state of public war immediately ensues.

In a Federal State the possibility of enforcing national
authority by proceeding directly against the recalcitrant
commonwealth is not excluded. Indeed, express provision
was made for this in the constitution of the German Empire, Article 19 of which declared that: "If the States of
the Confederation do not fulfil their constitutional duties,
they may be compelled to do so by execution. This execution shall be decided upon by the *Bundesrath,* and carried out by the Emperor." It is quite logical that this
provision for commonwealth coercion should have been
made in view of the fact that, in general, in Germany,
federal laws were carried into execution through the governmental agencies of the member commonwealths.

In the United States, with but few and unimportant

exceptions, federal laws are executed through Federal Governmental agencies and federal officials. It has thus resulted that the constitutional principle has become fixed that the supremacy of the national will is to be maintained, not by direct action against the member States, but by proceedings against individuals, anything in the Constitution or laws of any State to the contrary notwithstanding, and irrespective of what may be the opinions of those exercising the political powers of those States.[25a]

The individual States, having a political status only as members of the Union, have not the legal power to place themselves, as political bodies, in opposition to the national will. Their legislatures, their courts, or their executive officials may attempt acts unwarranted by the federal Constitution or federal law, and they may even command that their citizens generally shall refuse obedience to some specified federal laws or to federal authorities generally, but in all such cases such acts are, legally viewed, simply void, and all individuals obeying them subject to punishment as offenders against national law. The fact that their respective States have directed them to refuse obedience or to offer resistance to the execution of the federal laws can afford them no immunity from punishment, for no one can shelter himself behind an unconstitutional law, such a law being, in truth, as we have seen, not a law at all, but only an unsuccessful attempt at a law.

Thus, President Lincoln, in his first inaugural message, assumed a correct constitutional position when he declared that the Federal Government could not wage public war against a State, not, however, because of a lack

---

[25a] A possible exception to the generality of the foregoing statement would be with reference to suits in the Supreme Court of the United States by the United States or by a State of the Union against another State of the Union.

of constitutional authority to maintain in every respect federal supremacy, but because, from the very nature of the Union, there could not be a public war between the Union and its member States. After an argument tending to show the sovereign character of the Union, and that it was intended to be perpetual, he declared: "It follows from these views that no State upon its own mere motion can lawfully get out of the Union; that resolves and ordinances to that effect are legally void, and that acts of violence within any State or States against the authority of the United States are insurrectionary or revolutionary, according to circumstances. I therefore consider that, in view of the Constitution and the laws, the Union is unbroken, and to the extent of my ability I shall take care, as the Constitution itself expressly enjoins upon me, that the laws of the Union be faithfully executed in all the States. . . . In doing this there needs to be no bloodshed or violence, and there shall be none unless it be forced upon the national authority. The power conferred upon me will be used to hold, occupy and possess the property and places belonging to the Government and to collect the duty and imposts; but beyond what may be necessary for these objects, there will be no invasions, no using of force against or among the people anywhere."

In taking this position Lincoln had to treat the war that had begun as merely an insurrection in which the coercion and punishments were to be applied to individuals. Thus he began his Proclamation of April 15, 1861, in which he called for seventy-five thousand of the militia of the States, by saying: "Whereas the laws of the United States have been for some time past and now are opposed and the execution thereof obstructed in the States of South Carolina, Georgia, Alabama, Florida, Mississippi, Louisiana and Texas, by combinations too powerful to be suppressed by the ordinary course of judicial proceedings;" and closed by commanding "the persons composing the combinations aforesaid to disperse and retire peaceably to their respective abodes within twenty days from this date."

As further showing the theory as to the nature of the contest that was held by the National Government is the fact that Congress did not "declare war" against the South, or, when the struggle was over, enter into a treaty of peace with the Southern Confederacy. The United States did not recognize that the Confederacy had or could have a standing as a political power with which it might deal as with a foreign State. One after another, the surrender of his forces by each Confederate general was accepted as an act of war and thus the Confederacy left to collapse and disappear without any formal, official act to mark its demise.

The possession by the Federal Government of full power to protect any right and enforce any law of its own at any time, and at any place within its territorial limits, any resistance of private individuals, or state officials, acting with or without the authority of state law to the contrary notwithstanding, has been uniformly asserted by the Supreme Court whenever such an assertion has been necessary.[26]

Powers Necessarily Possessed by a Federal Government. Although it is not possible to distinguish a sovereign Federal State from a Confederacy upon a purely quantitative comparison of the functions exercised in each by the central government, there are certain powers which, as a practical proposition, the central government of a Federal State must possess and directly exercise.

[26] See the chapter immediately following, and the author's *Constitutional Law of the United States*, vol. I, chap. IV, "The Supremacy of Federal Authority."

It has already been seen that the National Government must have the right to determine finally and conclusively the extent of its own legal powers as well as those of the member States, and there must also exist legal processes by means of which these final decisions as to constitutional competency may be enforced. Negatively stated, this means that the member States shall not have a legal right, under any circumstances, to "nullify" a federal law. Together with this legal right of final determination of conflicts of jurisdiction between national and State government must go the possession by the Federal Government of an adequate military force to enforce its decisions.

It is practically imperative that, in a federal State, the control of foreign affairs should be in the hands of the central government. In some federal States the member States are permitted to have intercourse with foreign States and even to enter into treaties with them with regard to certain local purposes, but in no case are these individual States allowed to have direct relations with foreign States with regard to matters of general political importance, and in all cases the National State is held responsible by foreign States for any breaches of international right or treaty obligations which the individual States may have authorized or which have been committed within their several borders. In the United States this international responsibility of the Federal Government has at times given rise to very serious embarrassments upon its part, for upon these occasions it has found itself internationally responsible for conditions which it was legally unable to control. This legal incompetence has been due, however, rather to the failure of Congress to enact the necessary legislation than to an absolute lack of constitutional authority in the Central Government.

As the sole representative of the Nation in its international dealings it is of course necessary that a Federal Government should possess adequate military forces for purposes of both offense and defense—or at least it should possess the constitutional authority to provide for and maintain an adequate army and navy when the occasion for their use arises.

As a practical proposition it is also necessary that the Federal Government should be constitutionally empowered to raise an adequate income, either by taxes or loans or both. It is, of course, possible to provide that the financial needs of the general government shall be met by assessments levied upon the States as such, and apportioned among them according to their size, wealth, population or any other principle that seems just and politically expedient. This, in part, was the plan pursued in the German Empire. In Germany there were special reasons why "matricular" contributions of the States, as they are called, were provided for, but, in general, it may be said that it is expedient that the National Government should be able to provide itself with funds without needing in any way the cooperation or acquiescence of the federated States. So important is this principle felt to be in the United States that the individual States are not permitted to levy the smallest tax upon the bonds or other evidences of indebtedness of the Nation, or upon the income derived from them.

Though perhaps not indispensable, experience has shown that it is highly desirable that, in a Federal State, the General Government should be authorized to regulate trade and commerce among the States, including, if found expedient, the construction, ownership and direct operation of inter-state railways and steamship lines, the telegraph, telephone, wireless and other means of communication. An opinion, is, indeed, widely held that this

authority should include as well those instrumentalities
of trade and communication which operate wholly within
State lines, for, in the present day, so intimate are inter-
State and intra-state commercial relations, a severance
of the two, placing the regulation of the one in the hands
of the General Government and of the other in the hands
of the several State Governments, is often impossible
and, where possible, not desirable.

It is also very desirable, though not absolutely necessary, that, in a Federal State, the control of the currency
should be subject to the regulation, if not exclusively
vested in the hands, of the National Government. The
reasons for this require no elaboration.

One other power which it is highly important that a
Federal Government should possess is the right to require
that the citizens of each State in the Union shall be accorded in all the other States of the Union those civil
rights of residence, ownership and use of property, freedom of contract, guarantees of rights of speech and press,
due process of law, etc., which those States accord to their
own citizens. In fact, no State should be permitted to
discriminate in any way, except as to political rights, between its own citizens and those of the other States. And
even as to these political rights provisions should exist
whereby, without onerous restrictions, the citizens of one
State may obtain citizenship in another State and thereby
become entitled to the political rights which appertain to
that status.

In all the federal States which now exist care is taken
to provide for this inter-state comity. Thus, in the
United States, it is constitutionally established that a
State cannot forbid the citizens of other States of the
Union from establishing their residence within its borders
and thereby becoming its citizens; and it specifically provided that no State shall "deny to any person within its

jurisdiction the equal protection of the laws," and, furthermore, that "full faith and credit shall be given in each State to the public acts, records and judicial proceedings of every other State"; and that "the citizens of each State shall be entitled to all privileges and immunities of citizens in the several States." With reference to this last requirement we have the statement of the Federal Supreme Court that "It has been justly said that no provision of the Constitution has tended so strongly to constitute the citizens of the United States one people as this. Indeed, without some provision of the kind, removing from the citizens of each State the disabilities of alienage in the others, and giving them equality of privilege with citizens of those States, the Republic would have constituted little more than a league of States; it would not have constituted the Union which now exists." [27]

Disadvantages of the Federal System of Government. The disadvantages of the federal system of government are obvious. It necessarily means, to a considerable extent, a duplication of governmental machinery, and this is especially so in a federation of the American type, in which practically all the national functions are exercised through national agencies.

A federal government is thus a complicated as well as an expensive method of political rule. In addition, it is politically and administratively weak. It is politically weak because authority is divided, and there is ever the danger that the member States will refuse to fulfil their constitutional duties, or, at least, will be negligent and lax in so doing. In the United States, as is well known, there were numberless conflicts between federal and State authorities which aroused bitter feelings and finally led to the bloody four years' Civil War of 1861-65. And, as

[27] *Paul v. Virginia,* 8 Wallace 168.

has been earlier adverted to, there have been not a few occasions upon which the federal government has been greatly embarrassed in its dealings with foreign nations by the failure or open refusal of the States to give full recognition within their borders to the international rights of resident aliens. And there are pending at this time questions of this sort for which no fully satisfactory solution has been found.

Administratively viewed the federal system is an unsatisfactory one because State borders constitute jurisdictional lines which State authorities cannot cross. This greatly hinders the administration of justice, making difficult and often impossible the serving of that notice upon defendants of the beginning of judicial proceedings which must be had in order that jurisdiction may be obtained to proceed against them; the attendance of unwilling witnesses in another State cannot be obtained; property removed from one State to another in order to escape taxation or liability for seizure in payment of a debt or legal judgment is difficult to reach; when a personal judgment is obtained in one State it cannot be enforced in another State except by instituting a new suit upon it in the State in which its enforcement is sought; and, finally, troublesome extradition proceedings must be gone through with before fugitives from the justice of one State can be apprehended in a State to which they may have fled.

When, as in the United States, each State determines for itself the private laws, civil and criminal, which are to have validity within its limits, the practical disadvantages of the federal system are multiplied. To mention but a few of the disadvantages thus arising: legal instruments, including wills, deeds and all sorts of commercial contracts may be valid in some States while inoperative in others; common law principles receive different interpretations in the different States; statutory laws are alike in no two States; a child may be legitimate in one State and illegitimate in another, and a man may be deemed married or unmarried according to the State he is in,—he may even be regarded as married to one woman in one State and the husband of another woman in another State; a corporation having a legal existence in the jurisdiction of its birth has no right to do business in another State without its consent unless it happens to be engaged in interstate commerce which activity, fortunately, is placed within the regulating control of the General Government. In the United States the attempt is made to overcome some of this diversity of State law by the drafting of model acts dealing with some of the more important subjects, such as negotiable instruments, marriage and divorce, and securing their adoption in identical terms by the several States. This, however, is a very tedious and slow process, and, even when uniformity has been thus secured, it is impossible to maintain it, for there is no constitutional way of guaranteeing that the statutes thus adopted will receive the same interpretation by the courts of the different States. The only real solution of this evil is, therefore, to transfer the control or regulation of these matters to the legislative power of the central government whose laws will have validity throughout the Union. And, in this connection, it may be remarked that, in all the Federal Unions of the world, the tendency has been to extend the scope of the federal power.

To make more nearly complete the enumeration of the disadvantages inherent in the federal system, the fact needs to be pointed out that federalism necessarily leads to innumerable technical controversies between the States themselves, and between them and the Union as to their respective spheres of authority. As Dicey has said, "federalism means legalism," that is, the settlement by juristic interpretations of disputes which, in other States, are disposed of upon a basis of equity, compromise and political expediency. It is certain, therefore, that, irrespective of any other considerations, the federal system is not suited to a people who are not habituated to the rule of law, trained in an appreciation of legal distinctions, and disposed to acquiesce in judicial determinations even with reference to matters of the greatest political importance.

Advantages of the Federal Form. The special advantage of the federal form consists in the fact that it permits the satisfaction in fuller form than is possible under any ordinary system of local government of the desire that may be felt by the citizens of the individual States to preserve their rights of self-government while at the same time yielding obedience, as to certain matters, to a common political authority.

It is, however, to be observed, that, legitimate though this desire may be, it is one which is founded upon sentimental grounds rather than upon considerations of governmental efficiency. And this is shown by the significant fact that the federal system has seldom been adopted save as a means of securing cooperation between bodies-politic which were previously independent of one another, and around which have grown feelings of loyalty and affection which have made their citizens unwilling to purchase national unity and strength if that was to mean a total destruction of their several States as distinct political entities. This has been the case with the United States, Germany, Switzerland, Canada and Australia. With reference to all of these, the federal form was thus adopted, not willingly as the best possible form of political rule, but more or less unwillingly as a means of securing the amount of national strength and unity that circumstances made indispensable, while preserving, as far as possible, the independence of the several States to which their citizens had become historically attached. Thus it has been said of the American Union that it was "wrung from the grinding necessities of a reluctant people"; and, as we know, the feeling that their primary and truest allegiance belonged to their individual States rather than to the National Government persisted in the minds of many long after the national constitution was adopted, and seventy years later was strong enough to lead the citizens of eleven of the States to secede from the Union and attempt, at an enormous sacrifice of human lives and property, to maintain their independence.

CHAPTER XIV

THE UNITED STATES OF AMERICA

ASIDE from the intrinsic importance of the inquiry, an examination of the juristic nature of the American Federal Union is of value to the analytical jurist because of the excellent opportunity it offers him to apply and test the value of the abstract doctrines he has deductively obtained.[1]

The States' Rights Theory. In the controversies which have been waged as to the nature of the American Union, the so-called States Rights school advanced a single and logical theory. According to this theory the Constitution was declared to have been a compact to which the original States, acting as severally sovereign political bodies, were the contracting parties, and that it was not intended by these States, by the agreement into which they entered, to create a political entity that would be legally superior to themselves, and, therefore, in derogation of their own several sovereignties. Starting from this premise, this school deduced from it the essentially confederate nature of the Union and the denial that secession from it by any State at any time would be an illegal act.[2]

---

[1] In this chapter the author has drawn liberally upon chapter II of his volume, *The American Constitutional System,* published in 1904.

[2] This last conclusion was generally stated as an assertion that the States had a legal "right" to secede. This was not an exactly correct way of stating the proposition, for, the Union not being, *ex hypothesi,* a legal one, there could be no legal right in relation to it. All that could properly be said was that secession would not be a legal wrong.

As to the States subsequently admitted to the Union, it was argued that they obtained the same status as that of the original framers of the Constitution: that instrument, it was argued, implies in all its pro-

This juristic interpretation of the nature of the union entered into in 1789 was explicitly put forth as early as 1798 in the "Resolutions" of the legislature of the State of Kentucky which asserted: "That the several States comprising the United States of America are not united on the principles of unlimited submission to their General Government for special purposes. That to this compact each State acceded as a State and as an integral party, its co-States forming, as to itself, the other party." In the Resolutions adopted by the Virginia legislature the same year it was declared: "That this Assembly doth explicitly and peremptorily declare that it views the powers of the Federal Government as resulting from the compact to which the States are parties."

This doctrine was still more explicitly stated in 1803 by the first commentator upon the new Constitution, St. George Tucker.[3] He said: "The Constitution of the United States is an original, written, federal and social compact, freely, voluntarily and solemnly entered in by the several States and ratified by the people thereof respectively. It is a federal compact; several sovereign and independent States may unite themselves together by a perpetual confederacy, without each ceasing to be a perfect State. The Union is, in fact, as well as in theory, an association of States, or a Confederacy."

In another place he said: "The Federal Government, then, appears to be the organ through which the United Republics communicate with foreign nations, and with each other. Their submission to its operation is voluntary; its councils, its engagements, its authority, are theirs, modified and united. Its sovereignty is an emanation from theirs, not a flame in which they have been

visions an equality of rights upon the part of the States. This constitutional principle has, in fact, been declared by the Supreme Court of the United States.

[3] In an appendix to his edition of Blackstone's *Commentaries*.

consumed, nor a vortex in which they are swallowed up. Each is still a perfect State, still sovereign, still independent, and still capable, should the occasion require, of assuming the exercise of its functions, as such, to the most unlimited extent."

Calhoun. States' Rights assertions of a similar tenor continued from time to time to be made but the theory did not receive its final elaboration until John C. Calhoun took up the argument in behalf of the State of South Carolina in the controversy which had arisen between that State and the Federal Government with reference to a protective federal tariff.[4]

Nationalistic Theories. Those who have asserted the legal supremacy of the United States as a single sovereign State have advanced a number of theories, not always concordant with one another, and have put forward varying interpretations of the circumstances attending the historical birth of the Union. The chief of these theories and statements of alleged fact will be discussed.

The Constituent States Sovereign in 1789. By some it was declared that the original thirteen States never were severally sovereign bodies-politic, and that therefore the General Government, created in 1789, could not have been the product of their compacting sovereign wills. This statement of fact, it is now generally agreed, cannot be substantiated. There has, of course, been no difficulty on the part of those who have asserted the theory in showing that the independence of the original States from the dominion of Great Britain was, and could have been, obtained only by cooperative and associated action, but there is practically no evidence to show that a single sovereignty was created or intended to be created. The

---

[4] Calhoun's constitutional doctrines in their final form are to be found in his *Disquisition on Government* and his *Discourse on the Constitution and Government of the United States,* both of which are to be found in vol. I of his Collected works, published in 1853.

most that can be claimed is that common governmental
agencies were established for the convenient and effective
execution of the several but identical aims of the original
thirteen bodies-politic which had been brought into being
when the single legal bond which had previously united
them (common subordination to British dominion) was
removed. Furthermore, all jurists are agreed that, whatever may have been the legal situation prior to 1781, the
Articles of Confederation, which were adopted in 1781
and which remained in force until replaced by the present
constitution of the United States made provision for
a Confederacy and not a sovereign federally organized
State. In other words, that the thirteen States were then
severally sovereign.[5]

Their Sovereignty Not Usurped. Some writers have
attempted to overcome this conclusion as to the sovereignty of the individual States during the years immediately prior to the adoption of the present Constitution,
by asserting that, during those years, the States had
"usurped" the attributes of sovereignty that rightfully
belonged to that single national sovereignty which, they
have declared, came into existence as a result of the
American Revolution. Thus, Pomeroy, in his treatise on
"United States Constitutional Law," declares: "However
much the States may have exercised usurped attributes
of sovereignty during the unhappy Confederation; however much the conception of one people acting as a unit
may have been forgotten or abandoned amid the jealous-
ies and destructive rivalries of the commonwealths claiming substantial independence, the people had now [with
the adoption of the Constitution in 1789] arisen, reas-

[5] For example, such a staunch Nationalist as Chief Justice Marshall
felt constrained to admit this. In *Gibbons v. Ogden* (9 Wh. 1), speaking for the whole Supreme Court, he said, "It has been said that they
[the States] were sovereign, were completely independent, and were
connected with each other by a league. This is true."

serted the original idea, repudiated the assumption of local supremacy, and uttered their organic will in terms which we hope will have a meaning and power to the end of time." Van Holst, speaking of the establishment of the Confederation under the Articles, says that the Continental Congress "exhorted the legislatures, by an act of public usurpation against the legal consequences of historical facts, to transform the Union into a league of States, and the legislatures recklessly responded to this demand." [6]

Little argument is required to show the futility of such an attempt as is indicated in these quotations to escape from the juristic consequences of the facts which their authors were constrained to admit. Whatever may have been the wisdom or propriety of entering into an association under which the States were to be severally sovereign, and whatever effect this may have had upon a previously existing national sovereignty—granting, *arguendo,* that such a sovereignty had come into being— the juristic fact that the States were severally sovereign in 1789 at the time the new Union was entered into would not be disturbed.

Views of Burgess Examined. Most unsatisfactory is the reasoning of Burgess. In his *Political Science and Comparative Constitutional Law,* published in 1891, he asserts that a true National State was created at the time of the establishment of the first Continental Congress in 1774, that is, even before the Colonies had declared their intention to obtain legal separation from Great Britain. "From the first moment of its existence," he declares, "there was something more upon this side of the Atlantic than thirteen local governments. There was a sovereignty, a State, not in idea simply, or upon paper, but

---

[6] *Constitutional Law of the United States,* p. 9. See also vol. I, chap. I, of his *Constitutional History of the United States.*

in fact and organization." "The first paper constitution enacted by the American State," he continues, "was that of November, 1777, called the 'Articles of Confederation.' The one fatal and disastrous defect of this organization was that it provided no continuing organization of the State. It created only a central government, and that, too, of the weakest character. When, therefore, the Continental Congress, the revolutionary organization of the American State and its revolutionary central government gave way, in March of 1781, to the central government created by this constitution, the American State ceased to exist in objective organization. It returned to its subjective condition merely, as 'idea in the consciousness of the people.' From the standpoint of political science, what existed now, as objective institutions, was a central government and thirteen local governments. From the standpoint of public law, on the other hand, what existed as objective institutions, was thirteen States, thirteen local governments, and one Central Government. This was a perfectly unbearable condition of things in theory, and was bound to become so in fact." [7]

The sense of the phrase "unbearable condition of things in theory," is difficult to discover. A given theory explaining a given institution may be valid or invalid, according to whether or not its premises are correctly assumed and its deductions logical. But, as a theory, it is a mere matter of reasoning, and as such, how can it properly be spoken of as unbearable? The facts which lead to the theory may be unbearable, but not the theory which explains them. Probably, however, what Professor Burgess had in mind was that, viewed in the light of what we know generally regarding the requirements of political order and development, the condition of the American States during the period when the Articles of Confedera-

[7] *Op. cit.*, I, p. 101.

tion were in force was bound to lead to unsatisfactory results. Also the distinction which Professor Burgess makes in this connection between the viewpoint of public law and the viewpoint of political science is not clear. Apparently he holds that during these eight years there existed in theory no sovereign power whatever. If this be so, then, logically, he would have to hold that there existed neither laws nor governments, for, without a sovereign to declare and support them, there could have been no laws, and without a State to recognize and endow them with powers, there could have been no governments having a legally valid claim to existence. If Professor Burgess had said that, during this period, there existed in the minds of the Americans a certain amount of national feeling and desire for national unity, and that thus was furnished the psychological and moral basis upon which a national State might be, and was to be, founded, he would have been correct. But the existence of this sentiment which had not yet led to a realization of the desires which it prompted, even when coupled with the admitted necessity for a better form of union than that supplied by the Articles, cannot be said to have indicated the actual absence of sovereignty in both the Central Government and the individual States. For, if this be a valid conclusion, when is one safe in affirming, from the viewpoint of political science, the existence anywhere of sovereignty? In no State in the world are political conditions completely satisfactory, and, this being so, what definite criteria does Professor Burgess furnish for determining when political inefficiency is sufficient to warrant one in denying the existence of sovereignty over a given territory and people? Would he hold that at the present time there is not a State in Russia, or in the Chinese Republic, or in the considerable parts of Central and South America? If he would affirm this, then the ordinarily accepted definition of a State must be radically modified. Yet this relation of political efficiency to sovereignty Professor Burgess certainly holds, for he does not deny sovereignty to the thirteen States during the years from 1781 to 1789 because of the possession of sovereignty by the central power; instead, he declares that they were not States because the thirteen local units were not able to secure certain desirable results.

In truth it may be pointed out that Professor Burgess' assumption that there existed at this time a national State in a "subjective condition," as "idea in the consciousness of the people," may be denied. The allegation of the existence at a given time in the minds of a group of persons, now all dead, of a certain idea or sentiment is, of course, one incapable either of absolute proof or absolute disproof, but certainly there cannot, with confidence, be claimed to have existed in the minds of the Americans of the period a desire for national unity of a sufficient intensity to warrant one in declaring that there then existed, subjectively, a national sovereignty, when, in fact, during those years the several sovereignties of the thirteen States were recognized and obeyed by those very people without a single suggestion upon their part, so far as we now know, that the authorities thus recognized and obeyed were not entitled to their allegiance; and when, upon the contrary, it is known that it was only after strenuous exertions upon the part of their leaders that they were finally led to establish a central sovereignty which, more or less to their surprise, they were later to find resulted in the destruction of the sovereignties of the thirteen commonwealths.

It may be said, however, that Professor Burgess admits that, from the viewpoint of public law, there did then exist, as objective institutions, thirteen States as well as one central and thirteen local governments. But it would seem that he means that this was true only in a formal and not an essential sense,—only on paper and not in fact, for the real basis upon which the thirteen States founded their several sovereignties he declares to have been destroyed by the existence of this predicated national sovereignty, which, however, had not yet obtained for itself an organ through which it might be expressed and executed.

Turning to the question of the source whence the Constitution derived, and was at the time conceived by the American people to have derived, its force as fundamental law, Professor Burgess declares that the adoption of the Constitution was a purely national act. Furthermore, according to his view, the Constitution derived its validity, not, as its own terms assert, from the ratifications of the necessary number of State conventions, but from the authority of the federal constitutional convention; in other words, that the Convention not only drafted the instrument, but breathed into it its legal life. He writes: "I have endeavored to show that the real organization of the United States as the sovereign, the State, in our present system, was in the constitutional convention. This, like the Continental Congress, was a single body, representing the whole people of the United States and passing its resolves by simple majority. The people of the United States were behind this body, and gave it the power to ignore practically the Confederate Congress and the legislatures of the commonwealths, and, while formally submitting its work to ratification by the immediate representatives of the people in the commonwealths, chosen by the people for that special purpose, to really ordain the Constitution." [8]

It is difficult to have patience with such a position, contradicted as it is by the very terms of the instrument

[8] *Op. cit.*, I, p. 143.

itself, by the unambiguous acts of the convention, and unsupported by a single recorded expression of contemporaneous opinion.[9]

Theory That the Adoption of the Constitution Was a National Act. A second group of nationalistic publicists or politicians have said that, even if it be admitted that the States were severally sovereign prior to 1789, and that the Constitution then adopted was a product of their compacting wills, nevertheless, by that act, they created a truly sovereign national State to which they surrendered up their own several sovereignties. The juristic impossibility of such an act we have already seen, and, in fact, after the logic of Calhoun's reasoning had made this plain, the Nationalist School, in general, fell back upon a third theory, which was the one that Webster relied upon in his famous debates in the Senate. This theory was that, though the States existed in 1789 as thirteen severally sovereign bodies politic, and though the Constitution was formally ratified by conventions convened for that purpose in and by each of such States, the act of adopting the Constitution was, in essence, not the act of the several States but of the whole American people united into a single political body by that subjective feeling of, or desire for, political unity which is the ultimate factual foundation of every sovereign State. In other words, this theory asserted that, prior to 1789, a National State existed subjectively in the minds of the people, and was made objectively manifest by the creation of a National Government, and that the existing political machineries of the then thirteen States were used merely as convenient means for realizing this end. This view, it will be seen, admitted that the States were sovereign in 1789 and, therefore, by necessary implication, conceded that, as to them, the establishment of

[9] Professor Burgess does not attempt to adduce historical evidence in its support.

the new National State was an illegal or revolutionary act.

Regarding this theory the point especially to be observed is that it put the controversy upon a plane where absolute demonstration, either for or against, was rendered impossible. The allegation that, though the Constitution which had been drafted by the Convention of 1787 was ratified by conventions assembled in the several States, the peoples of those States believed themselves to be acting, and intended to act, as a single national body, is an assertion that can be proved or disproved only by determining the state of mind of the participants as evidenced in the historical records that have been preserved. Unfortunately, however, the statesmen of those times were neither skilled in juristic distinctions nor gifted with a foresight that would lead them to render perfectly explicit what they conceived to be the essential character of the constitutional transaction upon which they were engaged. Whatever the reasons may have been, the fact remains that neither the records of what was said at the time, nor the language of the Constitution itself, furnishes conclusive evidence as to what were the beliefs and intentions of the statesmen of the time as to the juristic relation the newly established Union was to bear to the individual States.

Though, from the nature of the case, it is impossible to demonstrate the invalidity of this nationalistic interpretation of the nature of the constitutive act of 1789 in the conclusive manner in which an alleged mathematical or other purely logical proposition may be exposed, it may be pointed out that the burden of proof would seem to rest upon those who assert that the adoption of the Constitution, though in form that of thirteen bodies-politic was, in reality, that of a single national unit. There is, however, no record of a declaration, contemporaneously made, that the peoples of the thirteen States felt or believed that they were acting otherwise than as distinct bodies-politic. Upon the contrary, there were repeated contemporaneous statements of the view that the Constitution was a compact between the States. In fact, that instrument itself declares that its ratification by conventions of nine States would be sufficient for its establishment as "between the States so ratifying the same." [10] Furthermore, as has been already pointed out, this compact doctrine was explicitly asserted in 1798 and 1799 by the legislatures of the States of Virginia and Kentucky. It is true that the other States of the Union which replied to these Resolutions did not agree with the deductions which the Resolutions drew with regard to the action that the States of the Union might rightfully take with regard to national measures deemed by them unwarranted by the Constitution, but none of those replying States, with the possible exception of Vermont, expressed any dissent from the premise that the Union resulted from a compact between its constituent members.[11]

A National State Intended. Even if it be accepted that the preponderant historical evidence is in favor of the view that, in 1789, the American people believed that the new Constitution resulted from, and was, in essential character, a compact between the thirteen severally sovereign peoples of the original States, it does not follow that they believed that they were creating only a league or confederacy in which the States were to remain sev-

---

[10] Article VII.

[11] Vermont declared: "the old Confederation, it is true, was formed by the State legislatures, but the present Constitution was derived from a higher authority. The people of the United States formed the federal Constitution, and not the States, or their legislatures." But even this assertion probably meant nothing more than that the new Constitution rested upon the assent of the sovereign peoples of the States and not merely upon the sanctions of the Governments of those States.

erally sovereign, and by which no national sovereignty was to be brought into being. Upon the contrary, there is considerable and perhaps preponderant historical evidence to show that the statesmen of that time intended to establish, and believed that they were establishing, not simply a central governmental organization that was to act as the common agent of the States for the attainment of certain common ends, but a true National State, withdrawal from which by a State would be an illegal act. To be sure, as is now generally agreed by jurists, these two views that the Union was a product of the compacting wills of severally sovereign States, and that a National State was thereby created, were logically inconsistent with each other, but this does not argue against the historical fact that both views were held.

Influence of the Social Compact Theory. It is well known that the political and juristic thought of that time was saturated with, and largely dominated by, doctrines of natural rights, and by the theory that political authority is legitimized by mutual agreements between the governed, or between them and their rulers. If, then, it was generally held that a public will could be created by a union of private wills, and that public rights could be based upon a surrender of rights by individuals originally and severally sovereign, it was but natural and logically consistent that it should also have been believed that a national sovereignty could be created by a mutual agreement between a number of severally sovereign bodies-politic. The reasoning which supported the one view would equally support the other.

There were, this theory admitted, certain practical considerations which made those who favored the adoption of the Constitution provide that it should be ratified by conventions specially assembled in the several States, rather than by the legislatures of those States, but, it was argued, the decisive reason why this mode of ratification was decided upon was because of the general conviction that though the existing governments of the States might be constitutionally competent to create a league or confederation of the respective States which they represented, only the citizen bodies of those States, acting in their original sovereign capacities could, as a matter of inherent political right, create a genuine National State; for, according to then prevailing political thought, this sovereignty, which the peoples of the States were conceived to possess as an original right, could be exercised by them only directly, or through conventions specially assembled for the express purpose.

In the Constitutional Convention of 1789 Madison said that "he considered the difference between a system founded on the legislature only, and one founded on the people, to be the true difference between a league or treaty, and a constitution." Rufus King declared that a proper ratification was the surest way of dispelling "all doubts and disputes concerning the legitimacy of the new Constitution."[12] As Chief Justice Marshall later said in his opinion in the case of *McCulloch v. Maryland*,[13] "To the formation of a league such as was the Confederacy, the State sovereignties were clearly competent. But when, in order to form a more perfect union "it was deemed necessary to change this alliance into an effective government, possessing great and sovereign powers and acting directly on the people, the necessity of referring it to the people, and of deriving its powers directly from them, was felt and acknowledged by all."

Secession. Whether or not the view was held at the

---

[12] The Articles of the Existing Confederation provided that they might be amended only by a unanimous vote of the States. The proposed new Constitution provided that it should go into effect when ratified by nine States, as between the States so ratifying.

[13] 4 Wheaton 316.

time of the adoption of the Constitution that the States, having once entered the Union, would be legally able to escape from it by secession, will always remain a matter for discussion. It is, however, worthy of remark that there is no record that such a right was explicitly declared, although several of the States, in their resolutions of ratification, did assume a moral and revolutionary right upon their part to reassume the powers they were parting with should they be used by the National Government to injure or oppress the governed. Furthermore, there are recorded statements in which a legal right of secession upon the part of the States was expressed and explicitly denied. A conspicuous instance of this was in the reply which Madison made to the inquiry of Hamilton as to the propriety of giving to the States, for a limited time, the right to withdraw from the Union should certain suggested amendments to the Constitution as drafted by the Convention be not adopted. Madison said: "The Constitution requires an adoption *in toto* and for ever. It has been so adopted by the other States. An adoption for a limited time would be as ineffective as an adoption of some of the articles only; in short, any condition whatever must vitiate the ratification." This letter was read to the New York Convention prior to its ratification of the Constitution, and its contents were well known to the peoples of the other States who, so far as is known, did not deny the doctrine it declared.

A Divided Sovereignty Intended. One further fact regarding this theory as to the nature of the constitutive act of 1789 is to be observed. Though the people of that time almost indubitably intended to create, and believed that they were creating, a true National State, it is reasonably certain that they thought that they were establishing a political entity that would not possess supreme or sovereign authority over all possible matters of legal regulation. The doctrines that sovereignty necessarily denotes unlimited legal competence, and that it is a quality or power not susceptible of division, were not then held. Instead, there is abundant evidence that, influenced by the theories of Locke, the American people believed that individuals, when creating a State by their common agreement, might exempt certain interests from its sphere of legitimate legal control, with the result that the regulation of these interests were to be regarded as reserved to the individual citizens. Thus, when the thirteen States were conceived of as creating, by their joint agreement, a National State, it was but natural that they would deem it possible to exempt from national control the exercise of certain legal rights of regulation, and to reserve these powers to the compacting States or to their respective citizen bodies. Thus, in the ninth and tenth Articles of Amendment to the Constitution which, at the time of the adoption it was understood would be added to that instrument, it was provided that the enumeration of certain rights in the Constitution was not to be construed to deny or disparage others retained by the people, and that "the powers not delegated to the United States by the Constitution, nor prohibited by it to the States, are reserved to the States respectively, or to the people." It was this reasoning which, as we shall presently see, made possible the holding of a theory of divided sovereignty which, after the adoption of the Constitution, played such a conspicuous and detrimental part in the constitutional history of the United States.

Space will not permit the presentation of all the historical evidence that might be advanced to show that the doctrines which have been described were the ones generally held by the statesmen of the period under discussion. A few illustrative examples may, however, be given.

Pelatish Webster, in his *Dissertation on the Political Union and Constitution of the United States,* published in 1783, and in which he urged the calling of a convention to frame a new Constitution, declared: "A number of sovereign States uniting into one Commonwealth and appointing a supreme power to manage the affairs of the Union, do necessarily and unavoidably part with and transfer to such supreme power so much of their own sovereignty as is necessary to render the ends of the Union effectual. . . . In like manner, every member of civil society parts with many of his natural rights that he may enjoy the rest in greater security under the protection of society."

James Wilson, in the Constitutional Convention, declared that "Federal Liberty is to the States what civil liberty is to private individuals; and States are not more unwilling to purchase it, by the necessary concession of their political sovereignty, than the savage is to purchase civil liberty by the surrender of the personal sovereignty which he enjoys in a state of nature." [14]

Washington, writing to the Congress of the Confederation, said: "It is . . . impracticable in the federal government of these States, to assure all its rights of independent sovereignty to each, and yet provide for the interest and safety of all. Individuals entering into society must give up a share of liberty to secure the rest." [15]

In the very ratification of the Constitution the compact theory was stated by some of the States. Thus Massachusetts, when giving her assent, spoke of the States as entering into an "explicit and solemn compact with each other," by assenting to and "ratifying the new

[14] *Madison Papers,* vol. II, p. 824.
[15] *Elliot's Debates,* vol. I, p. 305. For reference to other statements showing the application of the social compact theory to the formulation of a federal State, see the scholarly article by Professor McLaughlin in the *American Historical Review* for April, 1900, entitled "Social Compact and Constitutional Construction."

Constitution." To the same effect spoke New Hampshire.

Conclusion. In result, then, it seems reasonably certain that, so far as the intentions and beliefs of those who framed and adopted the Constitution are concerned, the view was held that a true National State was created, but that it was to be sovereign only as to the powers expressly or by necessary implication granted to it. All other powers were deemed to be reserved by the States or by their peoples.[16]

Constitutional Fathers Left Indeterminate the Situs of Sovereignty. It is not reasonable to believe that it wholly escaped the thought of the constitutional fathers that, ultimately, there must be, in every civil society, some single final source of political authority. But it would appear that they deemed this logical necessity sufficiently satisfied by the premise that all right to exercise political authority is drawn from the consent of the governed and remains subject to their will. It further appears that they did not foresee the disputes that were later to arise as to whether this ultimate basis of right for the National State was to be found in the general will of the governed conceived of as a single national body, or as grouped into thirteen or more distinct bodies-politic. Thus both the Union and the State were regarded as agencies for the exercise of sovereignty rather than as possessors of sovereignty. Instead of giving a real answer to the question of the ultimate location of sovereignty in the United States, men of the time merely pushed the problem one step further back and left it still undetermined. Because they did not appreciate this, they did not take the care that they otherwise might have done so to word the Constitution itself, or their acts of

---

[16] As to the general acceptance of this doctrine of divided sovereignty see Merriam, *History of American Political Theories,* chap. VII.

ratification of it, as to place beyond all possible controversy the constitutional status that the member States
were to have in the Union, and the legal action that
they might take in case they should deem that the National State was attempting to exercise powers not constitutionally vested in it.[17]

By adopting the explanation which has been given of
the political doctrines and intentions of those who established the American Union in 1789, we seem to be put
in the peculiar position of holding that the statesmen
of that time intended to obtain, and thought that they
were obtaining, a result which we now know to have been
a logical impossibility, and which, in fact, as events soon
showed, was one which it was in practice impossible to
maintain. If, then, we are asked to decide, from the
strictly juristic point of view, what was the character
of the Union at the time it was entered into, we can only
answer that it is impossible to say. This, however, is not
a surprising confession, for, as we have earlier learned,
the existence of sovereignty is a fact which, by its very
nature, is one that cannot be determined by the historical processes that have brought a political organisation
into being. The existence of sovereignty, in other words,
is a fact that is made manifest by the legal competence
that is effectively asserted by a political organization,
and especially, whether this is claimed as originating in
itself and not by way of delegation from any other po-

[17] Some few writers have asserted that the men of the time perceived
that they had left this matter undetermined, but that, for reasons of
practical expediency, they deliberately left it in that condition. This is
the view, for example, of A. H. Small, in his monograph, *The Beginnings of American Nationality,* published in the Johns Hopkins University *Studies in Historical and Political Science* (vol. VIII); and of
Francis A. Walker in his article *"The Growth of American Nationality,"*
published in 1895. There is no historical evidence to support this opinion, and it seems to the writer almost inconceivable that, if this had
been a policy deliberately pursued, there would not have come down
to us, in the notes or writings of the men of that time, some record
of it.

litical authority. This being so, it may easily happen that, when several governmental organizations are in close association with one another, uncertainty may exist as to which of them is or are sovereign. Indeed, as has already been pointed out in the discussion of the distinction between governments *de facto* and governments *de jure,* the political entities that lie back of these governments may or may not be considered as sovereign political persons, according to the point of view of the persons regarding them. So, similarly, with respect to such a federal form of political organization as that exhibited in the United States after 1789, it was possible that a portion of the people should regard the National Government as nothing more than a common agent of the severally sovereign States, and, therefore, that these States might, without legal wrong upon their part, either refuse obedience to federal commands of which they disapproved, or refuse longer to cooperate with the other States of the Union. At the same time, another portion of the people could regard the National Government as the agent of a true National State, possessing sovereignty in its own right, and, in this respect, superior to the member States of the Union. Still a third portion of the people could regard the National State and the individual States, as having the same juristic status, coordinate in authority, and each possessing supreme legal authority within their respective spheres as marked out by the Constitution. This condition of affairs could, and did, exist in the United States until the necessities of practical political life made it imperative that a choice should be made between these views; that is, until political action had to be taken which could be legally justified only by assuming one of these views rather than the others to be the correct one.

The Manifestation of National Sovereignty. The necessity for taking action that indicated, if it did not conclusively determine, which of these views was to be the one in accordance with which the constitutional life of the American people was to be conducted, arose very soon after the establishment of the Union. The view thus selected and acted upon was that there existed a national authority which was legally superior to that of the individual States. For years, however, lip service continued to be given to the doctrine of a sovereignty divided between the Union and its constituent States, although, whenever an issue arose between the two, the legal supremacy of the former was vindicated.

A liberal construction of national power by the National Congress and by the federal Executive was at once shown by the provision of the Judiciary Act of 1789, which provided for a final determination by the federal Supreme Court of all cases in which state Courts might render decisions adverse to claims by litigants of federal rights, privileges or immunities,[18] and by the establishment, in 1791, of a National Bank.

In 1793 the federal Supreme Court asserted its jurisdiction to give judgment in a suit brought by a citizen of one State of the Union against another State of the Union, despite the claim by the defendant State that such a proceeding was practically a denial of the sovereignty which it claimed to possess.[19]

The next year resistance to a federal tax law upon the part of the people of the State of Pennsylvania was overcome by a display of military force, summoned to the field by the Federal Government.

In 1798-1799 occurred the vehement protest of the States of Virginia and Kentucky against certain acts of

[18] The crucial importance of this assertion of federal right of determination will presently be discussed.
[19] *Chisholm v. Georgia*, 2 Dall. 419,

the federal Congress which they declared unwarranted by the federal Constitution. The resolutions, in which these protests were made, were submitted to the other States for their approval, but the conclusions which they declared, involving as they did a threat of refusal of obedience to the laws in question, were repudiated by the other States.

The year 1803 witnessed the acquisition by the United States of the vast Louisiana Territory and the passage by Congress of the Cumberland Road Act, both of which measures required, in order to sustain their legality, a very liberal interpretation of federal powers as defined by the Constitution.

In 1803 came also the decision of the Federal Supreme Court in the famous case of *Marbury v. Madison* [20] in which, for the first time, an act of Congress was declared void because not warranted by the federal Constitution. The significance of this case, as regards the matter of the location of sovereignty in the American Union, was that it pointed to the federal court as the proper tribunal for the final and authoritative construction of the provisions of the federal Constitution.

A few years later the State of Pennsylvania attempted to prevent the enforcement of a decree of a federal court, and, in fact, by an act of its legislature denied the authority of the federal court in the premises and directed the executive of the State to prevent, by force of arms if necessary, the execution of the federal decree that had been rendered. A writ having been asked of the federal Supreme Court to compel the lower federal court to proceed with the enforcement of its decree, the Supreme Court, in 1809, declared that the act of the Pennsylvania legislature was a legal nullity; that the State possessed no constitutional right to resist the legal process of a

[20] 1 Cr. 137.

federal court; and that a peremptory mandamus should issue.[21] In obedience to this order the lower federal court issued a writ of attachment, the service of which was at first sought to be prevented by state troops which had been called out by the Governor of the State. However, a comitatus of two thousand men having been summoned by the federal marshal, and the President of the United States having been appealed to in vain by the State Governor, the Pennsylvania authorities ceased their resistance which they saw would be futile, and the supremacy of the federal authority was thus fully vindicated.

In 1810, in the case of *Fletcher v. Peck*,[22] the federal Supreme Court again asserted and exercised the right to treat as void an act of a State legislature which the Supreme Court deemed unwarranted by the federal Constitution.

In 1819 was decided the case of *McCulloch v. Maryland* [23] in which it was held that a State of the Union could not, even in the exercise of such an important power as that of taxation, interfere in any way with the efficient operation of any agency of the Federal Government, even though the existence of that agency might not be an essential part of the federal machinery of government, and, indeed might be one which the United States could be conceded the right to maintain only by a very liberal definition of the so-called implied powers provided for in Clause 18 of Section 8 of Article I of the Constitution. [24]

---

[21] *United States v. Peters,* 5 Cr. 115.

[22] 6 Cr. 87.

[23] 4 Wh. 316.

[24] "Congress shall have power to make all laws which shall be necessary and proper for carrying into execution the foregoing specifically enumerated powers and all other powers vested by this Constitution in the Government of the United States, or in any department or office thereof."

This holding of the federal Supreme Court squarely declared the doctrine that the individual States and the United States were not to be regarded as upon a plane of constitutional equality, for, as has been said, it was held that when the powers of the Union came into conflict with those of the States, the exercise of the latter would have to be foregone.

In 1816, in *Martin v. Hunter's Lessee* [25], and again, in 1921, in *Cohens v. Virginia* [26] the federal Supreme court upheld the constitutionality of that provision of the Judiciary Act of 1789, which has been earlier referred to, according to which the Supreme Court was given the right to decide, upon writ of error, whether state Courts have denied to litigants federal rights, privileges or immunities which they had rightfully claimed. This assertion that, as to such claims, the States were not to have the final decision, even in cases arising in their own courts, was a crucial matter. Calhoun saw clearly the decisive character of this assertion of federal right. "The effect of this is," he wrote, "to make the Government of the United States the sole judge, in the last resort, as to the extent of its powers, and to place the States and their separate Governments and institutions at its mercy." "It would be a waste of time," he continued, "to undertake to show that an assumption that would destroy the relation of coordinates between the Government of the United States and those of the several States—which would enable the former, at pleasure, to absorb the reserved powers and to destroy the institutions, social and political, which the Constitution was ordained to establish and protect—is wholly inconsistent with the federal theory of government, though in perfect accordance with the national theory. Indeed, I might

[25] 1 Wh. 304.
[26] 6 Wh. 264.

go further and assert that it is, of itself, all sufficient to convert it into a national, consolidated government."[27]

In the years next following the federal Supreme Court repeatedly exercised the right to hold invalid laws of the States which it deemed not warranted by the federal Constitution.[28]

In 1832 the question as to where rested the real sovereignty in the American Union was put to a still more decisive test. In 1828 Congress had enacted a tariff law which was very objectionable to the State of South Carolina, and which contained features which that State declared were not warranted by the federal Constitution. Its legislature thereupon adopted an "exposition," drawn up by Calhoun, which explicitly asserted the legal right of a State of the Union to refuse obedience, and to direct its citizens to refuse obedience, to national acts which the States should deem unconstitutional. This assertion of the right of "Nullification" led, in 1830, to the famous debate in the United States between Webster and Hayne. In 1832 the people of South Carolina assembled in convention and issued "an ordinance to nullify certain acts of the Congress of the United States purporting to be laws." This ordinance went on to declare that "it shall not be lawful for any of the constituted authorities, whether of this State or of the United States, to enforce the payment of duties imposed by the said acts within the limits of this State"; and concluded with the statement that any attempt upon the part of the National Government to enforce the law within the limits of South Carolina will be "inconsistent with the longer continuance of South Carolina in the Union; and that the peo-

[27] *Discourse on the Constitution and Government of the United States.* Works of Calhoun, vol. I, p. 338.
[28] See for example *Osborn v. Bank of the United States* (9 Wh. 738), *Weston v. Charleston* (2 Pet. 449), *Gibbons v. Ogden* (9 Wh. 1); *Green v. Biddle* (8 Wh. 1); and *Craig v. Missouri* (4 Pet. 410).

ple of South Carolina will henceforth hold themselves absolved from all further obligation to maintain or preserve their political connection with the peoples of the other States, and will forthwith proceed to organize a separate government, and do all other acts and things which sovereign and independent States may of right do."

In pursuance of this ordinance the legislature of the State enacted laws which, as was said at the time, legislated the Federal Government out of the State.

South Carolina sent the proclamation of her ordinance to the other States. Without exception those which answered it condemned the doctrines it enunciated. This was true no less of the Southern than of the Northern States. Furthermore, Andrew Jackson, then President of the United States, in unmistakable terms declared his intention to enforce the federal law, whatever might be the attempted resistance of South Carolina. In result, that State was obliged to abandon any attempt to make good the threats it had made.

Reviewing the events that have been summarized, it would seem that proof had been piled upon proof that the claim that the States of the Union had a legal status coordinate in authority with that of the United States was not consistent with the actual facts of the case. History brought it about, however, that those who were still unwilling to admit the juristic conclusion that logically followed from these successive events, should subject the controversy to the final physical test of war. Claiming that, whatever constitutional concessions the States might have made in the past, they still had reserved to themselves a legal right of secession from the Union, eleven of the States, constituting a compact body in the South, and exercising what they claimed to be a right belonging to them as severally sovereign bodies-politic, seceded from the Union in 1861, and for four years by force of arms resisted the efforts of the National Government to enforce its law and authority within their limits.

The result of this Civil War is well known. Federal authority was finally re-established, and, since that time, there has been no serious claim from any quarter that the United States is not a sovereign State and that the individual States of the Union have any other political status than that of non-sovereign bodies-politic within the Union and subject to its superior authority.

Tests of Sovereignty. If it be asked by what tests at the present time it can be determined that sovereignty inheres in the United States as a single national State, and not in the individual States of the Union, the following facts of juristic significance may be pointed to.

Under the amending power, by a vote of three-fourths of the States acting through their legislatures or specially convened conventions, according as the one or the other method is proposed by Congress, it is possible to take away from any given State, against its will, and by a perfectly legal process, any or all of the powers which it now possesses, and from this result the objecting State has no legal means of escape by secession from the Union or otherwise. Also, there is no legal process by means of which a State, solely through its own legal will and legal competence, can draw to itself any of the powers not now constitutionally possessed by it. Furthermore, no State can in any way, or upon any pretext, offer legal resistance to the operation within its limits of a national law.

As regards the rights of a federal government, such as the United States is now conceded to be, to enforce its laws within the States and against any opposition that may be raised against them, we may quote the following striking language of the federal Supreme Court, in the so-called Debs Case: [29] "The entire strength of the Nation may be used to enforce in any part of the land the full and free exercise of all national powers and the security of all rights intrusted by the Constitution to its care. . . . If the emergency arises, the army of the Nation and all its militia are at the service of the Nation to compel obedience to its laws."

It is therefore plain that the constituent States have no sovereignty of their own, and that such autonomous powers as they now possess are had and exercised by the express will or by the constitutional forbearance of the national sovereignty. The Supreme Court of the United States has held that, even when selecting members for the national legislature, or electing the President, or ratifying proposed amendments to the federal Constitution, the States act, *ad hoc,* as agents of the National Government.

Putting the matter in affirmative terms, the sovereignty of the United States is fixed by the fact that it determines, through its own tribunals, the extent of its constitutional powers, and has the legal power to enforce its will without regard to the will or judgment of the States as to the constitutionality or wisdom of its acts. And, through the process provided for amending the federal Constitution, it has the legal right to vest in its own Government any power now entrusted for exercise to the State governments, or reserved to the people. In connection with the Nineteenth Amendment to the federal Constitution, ratified in 1920, the argument was put forward that there are inherent limitations upon the amending power—that there are some matters which can not be legally justified even by a constitutional amend-

[29] *In re Debs,* 158 U. S. Reports, 564.

menⱱ, but this view has been emphatically rejected by the federal Supreme Court.[30]

The foregoing facts are sufficient to fix the juristic character of the American Union and to determine the subordinate status of its individual State members. Of further significance, however, is the fact that the United States has not only the exclusive and unlimited power to determine the territorial extent of its authority, but also to declare what persons shall be deemed its own citizens, as well as the citizens of the States. The Fourteenth Amendment made this no longer debatable by the provision that "all persons born or naturalized in the United States, and subject to the jurisdiction thereof, are citizens of the United States and of the States wherein they reside." [31]

That the right of permitting the naturalization or expatriation of citizens is an exclusive federal right has been judicially determined, as has also been the doctrine that a State has not the constitutional right (except perhaps as a police measure with reference, for example, to persons with infectious diseases) to prevent persons obtaining residence within its limits. Thus, in result, the States are not able to determine who shall be their own citizens; whereas the United States, through its own constitution and statutes, has complete discretion in the matter.

This is the situation at the present time. The sov-

[30] Article V of the federal Constitution, which relates to amendments, provides that "no State, without its consent, shall be deprived of its equal suffrage in the Senate." It has been suggested that even this limitation upon the amending power can be overcome by first amending Article V so as to delete this limitation.

[31] In the *United States v. Wong Kim Ark*, 169 U. S. 649, the Supreme Court said that the real object of the words "and subject to the jurisdiction thereof" was to exclude by the fewest and fittest words possible, members of Indian tribes, children born of alien enemies in hostile occupation, and children born of diplomatic representatives of foreign powers—persons generally recognized by American as well as by foreign law as exceptions to the fundamental *jus soli* rule of citizenship.

ereignty of the United States and the non-sovereign status of the individual States is no longer contested. Thus, even though it be admitted, as it must be admitted, that there are grounds for holding that, originally, the United States was a confederacy of sovereign States united only by a treaty or compact, it nevertheless is a fair juristic reference from the events that occurred soon after the Union was established, that the confederate conception of the Union was no longer in consonance with the facts, and that the opposing nationalistic conception had been impliedly accepted by the American people when they acquiesced in the powers which the National Government had asserted and exercised. Certainly this establishment of a national sovereignty had been made sufficiently manifest before 1861 by the events that have been referred to. It would seem, therefore, that the supporters of the National sovereignty had good reason for saying that the leaders of the secessionist movement in 1861 were fairly estopped, at that late time, from claiming, on behalf of the States, a juristic status of sovereign bodies-politic.

This much, however may be said for the States' rights position. If it be admitted that the Union was originally a league or confederacy of several sovereign States, the establishment of the national sovereignty, however peaceably brought about or clothed in apparent legal form, was, as to those States, an essentially illegal or revolutionary act. As regards the victory of the National Government in the Civil War of 1861-1865, it can be said that its result determined the fact that henceforth there was to be no dispute as to the sovereignty of the United States; but it is not correct to say that that result operated to render legally valid the exercise by the National Government of powers that otherwise might have been regarded as illegal. No physical force of coercion, how-

ever overwhelmingly applied, can possibly transmute a
legal wrong into a legal right. The quality of legality is
so distinct, *in genere,* from that of physical might, that
the two can have no effect upon each other. All that
physical force advocated by those who claim a legal
right to exercise it, is able to do is to overcome the physical force of those who deny this legal right, and possibly,
to convince them of the practical futility or inexpediency
of further attempting to urge the correctness of their
own view of what are their legal rights. The real result,
then, of the American Civil War was to produce this conviction in the minds of those who had previously believed
that the States of the Union were sovereign bodies-politic
and could, without legal wrong upon their part, withdraw at will from the Union.

CHAPTER XV

NON-SOVEREIGN BODIES-POLITIC

THE discussion of the juristic nature of the federally organized State has raised the important question whether it is proper to designate its members as "States." And the same query may be raised with reference to those bodies-politic such as the Dominion of Canada, the Commonwealth of Australia, New Zealand, or the South African Union, which, though falling within the general category of dependencies or colonies, nevertheless possess very wide autonomous powers.

In Switzerland the federated units are known as Cantons; in Canada and the Argentine they are known as Provinces, but in Mexico, Australia, Germany and the United States they are termed States. Upon the other hand it is universally conceded that the administrative subdivisions of a sovereign State are not entitled to be designated as States, notwithstanding the fact that they may exercise a wide measure of self-governing, discretionary powers. In order, then, to concede the title of States to the units of a Federal Union and deny it to all other subdivisions of a sovereign State, it becomes necessary, if the term is to be used with scientific strictness, to find some juristic attribute or attributes which distinguish the constituent members of a *Bundesstaat* from other non-sovereign bodies. If such an attribute or attributes can be found it will be possible to draft a definition of the term State from which the concept of sovereignty is excluded, with the result that it will be proper to speak of non-sovereign as well as of sovereign States. If, however, it be found that, having once jettisoned the attribute of sovereignty, it is impossible to distinguish juristically such bodies as the members of a Federal State, or autonomous colonies, from other and less important non-sovereign units, then we shall be forced, in order to preserve any sort of exact meaning to the term "State," to deny its applicability to any but sovereign bodies-politic.

Brie and Rosin. Those writers who have sought to designate as "States" certain non-sovereign bodies have not agreed upon the criteria which are to be regarded as distinguishing those bodies from other politically inferior political units to which they do not concede this title. Thus, to give but a few examples, Brie [1] and Rosin [2] find the essential characteristic of a State, whether sovereign or non-sovereign, in its aim or end. Brie describes this state aim as a national as distinguished from a local one; while Rosin speaks of it as universal as distinguished from particular. Rosin writes: "The Commune (*Gemeinde*) is the organism of the local community; the State is the organization of the Nation. . . . Whereas the satisfaction of common interests resulting from the fact of a union of individuals in the same place and in adjoining places is the aim of the commune, the State has for its aim the task of realizing the genuine national interests of a people united in its quality as a national collectivity."

The unsatisfactory character of attempts such as these to find the essential mark of statehood in the aim or purpose of the group is at once evident. Not only is a juristic distinction thus based upon a quality that is without juristic connotation, but the attribute itself is one that may not be certainly or precisely determined. What are the marks which indubitably differentiate national from local aims? Are such political units as the Australian

[1] *Theorie der Staatenverbindungen.*
[2] *Souveränität, Staat, Gemeinde, Selbstverwaltung.*

Commonwealth or the Dominion of Canada without national aspirations? Can these great political bodies be said to be without national aims when such diminutive States as San Marino or Monaco are said to possess them? Rosin himself admits that, in a State composed of States, there are national interests superimposed upon national interests. If so, how distinguish the one from the other?

Brie criticizes Rosin's doctrine of national aims as too vague, but his substitution of universality of purpose is hardly an improvement. He writes: "Die allseitige ergänzende Natur des Staatszweckes ist das für den Begriff des Staats principale Moment, wodurch sich ins besondere auch seine Eigenart gegenüber allen anderen menschlichem Gemeinwesen bestimmt." And, as he goes on to assert, to this universality of aim is necessarily added a corresponding legal competency. But this, it would seem, if logically pursued, again brings in the attribute of sovereignty as the distinguishing criterion of statehood—the very position he has been seeking to avoid.

Laband. The leading commentator upon the German imperial constitution, Laband, argues that the members of the Empire might properly be termed States because they possessed rights of their own. "Own rights" he defines as those which originate in the subjects who exercise them; and, that the members of the Empire were thus endowed, he deduces from the fact that they existed as sovereign and independent States before the Union was formed.

The conclusions which we have earlier reached in this treatise are sufficient to show the invalidity of Laband's reasoning. Aside from the fact, which logic has forced upon us, that, in a Federal State, the constituent members must be juristically regarded as deriving their existence as well as their powers from the sovereignty of the

Federal State, Leband's position is unsatisfactory because the attribute which he predicates of the constituent members of the Empire is one that, in many cases, may also be ascribed to certain portions of unitary States—portions which originally existed as independent and sovereign bodies-politic. Furthermore, Laband's doctrine would make it necessary to hold that, whereas, in certain Federal States, the member units may be termed States, in other Federal States they may not. Thus, for example, it could not be maintained that the "States" of the Mexican Union enjoy rights of their own, since they never were independent and sovereign political entities. And, what is still more unsatisfactory from the standpoint of juristic analysis, one would be obliged to assert that, in the American Union, the original thirteen States together with Texas, alone, among the forty-eight members of the American Union, are entitled to the term States, since they alone ever enjoyed that original sovereignty and independence from which the possession of "own rights" may be deduced. In other words, the theory of Laband leads to the result, not simply that juristic analysis of *Bundesstaaten* leads, in different instances, to different conclusions, but that, as applied to unions such as the United States, certain of the members have a juristic status different from that of the others, although constitutional doctrine and uniform practice recognize that they all have the same legal status.

The objections, as above outlined, to Laband's definition of the non-sovereign State, as originally advanced by him, led him, in later editions of his work, to modify them somewhat,—not, however, by way of wholly abandoning his criterion of "own right," but by rendering it somewhat less important. Thus, in these later editions, he says that the essential characteristic of the State is its own right of domination. Domination thus becomes the essential characteristic of statehood, and this attribute he defines as an original legal superiority of the dominating political person over the dominated persons, coupled with the power to coerce those to whom its commands are addressed. The fact, says Laband, that, within this sphere of dominance, the non-sovereign State is controlled by certain prescriptions or limitations imposed upon it by a superior State is not destructive of the statehood of the inferior State. It still remains a State and generically distinct from a mere administrative subdivision of a State by reason of the fact that it has, by its own right, the faculty or power, which the administrative subdivision does not have, to constrain the persons to whom its commands are addressed, that is, to exercise this power without appealing to any other political authority for its permission or sanction. [3]

[3] Laband, in his *Deutsches Reichstaatsrecht*, published in 1907, p. 17, says: "Es ist die Frage zu beantworten, welches Kriterium für den Staat übrig bleibe, wenn man die Souveränität für nicht wesentlich erklärt, und durch welches durchgreifende Merkmal sich der 'nicht souveräne Staat' von Provinzen, Kreisen, Gemeinden und dergl. unterscheide. Dieses Merkmal ist darin zu finden, dass die Staaten eine öffentlich rechtliche Herrschaft kraft eigenen Rechts haben, nicht durch Uebertragung, nicht als Organe, deren sich eine höhere Macht zur Erfüllung *ihrer* Aufgaben, zur Durchführung *ihres* Willens bedient, sondern als selbständige Rechtssubjekte mit eigener Rechtssphäre, mit eigener Willens—und Handlungsfreiheit. Das Wesen der Herrschaft aber besteht in dem Recht freier Personen (und Vereinigungen von solchen) Handlungen, Unterlassungen und Leistungen zu befehlen und sie zur Befolgung derselben zu zwingen. Das Privatrecht kennt freien Personen gegenüber nur Forderungen, welche kein Zwangsrecht gegen den Schuldner enthalten und die nicht die Rechtsmacht in sich schliessen, ihm etwas zu befehlen; in obligatorischen Verhältnissen sind Gläubiger und Schuldner einander gleich geordnet; der Gläubiger hat keine Macht über den Schuldner. Das Wesen des Hoheitsrechts dagegen besteht in der rechtlichen Macht der Obrigkeit über den Unterthan, in der rechtlich anerkannten Gewalt über ihn, kraft deren derselbe gezwungen wird, dem an ihm ergangenen Befehl zu gehorchen. Herrschaft in diesem Sinne ist im heutigen Recht das spezifische Vorrecht des Staates, das er mit Niemandem teilt. Sein Wille allein hat die Kraft, den Willen der Individuen zu brechen, über Vermögen, natürliche Freiheit und Leben derselben zu verfügen. Weder die Gemeinde noch irgend ein anderer gemeindeähnlicher Verband hat dieses Recht als ein eigenes, auf sich selbst beruhendes und nach freiem Willen auszuübendes. Eine Gemeinde mag befugt sein, Verordnungen zu erlassen; Erzwingbarkeit erhalten dieselben immer nur durch das

Laband's attempted distinction between non-sovereign bodies and mere administrative subdivisions of sovereign States so closely resembles that of Jellinek, we may postpone our criticism of it until we have stated Jellinek's position and argument.

Jellinek saw the error of Laband's original doctrine that purely historical facts can play a decisive part in a matter of juristic status. He agreed, however, with Laband that there might be non-sovereign States, that the constituent members of a *Bundesstaat* fall within this class, and that the attribute which distinguishes non-sovereign States from other non-sovereign political bodies is the possession by them of "own rights."

In order to detect this distinguishing quality in non-sovereign bodies, Jellinek in his earlier work says: "It is not essential to the conception of one's own right that it should have arisen in the person of its possessor; furthermore it is not necessary that it should be such as cannot be again withdrawn against its own will. . . . The essence of one's own right consists neither in its originality nor in the impossibility of its being withdrawn. Its specific characteristic is solely and entirely that the

Gebot des Staates. Gemeinden können auf einem grossen Gebiet des politischen Lebens ein eigenes Recht zur Verwaltung, zur autonomischen Festsetzung von Statuten, ja selbst zur Rechtsprechung haben; sobald es aber darauf ankommt, ihren Befehlen Gehorsam zu verschaffen, muss entweder die zuständige Behörde des Staates darum angegangen werden oder dem Kommunalverbande muss vom Staate die Handhabung seiner Herrschermacht für gewisse Anwendungsfälle übertragen sein. Wenn die Gemeinde befugt ist, mit Rechtskraft (Erzwingbarkeit) zu befehlen und ihre Befehle nötigenfalls mit Gewalt durchzuführen, so handelt sie im Namen und Auftrag des Staates, in Stellvertretung oder Kraft Delegation desselben; es ist nicht ihre Macht, sondern die des Staates, welche sie in Bewegung setzt; es ist nicht ihr eigenes Recht, sondern ein fremdes, welches sie geltend macht. Die Gemeinde hat keine Untertanen; sie ist bei Ausübung ihrer Rechte ebenso machtlos, wie der Gläubiger seinem Schuldner gegenüber; Vollstreckungsgewalt findet sie einzig und allein beim Staate."

For a statement and criticism of other views upon this distinction see Laband's larger work, *Das Staatsrecht des Deutschen Reiches*, 4 Aufl. vol. I, p. 60 *et seq.*

one to whom it belongs is legally unanswerable for its exercise." [4]

In his later work, *Das Recht des Modernen Staates,* in which he says that he has definitely summed up his political philosophy, Jellinek returned to this subject, but did not substantially modify the views previously expressed, although he developed them somewhat.

The essential characteristic of a State, Jellinek says, is the possession of a power to command which is not derived from any other source—the authority to command by reason of its own power, and, as a consequence, according to its own right. The content of this power is not a matter of significance. Whenever there is a community which is able to exercise its dominion according to an order which is valid by reason of an original authority and also by original means of restraint, that community is a State.

The existence of this decisive political power, he says, is manifested by the existence of an independent organ, charged with the exercise of this power. An organization of its own and the enjoyment of this power which is tied to it is, then, the prime characteristic which distinguishes a State from a group which is not a State. Whenever, therefore, a political body receives its constitution from another power in such a manner that this constitution rests not upon the will of that political body but upon a law emanating from a foreign power, we have an example, not of a State, but of a constituent part of a State. Consequently, the members of the German Empire were States, since they were able to organize themselves according to constitutions which were based exclusively upon their own wills, and these constitutions were their own laws and not those of the Empire. Likewise, the constitutions of the Cantons of Switzerland and of the

[4] *Die Lehre von den Staatenverbindungen,* pp. 41-42.

several States of the American Union are State Constitutions properly so-called since they rest exclusively upon the laws of the States and not upon the will of the Federal State which is superimposed upon them.

The fact that it is required by the American and Swiss Federal Constitutions that the member States shall maintain governments republican in form, Jellinek declares, is not inconsistent with the assertion that the constitutions of the member States rest exclusively upon their own will. The same is true when wholly foreign States have joined in the establishment of a constitution for another community. This community, he asserts, remains a State if its constitution is considered, *pro futuro,* as exclusively an original act of its will, so that it may be able to alter it without obtaining any external consent.

Turning now to political units which may not properly be termed States, Jellinek holds that these groups receive their organization from a superior legal source. Thus, Alsace-Lorraine, while it remained a part of the German Empire, was not a State, nor are the English dominions of Canada and Australia, notwithstanding the very considerable autonomous powers with which they are endowed. For their constitutions are acts of the parliament of Great Britain. So, also, the kingdom and countries of the former Austrian Empire possessed constitutions which had been proclaimed as fundamental laws of the State, but these laws had been given by the Emperor and not by the chief authority of each of the States themselves, and, for their amendment, there was required the imperial consent. These communities, therefore, lacked the character of statehood.

Further elaborating his position, Jellinek says that, in order to attribute statehood to a political group, it is essential that its highest organ of government—that which assures its perpetuity—should be independent.

This organ may not coincide with the organ of another State. Thus, before 1918, Croatia, by its relation to Hungary, and Finland, by its relation to Russia, were not States, since the King of Croatia was juridically the King of Hungary, and the Prince of Finland was juridically the Tsar of Russia.

The first quality of the independent authority which characterizes the State, says Jellinek, is the right to create for itself all the organs materially essential to the laws which the State provides. It is therefore necessary that a veritable State should be so organized that it may be placed within a definite class as regards its governmental organization. Thus Würtemburg and Baden were monarchies; Hamburg, Berne and Pennsylvania were republics. Furthermore, non-sovereign bodies, in order to be entitled to be termed States, must be so completely organized governmentally that they will be able to stand forth as sovereign and completely organized States immediately upon the disappearance of the sovereign authority to which they have been subjected. This is not true of autonomous bodies which have not the character of States. These autonomous bodies, moreover, though able to issue orders with penalties prescribed for their violation, have the authority to enforce them only by reason of power delegated to them by the superior political State, and it is this lack of power to command in an absolute manner, and with a legally irresistible right of coercion that denotes their non-statehood. Thus, as distinguished from Laband, Jellinek emphasizes not so much the idea that the legal powers of the non-state entities are granted or delegated to them by political entities which are entitled to be termed States, as that these non-state bodies have no original coercive authority to execute such orders as they are conceded to have the legal right to issue. In short, the non-sovereign body which is entitled to be termed a State, as distinguished from the non-sovereign body, which is not so entitled, has, according to Jellinek, an original legal right of its own to provide for itself a complete governmental organization, with executive legislative and judicial powers. It thus has, of its own right, authority to enforce, as well as to create, legal obligations and rights. It is distinguished from the sovereign State only by reason of the fact that its sphere of legal authority is a limited one—limited by the authority of the sovereign State to which it is subordinated.

In order that we may have clearly before us Jellinek's doctrine, as stated in his last published work, the following is quoted from his *Allgemeine Staatslehre:*

"Wo ein Gemeinwesen aus ursprünglicher Macht und mit ursprünglichen Zwangsmitteln Herrschaft über seine Glieder und sein Gebiet gemäss einer ihm eigenthümlichen Ordnung zu üben vermag, da ist ein Staat vorhanden. Das Dasein einer Staatsgewalt äussert sich zunächst in dem Dasein selbständiger, sie versehender Organe. Eigene Organisation und die mit ihr verknüpfte Machtverteilung ist das erste Merkmal, um den Staat vom nichtstaatlichen Verbande zu trennen. Wo immer daher ein Gemeinwesen seine Verfassung von einer andern Macht erhält, so dass sie nicht auf seinem Willen, sondern dauernd auf dem Gesetze dieser Macht ruht, da ist kein Staat, sondern nur das Glied eines Staates vorhanden. Daher sind die deutschen Gliedstaaten Staaten, denn sie können sich durch ihre eigenen, ausschliesslich auf ihrem Willen beruhenden Verfassungen organisieren, die ihre Gesetze, nicht die des Reiches sind. Ebenso sind die Verfassungen der schweizerischen Kantone, der Einzelstaaten der amerikanischen Union Staatsverfassungen, denn sie beruhen ausschliesslich auf ihren eigenen Gesetzen, nicht auf dem Willen des übergeordneten Bundesstaates. Es können Schranken in den bundesstaatlichen Gesetzen für die Verfassungen der Gliedstaaten gezogen sein (z. B. Verbot einer anderen als der republikanischen Staatsform, wie in der Schweiz und in den Vereinigten Staaten): sie bleiben trotzdem ausschliesslich Gesetze der Gliedstaaten. Selbst wenn ein Gemeinwesen unter der Mitwirkung fremder Staaten seine Verfassung empfangen hat, so ist es Staat, wenn diese Verfassung pro futuro ausschliesslich als sein originäler Willensakt anzusehen ist, so dass sie von ihm ohne weitere Ermächtigung abgeändert werden kann.

"Wo hingegen ein Herrschergewalt übender Verband seine Organisation von einem über ihm stehenden Staate als dessen Gesetz empfangen hat, da ist kein Staat vorhanden. So vor allem bei den Kommunen, deren Verfassung stets auf Staatsgesetzen ruht, die höchstens in untergeordneten Dingen eine begrenzte Organisationsbefugniss zugestehen. . . . Daher ist Elsass-Lothringen kein Staat, . . . daher sind die mit weitestgehender Autonomie ausgerüsteten englischen Charterkolonien, wie Kanada, die südafrikanische Union, Australien, keine Staaten, denn ihre Verfassungen sind in englischen Gesetze enthalten, in Parlamentsakten Grossbritanniens, die rechtlich jederzeit vom Parlament wieder geändert werden können, ohne dass der betreffenden Kolonie ein gesetzliches Mitwirkungsrecht an solcher Verfassungsanderung zuständе." [5]

As regards the status of the constituent units of a Bundesstaat, Jellinek, in another place, declares that they are to be viewed as States with respect to certain of their functions, and as mere organs of the superior sovereign State as to other of their activities. He says: "Die Glieder des Bundesstaates sind als solche, soweit sie an der Herrschaft des Bundes teilnehmen, nicht Staaten,

[5] *Allgemeine Staatslehre* (ed. 1922), p. 490. See also Jellinek's short treatise, published in 1896, entitled *Ueber Staatsfragmente,* pp. 11-17.

sondern Organe des Bundesstaates und, soweit sie unterworfen sind und überhaupt noch einen selbständigen Willen aüssern können, nichtstatliche Verbände, und nur die physische Identität dieses Verbandes mit dem Gliedstaate führt zu der ungenauen Vorstellung, dass der Gliedstaat als solcher dem Bundesstaate unterworfen sei. Daher hat der Gliedstaat nur nach zwei Richtungen hin staatlichen Charakter: als Gemeinwesen, das von der Bundesstaatsgewalt frei ist und als Träger von öffentlich-rechtlichen Ansprüchen an den Bundesstaat gemäss dessen Verfassung." [6]

Criticism of Laband and Jellinek. It will have been seen that both Laband and Jellinek seek to invest the non-sovereign State with at least a certain sphere of legal authority that may truly be spoken of as, legally if not historically, underived from and uncontrolled by the superior State under whose sovereignty it exists, and that it is the possession of this authority that distinguishes it from the mere administrative agency of a sovereign State. It would seem, however, that the attempt to draw this distinction is an unsuccessful one. Unless one is willing to concede that sovereignty is divisible, which Laband and Jellinek are unwilling to do, and which, if admitted, would mean that the notion of sovereignty must be given a juristic meaning quite different from that which is attached to it by practically all publicists, it is futile to speak of a political entity as possessing original powers or rights of its own when these powers may be exercised only within a limited sphere of political control, and when the extent of this sphere is legally determined, and may be further curtailed or even wholly destroyed, by an exercise of the legal will of another political body. If this is the case, then it is not correct to say that certain subordinate or non-sovereign political bodies can ex-

[6] *Allgemeine Staatslehre* (1922), p. 773.

press independent wills of their own as to any matter whatsoever. Therefore, the threefold division of political bodies into those which can exercise an independent legal will as to all matters (sovereign States); those which can exercise it as to some matters (non-sovereign States); and those which can exercise it as to no matters (non-States) is logically an impossible one. If the body that is termed a non-sovereign State retains such powers as it has only by the legal sufferance of the sovereign State whose sovereignty it recognizes, its legal powers are as much dependent upon the will of the sovereign State as are those of the lowest administrative agency of that State. To both of them may be granted by that State a discretion as to how or when the rights vested in them are to be exercised, but this does not alter the fact that the legal will that is exercised is, when traced back to its ultimate source, that of the sovereign State.

If it be declared that the activities of the non-sovereign State, when acting within its constitutionally determined sphere of authority, are not subject to the control of the sovereign State, whereas the activities of the mere administrative agency or local governing body are or may be constantly controlled, and that this constitutes an essential distinction, the answer is that, in fact, the right of the sovereign State to control exists in both cases, and the only difference is as to the manner in which, under the law as it exists at any given time, it may be legally exercised. So long as an administrative agency keeps within the field of discretionary action granted by law, its acts are legal, whatever they may be. But, as a rule, this discretionary authority may be readily abridged or destroyed by an ordinary statute or order of an administrative superior. In the case of the so-called non-sovereign State, existing law may provide that its legal competency may be changed only by the more difficult process of amending existing constitutional provisions, but that this is a difference which does not create an essential juristic distinction, our earlier discussion of the nature of constitutional law as compared with ordinary law, must have made plain. In both cases the legal competency of the inferior is determined by the will of the superior body, although, in the one case, a greater degree of formality surrounds the alteration of such competence than it does in the other.

If it were true that, in the operation of a sovereign upon a non-sovereign entity, the sovereign entity had only the power of preventing the non-sovereign entity from exceeding its constitutional powers, there might be warrant for claiming an essential distinction between such a non-sovereign political being and a mere administrative district. But, as a matter of fact, the sovereign State always and necessarily possesses, in addition to this negative and prohibitory power, the ability to alter at will the legal competence of the subordinate body, even to the extent of utterly destroying it. As Jellinek himself says in another work, "The sovereignty of the superior State as contrasted with the non-sovereign State, appears in three ways: first, in a negative control by it of the activities of the latter; second, in the power of the sovereign State to use the non-Sovereign State for its own ends, be it as the direct object of its will or as a relatively independent member of a federal union; thirdly, the sovereign State has at all times the right to draw to itself in a constitutional manner the highest rights belonging to the non-sovereign State. The existence of the non-sovereign State as a State is therefore itself determined by the sovereign will of the supreme State, to an extent to which no formal *a priori* legal limit can be set."[7]

Woodrow Wilson, who accepts Jellinek's reasoning

[7] *Gesetz und Verordnung,* p. 203.

upon this point, says, "In the federal State, self-determination with respect to their law as a whole, has been lost by the member States. They cannot extend, they cannot even determine, their own powers conclusively without appeal to the federal authorities." But, he continues, "They are still States because their powers are original and inherent, not derivative; because their political rights are not also legal duties; and because they can apply to their commands the full imperative sanctions of law. But their sphere is limited by the presiding and sovereign powers of a State superordinated to them, the extent of whose authority is determined under constitutional forms and guarantees, by itself."[8]

"Their powers are original," Wilson says. But, are they? If the States have their status as political bodies only in the Union, as Lincoln declared, in what sense can their powers be said to be original, except in an historical sense, as related to the time when they were independent States, if ever they were? Juristically viewed, the legal competence of the members of the composite State is derived from the federal Constitution.[9] Secondly, Wilson says, they are States, "because their political rights are not also legal duties." If the writer correctly understands this, it is meant that, to a very great extent, the exercise or non-exercise, or the manner of exercise of their powers is left to their own discretion. But is not this true as well, to a considerable extent at least, of such bodies as cities and counties, which all would concede to be merely administrative units? Finally, Wilson says, these non-sovereign bodies are States because, "they can apply the full imperative sanctions of law." In other words, that all rules of conduct

[8] *An Old Master and Other Essays,* chapter on "Political Sovereignty," pp. 93-94.

[9] In what sense, it may be asked, can those present members of our Union, which have been admitted since 1789, be said to have possessed "original" powers?

promulgated by them within their legal competence are valid as laws. But this is no less true of all administrative bodies.

It thus appears that, from a juristic standpoint, no fundamental distinction can be drawn between non-sovereign members of a federal State and their administrative units. What difference there is, aside from historical associations, is one of degree, that is, as to the scope and powers and the ease with which the superordinated power may alter this competence. As a matter of fact, in several of the so-called States of the American Union, various of their urban districts are protected in their administrative competences by provisions in the constitutions of their respective Commonwealths. This is true in more than twenty States.[10] But we do not, for this reason, consider such protected districts any less purely administrative units, or to be distinguished in specific character from other less favored towns and counties.

A question which remains to be answered is: What effect should the conclusion that has been reached have upon political terminology? In other words, does it become necessary rigorously to confine the use of the word "State" to those bodies-politic or political persons that may properly be said to possess sovereignty? If the term State is to be regarded as a technical one, scientific accuracy would seem to demand that this be done, for, as has been seen, if it be employed in a sense that is in anywise broader, it becomes impossible to refuse to apply it to political units or organizations which political scientists in the past have never so dignified. Upon the other hand, if only those political entities are to be des-

---

[10] Commenting upon this fact, Professor Burgess says: "This is a most serious question. It demonstrates the fact that the government of the Commonwealth has ceased to be, in many respects, the natural local government." Article "The American Commonwealth," in *Pol. Sci. Quar.*, vol. I, No. 1.

ignated as States which are sovereign in character, common usage will be equally violated by excluding from its application many political units which have been almost universally so denominated. The only escape from these two alternatives, both of them highly objectionable, would seem to be for the analytical jurist to abandon the effort to give scientific precision to the term State and to obtain accuracy of expression by qualifying it when necessary, with such adjectives as sovereign, non-sovereign and the like. If one were starting with a clear sheet, or essaying to formulate a scientifically exact terminology for the analytical jurist there can be little doubt that it would be wise to refuse to designate as States those political entities in which sovereignty does not inhere, but, as it is, with a wider but less precise usage practically universal, such a restriction is not practicable. This conclusion the present author has been reluctantly compelled to accept.[11]

[11] Professor Burgess has suggested that the units of a sovereign federally organized State might be known as "commonwealths," and thus the necessity of designating them as States avoided. Reviewing Laband's *Deutsches Reichsstaatsrecht* in the *Pol. Sci. Quar.* (vol. III, p. 128), he says: "The learned author betrays much anxiety to preserve to the separate States the character of real States, while he denies to them the possession of any sovereign power. The jurist comes again to the front, and rescues the State from the category of organizations having only derived powers by the proposition that the distinguishing characteristic of the State in general is not sovereignty, but the power to command and compel obedience to its commands from the free subjects of the State. It seems to me that his distinction will not hold. If this power to command and to compel obedience be underived and independent, then it is sovereignty pure and simple. If, on the other hand, it be in any sense derivative, then the criterion of distinction which Dr. Laband sets up between the relation of the States to the Union and that of the municipal divisions of the State to the State largely breaks down, since these municipal divisions have also the power to command and compel obedience to their commands from the free subjects of the State, and in their case this is clearly a vested power. If sovereignty in the federal system be exclusively in the Union, then it seems to me that this makes the Union the only real State, and that the only distinction which remains between the separate States and the municipalities lies in the fact that, while the municipalities derive their authority from the States in a positive and

Federal Government and Local Government as Distinguished in Practice. The description which has been given of a federal system is sufficient to show that, in such a scheme of government, the member States occupy a position which resembles that of the local government areas of unitary States to which considerable autonomous powers are given. One is therefore justified in asking what precisely are the characteristics which distinguish a federally organized government from a unitary government in which wide discretionary powers and liberal rights of self-government have been granted to local areas? Or, to state the question in another form, in just what respects do the member States of a federally organized State differ from the autonomous administrative areas of a unitary State?

The difference is considerable, but, as has been already pointed out, the distinction does not lie in the possession by the member States of any part of a sovereignty which is not possessed by the local governing areas. Both the member States and the local areas derive such powers as they possess from the sovereign State of which they are constituent parts. The governments of both are local agencies for the purposes of the central government. Their political powers are emanations from the sovereignty of the National State. They have a legal status only as parts of the Government of that State, and no status independently of it. In these juristic aspects they are alike. As a matter of practical fact, however, there are important differences between the members of a

definite manner, the States derive their power from the Union in a permissive and general manner. To be completely scientific, then, in our nomenclature and emancipate ourselves completely from the power of customary phrases, we should give the name State only to the Union and find some other term to designate its members. In America we have already the suitable title Commonwealth.' "

This is an interesting suggestion, but for the reasons indicated above, not a practicable one.

Federal Union and the autonomous administrative districts of a unitary State.

In the first place, though not recognized as sovereign entities, the members of a federal State so far resemble sovereign States that, except as qualified by federal obligations, they usually stand towards each other as independent and foreign powers. This means that each member body constitutes a jurisdiction outside of which none of its acts,—executive, legislative or judicial,—have any force. Thus, a law enacted by one of the federal units, or a writ issued by one of its courts, has no operative force outside of its own territorial limits, and no one of its officials can exercise any official authority beyond such borders. This is the general principle which applies between sovereign States, and it applies to the members of a federated union subject only to such provisions as may exist in the national Constitution with regard to inter-member relations. Thus, in the United States, notwithstanding the constitutional provisions which have been cited with regard to interstate comity, and to the giving of full faith and credit by each State to the public acts of the other States, it still remains true that the States are without the legal power to issue a judicial writ upon which the presence of a witness who is in another State may be obtained, and a notice of the beginning of a suit against a non-resident does not give jurisdiction to the courts of a State except in those cases which are known as actions *in rem*. And a judgment obtained in the courts of one State will not, as such, be executed by another State. A suit must first be brought upon that judgment, as one would upon a promissory note, in the State in which enforcement is sought.[12]

---

[12] The clause of the federal constitution which decrees that full faith and credit shall be given to the public acts of the other States then applies so that in the suit thus instituted, the judgment may not be attacked upon its merits.

Nor can one State compel another State to return to it fugitives from its justice.[13]

A further respect in which the members of a federal State are distinguished from local government areas, and in which they resemble sovereign States, is that they have, as has been earlier pointed out, a citizenship of their own. And this citizenship imports such an allegiance upon the part of the citizens that a breach of it may probably be punished as high treason.

As distinguished from local government areas, the States of a federal union usually hold such self-governing powers as they have in firmer legal possession. This is due to the fact that these rights are enumerated and guaranteed in the written constitution upon which the Federal Union is itself based. Thus the Supreme Court of the United States has declared that the United States is an "indestructible union composed of indestructible States." This is possibly a somewhat exaggerated statement, since, by amendment of the federal Constitution, it is conceivably possible, by strictly legal means, to deprive the States of any or all of the self-governing powers which they possess, and this could be done against the will of any particular State, since the unanimous approval of the States to amendments of the federal Constitution is not required.[14] But, even if this be juristically possible, it still remains true that, as a practical proposition, the units of a Federation have a firmer pos-

[13] Interstate extradition is provided for by the federal Constitution, but it has been held by the Supreme Court that, though mandatory in terms, there is no constitutional means by which the States may be compelled to fulfill the obligations thus laid upon them.

[14] Possible exceptions to the above statement are exhibited in the constitutional provisions that no State shall be deprived of its right to equal representation in the Senate, and that new States shall not be erected out of parts of the original States or by the union of two or more of them, without the consent of the States thus concerned. It is, however, arguable that even these inhibitions can be overcome by first deleting them from the Constitution by the ordinary process of constitutional amendment.

session of their several jurisdictions than have the local governing bodies of administrative areas.

This constitutional security of the members of a federal union is, in most cases, rendered still more firm by reason of the fact that, before the establishment of the Union, they were independent States, and were, in historical fact, if not in juristic interpretation, the creators of the Union. They thus have back of them a political sentiment in support of their self-governing status to which local government areas can seldom lay claim. Not in all cases, however, have the member States of federal unions originally been independent States. Thus, in the United States, only fourteen of the present members can be said to have been originally sovereign bodies-politic; and, in the Dominion of Canada, only Ontario, Quebec, Nova Scotia, Prince Edward Island, and New Brunswick were originally separate colonies; and none of the present States of Mexico, Argentine and Brazil can lay claim to having had an independent existence prior to the establishment of the Union of which they are the constituent parts.

Another and most important distinction which places the member States of a federal union upon a plane of dignity and importance far above the most autonomous local government areas is that, subject to few restrictions, each federated body is able to determine for itself the form of its own government,—a right which includes also the authority to establish for itself such local government agencies as it sees fit. Thus, each State of Germany, or of the United States, or of Australia, and each Canton of Switzerland or Province of Canada, has its own distinct body of constitutional law which determines not only its form of government, but the principles in accordance with which it is to be operated. In sharp contrast with this is the principle that the local subdivisions of unitary States have their forms of government determined for them by national law.

A further respect in which the member States of such federations as the United States, Canada, and Australia occupy a more independent existence than do the local government areas of any unitary States is that legislative authority is given to each federated State to determine for its own inhabitants the great body of the law, civil and criminal, substantive and procedural, which regulate their private relations, whereas local government agencies have no option but to enforce the laws which they receive from the central government. In Germany and Switzerland the entire body of the private law is placed within the legislative competency of the central government, and, in this respect, therefore, the Swiss Cantons and the individual German States resemble the local governments of unitary States. But, upon the other hand, as has been earlier pointed out, these nationally created laws are interpreted and enforced almost wholly through the governmental agencies of the States which thus gain in executive importance what they have lost legislatively as compared with the States of Australia and of the United States, or the Provinces of Canada.

In this connection it may be said generally, although the principle cannot be laid down in precise terms, that local governments, however autonomous, are conceived of as primarily the agents to carry out, within their respective areas, the will of the central government. It may be that they are permitted in large measure to select for themselves the public officials by whom they are to be locally governed, and with regard to purely local matters they may be given discretionary authority as to what regulations shall be issued and enforced, but it remains true that their several governing agencies are conceived of as acting, *ad hoc,* as mere agencies of the central government.

As thus regarded, the operations of local governments are commonly subject to greater supervision and control by the central authorities than are the activities of the member States of a federal union. Ordinarily the acts of federated States, if falling within the constitutional fields marked out for them by the national constitution, are not subject to censure or annulment by the central government. It is only when some prohibition of the national constitution is violated, or some national right invaded, that a cause for national intervention arises. With regard to local governments, however, the central government usually exercises a continuous and comprehensive supervision.

For the most part it is within the discretion of the federated States to determine whether or not their constitutional powers shall be exercised. For local governments there is usually no such option. To them their duties are more often mandatory in character, and, when there is a failure upon their part to carry out the orders which they have received, the correction usually comes in a more direct and summary manner than is the case when the States of a federal union are derelict in the fulfillment of their federal obligations.

Because of the wide range of their autonomous powers, the member States of all federated unions are equipped with practically complete frame-works of government,— executive, legislative and judicial,—so complete, in fact, that, should the central government be destroyed, these States would be practically ready at once to exercise through their existing governments the functions previously performed by the general government, and thus to stand forth as fully organized bodies-politic. Strongly contrasted with this completeness of organization are the governmental agencies of the most autonomous and self-governing administrative areas. In very many cases, indeed, local governments possess no real legislative bodies, but only executive officials who have ordinance-making powers. Thus, in the entire United States, there is not a single local government, if we except the cities, which is provided with a legislative body, distinct from the executive agents, and composed of elected representatives of the people; although there are in the "Towns" brief annual meetings of the citizens or taxpayers. In England, since 1888, there have been locally-elected "County Councils," and, since 1894, "District Councils," but these have had administrative rather than legislative powers and they operate almost wholly through committees.

CHAPTER XVI

LAW AND SOVEREIGNTY AS ENVISAGED BY INTERNATIONAL LAW

Thus far, in considering the sovereign State as a concept of public law, we have been dealing with it in its national aspect, and have found it to be conceived of as a legal person possessing a legally supreme will, and its commands as having the force of positive law. We come now to consider in what sense and to what extent a similar conception is applicable when the State is regarded, not in its relations to those individuals who are within the control of its municipal law, but as *vis-à-vis* to other States which are similarly sovereign with regard to their respective citizens or subjects.

From what has been already said, it will have appeared, first of all, that, in International Law, the State is envisaged as a "person." It is an entity viewed as possessing a will, and as the subject of rights and obligations. This personality is similar in its conceptual character to that of the State of municipal law, and, in the great majority of cases, the sovereign municipal person has also an international personality. The two personalities are, however, distinct, and only error can result from confusing or identifying them. The rights and obligations which are connoted by international personality are different, both in essential nature and in content, from those which spring from municipal personality, and they are created, applied and enforced by different means.

Based upon its predicated sovereignty, the State of national or municipal law asserts that there are no limits to its will, and that the expressions of that will operate as commands to all those over whom it chooses to claim authority. The State, municipally considered, is not the creation of law, but lives and has its being in the realm of law, for, at the same time that it is the sole and ultimate source of all law it is, by its very nature, compelled to operate according to the rules thus laid down. It is able to act only through its Government, and an act unauthorized by law, even though committed by a government official, is not an act of the Government or of the State of which it is the agent.

As contrasted with this municipal conception of the State, the State of International Law asserts that it has *de facto* power or control over a given territory, and that it will not tolerate within its limits the exercise of any political authority save such as it consents to. Reciprocally, it holds itself responsible to other States for the manner in which, in the exercise of such exclusive jurisdiction, it may affect the rights or interests of other States.

This may be said to be the central conception of International Law, and, if all States were content with their existing territories, if boundaries were certain and undisputed, and if each State held itself unconcerned with whatever action might be taken by other States within their several limits, no opportunity for international discord would be presented. But, in fact, territorial boundaries have not been certainly and finally fixed, and, until the present, there have been vast areas of lands in Asia and Africa and elsewhere which have had no governments the rights of which have been recognized by the greater States of the world, and there has been a constant struggle between these greater States to bring within their respective controls the areas which by practically common consent have been considered as appropriate for annexation. Also, there have been the high seas, which are treated as subject to no sovereign control and as therefore open to free and common use by the citizens of all the States. These waters, however, have not been neutralized in the sense that in time of war belligerent operations upon them may not be conducted.

Furthermore, although each State claims exclusively jurisdiction over its own territories, it does not hold itself indifferent to what other States may do within their respective territories. Over those persons whom, according to its own municipal law, it claims as its own citizens and as owing primary allegiance to itself, each State asserts a right to exercise a certain amount of guardianship wherever they may be. And, in addition to this, it is urged as a matter of international comity, if not of strict right, that, subject to reasonable police restrictions, other States should permit these citizens to travel and reside and carry on business within their several jurisdictions. Thus it has come about, especially during recent years when the means of transportation and communication have been highly developed, that every great State has a considerable number of its citizens travelling or residing in the other States of the world. And, even when its citizens are not thus abroad, they have many commercial relations with the citizens of other States or directly with those States themselves.

In all these cases, each State asserts the right to see that the persons and property of its respective citizens are reasonably protected against violence or unduly discriminative treatment. Finally, all the States of the world have entered into many special treaty relations with one another whereby their general international rights and responsibilities have been modified. Thus it has come about that international relations have become highly complicated and furnish many opportunities for inter-state friction and discord. In order to reduce this friction and possibility of strife to a minimum the statesmen and publicists of all nations have sought to render as definite, and, in their operation, as reciprocally beneficial, as possible the rules and principles that are to be commonly recognized as determining the rights and duties arising out of the inter-relations into which, in modern times, the different States of the world and their citizens are brought.

When disputes have arisen, the effort has been to provide orderly and equitable modes for the settlement; and, finally, when these have failed and war, the *ultima ratio,* has been resorted to, the attempt has been made to establish rules for the conduct of warfare which will limit its horrors to the combatants, and to minimize its devastating effects upon non-combatants. In almost all wars the interests of neutral States become necessarily involved, and, for the determination of the reciprocal rights and responsibilities thus created, another large body of rules and principles has been evolved.

The total result thus is that, though starting from an essentially individualistic doctrine of State exclusiveness and independence, a great and complicated corpus of technical international principles has come into being. It still remains true, however, that the doctrines of exclusive territorial jurisdiction which have been outlined, and of the State as an international entity or person which is the bearer or "subject" of certain rights and corresponding duties, are the fundamental concepts, from which, by logical deduction, are explained and justified the special rules which regulate international relations. The more complicated and technical these provisions of international law, the more important it becomes that the basic ideas upon which they rest should be searched out and clarified.

Municipal and International Jurisprudential Concepts Distinguished. Leaving the domain of municipal life, and entering the field of international law, one finds the principles which regulate the relations of States *inter se* approximately as definite and as formalistic in character as are those which constitute the body of municipal law. Moreover, they are, in general, amenable to much the same analysis as that applicable to municipal law. Furthermore, the concepts that they connote, such as rights, obligations and the like, seem much the same. When, however, we subject these ideas to careful scrutiny, we find, in fact, that we have to deal with principles and concepts which have only a superficial or analogous resemblance to those of municipal law,—that, fundamentally, there is a difference between these two fields of jurisprudence which makes necessary the formation of new definitions of law, of legal rights, and of legal obligations, and a new conception of the State as the subject and object of these rights and obligations.

When we forsake the field of constitutional or municipal law and enter that of international relations we no longer have to deal with legal superiors and legal inferiors. Here we find no supreme will, but, legally speaking, a collection of equal wills, and the conflict, or at least the interplay, of independent powers. This is the fundamental premise of those who attempt the systematic statement of the principles which govern the relations of States to one another. It is true that the more developed and civilized States of the world are spoken of as forming a "Family of Nations," and that from this fact it is quite proper to argue that *ubi societas, ibi jus est.* But the *jus* which is thus brought into being has not the same essential character as has that of municipal life. Especially is this shown in the origin of International Law, although the manner in which it is determined and enforced is not without significance.

As regards their origin, the laws governing international relations do not find their birth in the mandatory utterances of supreme wills declaring to inferior persons what for them shall be deemed legally right and legally wrong. Instead, they derive their force from the fact that they have been accepted by those political persons —the States—whose actions they regulate. This acceptance may, indeed, be one which, for the most part, the States may not find it practicable to avoid, even should they so desire, and thus, in fact the rules of international intercourse may, *arguendo,* be admitted to be as definite, and, in general, as uniformly conformed to as are the provisions of the municipal law of the most orderly State. This, however, does not change the essential character of those international laws as rules which obtain between equals rather than as commands addressed by a superior legislative will to persons who are conceived of as subject to its control.

It would plainly appear, then, that the idea of Sovereignty, as it is found in constitutional law, can find no proper place among international conceptions. The word is, indeed, generally used in the literature of international jurisprudence, but, when thus employed, it has a meaning which is so different from that which it has in the municipal field that it is most unfortunate that it should ever have obtained this currency. It would have been far better if some such term as Independency had been employed. This word, far better than Sovereignty, would indicate the fact that, regarded from the point of view of positive law, complete individualism prevails in the international field. Socially, economically and morally there may be a family of nations,—a *societas maxima,*—but, looked at from the point of view of the constitutional jurist, international life is atomistic, non-civic, individualistic. Thus regarded, nations are, as individuals, in that "state of nature" in which Hobbes, Locke, Rousseau, and the other natural law writers placed primitive man. Even when, by formal treaties, independent States have established rules by which, with reference to the matters specified, their future dealings with one another are to be regulated, there has been no creation of law in a positive or Austinian sense, for, as to those matters, the contracting parties remain subject only to their own wills and not to that of an outside or foreign power. As Jellinek briefly puts it: "Der Staatenvertrag bindet aber er unterwirft nicht." [1]

The Relation Between International Law and Municipal Law. So independent and inherently diverse in character are international and municipal laws, it is not possible for the one to be created by the other; international law cannot be created by municipal law, and municipal law cannot owe its origin to international law. The two systems are, however, often brought into such close factual relations that the absence of this causal nexus is not always evident, and it is therefore necessary to justify somewhat more fully the truth of the proposition that has been stated.

Municipal Law Cannot Create International Law. That no one State can, by its own legislative fiat or judicial decree create international rules that are to bind the actions of other States is generally admitted. That such municipal acts may often have a strongly persuasive international force is granted, but that they may be determinative of the rights of other States is never conceded. It may, indeed, be pointed out that, were the

[1] *Gesetz und Verordnung,* p. 205.

doctrine once established that municipal law could create international law, the doom of international law as a fixed and generally binding body of principles would be at once pronounced. For not only would it thus be within the recognized right of each State to escape from the application of previously acknowledged rules of international law, but that law itself would lose its generality and have a content that would vary for each State.

So appropriate upon this point is the language of the Supreme Court of the United States in the case of *The Scotia*[2] that, though it may be superogatory, it will be quoted. Mr. Justice Swayne, who rendered the decision, was speaking of the maritime law, but the doctrine is applicable to general international law. "Undoubtedly," he says, "no single nation can change the law of the sea. That law is of universal obligation, and no statute of one or two nations can create obligations for the world. Like all the laws of nature, it rests upon the common consent of civilized communities. It is of force, not because it was prescribed by any superior power, but because it has been generally accepted as a rule of conduct."

International Law Cannot Create Municipal Law. That international law cannot create municipal law is not so generally admitted. Indeed, probably the greater number of writers assert that it has this force. In support of this contention attention is called to the many declarations of the national courts of almost all civilized States that international law is a part of the municipal law which they are called upon to apply when the rights of litigants before them are therein involved.

It is true that courts adopt and apply established principles of international law, but, in so applying and enforcing them, they consider them as having been first

[2] 14 Wallace 170 (1871).

impliedly adopted by the State as a portion of its own municipal law. Thus, though the principles which international laws embody are the product of international usage and agreement, their legal force, as rules controlling the administration of justice between litigants, is derived from the sanction of the State whose courts administer them, and by whose laws the courts themselves are created.

The adoption and modes of ascertainment of international laws by the courts are analogous to the manner in which the courts of Great Britain and the United States determine and enforce non-statutory common law principles. Just as the private common law may be modified by statute (though this must usually be by express declaration and not by implication), so a national legislature has full power to bind the courts by statutes which modify the generally accepted principles of international conduct. In the very early case of *The Charming Betsy*,[3] decided in 1804, it seems to have been accepted as a principle not needing argument that the court would be bound by an act of Congress providing a rule different from that laid down by international law, the only observation made being that "an act of Congress ought never to be construed to violate the law of nations if any other possible construction remains." In *The Nereide*[4] Marshall again declared: "Till an act [of Congress] be passed the court is bound by the law of nations, which is a part of the law of the land." In *Hilton v. Guyot*[5] the court said:

International law in its widest and most comprehensive sense—including not only questions of right between nations, governed by what has been appropriately called the law of nations, but also questions arising under what is usually called private international

[3] 2 Cr. 64.
[4] 9 Cr. 388.
[5] 159 U. S. 113.

law, or the conflict of laws, and concerning the rights of persons within the territory and dominion of one nation, by reason of acts, private or public, done within the dominion of another nation—is part of our law, and must be ascertained and administered by the courts of justice, as often as such questions are presented in litigation between man and man, duly submitted to their determination. The most certain guide, no doubt, for the decision of such questions is a treaty or a statute of this country. But when, as is the case here, there is no written law upon the subject, the duty still rests upon the judicial tribunals of ascertaining and declaring what the law is whenever it becomes necessary to do so in order to determine the rights of parties to suits regularly brought before them. In doing this, the courts must obtain such aid as they can from judicial decisions, from the works of jurists and commentators, and from the acts and usages of civilized nations.

In the case of *The Lottawanna,* sub nomine *Rodd v. Heartt*[6] is set out in the clearest possible manner the extent to which, and the manner in which, any body of law, not originally municipal, may, by adoption, become such. That case had reference to the adoption by the United States of the general principles of maritime law, but, as is pointed out in the argument, the principle is the same with reference to international law. Mr. Justice Bradley, speaking for the court, said:

The ground on which we are asked to overrule the judgment in the case of *The General Smith* is that by the general maritime law those who furnish necessary materials, repairs, and supplies to a vessel have a lien on such a vessel therefor, as well when furnished in her home port as when furnished in a foreign port, and that the courts of admiralty are bound to give effect to that lien.

The proposition affirms that the general maritime law governs this case, and is binding on the courts of the United States. But it is hardly necessary to argue that the general maritime law is only so far operative as law in any country as it is adopted by the laws and usages of that country. In this respect it is like international law or the laws of war, which have the effect of law in no country further than they are accepted and received as such; or, like the case

[6] 21 Wall 558.

of the civil law, which forms the basis of most European laws, but
which has the force of law in each State only so far as it is adopted
therein, and with such modifications as are deemed expedient. The
adoption of the common law by the several States of this Union
also presents an analogous case. It is the basis of all the State
laws, but is modified as each sees fit. Perhaps the maritime law is
more uniformly followed by commercial nations than the civil and
common law by those who use them. But, like those laws, however
fixed, definite, and beneficial the theoretical code of maritime law may
may be, it can have only so far the effect of law in any country
as it is permitted to have. But the actual maritime law can hardly
be said to have a fixed and definite form as to all the subjects which
may be embraced within its scope. Whilst it is true that the great
mass of maritime law is the same in all commercial countries, yet
in each country peculiarities exist either as to some of the rules or
in the mode of enforcing them. Especially is this the case on the
outside boundaries of the law, where it comes in contact with or
shades off into the local or municipal law of the particular country
and affects only its own merchants or people in their relations to
each other; whereas, in matters affecting the stranger or foreigner,
the commonly received law of the whole commercial world is more
assiduously observed—as, in justice, it should be. No one doubts
that every nation may adopt its own maritime code. France may
adopt one; England another; the United States a third; still, the
convenience of the commercial world, bound together, as it is, by
mutual relations of trade and intercourse, demands that in all
essential things wherein those relations bring them in contact, there
should be a uniform law founded on natural reason and justice.
Hence, the adoption by all commercial nations (our own included)
of the general maritime law as the basis and groundwork of all their
maritime regulations. But no nation regards itself as precluded
from making occasional modifications suited to its locality and the
genius of its own people and institutions, especially in matters that
are of merely local and municipal consequence, and do not affect other
nations. It will be found, therefore, that the maritime codes of
France, England, Sweden, and other countries are not one and the
same in every particular; but that, while there is a great correspondence between them, arising from the fact that each adopts the
general principles and the great mass of the general maritime law
as the basis of its system, there are varying shades of difference
corresponding to the respective territories, climate, and genius of

the people of each country respectively. Each state adopts the maritime law, not as a code having any independent or inherent force, *proprio vigore,* but as its own law, with such modifications and qualifications as it sees fit. Thus adopted, and thus qualified in each case, it becomes the maritime law of the particular nation which adopts it. And without such voluntary adoption it would not be law. And thus it happens that, from the general practice of commercial nations in making the same general law the basis and groundwork of their respective maritime systems, the great mass of maritime law which is thus received by these nations in common comes to be the common maritime law of the world.

The same principle which guides our courts in the adoption and enforcement of principles of international law is accepted by the courts of Great Britain, namely, the presumption that the State whose laws they apply has, by the fact of its existence as a member of the Family of Nations, accepted for its guidance in international matters the generally recognized rules of international law of procedure. When, however, as the State has by treaty or statute, or otherwise, shown that it does not accept a given international law principle, such principle does not receive judicial recognition.

A leading and often-cited English case upon this point is *The Queen v. Keyn,*[7] decided in 1876. The essential question involved in this case was whether, by the operation of the general principle of international law which treats the marginal waters of a country as territorial, the municipal court might, in the absence of any express statutory grant of power, exercise jurisdiction with reference to an act committed upon such waters. The court of last resort in its decision denied that the international law, however well established, could operate, *ex proprio vigore,* to extend the jurisdiction of a municipal court. In some way, it was declared, the assent of the State whose law the court is applying must be shown.

[7] *Law Reports, 2 Exchequer Division,* 68.

International usage, participated in by the State in question, may show this assent; but it is the assent of the State and not the international usage which erects the principle into a law recognizable and enforceable by the courts.

"To be binding," said Cockburn, C. J., "the law must have received the assent of the nations who are to be bound by it. This assent may be expressed, as by treaty or the acknowledged concurrence of governments, or may be implied from established usage—an instance of which is to be found in the fact that merchant vessels on the high seas are held to be subject to the law of the nation under whose flag they sail, while in the ports of a foreign state they are subject to the local law as well as to that of their own country. In the absence of proof of assent, as derived from one or other of these sources, no unanimity on the part of theoretical writers would warrant the judicial application of the law on the sole authority of their views or statements. Nor, in my opinion, would the clearest proof of unanimous assent on the part of other nations be sufficient to authorize the tribunals of this country to apply, without an act of Parliament, what would practically amount to a new law. In so doing we should be unjustifiably usurping the province of the legislature. The assent of nations is doubtless sufficient to give the power of parliamentary legislation in a matter otherwise within the sphere of international law, but it would be powerless to confer without such legislation a jurisdiction beyond and unknown to the law." [8]

By a law passed in 1878,[9] Parliament granted the jurisdiction which, in *Queen v. Keyn,* the court held itself to be without. The statement is sometimes made that the enactment of this law was equivalent to a parliamentary declararation of the erroneousness of the court's decision. This, of course, it was not. The preamble of that act does indeed declare that "the rightful jurisdiction of Her Majesty, her heirs and successors, extends and has always extended over the open seas

[8] In the instant case it was held that Parliament had given to the court only the jurisdiction formerly exercised by the Admiral which did not cover the case at bar.

[9] 41 and 42 Vict., chap. 73.

adjacent to the coasts of the United Kingdom," but this legislative declaration necessarily extended only to a denial of the fact upon which the court had founded its judgment, and not to an assertion of the fallacy of the *ratio decidendi* employed by the court. Indeed, it does not need to be said that it is not within the power of a legislature, whatever the extent of its law-making powers, to control processes of judicial reasoning. It may lay down laws by which the courts will in the future be bound, and it may even provide principles of statutory construction which shall henceforth be followed, but it cannot by any declaration render erroneous the process of reasoning which a court has employed. It may, for the future, with reference to specified matters, render inapplicable that reasoning, but cannot render it erroneous as applied in the past.

As a matter of fact the English courts have continued to the present day to assert the doctrine declared in *Queen v. Keyn*. In the very recent case of the *West Rand Central Gold Mining Co. v. King*,[10] the Lord Chief Justice, in his opinion, said:

The second proposition urged, that international law forms part of the law of England, requires a word of explanation and comment. It is quite true that whatever has received the common consent of civilized nations must have received the assent of our country, and that to which we have assented along with other nations in general may properly be called international law, and as such will be acknowledged and applied by our municipal tribunals when legitimate occasion arises for those tribunals to decide questions to which doctrines of international law may be relevant. But any doctrine so invoked must be one really accepted as binding between nations, and the international law sought to be applied must, like anything else, be proved by satisfactory evidence, which must show either that the particular proposition put forward has been recognized and acted upon by our country, or that it is of such a nature, and has been so widely and generally accepted, that it can hardly be

[10] L. R. (1905), 2 K. B. 391.

supposed that any civilized state would repudiate it. The mere opinions of jurists, however eminent or learned, that it ought to be so recognized, are not in themselves sufficient. They must have received the express sanction of international agreement, or gradually have grown to be part of international law by their frequent practical recognition in dealings between various nations. We adopt the language used by Lord Russell of Killoween in his address at Saratoga in 1896 on the subject of International Law and Arbitration: 'What then, is international law? I know no better definition of it than it is the sum of the rules or usages which civilized states have agreed shall be binding on them in their dealings with one another.' In our judgment, the second proposition for which Lord Robert Cecil contended in his argument before us ought to be treated as correct only if the term 'international law' is understood in the sense, and subject to the limitations of application, which we have explained. The authorities which he cited in support of the proposition are entirely in accord with and, indeed, well illustrate our judgment upon this branch of the arguments advanced on behalf of the suppliants. For instance, *Barbuit's Case*, Cas. Tal. 281; *Triquet v. Bath*, 3 Burr. 1478; and *Heathfield v. Chilton*, 4 Burr. 2016, are cases in which the courts of law have recognized and have given effect to the privilege of ambassadors as established by international law. But the expressions used by Lord Mansfield, when dealing with the particular and recognized rule of international law on this subject, that the law of nations forms part of the law of England ought not to be construed so as to include as part of the law of England opinions of textwriters upon a question as to which there is no evidence that Great Britain has ever assented, and *a fortiori* if they are contrary to the principles of her laws as declared by her courts. The cases of *Wolff v. Oxholm*, 6 M. & S. 92; 18 R. R. 313, and *Rex v. Keyn*, 2 Ex. D. 63, are only illustrations of the same rule—namely, that questions of international law may arise, and may have to be considered in connection with the administration of municipal law.

In *Mortensen v. Peters*,[11] decided in 1906, the High Court of Justiciary of Scotland said:

It is a trite observation that there is no such thing as a standard of international law, extraneous to the domestic law of a kingdom, to which appeal may be made. International law, so far as this court is concerned, is the body of doctrine regarding the international

[11] 14 Scots, L. T. R. 227.

rights and duties of states which has been adopted and made part of the law of Scotland.

The comparatively recent case of *The Zamora*,[12] decided by the Judicial Committee of the Privy Council, is fully consistent with the position here taken. In that case the central question was whether the British prize courts were to hold themselves bound by certain rules issued by the King in Council in exercise of his prerogative powers, that is, without express authorization so to do by act of Parliament. It was held that the court was not so bound. The Judicial Committee in the course of its opinion pointed out that, under the Act of Parliament, the Prize Court was obligated to enforce generally accepted rules of international law except insofar as these might be modified by the municipal law of Great Britain; that this law could not be determined by executive order; and that, therefore, except when otherwise provided by Parliament, the court was compelled to find its rules in the accepted doctrines of international law. "If," said the Judicial Committee, "an Order in Council were binding on the Prize Court, such court would be compelled to act contrary to the express terms of the commission from which it derived its jurisdiction." And, before this, the Judicial Committee had said: "Of course, the Prize Court was a municipal court and its decrees and orders owed their validity to municipal law. The law which it enforced might, therefore, in one sense, be considered a branch of municipal law."

In support of the position that international law is a part of municipal law the recent American case of *Paquete Habana* [13] decided by the Supreme Court in 1899 has been cited.[14] This case involved the question

[12] L. R. (1916), 2 A. C. 77.
[13] 175 U. S. 677.
[14] See, for example, the article by Dr. J. B. Scott in the *American Journal of International Law*, October, 1907, "The Legal Nature of International Law."

whether, in the absence of municipal law, the principle that fishing smacks belonging to an enemy are not subject to seizure had become so well recognized in international law as to warrant the courts in declaring illegal a capture made by the United States naval forces. In its opinion the court said:

> International law is part of our law, and must be ascertained and administered by the courts of justice of appropriate jurisdiction as often as questions of right depending upon it are duly presented for their determination. For this purpose, where there is no treaty, and no controlling executive or legislative act or judicial decision, resort must be had to the customs and usages of civilized nations, and, as evidence of these, to the works of jurists and commentators, who by years of labor, research, and experience have made themselves peculiarly well acquainted with the subjects of which they treat. Such works are resorted to by judicial tribunals, not for the speculations of their authors concerning what the law ought to be, but for trustworthy evidence of what the law really is.

In a dissenting opinion by the Chief Justice, Justices Harlan and McKenna concurring, the argument is not so much a denial that the exemption of fishing smacks from capture in time of war was a practice generally sanctioned by modern practice and by the opinions of international law writers, as that it lay within the discretion of the executive power to determine the rigors of war, and that, in the proclamation and directions which, in the exercise of that discretion had been issued, no such exemption had been expressly or impliedly authorized.

In this case we undoubtedly have the acceptance by our courts of an international usage as law, and that, too, a usage in whose favor neither universal and long-continued acceptance by nations nor unanimous advocacy by scientific commentators could be successfully urged. But this was by no means a repudiation of the principle declared by the Supreme Court in *The Lottawana*. The

Federal Constitution provides that Congress shall have the power to define and punish offenses against the law of nations, and to make rules concerning captures on land and water. Furthermore, it is declared that treaties made under the authority of the United States shall be the supreme law of the land. The courts have repeatedly held that effect of these clauses, which recognize the existence of a body of international laws and grant to Congress the power to punish offenses against them, is to adopt these laws into our municipal law *en bloc* except where Congress or the treaty-making power has expressly changed them. Furthermore, it is held that the commonly accepted principles of international law, insofar as they had been embodied in the English common law, have been adopted into American law with the acceptance, substantially *en bloc,* of that common law. When, then, Congress has not acted, the courts properly hold that it is its intention that the generally recognized principles of international conduct should be applied. In exactly the same way it has been held that, with reference to the regulation of interstate commerce, the silence of Congress is deemed equivalent to an expression of its will that commerce shall be free from control by the States of the Union. There was, therefore, in this Paquete Habana Case that acceptance by the State which the courts have consistently declared is required for the transmutation of an international rule into a municipal command.

When the doctrine is declared that municipal law may not be altered or determined by international law, no distinction is made between the general principles of international law and the special obligations which, by treaties, States see fit to impose upon themselves. It is true that treaties entered into by the United States become a part of its own municipal law, but this is the result of an express constitutional provision.[15] Where there is no such express provision in a State's own laws or constitution, it is universally held that the municipal law may not be altered by a treaty. This, for example, is emphatically asserted in *Walker v. Baird* [16] by the Judicial Committee of the Privy Council, affirming on appeal a judgment of the Supreme Court of Newfoundland. Commenting on this case, Cobbett points out that "it serves to show that international agreements to which this country [Great Britain] may be a party, and obligations arising therefrom, will not be regarded as a part of the ordinary law of the land, except insofar as they may have received the assent of the Legislature. Hence, in English law, treaties which affect private rights must have a legislative sanction. Thus, extradition treaties are carried into effect by Orders in Council, made under the Extradition Acts, 1870 to 1906; international copyright arrangements are carried out by Orders in Council under the International Copyright Acts, 1844 to 1866; whilst even commercial treaties are sometimes given effect to by act of Parliament."

And, in a subsequent note, Cobbett so excellently summarizes the true English doctrine that its quotation, *in extenso,* is justified. He says:

The true relation may perhaps be expressed in the following propositions: English Law recognizes the existence of International Law as a body of rules capable of being ascertained, and when ascertained as binding upon States either by immemorial usage [17] or by virtue of agreement. When once a rule of International Law is shown to have received the assent of civilized States, it will also be

[15] Art. VI, Sec. 2: "This Constitution and the laws of the United States which shall be made in pursuance thereof; and all treaties made, or which shall be made, under authority of the United States, shall be the supreme law of the land."

[16] A. C. 491 (1892). Cf. Cobbett, *Cases and Opinions on International Law,* p. 19.

[17] Which, of course, indicates assent.

deemed to have received the assent of the country, and will in that character be applied by English courts in cases coming before them to which such rule may be relevant. But there are certain rights and obligations arising out of international relations, or purporting to rest upon international law, which will not be deemed to be within the competence of municipal courts.[18] So in *Cook v. Sprigg* (1899 A. C. 572) it was held that annexation was an 'act of State,' and that obligations arising under a treaty to that effect were not of a kind which a municipal court could enforce. Moreover, the courts in interpreting and applying municipal law, whilst they will always seek to adopt such a construction as will not bring it into conflict with the law of nations, cannot of course give effect to its rules however clear, or to rights or obligations deducible therefrom, in cases where those rules derogate from or are inconsistent with the positive regulations of municipal law. With respect to treaties, in particular, the Crown or executive cannot claim, in virtue of any obligations arising out of a treaty not sanctioned by Statute, to modify or interfere with rights arising under the ordinary laws of the land. At the same time the inability of the courts to give effect to international obligations as against subjects will not, of course, have the effect of freeing a State from its international responsibility for their non-fulfillment. English law embraces a variety of Statutes which have been passed from time to time for the purpose of enabling the Crown and the executive to carry out more effectively its international obligations, and more especially to enter into and carry out particular treaty arrangements concluded with other States, and to this extent international law, and the obligations arising thereunder, will constitute a part of the law of the land to which the courts will in a proper case give full effect.[19]

Is International Law "Positive" in Character? In the preceding sections it has been shown that international law may not be assimilated to municipal law,—that it does not become positive municipal law until it has passed through the transmuting process of acceptance by the States whose courts enforce it. We have now to consider whether, without regard to its relation to municipal law,

---

[18] Citing *West Rand Central Gold Mining Co. v. The King*, 2 K. B. 391.
[19] *Op. cit.*, p. 21. Cobbett, in footnotes, gives references to authorities supporting each of these propositions.

it may properly be termed "positive" in character, that is, law in the strict Austinian or analytical sense.

Clearly it cannot be so regarded for it lacks the essential quality of embodying commands issued by political superiors to political inferiors. This, however, does not mean, as has been previously suggested, that the title "laws" should not be given to these international rules if it be borne in mind that the term, when so employed, has a meaning different from that which it has when used by the analytical jurist when speaking of municipal laws.

In order that the position taken in this treatise with regard to the juristic nature of International Law may be given its proper setting, it will be worth while to present and comment upon the typical arguments of publicists who have stated the contrary doctrine.

In his essay entitled "Methods of Jurisprudence," Pollock says: [20]

International Law is a true branch of jurisprudence, notwithstanding what may be said about its want of sovereign power and a tribunal. You may define it as 'positive international morality' not having the nature of law [as does Austin] but if you do the facts are against you. For what are the facts?

(1) The doctrines of international law are founded on legal not simply on ethical ideas. They are not merely prevalent opinions as to what is morally right and proper, but something as closely analogous to civil laws as the nature of the case will admit. They purport to be rules of strict justice, not counsels of perfection.[21]

(2) Since they have assumed a coherent shape they have been the special study of men of law, and have been discussed by the

---

[20] In his volume entitled *Oxford Lecturees*.

[21] This is an important point. Many writers appear to think that if international rules are denied the title laws in the positive or analytical sense, they are thereby declared to be nothing more than rules of morality. Austin is responsible for this mistake. International rules or principles are entitled to be termed laws, even though they may not properly be spoken of as laws in the sense in which that term is employed in municipal jurisprudence.

methods appropriate to jurisprudence, and not by those of moral philosophy.

(3) There is a practical test and a conclusive one. If international law were only a kind of morality, the framers of state papers concerning foreign policy would throw all their strength on moral argument. But, as a matter of fact, this is not what they do. They appeal not to the general feeling of moral rightness, but to precedents, and to opinions of specialists. They assume the existence among statesmen and publicists of a series of legal as distinct from moral obligation in the affairs of nations.

(4) Further, there is actually an international morality, distinct from, and incompatible with international law in the usual sense. As a citizen among citizens, so a nation among nations may do things which are discourteous, high-handed, savoring of sharp practice or otherwise invidious and disliked, and yet within its admitted right and giving no formal ground of complaint. There is a margin of discretionary behavior which is the province not of claims and dispatches but of "friendly representations" and "good offices."

These facts, thus stated by Pollock, may be at once and fully admitted, and the conclusion conceded that there is a body of international principles that may fairly be said to constitute a system of jurisprudence as distinguished from one of morality, and that Austin's designation of international law as nothing more than positive morality is therefore misleading, if not absolutely erroneous, but it is none the less true that these juristic principles do not come within the ordinary accepted definition of civil or municipal law. If the two bodies of law are to be brought under a single rubric it is necessary that a broader definition be given to municipal law than is ordinarily given it.

This is what T. J. Lawrence, Oppenheim, and many other publicists do. Thus, after defining International Law as composed of "the rules which determine the conduct of the general body of civilized States in their mutual dealings," and pointing out that by thus using the term "rules" instead of "laws" he is able to discard altogether the phrase "rights and obligations," Lawrence says: "If we are content with the definitions of Richard Hooker, the great Elizabethan divine, who spoke of law as 'any rule of canon whereby actions are framed,' we may apply the term to those regulations concerning international conduct which meet with general acceptance of civilized communities." [22]

Oppenheim defines law as "a body of rules for human conduct within a community which by common consent of this community shall be enforced by external power." [23] By this definition, as he points out, three essential conditions of the existence of law are posited,— a community, a body of rules for human conduct within the community, and a common consent to their enforcement by external power as distinguished from their enforcement by the internal conscience. These three essentials, he declares, are to be found in the rules which regulate the relations of States with each other: the civilized States do constitute a veritable community; they are definite rules that are accepted by common consent; and they are enforced by external authority.

The Development of International Law. If we date the rise of the science of international jurisprudence from the beginning of the seventeenth century, we find that, in its earlier phases, International Law was closely allied with, if not assimilated to, the moral or "natural" laws and that, during that period its rules presented a corresponding indefiniteness, their ethical sanction was *in foro interno,* and their actual observance was far from general or uniform. Indeed, at that time, the effort of such reformers as Grotius and his immediate followers was to escape from the international practices that prevailed

[22] *International Law,* sec. 9.
[23] *International Law,* 3d ed., sec. 5.

by appealing to principles founded in the very nature
of reason and morality. The uninterrupted tendency
since that time has, however, been to substitute the rules
manifested in actual practices for abstract principles, and
this tendency has been hastened by the increasing habit
of nations to provide by treaties conventional rules for
the guidance of their international affairs. These treaties
have, of course, served to create rules only for the States
parties to them, but where the same or substantially similar provisions have found a place in a number of treaties,
and especially where a considerable number of nations
have been parties to the treaties, the effect has been to
cause these provisions to be regarded as voicing the deliberate judgment of the international world. Thus,
whereas, in earlier times, treaties were but seldom entered into except at the termination of armed struggles,
and were limited in scope to the settlement of the
dynastic, territorial or other disputes, the modern world
has seen treaties employed for the purpose of establishing general rules for the future guidance of international
life. At first this wider and legislative function of treaties
was resorted to only when, upon the termination of some
general war, the nations found themselves convened for
the purpose of fixing the conditions of peace; but the
present age has witnessed the assembling of Conferences
embracing all or many of the members of the family of
nations for the sole purpose of the creating rules for the
regulation of international relations. Thus the general
will of the international world has shown an increasing
tendency to become articulate and legislative. Furthermore, as is well known, the attempt has been made, and
with no small degree of success, to establish tribunals
more or less judicial in character [24] for the settlement

---

[24] It is not necessary here to consider the distinction between "arbitration" and the "judicial settlement" of international controversies. It

of international disputes. And, finally, projects have been seriously discussed by publicists which would involve, if realized, the establishment of an international executive force for compelling obedience upon the part of recalcitrant nations to the generally recognized principles of international law. However, even were such an aim fully realized, it could hardly be said that international law would be thereby transmuted into positive law, unless the international judicial tribunals were given a general jurisdiction over international disputes, and unless, also, and what is still more important, the international legislative body, similar to the Hague Conferences, should have ascribed to them unlimited law-making powers, and, of course, its declarations given an immediate and not merely an *ad referendum* character. When, and only when, such conditions are met, will it be proper to say that a *civitas maxima* has been established with a territorial jurisdiction including the *orbem terrarum* and the utterances of its will entitled to be termed "positive" laws.

It none the less remains true, however, that, at the present time, there exists a body of rules regulating international relations which, though supported by the strongest feelings of morality and expediency, find their source no longer in abstract and vague doctrines of natural law, but in precedent and convention; which are sufficiently definite and susceptible of classification and logical arrangement; which for the most part may be referred back to, and supported by, fundamental propositions regarding the nature of the State as an international person, and with rights and obligations attaching

may be said, however, that while both methods have their special advantages and disadvantages the establishment of "judicial tribunals," as distinguished from courts or "boards of arbitration" would cause international more closely to approximate to municipal law as regards the mode of determination and its application to specific controversies.

to it as such; and which international rules are therefore susceptible of being brought together into a systematic and scientific whole. In short, the analytical political philosopher is provided with the material for a science of international law in as true a sense as he is when concerned with the construction of a philosophy of the State as nationally or municipally viewed.

It is further to be observed that what, in a comprehensive sense, is known as International Law is made up of several fairly distinct bodies of principles which vary as regards the obligatory and absolute force ascribed to them. Thus, just as in the field of national life there are many rules which Austin describes as rules of "positive morality," the justice and expediency of which are generally recognized, and which in fact are very generally conformed to, but which have not back of them the authority and sanction of the State; so, in the international field, there are many rules of what is known as international morality, or comity, the violation of which by one State is looked upon with disfavor by other States but not as illegal in a strict sense of the word. Thus, for example, principles of international comity provide that one State shall not refuse to have commercial or other dealings with other States, and that, subject to reasonable police regulations, it shall permit the nationals of those other States to travel or become domiciled and carry on business within its borders. Furthermore, this same comity demands that, in the privileges which one State extends to the subjects of other States, arbitrary distinctions shall not be made either between different classes of the subjects of the same State, or, generally between the nationals of different States. Thus, at the present time, Japan has shown dissatisfaction because the United States has denied to her subjects certain rights of immigration, naturalization, land-holding, and school privileges which are conceded to the citizens of other States. At the same time Japan recognizes that international law, in *sensu strictiore,* grants to each State a comprehensive right to exercise its full discretion with regard to these matters and that, therefore, strictly speaking, she has no legal claim to redress. Many instances, similar to this, could be cited in which international comity is recognized as creating what may be called moral rights, or obligations of friendship or respect as distinguished from those which international law, properly speaking, supports.

Another phase of international relations which deserves at least mention is the bearing which "national policies" have upon the rights of other nations as established by international law. Not infrequently the effect of these policies is to infringe the rights which, in principle, every independent State is conceded by international law to possess. A most conspicuous instance of this is furnished by the Monroe Doctrine as declared by the United States. Although it is conceded that every independent State has the right, as such, to acquire or dispose of territory as a result of a war, or by way of purchase and sale, the Doctrine amounts to a declaration that the United States will not permit other States to acquire additional territory or political control in the Western Hemisphere, by any means, or under any circumstances. The same general result follows in all those cases in which particular States lay claim to what are known as "Spheres of Influence." It is seen also in the notice recently (March 15, 1922) served upon the other Powers by Great Britain that, though it regards Egypt as now constituting a sovereign and independent State, "the welfare and integrity of Egypt are necessary to the peace and safety of the British Empire, which will therefore always maintain as an essential British interest the special relations between itself and Egypt long recognized by other Governments," and that, as so declared, the British Government "will not admit them to be questioned or discussed by any other Power." "In pursuance of this principle," the notice continues, "they [the British Government] will regard as an unfriendly act any attempt at interference in the affairs of Egypt by another Power, and they will consider any aggression against the territory of Egypt as an act to be repelled with all the means at their command." This declaration, it is to be observed, was a unilateral act upon the part of Great Britain and not one founded upon an agreement between itself and Egypt.

This general aspect of international life has recently been dwelt upon by Professor Jesse Reeves in a luminous paper in which he points out that, until this factor is taken into account, and the assertions of national policies brought into conformity with the general principles of international law, it is vain to hope that all international controversies may be brought within the jurisdiction of judicial as distinguished from arbitral tribunals. These national policies, he says, furnish the dynamic factors of international life, and, furthermore, "have to do not only with the relations of States with each other, a subject to which international law in the past has confined itself, but with the larger relations of groups to groups both within and without States, of individuals to individuals, of world-movements of population, of earthhunger and its appeasement, and of the strivings of international commercial competition. These things must be reduced to the régime of law, to an acceptance of a universal *status quo;* and in the past this has never come about except under a universal imperial dominion, or World-State. Slowly and painfully must the edifice be reconstructed, from foundation to superstructure. The basis of a régime of law among States must be those really juristic principles, recognized by the members of the world-society as not repugnant to the realization of national ideals on the one hand, and, on the other as fitting in with the generally accepted ideals of justice and of fair dealing on the part of peoples within a State."

"Finally," Professor Reeves points out, "there must be recognized what may be called the sphere of an international law of crime. It is possible that in combating Austin's doctrine that international law is not true law, we are in danger of neglecting what he claimed for it, a positive international morality. . . . Acts which shock the most obvious claims of humanity come to be looked at, not as international crimes, but as international torts, to be adjusted through diplomatic apology and assuaged by money payment. Anything, whether in the form of certain kinds of propaganda or in the smugly polished phrases of utterance, which glosses over the essentially anti-social and therefore criminal nature of certain international acts may contribute to a fatal confusion of ideas." [25]

[25] *American Political Science Review*, February, 1916 (vol. X, p. 70), "The Justiciability of international Disputes."

CHAPTER XVII

THE CONCEPT OF THE STATE IN INTERNATIONAL LAW

In the preceding pages the attempt has been made to determine the juristic character of the body of rules which regulate the relations of States to one another. In this chapter the aim will be to determine the conception which is held of the State as the subject of the rights and obligations which these rules recognize and create.

The concept of the State is the starting point of international as it is of municipal jurisprudence, for it is from the attributes which are ascribed to the individual political persons who constitute the international group that the most important principles of international law are directly or indirectly deduced. That, as members of the Family of Nations, States are envisaged as political persons is indicated by the language which has just been employed. Just as, in municipal law, they are regarded as the possessors of independent wills and as the entities in which are vested certain rights and responsibilities, so, in international law, they are viewed as political persons having definite rights and obligations. This status they have, however, in full effect at least, only insofar as they are regarded as members of what is known as the "Family of Nations," which Family does not include all the States of the world but only those nations which have reached a certain degree of civilization.

The States which are members of this narrower group have assumed to themselves the right to determine what other States shall be admitted to full membership with themselves. As the basis for this consent, they declare, to quote the words of Oppenheim, three conditions: "A State to be admitted must, first, be a civilized State which is in constant intercourse with members of the Family of Nations. Such State must, secondly, expressly or tacitly, consent to be bound for its future international conduct by the rules of International Law. And thirdly, those States which have hitherto formed the Family of Nations must expressly or tacitly consent to the reception of the new member." [1] Thus Turkey was not admitted to "the public law and system of Europe" until 1856, and Japan was not accorded this status until 1899.

With reference to the States that are still outside the Family of Nations, Cobbett points out that they can scarcely be held to be altogether outside the pale of international law. He says:

Such States may be said to occupy in the international system much the same position as persons subject to the disabilities of infancy or alienage occupy in municipal law, but their exact position is hard to define. . . . Such of them as are capable of independent relations are recognized as competent to enter into treaties and as being responsible for their observance; they send and receive ambassadors, and are held responsible for any invasion of the rights of embassy; whilst they are also held responsible for the security of foreigners residing within their limits, and as well as for other international delinquencies. They are also recognized as capable of making peace or war; and, in the case of a maritime war, a State like China, at any rate, would, if belligerent, probably be allowed to enforce and be expected to observe the customary rules with respect to neutral trade; whilst in the case of war between other States the obligations of neutrality would probably be enforced against her. On the other hand, their position differs from that of States within the Family of Nations in several particulars. Their territorial supremacy is less scrupulously respected; intercourse is not only often forced upon them, but Europeans and Americans living within their limits are also commonly exempted from

[1] *International Law*, 3d ed., p. 27.

the local jurisdiction and invested with the privilege of extraterritoriality; their conduct in relation to other States similarly situated, especially in time of war, would not, probably, be judged by ordinary international standards; nor do such communities generally participate in those forms of joint action and organization which constitute so strong a bond between civilized States. At the same time some of these traits are marks rather of political than of legal inequality; whilst others are mere incidents of their geo-political position.[2]

Territorial Integrity. The most important of the attributes conceded by international law to every member of the Family of Nations is that of territorial integrity,— the autonomous right of each State to exercise control over, and a corresponding responsibility for what occurs within, a given territory. The implications of this right and responsibility will be developed in later chapters which deal with Political Jurisdiction.

There are some authorities who hold that the occupation of a definite territory is not indispensable to international statehood. Thus Hall writes:

Abstractly there is no reason why even a wandering tribe or society should not feel itself bound as stringently as a settled community by definite rules of conduct towards other communities, and though there might be difficulty in subjecting such societies to restraint, or, in some cases, of being sure of their identity, there would be nothing in such difficulties to exclude the possibility of regarding them as subjects of law, and there would be nothing therefore to render the possession of a fixed seat an absolute condition of admission to its benefits.[3]

It seems to the author that this reasoning does not sufficiently recognize the principle which, since the beginning of the seventeenth century, has been accepted as a fundamental premise of international jurisprudence, that the recognition of one State by other States is predi-

---

[2] *Leading Cases on International Law,* 3d ed., p. 47.
[3] *International Law,* 6th ed., p. 19.

cated upon the demonstrated power of a given government to exercise effectual control over a given area, and that such government may therefore be held internationally responsible for what happens within this area. The only conceivable instance in which Hall's example of a wandering tribe, entitled to international recognition as a State, could be found would be where such a tribe is roving over territory which is not claimed as its own by any other member of the Family of Nations. But, in such a case, could it not be fairly said that the tribe in question has as its territorial basis the areas over which it roams? It is true that a State may, for reasons of its own, ascribe a quasi-independence to a group of individuals living within its midst and deal with those groups, in form at least, by treaties, as for many years was the practice of the United States with reference to many of the Indian tribes. The territorial State may permit such tribes to have direct relations with other States (which, however, the United States did not permit the Indians to do), but it is not conceivable that, even in such a case, the other States with which such tribes might have dealings would not hold the territorial State ultimately responsible for acts of those tribes which violated the international rights of those other States. For the State within whose territories the tribes dwelt would be held internationally responsible for whatever might happen within the territories which it claimed as its own; and, therefore, the treaties which those tribes might enter into would be held as entered into in behalf and with the sanction of the territorial State.

Recognition. Distinct from the question of admtiting a State to membership in the Family of Nations is that as to what government of State, being a member, is entitled to recognition by the governments of the other States as the mouthpiece or instrumentality for claiming the rights, or being held responsible for the performance of the duties, of such State as fixed by International Law.

International law, as fixed by international practice, determines in only a very general manner the conditions under which such recognition will be accorded, and there is no legal way in which this recognition, if deemed to be unjustly withheld, may be compelled. Furthermore, the action of one State in this respect, whether favorable or unfavorable, does not control, though it may influence, the action of other States.

As will presently be pointed out one State has no direct concern with the constitutional structure of another State, except, possibly, to assure itself as to the organ which has the authority to speak for the State in its international affairs. From this principle it follows that, to international law, the distinction between governments *de facto* and governments *de jure* is without juristic significance. Or rather we may say that a government which is recognized to be *de facto* is thereby *de jure* as well so far as its international status is concerned. When, therefore, one government is called upon to accord recognition to another government as the power with which to have dealings concerning a given territory and its people, the only question which the recognizing government needs to ask itself is whether the government which it recognizes is a *de facto* one to the extent that it is able to fulfill the obligations laid, by accepted international law, upon a government which asks international recognition as the power internationally responsible for what takes place within the territory over which it claims primary political control. President Wilson, therefore, went beyond the ordinary requirement of international practice, when, in the early part of his first administration, he declared that he would give international recognition to no government that might be established in Mexico, whatever its *de facto* control might amount to, which was not founded upon the will of the Mexican people and thus, in a constitutional sense, able to read its title clear. More recently, the American Government, through Secretary of State Hughes, has declared that, in the future, it will not give recognition to such South or Central American governments as may come into existence by the illegal or revolutionary overturning of previously existing governments. It will be remembered also, that for considerable periods of time, a number of the other governments of the world, including the United States, refused to have official dealings with the government of Greece after the return in 1920 of King Constantine. Only recently (1924) has Great Britain recognized the Soviet Government of Russia established in 1917, and a number of the other States, including France and the United States, still refuse to accord it this recognition. These instances of non-recognition are sufficient to show how discretionary, as exhibited in international practice, is the obligation of one government to give official recognition to the governments of other States. It appears, indeed, that this discretionary right is now more arbitrarily exercised than it formerly was.

States Not Concerned with the Constitutional Features of Other States. It is not merely with the juristic basis or origin of a State that other States have no concern; they are also, as a technical proposition, indifferent to its form of government, that is, to the distribution of powers amongst the several organs of government as provided for by its system of constitutional law. Each State, when it claims recognition as a member of the international society of States, asserts that it not only has the intention but that it possesses the ability, to fulfill all the duties which International Law lays upon it. Under no circumstances, then, is it permitted to plead a constitutional *non possumus* as an excuse for a failure to live up to the full measure of its international responsibilities. The application of this doctrine is of especial significance to Federal States, for it has several times happened that the United States, for example, has found itself placed in a most embarrassing international situation by reason of the fact that the provisions of its own constitutional law with reference to the powers of its individual member States has made it almost, if not quite, impossible to fulfill its international obligations. But the same difficulty can also arise in unitary States, as, for example, when, by treaty, certain obligations to another State are assumed the fulfillment of which requires legislation which the legislature refuses to enact. In all such cases it is recognized that the constitutional difficulty of the State is one that is self-created and may not be set up as an excuse for not carrying out the conventional or other obligations which its government has assumed or which are laid upon it by International Law.

It has sometimes been said that one State when dealing with another is presumed to know which organ of that other State is qualified to enter into treaties which will be constitutionally binding upon itself. Thus, for example, it has been asserted that, although the Crown in Great Britain possesses the full treaty-making power, the rulers of that country may be held to know that, in the United States, treaties, after negotiation and approval by the President and his advisers, require to be ratified by the Senate before they become constitutionally operative. This is probably a correct proposition, but it is also correct to say that, in any given case, one State is entitled to rely upon the assertion of the executive head of a State or of his plenipotentiary agent, that he is qualified to negotiate a treaty which will be immediately binding without *ad referendum* proceedings. The assertion thus made might be without constitutional warrant, but the State would none the less be internationally bound, for it could not be held that the other contracting State would be qualified or obligated to determine the question, which might be a very technical one, of the proper interpretation and application of the provisions of the other State's constitutional laws. Thus, for example, the many matters between the United States and China arising out of the Boxer troubles of 1900 were settled not by a treaty but by a *"protocol"* which, though a very important international agreement, was not submitted to the American Senate for approval. It must be assumed that those who acted on behalf of the United States assured all the other parties concerned that simple approval by the President was sufficient to bind the United States. The constitutional validity of this action has, indeed, never been contested in the United States, but had it been and had the courts of that country declared that, though termed a protocol, the agreement was, in fact, a treaty, and that, therefore, to be constitutionally binding, required the approval of the Senate, China and the other participating Powers would have a basis for a claim that whatever might be the constitutional situation according to its own municipal law, the United States was still internationally bound by the assertion of authority made by its official or organ which had acted as the agency through which negotiations with other States were to be carried on.

As a matter of fact, within recent years the Executive of China has entered into loan agreements with foreign bankers without securing the assent of the Parliament, although the Chinese Constitution has expressly declared that all such loans, in order to be legally binding, must be assented to by the legislature. It is certain, however, that, should China later attempt to deny its obligations under the loan agreements thus entered into, it would be held that it was internationally estopped from so doing by reason of the fact that the other contracting parties assumed, and were justified in assuming, that the organ of government which China held out as qualified to conduct the negotiations, had the authority which it claimed to have, namely, to act in behalf of, and to bind, the Chinese State.

The proposition, then, comes down to this: Peculiarities of constitutional structure of one State are without international significance to other States. Each State, as a member of the international society of States, has an organ of government through which it communicates with and enters into contractual and other relations with other States. Whatever undertakings are entered into by such organs are internationally binding upon the States which they represent.

Independence. In International Law "Independence" plays, in considerable measure, the part played by "Sovereignty" in Constitutional Law. In the great majority of cases a body-politic which, constitutionally speaking, has the status of a sovereign State in the international world, has also the status of an independent State. But the two ideas are not always and necessarily thus tied together. A number of illustrations will make this sufficiently plain.

In the first place, one may take the case of a colony or province which has repudiated the mother State as its *de jure* sovereign and has established a government of its own. Such a body, looked at from the point of view of its own constitutional law, is, as we have already seen, a sovereign State. It does not, however, become a State, internationally speaking, until at least one other State has accorded it recognition as such; and this may not happen for a considerable time.

Or, again, a Confederacy (*Staatenbund*), the general government of which possesses plenary powers with reference to international relations, is, indubitably, a State of international law, although, constitutionally, it has itself no existence as a sovereign State.

Viewed from this standpoint of International Law, a State is necessarily a unity. This is as true of an Empire with autonomous colonies and dependencies as it is of a Federal State or a highly centralized Confederacy. That government which holds within its hands the direction of foreign affairs will be held internationally responsible for all the claims that other Powers may have with reference to all the lands and all the peoples concerning which the given government claims authority internationally to deal. All those lands and their populations thus constitute, *ad hoc,* a single State or subject of International Law.

Thus it is that a political body which, constitutionally viewed, is a State, may not be a State in the eyes of International Law; and, conversely, a State or subject of International Law may not be a State when constitutionally regarded. In a Confederacy (*Staatenbund*) the member States, constitutionally viewed, are regarded as severally sovereign, and the instrument which unites them, though it may be termed a Constitution, is, in juridical fact, of an international contractual character. In either of these cases, however, the protecting and protected State, and the ensemble of confederated States, are deemed to constitute a single international person.

Some federally organized States permit their member States to enter into direct treaty relations with other powers. It is certain, however, that, in these cases also, the Federal State can be held responsible by other States for whatever its members may do or agree to do. Certainly, the sovereign federally organized State would not permit any foreign State to bring to bear force upon any one of its member commonwealths, for such an act would be a violation of its own territorial integrity which, of course, includes the several territories of all its member States.[4]

Another instance in which the constitutional and international conceptions of statehood do not correspond is in the case of what are known as Protectorates, or, at least, of those protectorates in which the foreign relations of the protected State are exercised by the guardian or patron State. Here, constitutionally speaking, the two States remain severally sovereign and separate from one another, and the bond which unites them is usually, in form at least, a contractual and not a legal one. [5] Inter-

[4] Upon the status of composite international persons Oppenheim writes: "Since it is always the Federal State which is competent to declare war, make peace, conclude treaties of alliance, and other political treaties, and send and receive diplomatic envoys, whereas no member-State can of itself declare war against a foreign State, make peace, conclude alliances or other political treaties, the Federal State, if recognized, is certainly itself an International Person, with all the rights and duties of a sovereign member of the Family of Nations. On the other hand, the international position of the member-States is not so clear. It is frequently maintained that they have totally lost their position within the Family of Nations. But this opinion cannot stand if compared with the actual facts. Thus the member-States of Germany, under the German Constitution as it existed before the World War, retained their competence to send and receive diplomatic envoys, not only in intercourse with one another, but also with foreign States. Further, the reigning monarchs of these member-States were still treated by the practice of the States as heads of sovereign States, a fact without legal basis if these States had been no longer International Persons. Thirdly, the member-States of Germany, as well as of Switzerland, retained their competence to conclude international treaties between themselves without the consent of the Federal State, and they also retained their competence to conclude international treaties with foreign States as regards matters of minor interest. If these facts are taken into consideration, one is obliged to acknowledge that the member-States of a Federal State can be International Persons in a degree. Full subjects of International Law—International Persons with all the rights and duties regularly connected with the membership of the Family of Nations—they certainly cannot be. Their position, if any, within this circle is overshadowed by their Federal State; they are part sovereign States, and they are, consequently, International Persons for some parts only." *International Law*, 3d ed., p. 89.

[5] In 1914, Great Britain, by a unilateral act, served notice upon the other Powers that it had established a protectorate over Egypt. By a similar unilateral act it terminated that protectorate in 1922.

nationally speaking, the two constitute a single State. This assertion, it may be said, is not supported by a line of established precedents, but it will be generally conceded that, where one State has within its hands the full control of the international relations of another State, other Powers will look to the dominant State, and not to the protected State for the fulfillment by it of its international obligations; and, reciprocally, it is equally certain that the guardian State will concern itself with any violation of international rights which the protected State may suffer. If this is so, then the international distinction between the two States is without real substantive content. It has, indeed, happened that where the guardian State has been at war, the protected State has been regarded as neutral. This is inconsistent with the proposition which has been here declared. Essentially speaking, however, this has been a matter of grace rather than the recognition of a technical obligation, for it may be confidently asserted that in those cases in which there is a substantial reason for declaring that the belligerency of the patron State carries with it *ex necessitate* the belligerency of the protected State, this doctrine will be applied. The logic of such a proposition is evident.

If one defines a juristic person as an entity in which legal duties and rights inhere, it would seem that there may be bodies-politic which, in the eyes of International Law, are not independent States, and which yet have a standing as persons in the international world. This occurs when, in the case of a civil war, the revolting party has been recognized as a belligerent. This gives to the belligerent a status, not as a State, but as a body-politic which, for the purposes of the war only, is entitled to exercise the rights of, and is under the obligations which apply to, States themselves when at war with one another.

At first thought it might appear that those States which, for various reasons, have not been admitted to fellowship with the members of the Family of Nations are illustrations of international persons which are not at the same time independent States. This, however, is not the case. Though these States do not have by international law an equality of rights with the other States, they are none the less sovereign States when viewed constitutionally; and are independent States when looked at internationally. For no other State claims a legal authority over them.

State Succession. It will have been seen that, to a very considerable extent, the distinction between State and Government so important to Constitutional Law, is without importance to International Law. International relations, it appears, are between governments, irrespective of their constitutional relations to the States back of and supporting them. In another sense, however, International Law may be said to have dealings only with States, for, according to its premises, the establishment of a new government in no way operates to invalidate, so far as the interests of other States are concerned, the obligations incurred or treaties entered into by the old governments. The governments succeed to one another but the State remains the same. Thus, when, by revolutionary means, one government is supplanted by another government, the new government is held responsible by the governments of other States for the acts of its predecessors, and should the former government re-establish its *de facto* control, it will be held internationally responsible for the acts of the government which it has overthrown even though, from its point of view, that government never had a legal existence. From the viewpoint of constitutional law however, the restored government need recognize the legal validity of the acts of the *de facto* government only insofar as it deems it equitable and expedient. Upon these grounds, municipal courts have held that the payment of taxes by individuals to a *de facto* government relieves those individuals from making subsequent payment to the re-established *de jure* government.[6]

The doctrine of continued State liability applies when the whole or a part of the territory of one State is taken over by another State. However, the question as to the extent to which a State which thus takes over the entire territory of another State (which State of course thereby goes out of existence) succeeds to the rights and obligations of the destroyed State as created by previous treaties or agreements with other States, is not without difficulty. Professor Max Huber who, in his *Die Staatensuccession,* has given us what is perhaps the best discussion of the fundamental principles or theory upon which the answer to the problems thus raised should be solved, lays down the following proposition.

The conception of succession is a general legal conception and belongs neither exclusively to private law nor to public law. Succession is substitution plus continuation. The successor assumes the place of the predecessor and continues his rights and obligations; to this extent public and private law are alike. There is, however, this distinction between succession in public and in private law. The private law successor steps into the place of his predecessor and takes his rights and obligations as though he were the predecessor. This, at least, according to the ruling theory is the "universal succession" in the Roman sense. The successor of International Law, however, assumes the rights and obligations of his predecessor as though they were his own. . . . When a State

---

[6] See, for example, the holding of the United States Supreme Court in the case of *United States v. Rice,* 4 Wheaton 246. Cf. Moore, *Digest of International Law,* vol. I, p. 21. This topic is more fully discussed, *post,* in chapter XX.

acquires territory, it is obtained by its own authority—it succeeds not by virtue of the authority of the former owner; its legal personality extends itself over the new area.[7]

This conclusion of Huber, it is seen, is in full agreement with the position assumed in the present treatise that one State cannot derive jurisdiction from any other source than its own sovereignty. From this conclusion it results that when new territory is acquired by a State— such territory being the whole or a part of the territory of another State—the acquiring State is, with reference to such new territory, bound by the treaties or other agreements of the original State with regard to such territory only insofar as such commitments are in consonance with the fundamental principles of its own public law.[8]

When a portion of the territory of another State is annexed which does not constitute an important part of the entire territory of the State from which it is taken, no questions of international right ordinarily arise. When, however, an obligation, such as a public debt, has been created with special reference to the area which is parted with, the question occurs whether the obligations should not be said to be appurtenant to that special area, and be carried with it, so that the annexing State may equitably be held responsible for it. This, however, is a matter that ordinarily is agreed upon, at the time of the

[7] *Op. cit.*, sec. 23.

[8] Westlake says: "The continued existence of concessions must depend on not being in conflict with the public law and policy of the annexing State, but if they are cancelled the persons interested will be entitled to such compensation as that State grants in cancelling a concession of its own." *International Law*, vol. I, p. 83. Westlake, it may be observed accepts the theory of Huber with certain qualifications, which, however, it is not necessary here to discuss. A. B. Keith, in his study entitled *The Theory of State Succession with Special Reference to English and Colonial Law* (1907), reviews the various theories which publicists have held, and himself holds that the correct doctrine is that "the annexing power seizes all the rights in the country which can be obtained by possession of the territory of the country and its material resources, but it does not succeed to the obligations of the conquered Government nor to such rights as were personal to that Government." (page 6.)

transfer, between the two States directly concerned. When, however, the part transferred constitutes, geographically or economically speaking, such an important part of the territory of the State from which it is taken, that that State, with the resources of the territory and people left to it, cannot reasonably be expected to be able to meet its previously assumed general liabilities, other States interested in the fulfillment of such liabilities are justified in interfering to the extent of demanding of the annexing State that it shall, together with the area which it had annexed, assume a proportionate part of the obligations of the parent State.

Equality of States. The members of the Family of Nations are commonly spoken of as all having the same international legal rights and duties without regard to their differences in territorial extent, population, economic resources and military strength. This, however, is not exactly correct. What is meant is that they have an equal capacity for rights. No one has made this more plain than has Professor N. D. Dickinson in his scholarly treatise, *The Equality of States in International Law*, published in 1920.

After a detailed critical and historical examination of the principle he says:

Very few publicists distinguish equal protection of the law and equal capacity for rights. Legal and political rights are almost always confounded. . . . Equality is variously described as an attribute, a right, or a principle. The first is unsatisfactory because it approaches the subject from the wrong angle, predetermines the issue, and confines discussion to pure abstractions. While equality may conceivably be an essential attribute of the theoretically perfect State, the really important consideration is the way in which the law of nations regards actually existing States. The description of equality as a right is a survival of naturalistic theories, and is quite inadequate. It leads to confusion of natural rights or essential interests with legal rights, induces unsound classifications, and raises the whole question of fundamental rights. Among a majority of the publicists equality is coming to be regarded as a principle or foundation rule, which contributes to determine the content of the mass of substantive rules of which the law of nations is composed. This description is adequate, and is free from the objections which may be made to the definition equality as a right or an attribute. . . . It is creating no end of difficulty to speak of equality of rights, as though persons could have identical rights in a world of realities. What is really meant is an equality of capacity for rights.[9]

As Professor Dickinson goes on to say, equality of capacity in municipal law applies only to those persons who are of the same juristic condition or status, and, therefore, the principle of legal equality, when recognized at all, means that all persons are entitled to the equal protection of the law, that is, they are equally entitled to be protected in the exercise of such rights as the law happens to regard them as invested with.

Equal protection of the law or equality before the law is essential to any legal system. In municipal law it is the alternative to an unguarded tyranny of magistrates. In the law of nations it is the necessary consequence of the denial of universal empire and of the claim of separate States to live together in an international society controlled by law. An equality of capacity for rights, on the other hand, is a postulate by no means essential to the rule of law. Within reasonable limitations it is commonly regarded as a desideratum, as an ideal toward which the law should seek to develop, assuming there is a certain homogeneity of characteristics among the persons included in the number of its subjects. In systems of municipal law history reveals that such an equality is never present in the rudimentary stages, and is only attained imperfectly as the law develops. It is a curious circumstance that in the law of nations what would seem to be the natural course of development has been turned about. Through the powerful influence of certain theories [natural law theories] . . . an absolute equality of capacity for rights among international persons was established as a fundamental postulate when the science was in a primitive stage. The subsequent

[9] *Op. cit.*, p. 148.

history of international relations shows a continuous struggle to impose limitations upon that equality.[10]

Of the value of a doctrine of legal equality of rights of all States as a norm to be approached as nearly as circumstances will permit, that is, as a principle to be applied in all cases except where special express, and imperative reasons otherwise provide, there would seem to be no doubt. The adoption, indeed, of some such general rule is indispensable if the rules of International Law are to be reduced to systematic and scientific statement. For it is only by starting with some such general aim, even though not absolute, proposition, that it becomes possible to deduce the particular international legal rights which the States may lay claim to, and the obligations which may be imputed to them. In fine, the rule has to be stated and then the exceptions specially justified.

Semi-Sovereignty, Suzerainty, etc. The terms Semi-Sovereignty or Part-Sovereignty, and Suzerainty have played and still play a considerable part in the literature of international jurisprudence. The attempt, however, to reduce these and similar terms to a definite juristic meaning is a hopeless one, and it is a reproach to the science of International Law that their continued use should be tolerated.

As has already been dwelt upon, the term Sovereignty should never have found lodgement in international legal nomenclature. Still more objectionable is the expression semi-sovereignty, which is a *contradictio in adjecto.* A State either is or is not sovereign. It either is or is not

[10] *Op. cit.,* p. 4. In Chapter VI of his treatise, Professor Dickinson discusses the extent to which the States of the world have, by constitutional provisions, limited their own freedom of action in foreign affairs; and, in Chapter VII, he shows the many ways in which, in actual practice, external limitations have been placed upon the equal capacity of States to exercise international legal rights. In a supplementary chapter he discusses the extent to which equality of status of all States received recognition or was denied in the treaty, drafted at Paris in 1919 between Germany and the Allies.

independent. If different political units are united by bonds which are legal they constitute parts of a single State. If the bond which unites them is of a conventional and non-constitutional character they remain severally sovereign and independent Nations.[11]

The word "suzerainty," while not bearing upon its very face the evidence of a *contradictio in adjecto,* is, nevertheless, a "term of art" even more worthless, if anything, than the term "semi-sovereignty." The term, in fact, has its proper place only in feudal law and is without significance in public law—either constitutional or international. Fortunately it is not often employed by constitutional law writers, and, in the international field, it is used rather to "save the face" of a State which has, in fact, lost its sovereignty over a portion of its territory than to fix the status of a nation to which it is applied. It will be amply sufficient if we quote the following from Cobbett: [12]

The term "subject to suzerainty" has, indeed, no fixed meaning; and is sometimes applied to communities which are not "States" in international law. But, in its most appropriate sense, it would appear to denote a State which, although once a part of the paramount State, has, as the result of agreement or disruption established itself as a separate political community, although without achieving complete independence in its international relations. The use of the term in relation to any political community is sometmes said to carry "a presumption against the possession of any given international capacity." But having regard to its numerous applications in practice, it would scarcely seem to imply any definite relation in law; whilst the question of capacity would appear to depend on the facts of each particular case. If we look to modern instances of "States under suzerainty," we shall find (1) that some possess no international capacity whatever, this being the case with the native States of India, which are officially declared to be

[11] See *ante,* chapter XIII, for a discussion of unions or associations of States.
[12] *Cases on International Law,* 3d ed., p. 59.

under the suzerainty of the Crown, but which are altogether subordinate and incapable of foreign relations; (2) that others are wholly independent, as was the case with the Kingdom of Naples in its relation to the Holy See down to 1818; and (3) that others, again, are really semi-sovereign, as was the case of Bulgaria from 1878 to 1908.[13]

[13] If desired, this subject may be further studied in the following works: Tischel, *Die Begriff der Suzeränität;* Sermagieff *De la Situation des États Mi-Souveraineä;* Boghitchevitch, *Halb-Souveränität;* and Bornhak, *Einsitige Abhangigkeitsverhältnisse unter den Modernen Staaten.* Professor R. T. Crane, in his study *The State in Constitutional and International Law* (Johns Hopkins University Studies), has, by his discussion of the various definitions given Suzerainty, shown the absolute confusion which exists with regard to the use of the term.

PART TWO

FUNDAMENTAL CONCEPTS APPLIED

CHAPTER XVIII

TERRITORIAL JURISDICTION

In this and the chapters that follow the leading cases in American and English courts will be examined in order to show the extent to which, and the manner in which, judicial application has been made of the doctrines which, in the Part One of this treatise, have been deductively obtained from the conceptions which Public Law employs. This examination will demonstrate the correctness of the assertion, made at the outset, that the doctrines of international and constitutional jurisprudence stand in such logical relations to one another, and to certain fundamental assumptions regarding the nature of the State and its legal competence, as to create bodies of coherent juristic thought.

The predication to it of Sovereignty necessarily implies that, from a standpoint of mere legal competence, the State has the power to determine, in every respect, what legal rights and obligations it will recognize with respect to itself. This means that it is legally qualified to claim either concurrent or exclusive jurisdiction over such persons and portions of the earth's surface, or the space above it as it may see fit. Each sovereign State thus has, *ex hypothesi,* the potential legal authority to subject to its legal control the entire surface of the globe and all those who dwell upon it. In other words, it is obligatory upon the judicial and executive officials of every sovereign State to recognize the validity of, and to the extent of their several actual powers, to give effect to, all declarations of policy of their respective governments, irrespective of what effect the carrying out of these policies may have upon the foreign relations of their respective States. Of course, in many cases there may arise questions as to the legal competence of the particular governmental organs or officials to issue the orders, or to enact or declare the policies involved, but these are matters wholly of constitutional limitations which the States have themselves laid upon their own governmental agencies, and do not disturb the postulate that there inheres in sovereign States the legal competence to remove these limitations if they so see fit, and thus to qualify their policy-forming or law-determining organs to assert, in behalf of themselves, whatever character or scope of jurisdiction, personal or territorial, they may deem desirable.[1]

This being the legal situation, it follows that, as long as there are a number of States, each with this unlimited potential jurisdictional competence, opportunity is provided for inter-State conflicts by reason of two or more States claiming exclusive or conflicting legal control over the same persons or the same areas. The adjustment or prevention of these conflicts is the task of international law, but the fact that the necessities of international life compel each sovereign State to refrain from the exercise, in certain respects, of a jurisdiction over persons and territory which it might, if it saw fit, bring within the scope of its legal will, does not in any wise, or to any degree, derogate from that legal omnipotency, which, from the municipal point of view, it possesses.

That the courts of a country are bound to follow the determinations of their respective governments with re-

[1] See the very valuable article by Professor Ernest Lorenzen, "Territoriality, Public Policy and the Conflict of Laws," in the *Yale Law Journal*, May, 1924, in which is pointed out the error of attempting to found systems of municipal law upon the promise that the jurisdiction of States is wholly territorial in character.

spect to the territorial extent of the jurisdiction claimed
by them is an accepted principle of the public law of all
States.

In *Foster v. Neilson*,[1a] the Supreme Court of the
United States, speaking of the existence of territorial
jurisdiction, said: "A question like this is, as has been
truly said, more a political than a legal question, and, in
its discussion, the courts of every country must respect
the pronounced will of the legislature." In *Ex parte
Cooper* [2], the same court considered itself bound by the
action of the political departments of the government in
claiming jurisdiction to an extent of fifty-nine miles from
the shores of Alaska. Most emphatic of all is the statement of the court in *Jones v. United States* [3]. In that
case, speaking for a unanimous court, Mr. Justice Gray
said:

Who is the sovereign, *de jure* or *de facto*, of a territory is not
a judicial, but a political question, the determination of which by the
legislative and executive departments of any government conclusively
binds the judges as well as all other officers, citizens and subjects
of that government. This principle has always been upheld by
this court and has been affirmed under a great variety of circumstances. . . . All courts of justice are bound to take judicial notice
of the territorial extent of the jurisdiction exercised by the Government whose laws they administer or of its recognition or denial of
the sovereignty of a foreign power, as appearing from the public
acts of the legislature and executive, although those acts are not
formally put in evidence, nor in accord with the pleadings.

Effect of Annexation on Laws of Annexed Territory. It
necessarily follows from the general principles of sovereignty that, after annexation, the laws previously
obtaining in a given territory no longer are able to draw
legal vitality from the former sovereignty, and that, in-

[1a] 2 Peters 253.
[2] 143 U. S. 472.
[3] 137 U. S. 202.

sofar as they are to continue to have legal power, they must look to the will of the new sovereign. This will may be expressed tacitly, or by affirmative expression, and as a matter of enlightened political practice, annexing States generally follow the rule that these laws, so far as they are not contrary to their own public policies, shall continue in force until expressly altered or repealed. Thus in the case of *Chicago, Rock Island and Pacific Railway Co. v. McGlinn*[4], the Supreme Court of the United States said:

The contention of the Railroad Company is that the Act of Kansas became inoperative within the Reservation upon the cession to the United States of exclusive jurisdiction over it. We are clear that this contention cannot be maintained. It is a general rule of public law, recognized and acted upon by the United States, that whenever political jurisdiction and legislative power over any territory are transferred from one nation or sovereignty to another, the municipal laws of the country, that is, laws which are intended for the protection of private rights, continue in force until abrogated or changed by the new government or sovereign. By the cession public property passes from one government to the other, but private property remains as before, and with it those municipal laws which are designed to secure its peaceful use and enjoyment. As a matter of course, all laws, ordinances, and regulations in conflict with the political character, institutions and Constitution of the new government, are at once displaced. Thus, upon a cession of political jurisdiction and legislative power—and the latter is involved in the former—to the United States, the laws of the country in support of an established religion or abridging the freedom of the press, or authorizing cruel and unusual punishments, and the like, would at once cease to be of obligatory force without any declaration to that effect;[5] and the laws of the country on other subjects would necessarily be superseded by existing laws of the new government upon the same matters.

[4] 114 U. S. 542. This case involved the cession to the United States by one of its own member-States of exclusive federal jurisdiction. The principles declared are, however, drawn from international jurisprudence.

[5] Laws of these kinds are forbidden by the United States Constitution.

In the case of the *United States v. Percheman,*[6] the Supreme Court was called upon to examine the validity of certain land grants of the Spanish governor of Florida issued prior to the annexation of that territory by the United States. In the opinion rendered by the Court, Chief Justice Marshall said:

It is very unusual, even in cases of conquest, for the conqueror to do more than displace the sovereign and assume dominion over the country. The modern usage of nations, which has become law, would be violated; that sense of justice and of right which is acknowledged and felt by the whole civilized world would be outraged, if private property should be generally confiscated, or private rights annulled. The people change their allegiance; their relation to their ancient sovereign is dissolved; but their relations to each other, and their rights of property, remain undisturbed. If this be the modern rule even in cases of conquest, who can doubt its application to the case of an amicable cession of territory.

This is strong language, but there is no suggestion that it does not lie within the legal power of the new government (subject, of course, to the limitations of its own constitutional laws) to act as it might seem fit with regard to the private as well as to the public rights of the inhabitants of annexed territories.

State Succession. In Part One of this volume the general principles governing the transfer of the obligations of a State whose territory is annexed in whole or in part by another State, have been stated and do not need to be here repeated. It will, however, be worth while to refer to the holding of the British court of King's Bench in the case of *West Rand Central Gold Mining Co. v. Rex,* decided in 1905.[7] This case is an interesting one not only as regards the matter of State Succession, but as exhibiting the nature of an "Act of State" as conceived of in English law (a topic later to be discussed) and also

[6] 7 Pet. 51.
[7] 2 K. B. 391.

as illustrating the relation of international law to the law of England. In this case, by a petition of right, the plaintiff sought to recover certain amounts of gold which, prior to the war between Great Britain and the South African Republic, had been seized by that government. The claim was that, by annexation of the Republic to Great Britain, the liability in the matter had been shifted from the former to the latter. On demurrer is was held that the petition disclosed no right which could be enforced against the King in any municipal court.

The court not only denied that there was any certainly established rule of international law requiring the assumption by a conquering and annexing State of the liabilities of an annexed State, but that, so far as such a rule could be said to be favored by international law writers, it was inconsistent with the law as recognized for many years by the English courts.

The case involved an alleged contractual liability. In the latter part of his opinion the Lord Chief Justice implied that had the interest been one based upon perfected title, especially to land, and therefore, an interest for the divesting of which affirmative state action would be required, the doctrine might have been a different one. He said: "It must not be forgotten that the obligations of conquering States with regard to private property of private individuals, particularly land as to which the title had already been perfected before the conquest or annexation, are altogether different from the obligations which arise in respect of personal rights by contract. As is said in more cases than one, cession of territory does not mean the confiscation of the property of individuals in that territory. If a particular piece of property has been conveyed to a private owner or has been pledged, or a lien has been created upon it, considerations arise which are different from those which have to be considered when the question is whether the contractual obligation of the conquered State towards individuals is to be undertaken by the conquering State."

As to the American cases [8] cited by counsel for the West Rand Co., the Chief Justice observed that they all related to landed property in annexed areas, and that, in all of them, the treaties of cession or subsequent statutes of the United States had declared that the rights of private property were to be respected, and that no question had been involved of the duty of the United States to fulfil the obligations of the former sovereignties.

Recognition of States. The same sovereign power which enables each sovereign State to determine for itself the extent of its territorial dominion, enables it to determine, in a manner conclusively binding upon its own courts, what other States it will recognize as sovereign, and the extent of their several territorial dominions. Those legally conclusive determinations are reached by the so-called political departments of government, namely, those having constitutional authority to deal with the relations of the State to other States. Furthermore, international law and practice, in agreement with national or municipal law, declares that such sovereign State must, and of a right should, determine for itself, in each particular case, whether or not recognition shall be accorded.[9]

[8] *United States v. Percheman,* 7 Pet. 51; *Mitchell v. United States,* 9 Pet. 711; *Smith v. United States,* 10 Pet. 326; *Strother v. Lucas,* 12 Pet. 410.

[9] "No new State has by International Law a right to demand recognition, although practically such recognition cannot in the long run be withheld, because without it there is no possibility of entering into intercourse with the new State. . . . History nevertheless records many cases of deferred recognition, and, apart from other proof, it becomes thereby apparent that the granting or denial of recognition is not a matter of International Law but of international practice." Oppenheim, *International Law,* vol. I, sec. 72 (2d ed.).

In *Williams v. Suffolk Insurance Co.*[10] the Supreme Court of the United States said:

Can there be any doubt that when the executive branch of the government which is charged with our foreign relations, shall, in its correspondence with a foreign nation, assume a fact in regard to the sovereignty of any island or country, it is conclusive on the judicial department? And in this view it is not material to inquire, nor is it in the province of the court to determine, whether the executive be right or wrong. It is enough to know that, in the exercise of his constitutional functions, he has decided the question. Having done this under the responsibilities which belong to him, it is obligatory on the people and government of the Union.

Earlier than this, in the case of the *Cherokee Nation v. Georgia*[11] the same court had said: "It is a rule which has been repeatedly sanctioned by this court, that the judicial department is to consider as sovereign and independent States or Nations those powers that are recognized as such by the executive and legislative departments of the government, they being more particularly entrusted with our foreign relations."

The English doctrine as to the conclusiveness, so far as the courts are concerned, of the determination of the political departments of the government is the same as that of the United States. In the case of *The Charkieh*[12] Sir Robert Fillimore took a different view, but he was expressly overruled in 1894 by the Court of Appeal in the case of *Mighell v. The Sultan of Johore,* Lord Esher, in that case, saying: "When there is an authoritative certificate of the Queen through her Minister of State as to the status of another sovereign, that, in the courts of this country, is conclusive."[13]

Recognition of Governments. The matter of the recognition of Government or heads of States as distinct from

[10] 13 Pet. 415.
[11] 5 Pet. 1.
[12] 1873, 4 A. & E. 39.
[13] L. R. 1894, 1 Q. B. 149.

the recognition of the States themselves will be discussed later on.[14]

Determination of Extent of Territorial Jurisdiction. Equally conclusive upon the courts are the determinations of the political department as to the territorial extent of the British dominion itself.

In *Regina v. Keyn*,[15] decided in 1876, one of the questions was as to the territorial jurisdiction of Great Britain over waters within three miles of her coasts. In the course of his opinion Chief Justice Cockburn said: "That such legislation [asserting jurisdiction], whether consistent with the general law of nations or not, would be binding on the tribunals of this country—leaving the question of its consistency with international law to be determined between the governments of the respective nations—can of course admit of no doubt."

In the same case Justice Brett, in a dissenting opinion—his dissent being based upon the denial of the position assumed by the majority that an affirmative act of Parliament asserting the jurisdiction and vesting in the court authority to adjudicate cases of the instant class was needed—said: "The question what is or what is not a part of the realm, is in my opinion not in general a question for a judge to decide. . . . What are the limits of the realm should in general be declared by Parliament."

So, also, the Judicial Committee of the Privy Council, the next year, in the case of *Direct United States Cable Co. v. Anglo-American Telegraph Co.*[16] said, with reference to the political status of the Bay of Conception: "Moreover, [a circumstance] which, in a British tribunal, is conclusive, the British Legislature has by act

[14] Post, chap. XX.
[15] Law Reports, 2 Ex. Div. 63. This case is often cited as *The Franconia*.
[16] 1877, 2 A. C. 394.

of Parliament declared it to be a part of the British territory."

Finally, by Section 4 of the Foreign Jurisdiction Act of 1891, the British Parliament expressly declared that whenever, in any civil or criminal proceedings, a question should be raised as to the existence of British jurisdiction, the decision of the Secretary of State should be taken as final by all tribunals.

Neutral or Belligerent Status. It has been seen that the courts of States are bound by the declarations of the so-called political departments of their own governments as to the extent of territorial jurisdiction claimed respectively by these States, and as to what foreign States are to be recognized as having sovereignty over particular foreign areas. Similarly, in times of war, all courts hold themselves bound by the decisions of their respective political departments as to whether given territories are to be regarded as having a neutral or belligerent status. The existence of a state of war between foreign States or with their own State is also a matter upon which the courts hold themselves conclusively bound by the determinations of the constitutionally competent political departments of their own governments.

Exclusiveness of Territorial Jurisdiction. That, within the area which it claims as peculiarly its own, a sovereign State will not permit, except with its own consent, the exercise of legal jurisdiction by any other State, is a principle of public law so universally advanced that it is scarcely necessary to vouch authorities in its support. It will be sufficient to give the classic statement of it by Chief Justice Marshall in the case of *The Exchange*.[17]

The jurisdiction of the nation within its own territory is necessarily exclusive and absolute. It is susceptible of no limitation not imposed by itself. Any restriction upon it, deriving validity from

[17] 7 Cranch. 116.

an external source, would imply a diminution of its sovereignty to the extent of the restriction, and an investment of that sovereignty to the same extent in that power which would impose such restriction. All exceptions, therefore, to the full and complete power of a nation within its own territories, must be traced up to the consent of the nation itself. They can flow from no other legitimate source. This consent may be either express or implied.

From this principle it follows that all those instances of what is termed extraterritorial jurisdiction which are commonly recognized by modern States, such as that pertaining to the persons of foreign sovereigns, to foreign ships of war in the ports or territorial waters of other States, the immunity of foreign diplomatic officials from local jurisdiction, etc., as well as those instances in which, in certain countries of the Levant and Eastern Asia, foreigners are suable only in the consular or other courts of their own countries and have applied to them only the laws of their own countries, are all to be deemed authorized by the express or implied consent of the local territorial sovereign.[18]

It would seem, then, that there is no necessity for the fiction, so often employed, that the public ship of a nation is to be deemed a part of the territory of the State to which it belongs, or that the residence of a diplomatic official is to be similarly viewed.[19]

[18] The juristic competency of a State to exercise extraterritorial authority will be later examined. See *post*, chap. XXII.

[19] W. E. Hall stands preëminent among English and American jurists as regards the attempt to found accepted rules of International Law upon basic juristic principles. In Chapter IV of his *International Law*, entitled "Sovereignty in Relation to the Territory of the State," with regard to the ordinarily recognized immunities which go under the name of extraterritoriality, he says: "The relation created by these immunities is usually indicated by the metaphorical term extraterritoriality, the persons and things in enjoyment of them being regarded as detached portions of the State to which they belong, moving about on the surface of foreign territory and remaining separate from it. The term is picturesque; it brings vividly before the mind one aspect at least of the relation in which an exempted person or thing stands to a foreign State; but it may be doubted whether its picturesqueness has not enabled it to seize too strongly upon the imagination. Extraterritoriality

Correlative Complete Responsibility. It scarcely needs to be said that the correlative to the claim of exclusiveness of jurisdiction is the strict accountability to which a State may be held by other States for the equitable and reasonable manner in which this jurisdiction is exercised over their own respective nationals and their property, or, indeed, with regard to any matters in which they conceive their just interests to be involved. Stated in other words, this doctrine is that no State is conceded by other States the right to plead either a *de facto* or constitutional *non possumus* as an excuse for failure to fulfill the obligations imposed upon it by generally recognized international law. From such a plea it is

has been transformed from a metaphor into a legal fact. Persons and things which are more or less exempted from local jurisdiction are said to be in law outside the State in which they are. In this form there is evidently a danger lest the significance of the conception should be exaggerated. If extraterritoriality is taken, not merely as a rough way of describing the effect of certain immunities, but as a principle of law, it becomes, or at any rate it is ready to become, an independent source of legal rule, displacing the principle of the exclusiveness of territorial sovereignty within the range of its possible operation in all cases in which practice is unsettled or contested. This course is conceivably its actual position. But the exclusiveness of territorial sovereignty is so important to international law and lies so near its root, that no doctrine which rests upon a mere fiction can be lightly assumed to have been accepted as controlling it."

After discussing the various grounds of expediency and courtesy which have led to the granting of these immunities, Hall says: "If the view that has been presented of the extent and nature of the immunities which have been hitherto discussed be correct, it is clear that the fiction of extraterritoriality is not needed to explain them, and even that its use is inconvenient. . . . The fiction is . . . inconvenient, because it gives a false notion of identity between immunities which are really distinct both in object and extent, and because no set of immunities fully corresponds with what is implied in the doctrine. Nothing in any case is gained by introducing the complexity of fiction when a practice can be sufficiently explained by reference to requirements of national life which have given rise to it; where the fiction fails even to correspond with usage, its adoption is indefensible."

The author of the present volume heartily concurs with these views.

In connection with this subject it may be said that exactness of terminology would require the use of the expression "exterritoriality" when immunity from local jurisdiction is referred to; and that "extraterritoriality" is the proper word when reference is had to the operation of municipal law outside of the territorial limits of the State creating it. In fact, however, this preciseness of terminology has not been generally attempted by International Law writers.

prevented by its claim of right to deny to all other States the exercise of jurisdiction within its own limits.

The United States has, at times, been greatly embarrassed by, but has not been able to escape from, the application of this principle, by reason of its peculiar constitutional system. Under this system it is with the National Government alone that foreign States have relations and to it alone they look for the fulfillment of international obligations, and yet, in fact, that Government has not, in all cases, had the constitutional or statutory power to protect or give adequate relief to resident aliens who have been injured by reason of the failure of state authorities to give them proper protection or, after injury, properly to punish those who have been guilty of the wrongs complained of.

Space will not permit even a brief account of the international controversies to which the United States has been a party, arising out of injuries received by aliens at the hands of mobs or in time of riots,[20] or even to discuss the embarrassing situation which arose by reason of the inability of the National Government to secure the release from the custody of the State of New York of one McLeod who was being criminally prosecuted for an act the responsibility for which had been assumed by the Government of Great Britain.[21] We may, however, quote the following from a communication of the British Foreign Office to the American Secretary of State, Daniel Webster: "Neither can Her Majesty's Gov-

[20] For instance, the New Orleans Spanish Riots of 1851, the Denver Chinese Riot of 1880, the Chinese Riot of 1885 at Rock Springs in the Territory of Wyoming, the Chinese Riot of the same year in Seattle, the lynching of Italians in 1891 at New Orleans. In these cases the United States was not willing to acknowledge in explicit language, its full international responsibility, but, in fact, in most instances at least, granted, *ex gratia,* pecuniary damages to the persons injured or to their families.

[21] As to this important case, see *British and Foreign State Papers,* vols. XXIX and XXX, and Moore, *Digest of International Law,* vol. II, p. 25, and authorities there cited.

ernment admit for a moment the validity of the doctrine . . . that the Federal Government of the United States has no power to interfere in the matter in question, and that the decision thereof must rest solely and entirely with the State of New York. With the particulars of the internal compact which may exist between the several States that compose the Union, foreign Powers have nothing to do; the relations of foreign Powers are with the aggregate Union, that Union is to them represented by the Federal Government, and of that Union the Federal Government is to them the only organ. Therefore, when a foreign State has redress to demand for a wrong done to it by any State of the Union, it is to the Federal Government, and not to the separate State that such Power must look for redress for that wrong. And such foreign Power cannot admit the plea that the separate State is an independent body over which the Federal Government has no control. It is obvious that such a doctrine, if admitted, would at once go to a dissolution of the Union so far as its relations with foreign Powers are concerned; and that Foreign Powers, in such case, instead of accrediting diplomatic agents to the Federal Government, would send such agents not to that Government, but to the Government of each separate State." [22]

[22] The American Government did not, in this case, seek to controvert the doctrine thus stated, but tried to shift the issue to a somewhat different ground. In the Cutting Case, arising in 1886, the United States took towards Mexico quite the same position that England had taken in the McLeod Case. In a careful document entitled *Report on Extraterritorial Crime and the Cutting Case*, Dr. John Bassett Moore, then Third Assistant Secretary of State, said (p. 19): "It is not proposed to discuss the extent of the control of the Federal Executive of Mexico over the authorities of the States which compose that Republic. This is a question of municipal law, which, in accordance with the rule that the authorities of a nation are the proper interpreters of its municipal regulations, may be left to the Mexican Government. But it should not be forgotten that, while a domestic difficulty may be accepted as a plea for delay, it cannot be set up as a bar to the ultimate performance of international obligations, and cannot, therefore, be held to prevent

It is seen, then, that when one Government is notified by another Government that it assumes responsibility for an act, the notified Government, as a matter of policy as well as of proper international procedure, will not attempt to hold personally responsible in its courts the individual who has committed the act, but, instead, if any issue growing out of that act is to be made, will consider the matter one to be dealt with directly between the two Governments. In other words, it is deemed a matter of comity, or of due respect to the dignity of a Government, that the propriety of acts which it has ordered or assumed responsibility for, should not be questioned in municipal courts. In the McLeod case the United States was so unfortunately circumstanced by its peculiar constitutional system it did not have the legal means of compelling the courts of one of the States of the Union to obey this direction of discontinuance. But that, as a matter of international comity, the judicial proceedings against McLeod should have been discontinued, the foreign office of the United States fully recognized. The American Secretary of State, Mr. Webster, said: "The Government of the United States entertains no doubt that after this avowal of the transaction as a public transaction authorized and undertaken by the British authorities, individuals concerned in it ought not by the principles of public law and the general usage of civilized States to be holden personally responsible in the ordinary tribunals of law for their participation in it."

Mutual Respect of States for Each Others' Sovereignty. A mutual respect by States of each other's sovereignty has led to the doctrine that the determinations of the courts of one State, when acting with regard to persons

a demand upon a Government for the fulfilment of those obligations. To hold otherwise would be to assert the supremacy of municipal regulations, and permit each nation to prescribe the measure of its international duty."

or property over whom they have obtained jurisdiction, will not be judicially questioned by the courts of other States.[23] If those other States feel themselves aggrieved by the acts of another State, whether executive or judicial, their only recourse is to diplomatic protest, and, if this fails, to force.

In *Dobree et als. v. Napier et al.*,[24] the British court held that, notwithstanding the provisions of a British Act of Parliament with regard to foreign enlistments, an action would not lie against a British citizen who, in the service of a foreign State, at peace with Great Britain, had captured upon the high seas a British vessel for breaking a blockade, and which was thereupon condemned by a prize court of the capturing State. The court said: "The sentence of a foreign court of competent jurisdiction, condemning a neutral vessel taken in war, as prize, is binding and conclusive on all the world; and no English court of law can call in question the propriety, or the grounds, of such condemnation."

This case is authority for the doctrine that acts upon the high seas done or authorized by a foreign sovereignty, and held legitimate by its courts cannot furnish ground for suits in the British courts.

In *Regina v. Lesley*,[25] decided in 1860, the Court for Crown Cases Reserved, upon the authority of *Dobree v. Napier*, held that a trespass committed on a British ship, under contract with a foreign State, while in the territorial waters of that State, and authorized by that State, could not furnish ground for an action in British courts against the trespasser; but that, upon the high seas, acts done in a British ship were to be regarded as governed by British law, and the authority of no foreign

---

[23] For a fuller discussion of this topic see *post*, chap. XVIII.
[24] 2 Bingham's New Cases 781.
[25] 29 L. J. M. C. 97.

State could extend to them so as to make them non-justiciable.

In this case it is clear that the doctrine was asserted that a State could not throw the mantle of its authorization over acts committed outside its own territorial jurisdiction. It would appear, however, that the doctrine does not apply to acts which involve more than private interests and rise to the dignity of matters of high policy, that is, where they concern questions which are normally determined by direct international dealings of States with one another, as, for example, was the fact in the McLeod Case.[26]

It is of course clear that one State has no legal authority directly to control proceedings in the courts of another State, and that, therefore, in case it desires them discontinued or otherwise controlled, it must ask the Foreign Office of the other State to cause the necessary direction to be transmitted to its judicial tribunals. It might be proper for the Government of one State to ask leave of the court of another State to intervene in a suit in order to file its statement that it assumed responsibility for an act upon which the instant proceedings were predicated, but, ordinarily, this statement would be filed by

[26] Moore, in his *Act of State in English Law*, p. 125, says: "Lesley's Case probably means no more than this: that the mere authority of the foreign sovereign, irrespective of the subject matter and the other facts of the case, does not constitute a justification, or put the matter out of court. There is, in fact, a distinction to be drawn between acts done or purporting to be done in the ordinary course of the country's law which is limited by the sovereignty of that country; and, on the other hand, acts to which we apply the term 'State' or 'high policy' or 'sovereign' which are recognizable as referable to the relations of States *inter se,* and as to which it is immaterial what is the attitude of the law of either of the countries concerned. Of the first class, the facts in Lesley's Case are an illustration. . . . . Illustrations of the second class may be found in such an avowed invasion of territory as the Jameson Raid. If in that case the British authorities had avowed and adopted the acts of Dr. Jameson and his associates, then, though a national act of invasion in the circumstances might have been treacherous and disgraceful to a civilized Power, the actual actors would not upon principle have been punishable in any court of the injured State. The classical case upon this subject is McLeod's Case."

the defendant by way of defense. In the United States the President has the authority to direct the Attorney General to cause a *nolle prosequi* to be entered in judicial proceedings, civil or criminal, instituted by the United States, but no such order of discontinuance could be issued to authorities of the States of the Union; nor, in most of the States, has the State executive such a power. In those cases, then, in which a foreign sovereign has assumed responsibility for an act, and in which the executive, federal or state, has not the legal power to control the judicial proceedings, it remains for the courts themselves to take appropriate action.

Quite different from the situation that has just been discussed is that presented when the civil liability that is sought by the plaintiff to be imposed upon the defendant is one that depends, for its existence, upon foreign law. In such a case the court has a discretionary right, the exercise of which is guided by principles of policy and international comity, as to whether or not it will recognize and enforce the liability thus accruing. Having this discretionary right, the refusal of a court to recognize and enforce the liability cannot be held to deny to the plaintiff a right to which, by law, he is entitled. It is not, therefore, a denial to him of due process of law.

It cannot, then, be contended that the obligation upon the part of one Government, at the request or demand of another Government, to discontinue judicial proceedings in its own courts against individuals who have violated its laws, has a basis of legal necessity, for, as has been said, there is no nexus between one State and the law of another State which will make it possible, legally speaking, for the first State either to control the governmental agencies of another State or to determine the legality of its acts as tested by the municipal law of that other State. It is, however, always within the political

or international right of one State to protest to another
State, and, in case that protest is not heeded, to take
whatever action it sees fit, if the judicial tribunals or
other governmental agencies of another State have taken
or are about to take action which the protesting State
deems prejudicial to its own interests or dignity, or to
the legitimate interests or dignity of its own citizens. In
such cases the point at issue is not the legality, *in sensu
strictiore,* of the action in question, but the propriety of
the exercise by the State of its sovereign rights,—a propriety that is to be determined by principles of international comity and usual international practice. Therefore, viewed simply as a principle of municipal law, as a
question of strict legal right divorced from considerations
of policy and comity, the New York State court was correct when, in the McLeod Case, it said: "England . . .
could legally impart no protection to her subjects concerned in the destruction of the *Caroline,* either as a party
to any war, to any act of public jurisdiction exercised by
way of defense, or sending her servants into a territory
at peace." And, later on in the opinion: "Whatever obligation his [the accused's] nation may be under to save
him harmless, this can be done only on the condition that
he confine himself within her territory." [27]

The McLeod case illustrates the class of cases in which
the act involved is committed within the territorial jurisdiction of the State whose courts are asked to take cognizance of it. A quite different question is presented
when the act is committed abroad and responsibility for
it assumed by the local sovereign. Here it is quite plain
that, in proceedings instituted in tribunals of another
State the *lex loci actus* should govern, and that the formal
approval of the local sovereign of an act should be deemed

---

[27] *People v. McLeod,* 1 Hill, 377, and 25 Wendell, 433; 37 *American Decisions,* 328.

conclusive of its legality as tested by the local law, and, if the subjects of other States are injured by such act they should be remitted to the political departments of their respective government for them to take such action as they may deem appropriate or feasible in the premises.

It is well established that this doctrine applies as well to acts ordered or approved by *de facto* governments as to those sanctioned by political establishments regarding whose legal status there is no question. A leading American case upon this point is *Underhill v. Hernandez*,[28] decided by the United States Supreme Court in 1897.

This case was an action brought by Underhill, an American citizen, against one Hernandez, who, while military commander, deriving his authority from a *de facto* government in Venezuela, had ordered Underhill's detention and confinement. The inferior court dismissed the action upon the ground that the act complained of had been that of the Venezuela Government, and the Supreme Court, affirming this decree, and speaking through Chief Justice Fuller, said:

Every sovereign State is bound to respect the independence of every other sovereign State, and the courts of one country will not sit in judgment on the acts of the Government of another State done within its own territory. Redress of grievances by reason of such acts must be obtained through the means open to be availed of by sovereign powers as between themselves. Nor can the principle be confined to lawful or recognized Governments, or to cases where redress can manifestly be had through public channels. The immunity of individuals from suits brought in foreign tribunals for acts done within their own States, in the exercise of governmental authority, whether as civil officers or as military commanders, must necessarily extend to the agents of Governments ruling by paramount force as a matter of fact. . . . If the party seeking to dislodge the existing Government succeeds, and the independence of the Govern-

[28] 168 U. S. 250.

ment it has set up is recognized, then the acts of such Government from the commencement of its existence are regarded as those of an independent nation. If the revolt fails of success, still, if actual war has been waged, acts of legitimate warfare cannot be made the basis of individual liability.[29]

This matter of the non-justiciability in municipal courts of acts of foreign sovereignties was again discussed by the United States Supreme Court in the case of *American Banana Co. v. United Fruit Co.*,[30] decided in 1909.

This was an action to recover damages provided for by the so-called Sherman Anti-Trust Act of 1890, and was based upon the claim that the defendant corporation had corruptly instigated the Government of Costa Rica to take action whereby the plaintiffs' properties were injured. Dismissing the complaint, the court said: "Not only were the acts of the defendant in Panama or Costa Rica not within the Sherman Act, but they were not torts of the place, and therefore were not torts at all, however contrary to the ethical and economic postulates of that statute. The substance of the complaint is that, the plantation being within the *de facto* jurisdiction of Costa Rica, that State took and keeps possession of it by virtue of its sovereign power. But a seizure by a State is not a thing that can be complained of elsewhere in the courts (*Underhill v. Hernandez*). The fact, if it be a fact, that *de jure* the estate is in Panama, does not matter in the least; sovereignty is pure fact. The fact has been recognized by the United States, and, by the implications of the bill, is assented to by Panama. The fundamental reason why persuading a sovereign power to do this or that cannot be a tort is not that the sovereign cannot be joined as defendant or because it must be as-

---

[29] Citing *U. S. v. Rice,* 4 Wheaton, 246; *Fleming v. Page,* 9 Howard, 603; *Thorington v. Smith,* 8 Wallace, 1; *Williams v. Bruffy,* 96 U. S. 176; *Ford v. Surget,* 97 U. S. 594; *Daw v. Johnson,* 100 U. S. 158.
[30] 213 U. S. 347.

sumed to be acting lawfully. . . . The fundamental reason is that it is a contradiction in terms to say that, within its jurisdiction, it is unlawful to persuade a sovereign power to bring about a result that it declares by its conduct to be desirable and proper. It does not, and foreign courts cannot, admit that the influences were improper or the results bad. It makes the persuasion lawful by its own act. The very meaning of sovereignty is that the decree of the sovereign makes law. See *Kawananakoa v. Polyblank,* 205 U. S. 349. . . . The acts of the soldiers and officials of Costa Rica are not alleged to have been without the consent of the Government, and must be taken to have been done by its order. It ratified them, at all events, and adopted and keeps the possession taken by them." [31]

In *Oetjen v. Central Leather Co.,*[32] the Supreme Court of the United States was called upon to consider the effect to be given in American courts to acts committed in Mexico under the authority of a Government which, at the time, had not been recognized as either *de facto* or *de jure* by the American Government, but which had later been so recognized. After referring to the principle that, in matter of recognition of foreign Governments the courts are conclusively bound by the determinations of the political departments of their own Government, and that recognition, when accorded, has a retroactive effect so far as concerns the acts of that Government, the Court said: "The principle that the conduct of one independent Government cannot be successfully questioned in the courts of another is as applicable to a case involving the title to property brought within the custody of a

---

[31] For a discussion of this case with reference to the possible extraterritorial force of the Sherman Act, see *post,* p. 408.
[32] 246 U. S. 297.

court, such as we have here, as it was held to be in the cases cited [33] in which claims for damages were based upon acts done in a foreign country, for it rests at last upon the highest considerations of international comity and expediency. To permit the validity of the acts of one friendly State to be re-examined and perhaps condemned by the courts of another would very certainly imperil the amicable relations between Governments and vex the peace of nations."

Aerial Jurisdiction. With the development of the art of navigating the air the extent to which it will be internationally, as well as nationally, expedient that a State should have jurisdiction over the air above its land area is a matter which as yet has not received clear determination. It does not appear, however, that the introduction of this new element into the political problem will make it necessary to change accepted fundamental notions of the State's jurisdictional powers. Before the Great War international conferences assembled at Paris and Verona with a view to seeing if all the States of the world, or a major part of them, might not come to some general agreement upon this subject and thus avoid occasions for dispute. The matter was also considered at various meetings of the Institute of International Law. At the Paris Peace Conference, in 1919, aerial jurisdiction was discussed and a convention drawn up and signed, October 13, 1919, to which the five principal Allied Powers were named as parties. The rules of this agreement apply only in times of peace, and, therefore, do not restrain the action of the parties to it in times of war either as neutrals or belligerents. But the convention does explicitly recognize, as a fundamental proposition,

---

[33] *Williams v. Bruffy*, 96 U. S. 176; *Underhill v. Hernandez*, 168 U. S. 250.

that each State has complete and exclusive jurisdiction over the air space above its land area and territorial waters.[34]

Garner [35] classifies as follows the various international law writers as regards the doctrines recommended by them for adoption by the nations of the world:

1. "Those who assert that the air is or should be absolutely free for purposes of aerial navigation by aviators of all countries."

2. "Those who assert the general principle of the freedom of the air subject to a certain right of control by the subjacent State over the superincumbent atmosphere up to a certain height. This area they call the 'territorial zone.'"

3. "Those who advocate the general principle of the freedom of the air but allow the underlying State to exercise control over it up to an indefinite height for purposes of self-protection and preservation."

4. "Those who contend for the absolute sovereignty of the underlying State for any and all purposes over the aerial domain above the territory."

5. "Those who contend for the principle of absolute sovereignty subject to the right of free passage. . . . This is the view embodied in the convention relating to international air navigation, agreed to by the representatives of the Allied and Associated Powers at the Peace Conference in 1919." [36]

The rule adopted by the Institute of International Law

[34] For a reference to the leading discussions of this topic see the third edition (1920) of Oppenheim's *International Law*, vol. I, pp. 352 et sec. Also see the article of Professor G. G. Wilson, "Aerial Jurisdiction" in the *American Political Science Review*, vol. V, p. 71 (May, 1911); G. G. Bogert, "Problems in Aviation Law" in the *Cornell Law Quarterly*, vol. VI, p. 271; and Garner, *International Law and the World War*, vol. I, p. 478, and numerous authorities there cited.

[35] *Op. cit.*, vol. I, p. 479.

[36] Garner lists the names of writers giving, respectively, their adherence to the enumerated doctrines.

in 1906 declares the air domain to be free in war as in peace, subject only to the right of underlying States to take appropriate measures to protect persons and property upon their respective soils.

Radio. The rapid development of radio communication throughout the world has rendered still more necessary an agreement of the nations upon some generally binding rules as to the use of the air for purposes of wireless operations, whether in times of peace or of war.[37]

[37] See the testimony of O. D. Young, of the Radio Corporation of America, before the Committee on Interstate Commerce of the United States Senate, 66th Congress, third session. (U. S. Government Printing Office, 1921.)

CHAPTER XIX

Citizenship. The juristic conception of the State which has been outlined emphasizes the fact that citizenship is a status imposed by the State upon such individuals as it desires to draw beneath its authority, and is not in any sense a status created by or dependent upon the consent of the citizens themselves.[1] From this it logically follows that each State is universally recognized to have the power of determining for itself who shall be deemed its subjects—whether according to the rule of *jus soli* or *jus sanguinis*, or of both; who may become its naturalized citizens, and under what conditions; what rights shall be granted to aliens, domiciled or undomiciled; who may enter or remain within its territorial borders; and whether or not the right of expatriation shall be recognized, and, if recognized, upon what conditions.

It has already been seen that it is a premise of public law that a sovereign political power has the legal authority to extend its political control over such territory and such individuals as it may see fit, and that it would thus be conceivably possible for any given State to extend its jurisdiction over all persons whomsoever. As a matter of practical fact, however, no State attempts to exercise this *plenitudo potestatis* and hence arises a distinction between those who are regarded as owing an allegiance to

[1] Credit is due to Professor R. T. Crane, now of the University of Michigan, for the clearness with which he pointed out that a citizen's allegiance to his State is in no wise to be construed as a contract between himself and the State. See Johns Hopkins University *Studies in Historical and Political Science*, Series XXV, pp. 329-330.

a given territory and those who do not. Those who are deemed to owe this allegiance are divisible into two classes. The first of these classes includes those who are deemed citizens or subjects, and who have obtained or have had imposed upon them their status as such by reason of the nationality of their parents or birth within the territorial jurisdiction of the State, or have been formally assimilated to these by adoption by the State by a process that is called "naturalization." Ordinarily, of course, this process of naturalization is one which is initiated and desired by the one thus seeking a new citizenship, but not infrequently this new citizenship is imposed without the desire or consent of the persons affected, as for example, when, by treaty or statute, the inhabitants of an annexed district are naturalized *en bloc*.

Never is it the case that one may claim citizenship as a legal right, nor may it be surrendered or in any way gotten rid of, save with the consent of the State to which it is due. This is a doctrine of public law enforced by all sovereign States.

The allegiance of citizens or subjects is thus, so far as the control over it by themselves is concerned, permanent in character, and independent of the place where they may happen to be. This legal control which a State may exercise over its own citizens whether within or without its own territorial limits has already been adverted to.

Furthermore, it is within the legal power and discretion of every State to group its own citizens into various classes and to award to the members of each special class such special public and private rights and duties as it may judge best. This, however, is a detail of a State's constitutional jurisprudence which has no bearing upon the essential nature of citizenship or allegiance. And equally immaterial upon this point is the question whether a State founds the status of citizenship upon the place of birth (*jus soli*) or the nationality of the parent or parents (*jus sanguinis*) or upon both. Also without significance are the special conditions, if any, upon which a State permits either naturalization or the renunciation of citizenship (expatriation).

Resident Aliens. The second class of persons who owe obedience to a State is made up of those persons who, though citizens of other States, are for the time being within the territorial limits of the State in question. These persons are universally held to be in genuine allegiance to this State, although it is an allegiance which lasts only so long as they remain within the borders of this State, and is somewhat qualified, in practice at least, by the rule that the local sovereignty will not compel aliens to bear arms except for the purpose of maintaining domestic order, in the benefits of which they themselves partake, or, possibly, to prevent invasion, but in no case are they required to fight against the countries of their natural allegiance.

It is, then, proper to hold that the *civitas*, or body-politic, of a State includes all persons who are within its territorial limits, as well as those of its own citizens who are beyond its borders.

The status of aliens with regard to their allegiance to the local sovereignty is not influenced by the fact whether or not they are domiciled.[2] Domiciliation, according to all developed systems of law, carries with it certain changes in the legal rights and responsibilities of the persons affected by it, but it does not increase or alter the

---

[2] "In its ordinary acceptation, a person's domicile is the place where he lives or has his home. In a strict and legal sense, that is properly the domicile of a person, where he has his true, fixed, permanent home and principal establishment, and to which, whenever he is absent, he has the intention of returning." *Anderson v. Anderson*, 42 Vt. Reports, 350. No term of actual residence is necessarily required in order to establish a domicile. It may be created the moment a person comes to a place *animo manendi*.

allegiance which the alien owes to the territorial sovereign. Nor is the existence of this allegiance placed in doubt by reason of the fact that, as a matter of international comity and expediency, a resident alien is not ordinarily called upon to perform certain military services which are, or may be, exacted of the citizen. The allegiance to the territorial sovereign which is imposed upon the resident alien finds its ethical or practical basis in the maxim *protectio trahit subjectionem et subjectio protectionem.* Thus Webster, when Secretary of State, in his report in Thrasher's case in 1851, declared:

Independently of a residence with intention to continue such a residence; independently of any domiciliation; independently of the taking of any oath of allegiance, or renouncing any former allegiance, it is well known that by the public law an alien, or a stranger born, for so long a time as he continues within the dominions of a foreign government, owes obedience to the laws of that government, and may be punished for treason or for such other causes as a native-born subject might be, unless his case is varied by some treaty stipulation.[3]

Double Citizenship. The ascription to resident aliens of allegiance to the local sovereign does not, of course, carry with it the annulment or even a temporary suspension of the allegiance due by those aliens to the States of which they may be citizens, although, as we have already seen, their native States are, as a practical fact, not able to exercise any jurisdiction over them, save with the consent of the local State.

Not simply a double allegiance, but a double primary citizenship is created when the citizens of a State which does not recognize the right of expatriation is naturalized by another State. In certain cases there may even be a triple citizenship, as, for example of

[3] Webster's Works 6, 526. For approvals of this doctrine by the United States Supreme Court, see *United States v. Carlisle,* 16 Wall 147; and *United States v. Wong Kim Ark.,* 169 U. S., 649.

a child born in England of American parents and residing later in France. And it may be possible to imagine cases, under the operation of varying municipal laws, in which the allegiance of an individual may be claimed by four or more States. It is possible for a person to be without any citizenship and thus to be an alien in whatever State he may happen to be. An illustration of this condition of statelessness is given in the *International Law Notes* for February, 1916, where it is said:

An illegitimate child born in Russia of an English mother is actually destitute of nationality because the English Common Law regards him as an alien and there is no statute to help him, while, according to Russian law, he does not acquire Russian nationality. Again, all individuals who have absolutely and finally lost their original nationality, without acquiring another, are, in fact, destitute of nationality. In Austria, for instance, one emigrating without permission of the State loses his nationality and so is destitute of nationality until he acquires another.

In practice the point is usually of little consequence, since such individuals are in most States treated in much the same way as subjects. Hall suggests the adoption of an International rule ascribing a nationality of domicile to such persons.[*]

To some writers this multiple citizenship has seemed abnormal and as indicating that the definition of citizenship has broken down. In truth, however, there is nothing that is confusing or that is logically inconsistent in this phenomenon of public law. When we revert to the fact that sovereignty, the relation of a political superior to a political inferior, is personal in character, that it is a purely legal concept, and that, as a concept, it is applicable only in the field of municipal law, and, especially, when we clearly apprehend the nature of that legal omnipotence which that legal theory predicates of the State, and distinguish this claim from exclusiveness of

[*] For other instances of "statelessness," see *Yale Law Journal*, vol. XXVII, p. 840.

territorial jurisdiction asserted in international law,—when these principles and premises are borne in mind, the difficulties conceived to surround the subject of citizenship and allegiance wholly disappear.[5]

In what has been already said, it has appeared that the essential status of the resident alien is not greatly different from that of the citizen. Such differences of rights and obligations as do exist are the creations of municipal law and are often no greater than those which exist between different classes of citizens. Thus, from the broad constitutional standpoint,the inhabitants of the Philippines, tribal Indians upon their reservations, the inhabitants of incorporated territories of the States of the Union, are all citizens or subjects of the United States. The differences in political and civil rights, however, which by the constitution and by statute separate them into distinct classes are certainly no greater or even as great as those which, in many of the States, mark off the domiciled alien from the general citizen body. And, in this connection, it may be remarked that there has been in modern times a marked and unbroken tendency among all civilized States to minimize the distinctions which municipal law creates between the citizen and the domiciled or even the undomiciled alien. Thus in England today the civil and political disqualifications of the alien, in times of peace at least, are very few and relatively unimportant; and, in a number of the States of the American Union, even the suffrage is granted to the aliens who have taken out what are called their "first papers," that is, have indicated that it is their intention to seek naturalization when their length of residence within the country, will, under federal statute, permit them to do so.

[5] Under the Aliens Restriction Act of 1914, in England, this point has been important in several cases where persons have attempted to prove that they have lost their original nationality.

Rights with Respect to Aliens. It is but reasonable that States, when they concede to other States the right to exercise jurisdiction over such of their own nationals as are within the territorial limits of such other States, should insist that those States should provide systems of law and of courts, and, in actual practice, so administer them, as to furnish substantial legal justice to alien residents. This does not mean that a State must or should extend to aliens within its borders all the civil, or, much less, all the political rights or privileges which it grants to its own citizens; but it does mean that aliens must or should be given adequate opportunity to have such legal rights as are granted to them by the local law impartially and judicially determined, and, when thus determined, protected.

Enlightened international practice during recent years has led States to grant to resident aliens most of the civil rights that are granted to their own citizens, but this has been the result of humanity and international comity, and not of a conceded juristic necessity. In other words, each sovereign State has a discretionary right to determine what, if any, civil and political rights aliens within its borders are to possess, and, indeed, whether, upon any terms, they are to be permitted to enter or remain within its borders. Thus, throughout the world, instances abound in which, for special reasons, aliens in general, or aliens of particular countries, are denied the enjoyment of specific legal rights, privileges, or immunities which the citizens of the countries in which they are freely enjoy. For instance, in the United States, the nationals of certain other countries are not allowed to enter at all. So, also, in addition to the specific civil disabilities suffered by all aliens, certain classes of aliens are not permitted to seek naturalization as American citizens, although this privilege is granted to all other resident aliens.

It is not surprising that the States whose nationals are thus selected out and denied the rights or privileges which are granted to the nationals of other States should feel aggrieved, and seek to have this inequality of treatment corrected. But, unless they are able to point to undertakings, in treaty form or otherwise, upon the part of the discriminating State, that such discrimination will not be made, the protesting States have no legal basis for complaint. There may, indeed, be a question whether they have even an ethical or economic ground of grievance. In other words, Constitutional Law recognizes the right of every sovereign State to determine not only who shall be deemed or permitted to become its own citizens, but to decide as a matter of discretionary policy what aliens, if any, shall cross its borders, and what legal rights, if any, shall be conceded to those who are tolerated within its territorial limits. And this unlimited constitutional right is reflected in the international doctrines that have been described. Publicists are therefore pretty well agreed that, prior to the Boer War, Great Britain had no legal ground of complaint against the Transvaal because of the severe restrictions laid by that Republic upon the right of British and other aliens to obtain naturalization as its citizens. Whatever other ground for complaint Great Britain may have had, she had a legal case only insofar as she could point to pertinent provisions of subsisting treaties between herself and the Transvaal.

In those countries which have not developed bodies of law and systems of courts which command the confidence of the other Powers, those other Powers, when possible, obtain by treaties the right to maintain their own courts for the trial of cases in which their own nationals are parties defendant. Where this extraterritorial jurisdiction does not exist, all States assert the right to take action, through their political departments, in cases in which they believe that their nationals have not been given full and fair hearing of their cases in foreign tribunals or have not had their rights determined in accordance with the *lex fori,* or where, as in the Cutting Case, later to be referred to,[6] it is held that the foreign courts have improperly asserted a jurisdiction over the nationals of the complaining State.[7]

It does not need to be said that the Government of one State will not, through its foreign office, make complaint to another State in all cases in which its nationals assert that the courts of that State have not properly weighed the evidence in the cases in which they have been parties, or have not correctly construed their own municipal law. It is only when it appears that there has been a gross miscarriage of justice, due to what strongly appears to be the incompetence, dishonesty, or partiality of the courts, that the Governments of the aggrieved nationals feel themselves warranted in making protest to foreign Governments because of action which their courts have taken.

"The regularity and legality of a court's practice and procedure are to be judged by the local law, which need

---

[6] *Post,* p. 413.

[7] Daniel Webster, Secretary of State, writing to the Minister of Spain, in 1843, said: "Nations are bound to maintain respectable tribunals to which the subjects of States at peace may have recourse for the redress of injuries and the maintenance of their rights. If the character of these tribunals be respectable, impartial, and independent, their decisions are to be regarded as conclusive. . . . If the tribunal be competent, if it be free from unjust influence, if it be impartial and independent, and if it have heard the case fully and fairly, its judgment is to stand as decisive of the matters before it. This principle governs in regard to the decisions of courts of common law, courts of equity, and especially courts of admiralty, whose proceedings so often affect the rights and interests of citizens of foreign States and Governments." Quoted by Moore, *Digest of International Law,* vol. II, p. 5. See also the statements of the American Secretary of the State in the Cutting Case, later to be quoted, p. 414.

not, however, manifest the liberal principles of Anglo-American law. For example, in countries in which the inquisitorial system of criminal law prevails, a fair application of the law to aliens and citizens alike removes all ground of complaint on the part of foreign countries, even of those adopting the accusatory system. Provided the system of law conforms to a reasonable standard of civilized justice and provided it is fairly administered, aliens have no cause for complaint.

"The personal acts of judges either in their private capacity or so grossly violative of their judicial functions that they may be held to be personal acts, do not entail any liability of the Government. For their private acts they are liable as other individuals." [8]

Some writers attempt to make a distinction between judgments of municipal courts which, though deemed unjust, have been reached without violation or misapplication of municipal or international law, and those which have involved violations or misapplication of law with a result that there has been a substantial denial of justice. This distinction would seem to be of value as a guiding principle, and to suggest that, as a rule, governments should confine their protests to the latter class of cases, but practically all Governments have, upon occasion, asserted the right to interpose in behalf of their nationals in extreme cases of the former class. Upon this general point, Borchard says: [9]

"While, on principle, the erroneous or merely unjust decision of a court involving no unlawfulness or irregularity in procedure should not involve the State in respon-

---

[8] Borchard, *Diplomatic Protection of Citizens Abroad,* p. 198. If the Government in question should accept the responsibility for such acts of its judges, or if there are not available to the aggrieved parties adequate judicial proceedings against judges, the matter becomes one which the Governments of the aggrieved parties can properly take cognizance of.

[9] *Diplomatic Protection of Citizens Abroad,* p. 197.

sibility, the failure of the higher courts to disapprove violations of national or international law by minor officials or other authorities fixes an international responsibility upon the State, and a flagrant or notorious injustice is not easily distinguishable from a denial of justice. Similarly, the judgment of a court in violation of a treaty or of international law serves to render the State responsible.

"It is a fundamental principle that the acts of inferior judges or courts do not render the State internationally liable when the claimant has failed to exhaust his local means of redress by judicial appeal or otherwise, for only the highest court to which a case is appealable may be considered an authority involving the responsibility of the State."

Effect of Military Occupation upon Allegiance. To what extent mere military occupation of a territory by the forces of a State, which does not claim to have permanently annexed such area to its own territory, operates to bring the persons within such occupied area under allegiance to the occupying State, deserves, perhaps, a word of discussion.

It is a doctrine of American constitutional law that mere conquest or military occupation of a territory of another State does not operate to annex such territory to the occupying State, but that the inhabitants of the occupied district, no longer receiving the protection of their native State, for the time being owe no allegiance to it, and, being under the control and protection of the victorious power, owe to that power fealty and obedience. As Chancellor Kent observes:

If a portion of the country be taken and held by conquest in war, the conqueror acquires the right of the conquered as to its dominion and government, and children born in the armies of a state, while abroad, and occupying a foreign country, are deemed to be born in the allegiance of the sovereign to whom the army belongs. It is equally the doctrine of the English common law that during such hostile occupation of a territory, and the parents adhering to the enemy as subjects *de facto,* their children, born under such a temporary dominion, are not born under the ligeance of the conquered.

And he adds that there is no reason why the same principle should not apply to the United States.[10]

In the quite early case of *United States v. Rice*[11] the effect of military possession was discussed with reference to the port of Castine, in Maine, which, for a time during the War of 1812, was in the possession of the British military forces, but, after the restoration of peace, was restored to the United States. In that case the court said:

It appears, by the pleadings, that on the first day of September, 1814, Castine was captured by the enemy, and remained in his exclusive possession, under the command and control of his military and naval forces, until after the ratification of the treaty of peace in February, 1815. . . . By the conquest and military occupation of Castine, the enemy acquired that firm possession which enabled him to exercise the fullest rights of sovereignty over that place. The sovereignty of the United States could no longer be rightfully enforced there, or be obligatory upon the inhabitants who remained and submitted to the conquerors. By the surrender the inhabitants passed under a temporary allegiance, to the British government, and were bound by such laws, and such only, as it chose to recognize and impose. From the nature of the case, no other laws could be obligatory upon them for where there is no protection or allegiance or sovereignty, there can be no claim to obedience. Castine was, therefore, during this period, so far as respected our revenue laws, to be deemed a foreign port; and goods imported into it by the inhabitants, were subject to such duties only as the British government chose to require. Such goods were in no correct sense imported into the United States. The subsequent evacuation by the enemy, and resumption of authority by the United States, did not, and could not, change the character of the previous transactions.

In *Fleming v. Page*[12] the question arose whether duties

---

[10] *Commentaries on American Law,* 6th ed., vol. II, p. 42.
[11] 4 Wheaton 246.
[12] 9 Howard 603.

levied upon goods entering the port of Tampico, Mexico, at the time it was in the military possession of the United States, were properly levied under the act of Congress laying duties upon goods imported from a foreign country. Chief Justice Taney, who rendered the opinion of the court, said:

It is true, that, when Tampico had been captured, and the State of Tamaulipas subjugated, other nations were bound to regard the country, while our possession continued, as the territory of the United States, and to respect it as such. For, by the laws and usages of nations, conquest is a valid title, while the victor maintains the exclusive possession of the captured country. The citizens of no other nation, therefore, had a right to enter it without the permission of the American authorities, nor to hold intercourse with its inhabitants, nor to trade with them. As regarded all other nations, it was a part of the United States, and belonged to them exclusively, as the territory included in our established boundaries.

But yet it was not a part of this Union. For every nation which acquires territory by treaty or conquest, holds it according to its own institutions and laws. And the relation in which the port of Tampico stood to the United States while it was occupied by their arms did not depend upon the laws of nations, but upon our own Constitution and acts of Congress. The power of the President under which Tampico and the State of Tamaulipas were conquered and held in subjection was simply that of a military commander prosecuting a war waged against a public enemy by the authority of his government. And the country from which these goods were imported was invaded and subdued, and occupied as the territory of a foreign hostile nation, as a portion of Mexico, and was held in possession in order to distress and harass the enemy. While it was occupied by our troops, they were in an enemy's country, and not in their own; the inhabitants were still foreigners and enemies, and owed to the United States nothing more than the submission and obedience, sometimes called temporary allegiance, which is due from a conquered enemy, when he surrenders to a force which he is unable to resist. But the boundaries of the United States, as they existed when war was declared against Mexico, were not extended by the conquest; nor could they be regulated by the varying incidents of war, and be enlarged or diminished as the armies on either side advanced or retreated. They remained unchanged. And

every place which was out of the limits of the United States, as
previously established by the political authorities of the government,
was still foreign; nor did our laws extend over it. Tampico was
therefore, a foreign port when this shipment was made.

Upon first thought it may appear that the doctrine
declared in *Fleming v. Page* is not in harmony with that
uttered in *United States v. Rice,* for, in the former case,
it was held that mere military occupation was not sufficient to annex the territory occupied to the United
States, whereas, in the latter case, it was declared that
military occupation by the forces of another state did
not operate to render the port foreign to the United
States. If these two decisions had been given by an international tribunal, and had had reference to the status
of the territories viewed internationally, they undoubtedly would have been inharmonious. Looked at
from the international side, a country belongs to that
power which is in effective control of it. Thus viewed,
therefore, Castine belonged to Great Britain while its
military forces were in paramount control of it. In like
manner, Tampico, viewed internationally, was a port of
the United States, and other States would have held the
United States responsible for anything that might have
occurred there while it was in possession. But when, as
was the case both in *United States v. Rice* and *Fleming
v. Page,* the question was purely one of domestic municipal law, it was within the province of the Supreme
Court to determine in each case the status of the territory
concerned according to the peculiar municipal or constitutional law which it was interpreting and applying. In
other words, in the *Fleming v. Page* case the Supreme
Court would not have been justified in declaring that
Tampico did not, during American occupancy, belong to
the United States in an international sense; whereas it
was justified in holding that, from the viewpoint of

American constitutional law, it was not a part of the
United States, any more than, for example, was Cuba
during the time of its administration by American
authorities.[13]

During the Great War the armed forces of Germany
were in occupation of all the territories of Serbia and
Montenegro. The question may be asked as to what
international status these States had during this period
of occupation. The answer is that, remembering that it
lies within the right of each International State to determine the other States which it will recognize as co-
equals with itself in the family of nations, it is certain
that as long as Serbia and Montenegro were in the com-

---

[13] For further discussion by the United States Supreme Court of the
cases referred to in the text see *De Lima v. Bidwell*, 182 U. S. 1. In
Neeley v. Henkel (180 U. S. 109), with reference to the status of Cuba
during American occupation, the Supreme Court said: "Cuba is none
the less foreign territory, within the meaning of the act of Congress,
because it is under a military governor appointed by and representing
the President in the work of assisting the inhabitants of that island
to establish a government of their own, under which, as a free and
independent people, they may control their own affairs without interference by other nations. The occupancy of the island by the troops
of the United States was the necessary result of the war. That result
could not have been avoided by the United States consistently with
the principles of international law or with its obligations to the people
of Cuba.

"It is true that as between Spain and the United States—indeed, as
between the United States and all foreign nations—Cuba, upon the
cessation of hostilities with Spain and after the treaty of Paris, was to
be treated as if it were conquered territory. But as between the United
States and Cuba that island is territory held in trust for the inhabitants of Cuba, to whom it rightfully belongs, and to whose exclusive
control it will be surrendered when a stable government shall have
been established by their voluntary action."

In *Dooley v. United States* (182 U. S. 222), one of the "Insular Cases"
decided in 1901, the doctrine of *Fleming v. Page* was applied in fixing
the status of Porto Rico while under the military government of the
United States, but prior to the ratification of the treaty of peace ceding
the island to the United States. The court said: "[During this
period] the United States and Porto Rico were still foreign countries
with respect to each other, and the same right which authorized us to
exact duties upon merchandise imported from Porto Rico to the United
States authorized the military commander in Porto Rico to exact duties
upon goods imported into that island from the United States. The fact
that, notwithstanding the military occupation of the United States,
Porto Rico remained a foreign country within the revenue laws, is
established by the case of *Fleming v. Page*."

plete military occupation of Germany, that country would not admit that these countries were international States *in esse;* although, if there was no intention of ultimate annexation, Germany might have admitted that they were international persons *in posse.* Certainly, however, the allies of Serbia and Montenegro would have continued to recognize their international existence. But this would have been not because they asserted that an international State could exist without territory but because they regarded Serbia and Montenegro as still entitled to the territories of which the Germans were in *de facto* but not in *de jure* occupation. In the case under consideration, the view of the allies would have been that the *de facto* military occupation by the Germans was a temporary and tentative one.

CHAPTER XX

Distinct from the question of the recognition by one State of another body-politic as a sovereign and independent State, is the question as to recognition of a given political organization as the Government of that independent entity. Here, as in the case of the recognition of the State itself, the matter is one for the determination of the political departments of the recognizing or non-recognizing Governments, according to their judgment as to what the facts warrant or their own public policies dictate.

The question as to the *locus standi* of foreign Governments is raised in the courts of other Governments when they are called upon to consider the right of the foreign Governments to sue, or their liability to be sued, and when the legal effect to be given to their acts is in question.

De Facto and De Jure Governments. In Part One of the present volume [1] the distinction between *de facto* and *de jure* Governments was discussed from the standpoint of municipal law, and the point emphasized that a given Government may be regarded as merely *de facto* if looked at from the point of view of those who deny its legal legitimacy, while it may properly be declared to be *de jure* in character when considered from the point of view of those who support it. When, then, a Government is spoken of as *de facto* merely, it is always to be understood, in municipal law, that it is viewed from the stand-

[1] P. 178.

point of those who give their adherence to another Government as the only political organization entitled, as of legal right, to exercise authority over the territories and persons concerned. In the present chapter we shall examine more carefully the legal deductions to be drawn from this distinction between *de facto* and *de jure* Governments, and also consider the significance of this distinction within the realm of international relations.

Varieties of De Facto Governments Municipally Viewed. The questions that arise in national or municipal law as to the legal effect to be attached to Governments which have maintained for a time, or in particular areas, a *de facto* political control in opposition to the *de jure* Government are illustrated in the two cases of *Thorington v. Smith* [2] and *Williams v. Bruffy*,[3] decided by the Supreme Court of the United States, and from whose opinion quotations of considerable length are justified.

In *Thorington v. Smith* the chief question before the court was as to whether a contract for the payment of Confederate notes, made during the Civil War, between private parties residing within the Confederate States, should be enforced in the courts of the United States. In the course of its opinion the court said:

There are several degrees of what is called *de facto* government. Such a government, in its highest degree, assumes a character very closely resembling that of a lawful government. This is when the usurping government expels the regular authorities from their customary seats and functions, and establishes itself in their place, and so becomes the actual government of a country. The distinguishing characteristic of such a government is, that adherents to it in war against the government *de jure* do not incur the penalties of treason; and under certain limitations, obligations assumed by it in behalf of the country, or otherwise, will, in general, be respected by the government *de jure* when restored. It is very certain that the Confederate Government was never acknowledged by the United States

[2] 8 Wall. 1.
[3] 96 U. S. 176.

as a *de facto* government in this sense. Nor was it acknowledged as such by other powers. No treaty was made with it by any civilized States. No obligations of a national character were created by it, binding after its dissolution, on the States which it represented, or on the National Government. From a very early period of the Civil War to its close, it was regarded as simply the military representative of the insurrection against the authority of the United States.

But there is another description of government, called also by publicists a government *de facto,* but which might, perhaps, be more aptly denominated a government of paramount force. Its distinguishing characteristics are (1) that its existence is maintained by active military power within the Territories, and against the rightful authority of an established and lawful government; and (2) that while it exists, it must necessarily be obeyed in civil matters by private citizens who, by acts of obedience, rendered in submission to such force, do not become responsible, as wrongdoers, for those acts, though not warranted by the laws of the rightful government. Actual governments of this sort are established over districts differing greatly in extent and conditions. They are usually administered directly by military authority, but they may be administered also by civil authority, supported more or less directly by military force. One example of this sort of government is found in the case of Castine, in Maine, reduced to British possession during the war of 1812. . . . A like example is found in the case of Tampico, occupied during the war with Mexico by the troops of the United States. It was determined by this court, in Fleming v. Page (9 How. 603; 13 L. ed. 276), that although Tampico did not become a part of the United States in consequence of that occupation, still, having come together with the whole State of Tamaulipas, of which it was part, into the exclusive possession of the national forces, it must be regarded and respected by other nations as the territory of the United States. These were cases of temporary possession of territory by lawful and regular governments at war with the country of which the territory so possessed was part. The central government established for the insurgent States differed from the temporary governments at Castine and Tampico in the circumstance that its authority did not originate in lawful acts of regular war, but it was not, on that account, less actual or less supreme. And we think that it must be classed among the governments of which these are examples. It is to be observed that the rights and obligations of a belligerent were conceded to it, in its military character, very soon after the war began, from motives of humanity and expediency by the United States. The whole territory controlled by it was thereafter held to be enemies' territory, and the inhabitants of that territory were held, in most respects, for enemies. To the extent, then, of actual supremacy, however unlawfully gained, in all matters of government within its military lines, the power of the insurgent government cannot be questioned. That supremacy did not justify acts of hostility to the United States. How far it should excuse them must be left to the lawful government upon the re-establishment of its authority. But it made obedience to its authority, in civil and local matters, not only a necessity but a duty. Without such obedience, civil order was impossible.

After describing the Confederate Government established, and the actual control exercised by, the insurgent States, the court said:

It was by this Government, exercising its power throughout an immense territory, that the Confederate notes were issued early in the war, and these notes in a short time became almost exclusively the currency of the insurgent States. As contracts in themselves, except in the contingency of successful revolution, these notes were nullities, for, except in that event, there could be no payer. . . . While the war lasted, however, they had a certain contingent value, and were used as money in nearly all the business transactions of millions of people. They must be regarded, therefore, as a currency imposed on the community by irresistible force. . . . Contracts stipulating for payment in this currency . . . have no necessary relations to the hostile Government. . . . They are transactions in the ordinary course of civil society, and, though they may indirectly and remotely promote the ends of unlawful Government, are without blame, except when proved to have been entered into with actual intent to further invasion or insurrection. We cannot doubt that such contracts should be enforced in the courts of the United States, after the restoration of peace, to the extent of their just obligation.

In the case of *Williams v. Bruffy*,[4] the Court was called upon to consider the legal effect to be given to a sequestration during the Civil War, by the Confederate Gov

[4] 96 U. S. 176.

ernment of a debt. Speaking of *de facto* Governments, the court said that they are of two kinds:

One of them is such as exists after it has expelled the regularly constituted authorities from the seats of power and the public offices, and established its own functionaries in their places, so as to represent in fact the sovereignty of the Nation. Such was the Government of England under the Commonwealth established upon the execution of the King and the overthrow of the Loyalists. As far as other nations are concerned, such a Government is treated as, in most respects, possessing rightful authority; its contracts and treaties are usually enforced; its acquisitions are retained; its legislation is in general recognized; and the rights acquired under it are, with few exceptions, respected after the restoration of the authorities which were expelled. . . . But the Confederate Government was not of this kind. It never represented the nation, it never entered into any treaties, nor was it ever recognized as that of an independent power. It collected an immense military force and temporarily expelled the authorities of the United States from the territory over which it exercised an usurped dominion: but in that expulsion the United States never acquiesced; on the contrary, they immediately resorted to similar force to regain possession of that territory and re-establish their authority, and they continued to use such force until they succeeded. . . .

The other kind of *de facto* governments . . . is such as exists where a portion of the inhabitants of a country have separated themselves from the parent State and established an independent Government. The validity of its acts, both against the parent State and its citizens or subjects, depends entirely upon its ultimate success. If it fail to establish itself permanently, all such acts perish with it. If it succeeded, and became recognized, its acts from the commencement of its existence are upheld as those of an independent nation. Such was the case of the State Governments under the old Confederation on their separation from the British Crown—no case has been cited in argument, and we think none can be found, in which the acts of a portion of a State unsuccessfully attempting to establish a separate revolutionary government have been sustained as a matter of legal right.

Referring to its holding in *Thorington v. Smith*,[5] the

[5] 8 Wall 1.

court said that all that had been held in that case was that, while the Confederate Government exercised actual supremacy of force in a given territory, obedience to its authority by the inhabitants of that territory was a matter of necessity, and, in the interest of order, a duty; but that no concession was made by the court as to the rightfulness of the authority exercised. So, also, in the *Prize Cases*,[6] all that had been recognized was that the Confederate forces should be treated as belligerents, and that a state of war existed such as warranted the treatment of the territory of the States in secession as enemy territory and its inhabitants as enemies, and their property on the high seas as subject to capture.

In *The Lilla*,[7] a District Court of the United States, sitting in admiralty, refused, in 1862, to admit that the Confederates in the American Civil War had established a Government to whose acts the United States Court could be called upon to attach a legal validity. It is true, said Judge Sprague, the Confederates were treated in some respects as belligerents, and therefore, their Government recognized as a *de facto* one for belligerent purposes, but, as held in the case of *The Amy Warwick*,[8] this did not import an abandonment by the United States of its claim of continued sovereignty over the areas and the inhabitants of the States which had attempted to secede from the Union. "Most assuredly," he said, "I shall not recognize the Southern Confederates as a nation or as having a government competent to establish prize courts. No proceedings of any such supposed tribunals can have any validity here, and a sale under them would convey no title to the purchaser, nor would it confer upon him any right to give a title to others."

Status of Conquered Domestic Territory. In *New Or-*

[6] 2 Beacks 635.
[7] 2 Spr. 177, Fed. Cas. no. 8348.
[8] 2 Spr. 123, Fed. Cas. no. 341.

leans v. New York Mail Steamship Co.[9] was considered the status of territory of the Southern Confederacy which had been conquered by the federal forces. The court held that the federal forces in possession might exercise the same absolute authority as in the case of territory conquered from a foreign State. The court said:

"Although the city of New Orleans was conquered or taken possession of in a civil war waged on the part of the United States to put down an insurrection and restore the supremacy of the National Government in the Confederate States, that Government had the same power and rights in territory held by conquest as if the territory had belonged to a foreign country, and had been subjugated in a foreign war. The *Prize Cases,* 2 Black 635; *Mrs. Alexander's Cotton,* 2 Wall. 404; *Mauren v. Ins. Co.,* 6 Wall. 1. In such cases the conquering power has a right to displace the pre-existing authority, and to assume, to such extent as it may deem proper, the exercise by itself of all the powers and functions of government. It may appoint all the necessary officers and clothe them with designated powers, larger or smaller, according to its pleasure. It may prescribe the revenues to be paid, and apply them to its own use or otherwise. It may do anything necessary to strengthen itself and weaken the enemy. There is no limit to the powers that may be exerted in such cases, save those which are found in the laws and usages of war. These principles have the sanction of all publicists who have considered the subject. They have been repeatedly recognized and applied by this court. *Cross v. Harrison,* 16 How. 164; *Leitensdorfer v. Webb,* 20 How. 176; *The Grapeshot,* 9 Wall. 129. In the case last cited the President had, by Proclamation, established in New Orleans a Provisional Court for the State of Louisiana, and defined its jurisdic-

[9] 20 Wall. 387; 22 L. ed. 354.

tion. This court held the Proclamation a rightful exercise of the power of the Executive, the court valid, and its decrees binding upon the parties brought before it. In such cases the laws of war take the place of the Constitution and laws of the United States as applied in time of peace."

De Facto and De Jure Governments Internationally Viewed. We have now to consider the significance in international relations of the distinction between *de facto* and *de jure* Governments.

Though often referred to, and without doubt of considerable political significance, it seems clear that, in municipal courts, the question whether another Government has been recognized by their own Government as *de jure,* as distinguished from *de facto,* is juristically unimportant. Indeed there is some difficulty in determining just what significance it attached to the distinction by the departments of government which control the foreign relations of States. Certain it is that when a Government "recognizes" another Government as either *de facto* or *de jure,* there is no pronouncement upon its part as to the legality of the steps by means of which that Government may have come into existence. Thus, as Oppenheim says: "Recognition of a new head of a State by no means implies the recognition of such head as the legitimate head of that State. Recognition is, in fact, nothing else than the declaration of other States that they are ready to deal with a certain individual as the highest organ of a particular State, without prejudice to the question whether such individual is, or is not, to be considered as the legitimate head of that State." [10]

The writer has not succeeded in finding an official or

---

[10] *International Law,* 3d ed., vol I, p. 528. Oppenheim here speaks of a head of a State, but as to the point under discussion there is no distinction between recognition of him and that of the Government he represents.

even quasi-official statement of just what is held to be the nature or political importance of the distinction between the recognition by one Government as *de facto* or as *de jure* in character, but it would appear that, from the point of view of another Government, a Government is regarded as *de jure* when it is given full and, presumably, permanent recognition as the organization qualified to speak and act for the territory and people over whom it claims jurisdiction, and especially when a particular individual is formally recognized as the titular head of that Government. Thus it has been officially held that the then existing Government of Mexico was recognized by the United States, October 19, 1915, as *de facto* in character, and, on August 31, 1917, as *de jure* when Carranza was recognized as its President.[11]

However, there have often occurred cases in which one Government, in order to show its displeasure with regard to something done by another Government, has with-

[11] On October 19, 1915, the American Secretary of State, in a letter to the representative of the Mexican Government, said:

"MY DEAR MR. ARREDONDO: It is my pleasure to inform you that the President of the United States takes this opportunity of extending recognition to the *de facto* government of Mexico, of which Gen. Venustiano Carranza is the Chief Executive.

"The Government of the United States will be pleased to receive formally in Washington a diplomatic representative of the *de facto* government as soon as it shall please Gen. Carranza to designate and appoint such representative; and, reciprocally, the Government of the United States will accredit to the *de facto* government a diplomatic representative as soon as the President has had opportunity to designate such representative."

On August 31, 1917, the President of the United States, communicating directly with General Carranza, and addressing him as President of the United Mexican States, said:

"Great and Good Friend:

"I have received the letter of the 1st of May last, in which Your Excellency announced your assumption of the Presidency of the Republic and your entrance upon the duties of the office.

"I cordially reciprocate the sentiments you express for the continuance of the friendly relations which have heretofore existed between the United States of America and the United Mexican States, and I assure Your Excellency of my best wishes for your personal welfare and for the prosperity of the Republic over which you have been called to preside."

drawn for a time its diplomatic representatives from the capital or court of that other Government, without thereby indicating, or intending to indicate, that it no longer recognized that Government as the *de jure* Government of the State in question.

When a Government has come into existence by the forcible or illegal overthrow of a former Government, and, for a time, maintains its authority, but is later overthrown by the former Government which re-establishes its authority, the first Government is spoken of in municipal law, as we have seen, as having had only a *de facto* existence, but, whatever sort of recognition it may have had from other Governments, those other Governments, as we shall presently see, will hold the re-established Government or, indeed, any other future Government of the State in question, responsible for the acts of the *de facto* Government. This results from the fundamental doctrine that a sovereign State is internationally responsible for what occurs within its own territory, and for acts of those who, in fact, exercise the dominant political control. In other words, a recognized Government in being is internationally liable not only for its own acts but for those of the Governments which it has overthrown or which have preceded it. And this principle applies equally to treaties or other agreements or undertakings into which the former Governments have entered. In domestic or municipal law, however, the doctrine is a very different one, the acts of *de facto* Governments which do not attain a *de jure* status, being held wholly illegal, and, therefore not such as to furnish a basis for the claim of legal rights.

Recognition. It would appear, then, that, in international relations the distinction between *de facto* and *de jure* Governments is of little, if any, legal significance. In either case, the recognition of the Government by the political department of another Government has substantially the same effect in and upon the courts of the recognizing State. The following are some of the cases which illustrate this.

Luther v. Sago & Co.,[12] decided in 1921, was an action brought to establish the plaintiff's title to certain goods imported into England from Russia by the defendant who had bought them from the Republican Government of Russia which, in 1919, had forcibly taken the goods from the plaintiff. The plaintiff contended that the Republican Government had no legal existence as the Government of Russia, and had not been recognized as such by the British Government. As an alternative plea, he contended that the decree of the Republican Government which had ordered the confiscation of his goods was not one which, upon moral grounds, should be given legal effect to by the British courts.

When this case came on for trial, in 1920, in the Court of King's Bench, the court was informed by the British Foreign Office that the British Government had not recognized the Soviet Government as the Government of the Russian Federative Republic or of any sovereign power or State. Mr. Justice Roche, thereupon, speaking for the court, said: "I am therefore unable to recognize it, or to hold that it has sovereignty, or is able by decree to deprive the plaintiffs of their property." However, by the time the case came on for a hearing in the Court of Appeal it appeared that the British Government had altered its position with regard to the Soviet Government. In a letter from the Foreign Office it was declared that the British Government had recognized the Soviet Government as the *de facto* Government of Russia, and, also that the "Provisional Government," which came into power in March, 1917, and remained in authority until

[12] 37 T. H. R. 777.

December of the same year, had been similarly recognized. The Court of Appeal thereupon, while holding that the decision of the lower Court had been a correct one in the light of the facts as they then stood, reversed its holding and held that the Soviet Government was one the legal validity of whose acts should be judicially recognized.

Attempt was made by the counsel for the respondents to draw a distinction, at least as to its retroactive effect, between the recognition of a Government as *de jure* and its recognition as *de facto* only. In his opinion Lord Justice Banks said:

"For some purpose no doubt a distinction can be drawn between the effect of the recognition by a sovereign State of one form of Government or of the other, but for the present purpose, in my opinion, no distinction can be drawn. The Government of this country having . . . recognized the Soviet Government as the Government really in possession of the powers of sovereignty in Russia, the acts of that Government must be treated by the courts of this country with all the respect due to the acts of a duly recognized foreign sovereign State."

As to the allegation that the decree of confiscation was so immoral as not to furnish a basis for rights that the courts of a foreign State could be called upon to give effect to, the Lord Justice said:

"The question before the court is not one in which the assistance of the court is asked to enforce the law of some foreign country to which legitimate objection might be taken, as in *Hope v. Hope,* 8 De Gex. Mac. and G. 731, and *Kaufman v. Gerson,* 20 Times L. R. 277 (1904), 1 K. B. 591. The question before the court is as to the title to goods lying in a foreign country [at the time of sale] which a subject of that country, being the owner of them by the law of that country, has sold under a f.o.b. contract for export to this country. The court is asked to ignore the law of the foreign country under which the vendor acquired his title, and to lend its assistance to prevent the purchaser from dealing with the goods. I do not think that any authority can be produced to support the contention."

In support of his judgment, the Lord Justice then quoted the following from the opinion of Mr. Justice Blackburn in *Santos v. Illidge* (8 C.B., N.S. 876):

"Assuming the taking to have been prohibited by a British Act, still the taking having been of property locally situated in a foreign country in a manner lawful according to the laws of that country, I apprehend that the property actually passed by the sale and vested in the purchasers, though they committed a felony according to our law by taking it. . . . Though the venders were British subjects, the validity of the transfer must, on every principle of law, depend upon the local law of Brazil and not upon that of the country of the purchaser."

In *Republic of Peru v. Peruvian Guano Co.*[13] Justice Chitty said:

One of the principal grounds relied on by the plaintiffs is that the agreement of compromise was made on behalf of the *de facto* Government of the Republic which was not the *de jure* Government. But the court is bound to take cognizance of the recognition of a *de facto* Government by the Government of this country, and it was admitted by plaintiff's counsel at the bar that the *de facto* Government was duly recognized by the Queen. So soon as it has been shown that a *de facto* Government of a foreign State has been recognized by the Government of this country, no further inquiry is permitted in a court of justice here. The court declines to investigate, and indeed has no proper means of investigating, the title of the actual Government of a foreign State which has been thus recognized. This attempted distinction between the *de*

---

[13] L. R. 36 Ch. D. 489 (1887).

facto and the *de jure* Government which runs through the statement of claim is untenable.

In *Ricaud v. American Metal Co.*[14] the Supreme Court of the United States, answering questions certified to it by a Circuit Court of Appeals, declared that the seizure, condemnation and sale of personal property in Mexico by agents of the Carranza Government, which was then seeking to overthrow the older Huerta Government, and which later was recognized by the United States as the *de facto,* and, still later, as the *de jure* Government of Mexico, operated to divest the title of an American citizen not in or a resident of Mexico when the seizure and condemnation occurred. If entitled to any redress, this citizen, it was declared, would have to seek it either in the courts of Mexico or through the political departments of the American Government. The court, speaking through Mr. Justice Clarke, said:

The revolution inaugurated by General Carranza against General Huerta proved successful, and the Government established by him has been recognized by the political department of our Government as the *de facto* and later as the *de jure* Government of Mexico, which decision binds the judges as well as all other officers and citizens of the Government. . . . This recognition is retroactive in effect and validates all the actions of the Carranza Government from the commencement of its existence. . . . It is settled that the courts will take judicial notice of such recognition as we have here, of the Carranza Government by the political department of our Government . . . and that the courts of one independent Government will not sit in judgment on the validity of the acts of another, done within its own territory. . . . This rule, however, does not deprive the courts of jurisdiction once acquired over a case. It requires only that when it is made to appear that the foreign Government has acted in a given way on the subject matter of the litigation, the details of such action or the merit of the result cannot be questioned, but must be accepted by our courts as a rule for their decision.

[14] 246 U. S. 304.   See also *Oetjen v. Central Leather* Co., 246 U. S. 297.

Local and General De Facto Governments. The international doctrine as to *de facto* Governments becomes one especially difficult to apply in the case of political organizations which, in opposition to the *de jure* governments, are able to maintain a *de facto* control over only a portion of the territory of the State concerned. In such cases they are spoken of as Local to distinguish them from General *de facto* Governments. Professor Borchard, in an able article [15] has dealt with this topic and from that article we quote the following:

A general Government *de facto*, having completely taken the place of the regularly constituted authorities in the State, binds the Nation. So far as international obligations are concerned, it represents the State. It succeeds to the debts of the regular Government it has displaced, and transmits its own obligations to succeeding titular Governments. Its loans and contracts bind the State, and the State is responsible for the governmental acts of the *de facto* authorities. In general its treaties are valid obligations of the State. It may alienate the national territory, and the judgments of the courts are admitted to be effective after its authority has ceased. An exception to these rules has occasionally been noted in the practice of some of the States of Latin America, which declare null and void the acts of a usurping *de facto* intermediary Government when the regular Government it has displaced succeeds in restoring its control. Nevertheless, acts validly undertaken in the name of the State and having an international character cannot lightly be repudiated and foreign Governments generally insist on their bending force. . . .

The responsibility of a State for the acts of a local *de facto* Government involves more delicate questions. . . . The power of such a *de facto* Government to involve the responsibility of the State depends largely upon its ultimate success, so that most of its international acts, e. g., treaties, etc., are affected with a suspensive condition. Nevertheless, even if it fails, definite executed results follow from its merely temporary possession of administrative control within a defined area.

[15] "International Pecuniary Claims Against Mexico" in the *Yale Law Journal*, March, 1917 (vol. XXVI, p. 339). In footnotes, Professor Borchard cites authorities supporting his propositions.

Thus, as Professor Borchard goes on to show, foreigners, as a matter of necessity, must submit to the jurisdiction thus exercised, and cannot be later punished or penalized by the *de jure* Government for so doing, and taxes thus paid cannot rightfully again be collected. As a general rule, however, a succeeding *de jure* Government is not liable for the debts contracted by the *de facto* Government which has been overthrown,—persons contracting with such a Government do so at their peril.

It is well established as a doctrine of International Law that when a *de jure* Government has been recognized as a belligerent by those who are in arms against it, it is thereby released from its liability to its own citizens for the acts of those in rebellion against its authority. However, it cannot thereby release itself from all responsibility to other Powers or to their citizens, for the acts of the belligerent authorities.

CHAPTER XXI

STATUS OF UNRECOGNIZED GOVERNMENTS

WHEN there exists in a foreign country a contest between two or more political organizations each claiming to be the legal Government of the State, the courts of other States will recognize that Government, if any, that has been recognized by the political departments of their own respective Governments.[1]

When, as a matter of fact, a recognized Government is overthrown, the Governments of other States may, nevertheless, continue to recognize the old, but actually defunct, Government. In such cases, the courts of those States continue to treat, as still existent in law, the old Government. This, for example, was for some years the attitude of the Government of the United States and its courts with reference to the Government of Russia which was overthrown in 1917. Thus, in *The Penza*[2], the court held that the Soviet Government of Russia could not maintain a maritime libel in the federal courts because it had not been recognized by the American Government. In that case the United States Department of State, in answer to an inquiry, had written as follows: "In reply the Department desires to inform you that the so-called

[1] "It is an axiom in international relations that a sovereign State cannot speak with two voices. For the Foreign Office to recognize a foreign community as a sovereign State, or a particular person or group of persons therein as entitled to act for that community, while the judges denied such recognition, would be an impossible situation." A. D. McNair in the *British Year Book of International Law*, 1921-1922, p. 65, "Judicial Recognition of States and Governments, and the Immunity of Public Ships."

[2] 277 Fed. Rep. 91 (1921).

Russian Federated Republic has not been recognized by the Government of the United States, nor is M. Recht recognized by it as an agent or attorney of the so-called Russian Socialist Federated Soviet Republic. The status of Mr. Bakhmetieff as Ambassador of Russia has not changed since this Department's letter to you of June 24, 1919."

A similar conclusion was reached by a New York Court in the *Russian Socialist Federated Government v. Cibrario.*[3] In this case, in affirming the judgment of the lower court, the Court of Appeals, speaking through Justice Andrews, as to the right of a government unrecognized by the political departments of the United States Government to sue in American courts, said: "We find no precedent that a Power not recognized by the United States may seek relief in our courts. Such intimations as exist are to the contrary. . . . A foreign Power brings an action in our courts not as a matter of right. Its power to do so is a creature of comity. Until such government is recognized by the United States, no such comity exists."

This decision is all the stronger in that it was rendered after the same court had held that the unrecognized Soviet Government might be sued.[4]

So, also, it was held in *Pelzer v. United Dredging Co.*[5] that an administratrix appointed by the unrecognized Government of Mexico could have no *locus standi* as plaintiff in the courts of New York.

In *Sokoloff v. National City Bank*[6] it was held by the New York Supreme Court that the defendant could not show that, by an act of the Soviet Government in Russia, the performance of an undertaking entered into by it had

---

[3] 191 N. Y. Supp. 543; 235 N. Y. 255 (March 6, 1923).
[4] *Wulfsohn v. Russian Socialist Federated Soviet Republic.* 234 N. Y. 372.
[5] 193 N. Y. Supp. 675.
[6] 119 Misc. Rep. 332 (1922).

been rendered impossible. "The impossibility of performance cannot avail the defendant," said the court, "unless such impossibility was created by act of the sovereignty, that is, by law." In the instant case, the Soviet Government had not been recognized by the political departments of the United States, and, therefore, the courts of the United States could not regard its acts as having had in Russia the force of law.

In *United States v. Trumbull*,[7] it was held that a foreign consul holding an unrevoked exequatur issued by the President of the United States must be recognized by the courts as such foreign consul even though the Government which sent him had been overthrown as a result of a successful revolution.

In *The Rogdai*[8] the court, sitting in admiralty, held that it was without jurisdiction to determine the right to a vessel, admittedly the property of the Russian Nation, as between the unrecognized Government of the so-called Soviet Republic, and the old Russian Government as represented by its duly accredited ambassador who was still recognized by the United States and still in actual possession of the vessel.

In *The Gagara*[9] the status of the provisional Government of Esthonia was raised in an English court. In response to an inquiry addressed to it by the court, the British Foreign Office declared that Great Britain had, with certain reservations, recognized the Esthonian Government as a *de facto* and independent body, and had received certain persons as its formal diplomatic representatives, and that it was the opinion of the British Government that the Esthonian Government was qualified to establish a prize court. The court thereupon held that a writ of arrest on behalf of former Russian owners

[7] 48 Fed. Rep. 94.
[8] 278 Fed. Rep. 294 (1920).
[9] 88 L. J. P. 101 (1919).

of a vessel, then in British waters, that had been seized and condemned as a prize of war by the Esthonian Republic, should be vacated.

In *The Annette* [10], decided at the same time, the status of the Provisional Government at Archangel was in question. Here the British Foreign Office had advised the court that "The Provisional Government of Northern Russia is composed of Russian groups who do not recognize the authority of the Russian Central Soviet Government established at Moscow. The seat of the Government is Archangel, and it extends its authority over the territory surrounding that port, and to the west of the White Sea up to the Finnish border. As the title assumed by that Government indicates, it is merely provisional in nature, and has not been formally recognized either by His Majesty's Government or by the Allied Powers as the Government of a sovereign independent State. His Majesty's Government and the Allied Powers are, however, at the present moment co-operating with the Provisional Government in the opposition which that Government is making to the forces of the Russian Soviet Government, who are engaged in aggressive operations against it, and are represented at Archangel by a British Commissioner. The representative of the Provisional Government in London is Monseiur Nabakoff, through whom His Majesty's Government conducts communications with the Archangel Provisional Government."

In the light of this communication the court held that the Archangel Government had not been so recognized as to give it a judicial *locus standi*.

Professor Borchard has criticized the holding of the New York court in *The Russian Socialist Federated Soviet Republic v. Cibrario* (*supra*) upon the ground that there are judicial means of proving the existence of a Govern-

[10] 88 L. J. P. 107 (1919).

ment other than by political recognition, and, in support of this contention, cites the early case of *Yrissarri v. Clement* [11] in which Chief Justice Best, in his opinion, had said: "If a foreign State is recognized by this country, it is not necessary to prove that it is an existing State; but if it is not so recognized, such proof becomes necessary. There are hundreds in India, and elsewhere, that are existing States, though not recognized. I take the rule to be this,—if a body of persons assemble together to protect themselves, and support their independence, and make laws, and have courts of justice, that is evidence of their being a State. We have had, certainly, some evidence here today that these provinces [Chili] formerly belonged to Spain; but it would be a strong thing to say, that because they once belonged, therefore they must always belong. We have recognized lately some of these States. It makes no difference whether they formerly belonged to Spain, if they do not continue to acknowledge it, and are in possession of a force sufficient to support themselves in opposition to it."

As has been seen from cases already cited, the position of the court in this case is scarcely in harmony with the body of judicial opinion. However, there is force in the statement of Professor Borchard that "where the plaintiff *de facto* Government does not claim as the legal successor of a prior government or as the legitimate Government between two opposing factions, but as the legal owner of property in its own right, it would seem that political recognition is immaterial. If it can prove its existence as a *de facto* Government and a property owner and its title to the property claimed, there seems to be no valid reason why it should not receive the aid of the courts in the protection of its property."

In *Wulfsohn v. Russian Socialist Federated Soviet Re-*

[11] 2 Car. & P. 223 (1825).

public,[12] an action for damages for seizing and converting to its own use goods of the plaintiff, a lower court of New York held that the unrecognized Soviet Republic could be sued even though it could not sue or have any of the other immunities of a sovereign State. In other words, the court conceded that, though unrecognized, the Soviet Government had a *de facto* existence. Judge Rich said:

"It is my opinion that the defendant is not entitled to immunity from suit, it is a foreign corporation aggregate, and, as such, for the time being, because it is representing the people of Russia, it is legal entity, for whose acts the nation is responsible. Like a foreign corporation which has failed to comply with the requirements of the general corporation law and the tax law [of New York] it cannot sue in our courts, but may be sued."

However, upon appeal, the Court of Appeals,[13] reversing the lower court, held that the unrecognized Soviet Government could not be sued in an American court. This it did, not upon the proper ground that, because unrecognized by the American Government, there existed no legal entity to be sued, but upon the ground that, being admittedly the Government which, in fact, was effectively exercising the supreme political power in Russia, it was a foreign sovereign entity, which, in conformity with the general principles of international comity might not have the legal quality of its acts questioned or itself subjected, without its consent, to legal process. The Court said:

"The Russian Federated Soviet Republic is the existing *de facto* Government of Russia. This is admitted by the plaintiff. . . . The plaintiff owned a quantity of furs. They were stored in Russia, and they were confiscated by the Russian Government. Treating this act as a conversion, the present action is brought. The litigation is not, therefore, with regard to title to property situated within the jurisdiction of our courts, where the result depends upon the effect to be given to the action of some foreign Government. Under such circumstances it might be that the theory of the comity of nations would have a place.[14] A different case is presented to us. The Government itself is sued for an exercise of sovereignty within its own territories on the theory that such an act, if committed by an individual here, would be a tort under our system of municipal law. It is said that, because of nonrecognition by the United States, such an action may be maintained. There is no relation between the premises and the conclusion. The result we reach depends upon more basic considerations than recognition or non-recognition by the United States. Whether or not a Government exists, clothed with the power to enforce its authority within its own territory, obeyed by the people over whom it rules, capable of performing its duties and fulfilling the obligations of an independent Power, able to enforce its claim by military force, is a fact, not a theory. For its recognition does not create the State, although it may be desirable. . . . Recognition may become important where the national existence of a Government created by a rebellion or otherwise becomes a political question affecting our neutrality laws, the recognition of the decrees of prize courts, and similar questions. But, except in such instances, the fact of the existence of such a government whenever it becomes material may probably be proved in other ways [15]. Here, however, we need no proof. The fact is conceded. We have an exist-

[14] Citing *The Annette*, L. R., 1919, Prob. Div. 105; *The Nueva Anna*, 6 Wh. 193; *Oetjen v. Central Leather Co.*, 246 U. S. 297; *Luther v. Sagor* (1921), 1 K. B. 456 S. C. (1921), 3 K. B. 352.

[15] Citing *Yrissarri v. Clement*, 3 *Bing.* 432; *The Charkieh*, L. R. 4 A. & E. 59. But see (the court says) *Mighell v. Sultan of Johore* (1894), 1 Q. B. 158; *Luther v. Sagor* (1921), 1 K. B. 456, 471.

ing Government, sovereign within its own territories. There, necessarily, its jurisdiction is exclusive and absolute. It is susceptible of no limitation not imposed by itself. This is a result of its independence. It may be conceded that its actions should accord with natural justice and equity. If they do not, however, our courts are not competent to review them. They may not bring a foreign sovereign before our bar, not because of comity, but because he has not submitted himself to our laws. . . . Concededly that is so as to a foreign Government that has received recognition. . . . But whether recognized or not the evil of such an attempt [to hold it amenable to suit] would be the same."

It seems quite clear to the writer that the reasoning of the Court of Appeals in this case is out of harmony with the line of judicial opinion shown in this chapter. The court, in effect, recognized the legal existence of a Government, which the court's own Government had refused to recognize. As has been above suggested the court could and should have reached the result it did reach by dismissing the action upon the ground that, in the eyes of the law, the defendant had no existence as a legal entity.

CHAPTER XXII

EXTRATERRITORIAL JURISDICTION

MOST writers do not attempt to distinguish in use between the two terms exterritorial and extraterritorial. There is, however, a clear distinction, and it is unfortunate that the latter term should so generally be used to cover the idea connoted by the former. When persons,—diplomatic officials for example,—are treated as exempt from the ordinary jurisdiction of the State within whose territory they are, there exists a situation that can properly be spoken of as exterritorial. This status has been earlier discussed. When a State asserts a jurisdiction over persons or things outside its own territorial limits, there is presented a case of extraterritoriality. It is with this type or phase of jurisdictional authority that the present chapter will be concerned, and first will be considered the actual exercise by one State of jurisdiction upon the soil of another State.

Instances of the exercise of this kind of extraterritorial jurisdiction are of two kinds, both being dependent upon the consent, express or implied, of the States in which the jurisdiction is exercised. First we have the authority exercised by the diplomatic and, in some cases, by other officials of a State when abroad, upon public vessels, and, to some extent, upon private vessels, in foreign territorial waters or ports. It has already been shown that the jurisdiction thus exercised is not inconsistent with the exclusiveness of the territorial sovereignty of the State in which it is exercised because that State gives its consent to it. It does, however, illustrate the fact that the exercise of a State's sovereign competence is not, by its very nature, confined within fixed territorial limits.

Ships in Foreign Ports. The correlative immunity from local jurisdiction that, according to general international practice, is granted to the public ships of one State in the ports or territorial waters of another State is practically complete. The immunity that is conceded to foreign merchant or other private ships is not so complete, and the obligation to grant any immunity at all appears to rest rather upon international comity than upon international law. This is not to say that States do not assert a right to extend the operations of their laws to acts committed upon their own private ships while in foreign ports or other territorial waters, but that the local sovereignties when they see fit claim a right to exercise a jurisdiction over those same ships.

The state of the law in this respect is illustrated by the case of *Regina v. Anderson*,[1] decided in 1868, in which the Court for Crown Cases Reserved asserted jurisdiction in the case of an American charged with murder committed on board a British vessel, upon which he had enlisted as a member of the crew, and while the vessel was within French territorial waters. C. J. Bovill, said:

Although the prisoner was subject to American jurisprudence as an American citizen, and to the law of France as having committed an offense within the territory of France, yet he must also be considered as subject to the jurisdiction of British law, which extends to the protection of British vessels, though in ports belonging to another country. . . . It appears that, with regard to offenses committed on board of foreign vessels within the French territory, the French Nation will not assert their police law unless invoked by the master of the vessel, or unless the offence leads to a disturbance of the peace of the port.

The two following cases are interesting as showing not only the character of questions of jurisdiction that may

[1] Cox, C. C. 198.

arise with reference to the ships of one State in the ports of another, but as having a bearing upon the control now asserted by the United States of America over foreign ships within its waters with reference to intoxicating beverages.

In *Caldwell v. Vanvlissengen*,[2] decided in 1851, the British Court of Chancery held that an alien defendant could be restrained from using upon his ship a device belonging to the plaintiff, patented by the British Government, when the ship was within British territorial waters, the ground for this holding being declared to be that an alien coming within the territorial jurisdiction of Great Britain became subject to its laws. To the suggestion that if foreign ships were prevented from using the British patented devices in British waters, without the consent of the patentee, foreign countries might, by their laws, prevent the use of such devices within their respective territorial waters, the Vice Chancellor, Sir G. T. Turner, said: "I think this argument resolves itself into a question of national policy, and it is for the legislature and not for the courts, to deal with that question: my duty is to administer the law and not to question it."

In a somewhat similar case[3] we find the United States Supreme Court saying: "We must interpret our patent laws with reference to our own Constitution and laws and judicial decisions. And the Court is of opinion that the right of property and exclusive use granted to a patentee does not extend to a foreign vessel lawfully entering one of our ports; and that the use of such improvement in the construction, fitting out, or equipment of such vessel, while she is coming into or going out of a port of the United States, is not an in-

[2] Hare, 415.
[3] *Brown v. Duchesne*, 19 How. 183.

fringement of the rights of an American patentee, provided it was placed upon her in a foreign port, and authorized by the laws of the country to which she belongs."

A careful scrutiny of this case shows that the decision turned rather upon a matter of statutory construction than upon a general principle of public law. Indeed, in the opinion we find the following: "The question depends on the construction of the patent laws. For undoubtedly every person who is found within the limits of a government, whether for temporary purposes or as a resident, is bound by its laws . . . A difficulty may sometimes arise, in determining whether a particular law applies to the citizen of a foreign country, and intended to subject him to its provision. But if the law applies to him, and embraces his case, it is unquestionably binding upon him when he is within the jurisdiction of the United States."

In this particular case, as has been seen, the Court found that the American Congress had not intended that the patent laws it had enacted should apply.

Another instance, besides that relating to intoxicating liquors, in which the United States has asserted and exercised a drastic control over the foreign ships and their crews while in American ports, is that presented by the Seaman's Act of March 4, 1915.[4] One section of this Act provides that every seaman, whether American citizen or not, on an American vessel, and on foreign vessels while in harbors of the United States, shall receive one half of the wages then earned by him at every port. In *Strathearn S. S. Co. v. Dillon*,[5] decided in 1920, the Supreme Court of the United States, upholding the validity of this provision as applied to a British subject on a British ship in an American port, said:

[4] 38 Stat. L. 164.
[5] 252 U. S. 348.

We come then to consider the contention that this construction renders the statute unconstitutional as being destructive of contract rights. But we think this contention must be decided adversely to the petitioner upon the authority of previous cases in this court. The matter was fully considered in *Patterson v. Bark Eudora*, 190 U. S. 169, in which the previous decisions of this court were reviewed, and the conclusion reached that the jurisdiction of this Government over foreign merchant vessels in our ports was such as to give authority to Congress to make provisions of the character now under consideration; that it was for this Government to determine upon what terms and conditions vessels of other countries might be permitted to enter our harbors, and to impose conditions upon the shipment of sailors in our own ports, and make them applicable to foreign as well as domestic vessels. Upon the authority of that case, and others cited in the opinion therein, we have no doubt as to the authority of Congress to pass a statute of this sort, applicable to foreign vessels in our ports and controlling the employment and payment of seamen as a condition of the right of such foreign vessels to enter and use the ports of the United States.

Extraterritorial Courts. The second kind of extraterritorial jurisdiction which a State exercises is that illustrated by the right enjoyed by States, in certain instances, to maintain judicial tribunals in other States for the trial, and, for the most part, according to its own laws, of its own nationals traveling or residing within such other States. Examples of this are the courts established and maintained until recently by Western European Powers and the United States in the Levant under the régime of "Capitulations," and in China and Siam, and, until 1899, in Japan, by express treaties with those countries.

In the case of *Ross v. McIntyre*,[6] decided in 1891, the question was whether an American citizen, tried in an extraterritorial court of the United States sitting in Japan, for a murder committed in Japan, was entitled to the benefit of the provisions of the United States Con-

[6] 140 U. S. 433. This case is sometimes cited as *In re Ross*.

stitution with reference to indictment and trial by jury.[7]
Under treaty agreements with Japan, the United States
had at that time the right to try, in its own consular
courts and according to American law, American citizens
committing offenses in Japan. The Supreme Court denied that Ross was necessarily entitled to the constitutional rights referred to, and said:

By the Constitution a government is ordained and established
"for the United States of America," and not for countries outside
of their limits. . . . The Constitution can have no operation in
another country. When, therefore, the representatives or officers
of our government are permitted to exercise authority of any kind
in another country, it must be on such conditions as the two countries may agree, the laws of neither one being obligatory upon the
other. . . . The framers of our Constitution who were fully aware
of the necessity of having judicial authority exercised by our consuls
in non-Christian countries, if commercial intercourse was to be
had with their people, never could have supposed that all the
guarantees in the administration of the law upon criminals at
home were to be transferred to such consular establishments, and
applied, before an American who had committed a felony there
could be accused and tried.

In effect, the Supreme Court, more or less coerced by a
practical necessity, decided, by what must be recognized
to be a forced construction of what were the intentions
of the framers of the Constitution, that the rights of
jury trial guaranteed to American citizens need not be
accorded them outside the territorial limits of the United
States. This being so there was no necessity for the
court to declare that the American Constitution had no
operative force outside of the United States. Such an
assertion was, in fact, both unfortunate and incorrect.
The truth is that the Constitution does, and of necessity

[7] Ross was, in fact, an English citizen and the offense was committed
on board an American merchant vessel in the port of Yokohama, but
it was held by the court that, inasmuch as Ross had enlisted as a member of the crew of the vessel, he had taken on the character of an
American citizen (without losing his English citizenship), and that the
offense was committed within Japanese jurisdiction.

must, operate throughout the world wherever official acts are committed by civil or military officials of the United States. If this were not so, such officials would *ipso facto* lose their public status and be without official authority the instant they crossed outside the territorial limits of the United States; for though their offices or appointments might not be specifically provided for in the Constitution, that instrument is the source of all legal authority that is exercised by American governmental officials. That instrument is also the ultimate source of all United States law, and, therefore, it must be deemed to operate in all those cases in which, as we have seen, the United States asserts and exercises the right to hold its citizens, or others, responsible for acts committed by them outside its borders.

Jurisdiction as to Acts Committed in Foreign Countries: General Consideration. We turn now to a consideration of the jurisdiction commonly exercised by States with reference to acts committed abroad.

The legal omnicompetence of a State within its own territory necessarily carries with it, as we have seen, a full jurisdiction over all persons within its borders, whether nationals or aliens, and whether these aliens be domiciled or only temporarily within its territory. From this general principle it results that it is within the complete legal discretion of each State to decide what legal responsibility, civil or criminal, it will impute to the acts of persons, whether nationals or aliens, over whom its courts obtain jurisdiction, and whether these acts are committed within or without the State's territory. Thus, for example, as will later appear in certain of the adjudications of American and British courts which will be reviewed, the bald fact that two aliens happen to be within the country, and are thus within the jurisdiction of the courts of that country, will warrant them in holding the aliens responsible for acts committed by them in other countries. And, *a fortiori*, similar jurisdiction is exercised when one or both of the parties to the controversy are citizens or subjects of the State where the court is sitting. It will be found that, very generally, in determining the legal character of such acts, the courts are guided by the law of the places where the acts are committed, but this is not always the case, and, when it is, it is a matter of discretion upon the part of the courts, and due merely to considerations of expediency or international comity upon the part of the States concerned.

In one sense the jurisdiction thus asserted, though with reference to acts committed abroad, is territorial rather than extraterritorial in character, since it is exercised by courts sitting within the respective territories of their several States, and always over persons over whom they have obtained control; and, furthermore, as hardly needs to be said, the judgments or decrees that are rendered are enforcible only within the territories of their respective States.[8] Nevertheless, it seems proper to de-

[8] These judgments, however, are construed to create an *obligatio* which will support a claim which the courts of other countries will enforce. Dicey, in his *Conflict of Laws* (p. 40), gives the following as a "General Principle": "The sovereign of a country acting through the courts thereof, has jurisdiction over, *i.e.*, has a right to adjudicate upon, any matter in regard to which he can give an effective judgment, and has no jurisdiction, *i.e.*, no right to adjudicate upon, any matter with regard to which he cannot give an effective judgment."

"An effective judgment means a decree which the sovereign, under whose authority it is delivered, has in fact the power to enforce against the person bound by it, and which therefore his courts can, if he choose to give them the necessary means, enforce against such person."

The only comment which the writer of this volume would make to this statement, and which would be a purely academic comment, is that it would be legally possible, but of course impracticable, for a sovereign State to give its courts jurisdiction to render decrees which either could not be enforced at all, or which, if attempted to be enforced, as, for example, within the territory of another State, would lead to protest and probable resistance upon the part of that other State. The principle stated by Dicey is undoubtedly the one followed by States as a matter of comity and expediency if not of legal necessity, at least with regard to States having reasonably effective forms of gov-

scribe as extraterritorial this exercise of jurisdiction since the indubitable effect of it is to determine by municipal law the legal character of acts or transactions committed or entered into upon foreign soil. It does not need to be said that in all these cases there is a double jurisdiction since the sovereignty of the place where these acts or transactions occur can of course control them by its laws and take cognizance of them through its courts.

However there occur dicta in decisions of the United States Supreme Court which suggest the doctrine that municipal law by its very nature cannot be held to determine the legal character of acts committed outside the territorial limits of the State concerned. It will, therefore, be necessary to consider whether these cases are, in fact, in irreconcilable conflict with the general doctrines of public law which have been arrived at in this volume.

Case of Rose v. Himely Examined. The case of *Rose v. Himely*,[9] decided in 1808 by the United States Supreme Court, is an interesting one since it raised the question whether the American courts might question the jurisdiction of a court of another State not simply upon the ground that it had not obtained sufficient jurisdiction of the parties or of the *rem* to render the judgment it had given, but because it had applied its own municipal law to a matter which municipal law, by its very nature, is not competent to control. In this case it would seem that the great Chief Justice Marshall did not exhibit his usual cogency of juristic thought.

The case arose in the following manner: While a war between France and Santo Domingo was in progress,

ernmental organization. States do often assume the right to enforce their laws and judicial decrees in those politically undeveloped countries which have no governments strong enough to make effective resistance, or which are themselves not qualified to administer effective justice.

[9] 4 Cranch 241.

the American ship *Sarah,* was seized upon the high seas by a French privateer for violation of a French municipal law, and was taken into a Cuban port and there sold by the captor. The cargo having been brought by the purchaser into American waters was there libeled in a court of admiralty by its original American owner. The purchaser defended his title by a reference to a sentence of condemnation of a French tribunal sitting in Santo Domingo pronounced after the property had been libeled in the American court, and also by the order of sale made by the agent of the French Government.

The majority of the Justices of the Supreme Court held this defense insufficient. Of these majority Justices three did so upon the ground that the seized vessel and cargo had not been immediately carried into the territorial waters of France. As to the validity of a seizure made on the high seas, under a municipal law, if the property were immediately carried into a port of the capturing vessel, they declared they expressed no opinion. Chief Justice Marshall, however, rested his concurrence in the judgment of the court upon the argument that it had not been within the sovereign power of France to extend the operation of its municipal law to the high seas; that international law did not support the jurisdiction that the French court had asserted, and that, therefore, that tribunal having been wholly without jurisdiction, its decree was to be deemed a nullity. Referring to the regulations for the violation of which the vessel and cargo had been seized and her cargo condemned, Marshall said:

Of its own jurisdiction, so far as depends on municipal rules, the courts of a foreign nation must judge, and its decision must be respected. But if it exercises a jurisdiction which, according to the law of nations, its sovereign could not confer, however available its sentences may be within the dominions of the prince from whom the authority is derived, they are not regarded by foreign courts. This distinction is taken upon this principle, that the law of nations is the law of all tribunals in the society of nations, and is supposed to be equally understood by all. It is conceded, [Marshall continued], that the legislation of every country is territorial; that, beyond its own territory, it can only affect its own subjects or citizens. It is not easy to conceive a power to execute a municipal law, or to enforce obedience to that law without the circle in which that law operates. A power to seize for the infraction of a law is derived from the Sovereign and must be exercised, it would seem, within those limits which circumscribe the sovereign power. The rights of war may be exercised on the high seas, because war is carried on upon the high seas; but the pacific rights of sovereignty must be exercised within the territory of the sovereign. If these propositions be true, a seizure of a person not a subject, or of a vessel not belonging to a subject, made on the high seas for the breach of a municipal regulation, is an act which the sovereign cannot authorize. The person who makes this seizure, then, makes it on a pretext which, if true, will not justify the act, and is a marine trespasser. To a majority of the court it seems to follow, that such a seizure is totally invalid; that the possession, acquired by this unlawful act, is his own possession, not that of the sovereign; and that such possession confers no jurisdiction on the court of the country to which the captor belongs.

In other words, that, though the foreign prize court had declared that, under its own municipal law, it had jurisdiction, the American court was not conclusively bound by that decision.

Mr. Justice Johnson dissented from the reasoning of Marshall upon grounds which he stated as follows:

A seizure on the high seas by an unauthorized individual is a mere trespass and produces no change of right; but such a seizure, made by a sovereign authority, vests the thing seized in the sovereign; for the fact of possession must have all the beneficial effects of the right of possession, as the justice or propriety of it cannot be inquired into by the courts of other nations. But as this principle might leave the unoffending individual a prey to the rapacity of cruisers, or a victim to the errors of those who even mean well, and as every civilized nation pretends to the character of justice and moderation, and to have an interest in preserving the peace of the world, they constitute courts with powers to inquire into the correctness of captures made under color of their own authority, and to give redress to those who have been unmeritedly attacked or injured. These are denominated prize courts, and the primary object of their institution is to inquire whether a taking as prize is sanctioned by the authority of their sovereign, or the unauthorized act of an individual. From this it would seem to follow, that the decision of such a court is the only legal organ of communication through which the sanction of a sovereign can be ascertained, and that no other court is at liberty to deny the existence of sovereign authority, for a seizure which a prize court has declared to be the act of its sovereign. The propriety of such an act may correctly become the subject of executive or diplomatic discussion; but the equality of nations forbids that the conduct of one sovereign, or the correctness of the principles upon which he acts, should be submitted to the jurisdiction of the courts of another. From these considerations I infer, that the capture and continued possession of *The Sarah* and her cargo, confirmed by the approbatory sentence of a court of the capturing power, vested a title in the claimant, which this court cannot, consistently with the law of nations interpose its authority to defeat.

It seems clear that, in this difference of opinion, Justice Johnson had the better of the argument. Marshall was in error when he declared that it was not competent for a State to give extraterritorial effect to its laws except as to its own subjects, and that, therefore, in order to obtain such extraterritorial jurisdiction recourse would have to be had to the principles of international law. Had Marshall not been thus misled as to the possible sphere of application of municipal law, he would almost certainly have agreed with Justice Johnson that it was not proper that the American court should differ with a foreign court as to the operation of its own municipal law upon the high seas. Even as it was, it would seem that Marshall should have felt constrained not to contest the correctness of the interpretation of a principle of international law by the foreign court, even as to a matter involving its own jurisdiction, but should have left it for the Foreign Office of the American Government to take up the matter with the other Government if it were believed that an unwarranted doctrine of international law had been applied by its court.

It is interesting to note that in the case of *Hudson and Smith v. Guestier*,[10] decided two years later, in 1810, the Supreme Court expressly overruled the doctrine of *Rose v. Himely* that a State cannot extend the force of its municipal laws to the high seas. Mr. Justice Johnson, rendering the opinion of the court, from which there was no dissent, said: "I am not able to perceive how it can be material whether the capture were made within or beyond the jurisdictional limits of France; or in the exercise of a belligerent or municipal right. By a seizure on the high seas she interfered with the jurisdiction of no other nation, the authority of each being there concurrent.[11]

The Apollon. In the case of *The Apollon*,[11] the Supreme Court of the United States, speaking through Justice Story, again declared, with reference to a vessel seized while in Spanish waters by American customs officials, that, "The laws of no nation can justly extend beyond its own territories, except so far as regards its own citizens. They can have no force to control the sovereignty or rights of any other nation, within its own jurisdiction. And, however general and comprehensive the phrases used in our municipal laws may be, they must always be restricted in construction, to places and persons, upon whom the legislatures have authority and jurisdiction."

This case was a libel brought by the master of a French

[10] 6 Cranch 281.
[11] 9 Wheaton, p. 362.

vessel against an American customs official for damages occasioned by a seizure upon his part of the ship while within the acknowledged territorial jurisdiction of Spain, upon the alleged ground that the ship had violated an American statute. It was with reference to the justification, under this law, of an extraterritorial seizure that Justice Story employed the language that has been quoted. Further along in his opinion he said: "It would be monstrous to suppose that our revenue officials were authorized to enter into foreign ports and territories, for the purpose of seizing vessels which had offended against our laws. It cannot be presumed that Congress would voluntarily justify such a clear violation of the law of nations."

Even here, it will be observed, Justice Story did not flatly deny the legal authority of Congress to authorize an extraterritorial seizure, but only that such an authorization, in absence of express direction, should not be presumed. In other words, the court was not confronted with a case in which its own Government had asserted, in language from which there could be no escape, a right to exercise jurisdiction beyond its own borders, or within the borders of another State, or with reference to persons not its own citizens. It is, however, unfortunate that Justice Story should have expressed himself as broadly as he did. It is possible, however, that he did not mean more than to say that one nation is not called upon to recognize the validity, or acquiesce in the enforcement within its own dominions, of the municipal laws of another State. This, of course, is correct, but is quite a different proposition from the one that asserts that one State cannot bind its own courts when it asserts an extraterritorial jurisdiction upon the high seas or even within the territorial limits of other States.

American Banana Co. v. United Fruit Co. In the case of the *American Banana Co. v. United Fruit Co.*,[12] decided in 1909, the plaintiff claimed damages, under the Anti-Trust Act of 1890, for certain acts committed or instigated by the defendant in a foreign country. The court in its opinion admitted that there were both American and British instances of the assertion of extraterritorial jurisdiction, but nevertheless seemed so strongly impressed with the merits of the doctrine that, as a rule, jurisdiction should be exercised by a State only within its own borders, that it described as "startling" the proposition that acts committed outside of the United States should be claimed to be controlled by an Act of its Congress. "Law," said Mr. Justice Holmes, who spoke for the court, "is a statement of the circumstances in which the public force will be brought to bear upon men through the courts. But the word commonly is confined to such prophecies or threats when addressed to persons living within the power of the courts. A threat that depends upon the choice of the party effected to bring himself within that power hardly would be called law in the ordinary sense. We do not speak of blockade running by neutrals as unlawful. And the usages of speech correspond to the limit of the attempts of the lawmaker, except in extraordinary cases. It is true that domestic corporations remain always within the power of the domestic law; but, in the present case at least, there is no ground for distinguishing between corporations and men."

This is strong language against the doctrine of extraterritorial jurisdiction and yet it is seen that Holmes himself admits that there may be "extraordinary cases" in which it may be asserted. Indeed, in another part of his opinion he mentions a number of such instances, both

[12] 213 U. S. 347.

British and American. It is, however, quite right that he should use his argument to support the doctrine that, unless the legislature has clearly expressed or implied a contrary intention, municipal statutes should be given only a territorial force. "The foregoing considerations," he says, "would lead, in case of doubt, to a construction of any statute as intended to be confined in its operation and effect to the territorial limits over which the law-maker has general and legitimate power. 'All legislation is *prima facie* territorial' (*Ex parte Blain*, L. R. 12 Ch. Div. 522). Words having universal scope such as 'every contract in restraint of trade,' 'every person who shall monopolize,' etc., will be taken, as a matter of course, to mean only everyone subject to such legislation, not all that the legislator subsequently may be able to catch."

In conclusion, then, of this point, we may say that there is nothing in the nature of sovereignty which confines the legal operation of its will, as expressed in the form of municipal law to its own citizens, or to its own territorial limits.

Criminal Jurisdiction as to Acts Committed Abroad. In criminal matters Great Britain and the United States act, in the main, upon the territorial principle, confining the jurisdiction of their courts for the most part to offenses committed upon British or United States soil as the case may be.

Russia, Austria, Italy, Norway, France (to a limited extent) and some of the Swiss Cantons, upon the other hand, claim and exercise a general criminal jurisdiction over their respective nationals wherever they may happen to be.[13]

"Some States, again," as Cobbett points out, "claim a criminal jurisdiction over offenses committed even by foreigners and on foreign soil, although this pretension

[13] Cf. Cobbett, *Leading Cases on International Law,* 3d ed., p. 226.

varies greatly in its scope. France, Germany, Austria, Italy, Spain, Belgium, and Switzerland appear to limit this to offences against the safety or high prerogatives of the State, in which case, if the offense has produced local effects its seat may perhaps be regarded as local. Russia, Italy, Mexico, Greece, and the Netherlands extend it to offences of a certain gravity, committed against their own subjects. Austria and Italy claim to take cognizance of offences committed by foreigners on foreign soil, which affect neither the State nor its subjects, so long as the offender has been arrested locally and an offer of extradition has been refused; a practice which makes a near approach to a cosmopolitan theory of criminal jurisdiction, as distinct from that which is wholly territorial or personal. The actual exercise of jurisdiction in such cases is subject to the condition that the offender shall have been arrested locally, for the reason that such claims would not generally constitute a good ground for a demand for extradition; and that he shall not previously have been tried elsewhere."[14]

[14] Cobbett, *op. cit.*, p. 226. For a more detailed statement of the laws of various States upon this matter, see Hall, *International Law*, 6th ed., pp. 207-210. Hall refers to the fact that, in 1879, the *Institut de Droit International* by a vote of 19 to 7 resolved that "tout état a le droit de punir les faits commis même hors de son territoire et par des étrangers en violation de ses lois pénales, alors que ces faits constituent une atteinte à l'existence social de l'état en cause et compromettent sa sécurité, et qu'ils ne sont point prévus par la loi pénale du pays sur le territoire duquel ils ont eu lieu." Cobbett enumerates the following classes of cases in which Great Britain has provided, by statute, for the trial and punishment through its own tribunals of offenses committed outside of British territorial limits: (1) Treason, (2) murder or manslaughter committed by British subjects on land outside the United Kingdom, (3) bigamy committed by British subjects anywhere [see especially Earl Russell's case, 1901, A. C. 446], (4) offences committed in territorial waters [these would hardly appear to be extraterritorial cases], (5) offences within section 4 of the Foreign Enlistment Act of 1870, committed by British subjects anywhere, (6) offences under the Slave Trading Act of 1824, if committed by British subjects or any person resident within the British dominions, (7) offences committed out of the British dominions by any seaman who at time of the offence or within three months previously has served on board a British vessel, (8) offences committed by British subjects in countries without regular government, and coming within the terms of the Foreign Jurisdiction

In the footnote just given a number of instances are given in which Great Britain and the United States assert extraterritorial jurisdiction notwithstanding the acceptance by them of the general rule that they will take criminal cognizance only of acts committed, or taking effect, within their respective territorial limits. Another recent American instance is that provided for in the so-called Webb-Pomerene Law of April 10, 1918, entitled "An Act to Promote Export Trade and for other Purposes."[15] By section 4 of this act the "unfair competition" clause of the Federal Trade Commission Act of September 26, 1914, was extended so as expressly to include prohibited acts committed without the territorial jurisdiction of the United States. Section 5 of the same Act also provides that the Commission shall have powers of investigation where "An Association, either in the United States *or elsewhere,* has entered into any agreement, understanding, or conspiracy, or done any act which artificially or intentionally enhances or depresses prices within the United States of commodities of the class exported by such association, or which substantially lessens competition within the United States, or other-

Act of 1890, and the Orders in Council passed thereunder, (9) certain other cases of minor importance. For a more complete list see Stephen, *Digest of Criminal Procedure,* pp. 3 et seq.

The following are instances in which the United States asserts extraterritorial jurisdiction: transportation of explosives on vessels or vehicles carrying passengers between the United States and foreign countries (*Criminal Code,* sec. 232); judicial authority of American diplomatic and other representatives in certain non-Christian, uncivilized countries (*U. S. Rev. St.,* secs. 4083-4088); islands having guano deposits discovered by an American citizen (*U. S. Rev. St.,* sec. 5576); murder on the high seas (*Crim. Code, secs.* 272, 273, 275); citizens voluntarily on board a foreign slave-trade vessel (*Crim. Code,* sec. 252); treason (*Crim. Code,* sec. 1); criminal correspondence with foreign governments (*Crim. Code,* sec. 5); perjury or forgery committed in connection with an oath, affidavit or deposition administered or taken by an American Secretary of legation or consular official abroad (*U. S. Rev. St.,* sec. 1750). This list is taken from the article "The Webb-Pomerene Law: Extraterritorial Scope of the Unfair Competition Clause," by William Notz, in the *Yale Law Journal,* for November, 1919, p. 38.

[15] 40 Stat at L. 516.

wise restrains trade therein." If, as a result of such investigation, the Commission finds that the law has been violated, it is authorized to recommend that the association change its practices so as to cease doing so; and, if this recommendation is not heeded, to refer its findings and recommendations to the Attorney-General of the United States for such action as he may deem fit.

With reference to the exercise by a State of criminal jurisdiction over its own citizens for offenses committed by them while outside its territorial limits, little, if any, objection is raised by the States within whose borders the offenses may have been committed. It scarcely needs be said, however, that this jurisdiction does not warrant the prosecuting State in violating the territorial jurisdiction of another State in order to obtain custody of the accused. Therefore, if the State whose laws warrant the prosecution wishes to proceed to judgment, except by way of default, it must wait until the accused voluntarily enters its territory, or until it obtains possession of him by regular extradition proceedings.[16]

It does not need to be said that the doctrine that, as a legal proposition, a State may exercise criminal jurisdiction over foreigners for acts committed by them upon

---

[16] In case of default, judgment by way of fine can be executed against any property that the defendant may have within the State. In some States, as for example was formerly the case in China, the relatives of the criminal or even his home community could be punished for his acts,—a doctrine of vicarious responsibility which, though perhaps not just in the eyes of the modern Western world, adds greatly to the effectiveness of the administration of criminal justice.

It would appear to be an established principle of law, not only in the United States but in other countries, that if possession of the accused be obtained by a State by forcibly abducting him from another State, or by other means in violation of the law of that State, the jurisdiction over him thus obtained is as complete as if he had been obtained by lawful means. In other words, such illegal or irregular means may constitute proper grounds for complaint upon the part of the State whose laws have been broken or jurisdiction violated, but they do not give to the defendant himself any legal right to defeat the jurisdiction of the State in whose custody he finds himself. As to this see *Mahon v. Justice,* 127 U. S. 700, and *Ker v. Illinois,* 119 U. S. 436, and other cases, British and American, therein cited.

foreign soil, does not carry with it a denial of the legal right of the States of which these same persons are citizens, or upon whose soil the acts complained of are committed, to resist the exercise of such jurisdiction by the first State, and, in case it is, or is attempted to be exercised, to make the matter one of international concern between the governments concerned. Protests thus made may be based upon the ground that the territorial sovereignty of the complaining State has been invaded, or that the rights of its citizens have been violated, or that the jurisdiction asserted is one that is not approved by international law or comity, whatever may be its validity as purely a matter of municipal law.

The Cutting Case. A controversy which, at the time, aroused considerable interest with reference to the extent to which one State will permit another State to exercise criminal jurisdiction over its (the first State's) own citizens for offenses committed outside the territorial limits of the prosecuting State is the Cutting case which arose in 1886 between the United States and Mexico.

That controversy grew out of the arrest in Mexico of an American citizen upon the charge of having published in the United States a libel upon a Mexican.[17] It clearly appeared that the Mexican law gave to its courts jurisdiction in the premises, but, none the less, the American Government strenuously protested and demanded the immediate release of its citizen. This it did not only upon the ground that Cutting had not been given a fair hearing, but upon the alleged ground that the attempt of Mexico to exercise such jurisdiction was, in itself, inter-

[17] The record of this case shows that the newspaper in which the libel appeared had circulated in Mexico, and, therefore, that the Mexican courts might have defended their jurisdiction wholly upon the ground that the offense charged against Cutting had been committed upon Mexican soil. This, however, the Mexican courts and the Mexican Government did not do, but insisted that jurisdiction under the Mexican law extended to the original publication of the libel in the United States.

nationally viewed, an unjustifiable one. The American Secretary of State, Mr. Bayard, writing to the American Minister at Mexico City, with reference to the character of the proceedings that had been had, said:

By the law of nations no punishment can be inflicted by a sovereign on citizens of other countries unless in conformity with those sanctions of justice which all civilized nations hold in common. Among those sanctions are the right of having the facts on which the charge of guilt was made examined by an impartial court, the explanation to the accused of these facts, the opportunity granted to him of counsel, such delay as is necessary to prepare his case, permission in all cases to go at large on bail until trial, the due production under oath of all evidence prejudicing the accused, giving him the right to cross-examination, the right to produce his own evidence in exculpation, release even from temporary imprisonment in all cases where the charge is simply one of threatened breach of the peace, and due security to keep the peace is tendered. All these sanctions were violated in the present case.

As to the right of the Mexican authorities to take any action whatever in the premises, Mr. Bayard, referring to the alleged libel, said:

The proposition that Mexico can take jurisdiction of its author on account of its publication in Texas is wholly inadmissible, and peremptorily denied by this Government. . . . To an assumption of such jurisdiction by Mexico neither the Government of the United States nor the governments of our several States will submit. They will mete out due justice to all offenses committed in their respective jurisdictions. They will not permit that this prerogative shall in any degree be usurped by Mexico, nor, aside from the fact of the exclusiveness of their jurisdiction over acts done within their own dominions, will they permit a citizen of the United States to be called to account for acts done by him within the boundaries of the United States. On this ground, therefore, you will demand Mr. Cutting's release.[18]

It cannot be denied that this was strong and unqualified language, but the doctrine declared was one by which

[18] *U. S. Foreign Relations,* 1886, p. 700.

the United States was qualified to assert that it would be guided in its dealings with other States. Consistency would require that it would make this a rule as to all other States, and that, upon its own part, it would not attempt the exercise of a jurisdiction such as that which Mexico had asserted. Mr. Bayard, it would seem, did not claim that this jurisdiction was one which had no support in the municipal practice of other States, or, indeed, international practice. He would, in fact, have had difficulty in successfully doing so. Leaving aside the character of the proceedings as regards fair hearing, etc., this was, indeed, the weak side, internationally speaking, of the American case, for, to the extent that the claim of jurisdiction such as Mexico had exercised, was made and acquiesced in by other States, the United States was put in the position of adopting an international policy that was not that of the rest of the world.

Immediate release of Cutting was refused by the Mexican Government; he was brought to trial in the Mexican court, jurisdiction was sustained, conviction was secured, and a punishment imposed of a year's imprisonment at hard labor, a fine of six hundred dollars (or, in default of payment thereof, a further imprisonment of one hundred days), and the payment of a civil indemnity to the person who claimed to have been injured by the publication. After quoting the section of the Mexican Penal Code which, in explicit language, gave the jurisdiction in question, the Mexican trial judge, in his decision, said:

Considering . . . that according to the rule of law *Judex non de legibus, sed secundum legem debet judicare*, it does not belong to the judge who decides to examine the principle laid down in said Article 186, but to apply it fully, it being the law in force in the State.

In the Supreme Court of Chihuahua, to which the case was taken on appeal, the decision of the court below was fully approved, but Cutting was released upon the ground that the aggrieved plaintiff had withdrawn from the prosecution of the suit, and that, therefore, there was no sufficient motive for its continuance.

This Cutting case was subjected to a very careful examination by Dr. John Bassett Moore, then Third Assistant Secretary of State, and the results of his inquiry published by the United States Department of State in a pamphlet entitled *Report on Extraterritorial Crime and the Cutting Case.*[19]

In this brief, Dr. Moore recognizes as customary and proper the punishment by States of certain acts committed outside of their respective territorial limits. One special instance of this which is noted is Piracy, which stands in a class by itself. "The scene of the pirate's operations being the high seas, which it is not the special duty or right of any nation to police, and his crime being treated as a renunciation of the protection of the flag which he may carry, he is regarded as a complete outlaw, and may be punished by any nation that captures him. Such an exercise of jurisdiction is both logical and necessary, and is recognized by all nations as a common duty and a common advantage." "It scarcely need be said," Dr. Moore adds, "that the exercise, as in the case of conventions for the suppression of the slave trade, of criminal jurisdiction by one country over the citizens of another, under a special treaty between the two countries, presents no conflict of jurisdiction, and is simply a question of expediency to be considered by the parties to the agreement."

Dr. Moore is, however, obliged to recognize that there are still other cases in which States are accustomed to punish, when able to do so, offenses defined by their own laws, committed by foreigners upon foreign soil. These cases relate generally to the counterfeiting or forging of

[19] U. S. Government Printing Office, 1887.

national seals and securities, and offenses against the
safety of the State itself. This jurisdiction, says Dr.
Moore, is to be regarded as exceptional and is defended
"upon the high ground of necessity and self-defense."

After an examination of the laws of other States, Dr.
Moore says that it appears that only Russia and Greece
assert an extraterritorial jurisdiction as broad as that
claimed by Mexico, that is, one covering not only crimes
against the safety of the State and its coinage, but, in
general, misdemeanors as well as felonies committed outside the country against its own citizens. The law of
Norway and Sweden and of Hungary approximates that
of Mexico, falling short of it only by the provision that
prosecutions shall be initiated only if ordered by the
King, or, in the case of Hungary, by the Minister of
Justice. "Austria punishes only *crimes* not *délits* or misdemeanors, and then, except in the case of *crimes* against
the safety of the State, or coinage felonies, only after an
offer of surrender of the accused person has been made
to the State in which the *crime* was committed, and has
been refused by it. The same principle is found in the
law of Italy, with almost the same definition of jurisdiction. Brazil makes the assertion of extraterritorial jurisdiction over foreigners in similar cases depend upon the
assertion of a like jurisdiction by the criminal's country."

After an examination of various arguments that had
been advanced by the Mexican Government in support
of the propriety of its conduct, Dr. Moore says that the
general proposition that the judicial tribunals of a
country are bound, as to their competence and forms
of procedure, by municipal law, is incontestable. "There
is no doubt that, under the law of Mexico, the courts of
Chihuahua are competent to try a foreigner for offenses
begun and consummated in his own country against a
Mexican. But this is not the question raised by the

United States in the case of Mr. Cutting. That question is whether the provisions of the law of Mexico, as contained in Article 186 of the Penal Code, are in contravention of the rules of International Law."

It will thus be seen that the position of the United States in this case was in full conformity with the juristic conclusions which have been reached in the present treatise. Whether or not the practice of which the United States complained in the Cutting case was or was not in conformity with the best practice and generally accepted doctrines of International Law, is a fact of importance, but not one the decision of which either way affects the conclusions which have been reached with regard to the jurisdictional powers, constitutionally considered, of the legally sovereign State. It is, however, significant that extraterritorial jurisdiction, even with reference to foreigners, is asserted by practically all sovereign States, for this fact is sufficient to show that it is, after all, a matter of expediency or international courtesy, and not of absolute legal limitation, which causes the sovereign State to confine the exercise of its jurisdiction to its own territory or to its own citizens.

Civil Jurisdiction of Acts Committed Abroad. As regards generally the enforcement by one State of obligations incurred in another State, a distinction is made between actions that are termed local and those that are described as transitory in character. Local actions are those, which, from their very nature, can arise in only one place, as, for example, to recover possession of, or damages for trespass upon, specific pieces of land. Transitory actions are those which might arise anywhere. When there is doubt as to whether a given cause of action should be deemed transitory or local in character, the *lex fori* is usually held to govern.

As a general rule, actions founded upon tort are deemed

transitory in character and may be entertained wherever the court can obtain jurisdiction of the parties. The same is true of actions *ex contractu,* irrespective of where the contract is made or where it is to be performed, or where the act constituting the breach may have occurred. In early times in England the venue for these personal actions, whether contractual or delictual, was secured by a fictitious allegation, which was not traversable, that the place where they arose was situated in one of the counties of England, but for many years now the necessity for this fiction has disappeared.

This jurisdiction to sue upon non-penal transitory causes of action accruing abroad attaches even if both of the parties are aliens and only transiently within the country, provided personal service upon the defendant has been had.[20] However, the jurisdiction thus assumed would appear to be a discretionary one on the part of the courts, and, therefore, not one which the plaintiff may, as a matter of legal right, demand to be exercised.[21]

In actions *ex contractu,* the agreement sued upon must have been valid by the law of the country in which it was entered into, and not of a character to bring it into opposition to the public policy of the country where its enforcement or the assessment of damages for its breach is sought.

As regards civil liability for tort, the English doctrine would appear to be that the action complained of must be actionable according to the *lex fori,* and not affirma-

[20] France seems to be an exception to this, her courts not allowing aliens to sue each other in them. American courts assume jurisdiction of torts committed on board a foreign vessel on the high seas even when both of the parties are aliens. *Gardner v. Thomas,* 14 Johnson 134; 7 Am. Dec. 445.

[21] "Where the parties were non-residents of the United States at the time when the tort was committed, and the tort was committed abroad, a court of this country will entertain jurisdiction only as a matter of comity and not as a matter of right." *Miller v. Great Western R. Co.,* 1 Mich. n. P. 177.

tively justified by the law of the place where committed. As regards this latter requirement it has been held that an action may be sustained in the English courts even if, by the *lex loci actus*, no civil liability would have accrued. It has been deemed sufficient that the act is not affirmatively justified by the local law. Thus in *Scott v. Seymour*,[22] we find Justice Wightman saying: "Since the case of *Mostyn v. Fabrigas*,[23] I am not aware of any rule of law which would disable a British subject from maintaining an action in this country, or from obtaining damages against another British subject for assault and battery committed by him in a foreign country, merely because no damages for such trespass were recoverable by the law of that foreign country, and without any allegation that such trespass was lawful or justifiable in that country. By the law of England, an action to recover damages for assault and battery is maintainable; and whatever may be the case as between two Neapolitan subjects, or between a Neapolitan and an Englishman, I find no authority for holding, even if the Neapolitan law gives no remedy for assault and battery, however violent and unprovoked, for recovery of damages, that therefore a British subject is deprived of his right."

Scott v. Lord Seymour did not decide the question whether the action for damages would have been maintainable in England if the assault and battery had been affirmatively lawful or justifiable according to the local law. In *Phillips v. Eyre*,[24] this point was passed upon, Mr. Justice Willes saying: "A right of action whether it arises from contract governed by the law of the place, or from wrong, is equally the creature of the law of the

[22] 32 L. J. Ex. 61; English Ruling Cases, I, 533.
[23] K. B. 1775. I Smith Leading Cases; Cowper, 161. In this case the English court sustained an action for trespass and false imprisonment, committed by the defendant in Minorca upon the plaintiff, a native of that island.
[24] 10 B. & S. 1004; L. R. 6 Q. B. 1 (1870).

place and subordinate thereto . . . The civil liability
arising out of a wrong derives its birth from the law of
the place, and its character is determined by that law.
Therefore an act committed abroad, if valid and unques-
tionable by the law of the country where it is done, cannot, so far as civil liability is concerned, be drawn in
question elsewhere, unless by force of some distinct independent legislation superadding a liability other than
and besides that incident to the act itself. In this respect no sound distinction can be suggested between the
civil liability in respect of a contract governed by the
law of the place, and a wrong. . . . As a general rule
in order to found a suit in England for a wrong alleged
to have been committed abroad, two conditions must be
fulfilled. First, the wrong must be of such a character
that it would have been actionable if committed in England[25] . . . Secondly, the act must not have been justifiable by the law of the place where it was done."

It will have been observed that Justice Wightman in
the passage that has been quoted from *Scott v. Seymour*,
does not attempt to state what would have been his
holding if the parties in that case had been aliens. We
have, however, the following dictum from Justice Blackburn in that case: "I cannot think that the fact of the
parties being British subjects made any difference at all.
As at present advised, I think that when two Britons go
into a foreign country, they owe local allegiance to the
law of the country, and are just as much governed by
that law as foreigners. That point is not at present
raised."

In *Machado v. Fontes*,[26] the Court of Appeal held that
an action would lie in a British court for a tort committed
outside of British territory, if the tort were wrongful by

[25] See *The Halley*, 57 L. J. Adm. 33.
[26] 2 Q. B. Div. (1897) 231.

both the *lex fori* and *lex loci actus,* but that it was not necessary that, by the latter law, the act in question should have been the subject of civil proceedings. L. J. Lopes said: "In the present case the action lies for it complies with both of the requirements which were laid down by J. Willes [in *Phillips v. Eyre*]. The act was committed abroad, and was actionable here, and not justified by the law of the place where it was committed." L. J. Rigby said: "I will assume it [the case] to involve that no action for damages, or even no civil action at all, can be maintained in Brazil in respect of a libel published there. But it does not follow that that libel is not actionable in this country under the present conditions, and having regard to the fact that the plaintiff and defendant are here."

The American doctrine upon the point under consideration is that, in order to sustain an action in the American courts, the contract or act complained of must have been sufficient to support a civil action according to the law of the place in which it is entered into or committed. Indeed, the American courts go further than this in the respect they pay to the foreign law, and hold that, provided there is involved no matter opposed to the "public policy" of the forum, jurisdiction will be entertained and relief given even though, according to the *lex fori,* no cause of action is created. However, pains have been taken to make clear that this enforcement of contracts entered into or the awarding of damages for tortious acts committed in foreign countries is always a matter of comity and not of necessary legal obligation.

That a cause of action must have accrued under the *lex loci actus* has been repeatedly asserted by the American courts, and, as typical, may be quoted the following from a decision of a Rhode Island court: "The cause of action accrued in Massachusetts under and in virtue of the law in force there, and if, under the law of that State, the action no longer exists there, it no longer exists here. . . . It is not strict right, but comity, which enables a person who has been tortiously injured in one State to sue for damages for the injury in another; and of course after the cause of action has become extinct where it accrued, it cannot, as a mere matter of comity, survive elsewhere."[27]

In another well considered case,[28] in which it was held that a statute of the forum was not applicable to affect a contract which was valid in the State in which it was entered into, the court said:

It is too well settled to require citation of authority that the statutes of a State have no extraterritorial operation, and cannot invalidate contracts made and to be performed in other jurisdictions. The courts of this jurisdiction might be forbidden by the laws of this state, in the absence of constitutional obstacles, to enforce particular contracts, although made in other jurisdictions, by the laws of which they would be valid. The rule by which courts of one country test the validity of contracts made and to be performed in other countries, in accordance with the laws of such countries, is one of comity only, and cannot be applied in opposition to the positive law of the forum.

In the instant case, however, no such statutory intention was found to exist.

As to the necessity that a cause of action should exist according to the *lex loci actus* or *lex loci contractus,* the American cases are so numerous as scarcely to need citation. Many of these are referred to in *Pendon v. V. & B. American Machine Co.*[29]. In *Burns v. Grand Rapids & I. R. Co.,*[30] the court said:

All the cases agree that, whatever the law of the forum may be, the plaintiff's case must stand, if at all, so far as his right of action

[27] *O'Reilly v. N. Y. N. E. R. Co.,* 5 L. R. A. 364.
[28] *Chicago, R. I. v. P. R. Co.,* 7 L. R. A. n. s. 191; 97 S. W. Rep. 459.
[29] 35 R. I. 321; L. R. A. 1916, A. 428.
[30] 113 Ind. 169; 15 N. E. Rep. 230.

is concerned, upon the law of the place where the injury occurred.
. . . Unless the alleged wrong was actionable in the jurisdiction in
which it was committed, there is no cause of action which can be
carried to and asserted in any other jurisdiction.

In *The Lamington*,[31] a Federal district court, sitting in
admiralty, with reference to an action *in rem* brought by
a seaman on a British ship, injured on the high seas by
the alleged negligence of the owner of the ship, held
that the action, to be maintainable in the American court,
must be maintainable by British law as well as by American law. In effect, it was held that the accident occurred,
constructively, within the exclusive jurisdiction of Great
Britain. The court said:

If, now, the law of Great Britain does not permit an action *in rem*,
the present action must fail, unless it appear that such action is not
of the substantive law of the country, but is a form of procedure or
process of the court of the country whose jurisdiction is invoked.
There is no doubt that a lien, if it exists at all, must inhere in some
right of the injured person, that it remains inchoate until the
right has been invaded, and thereupon matures. No process nor
procedure of the court gives life to the lien, but the lien, of its own
force, justifies the procedure *in rem*. Hence, if the lien have no
existence, the procedure *in rem* can give it none.

In *Dennick v. N. J. Central R. Co.*[32] the Supreme
Court of the United States, speaking through Justice
Miller, said:

Whenever, by either the common law or the statute law of a
State, a right of action has become fixed and a legal liability incurred,
that liability may be enforced and the right of action pursued in
any court which has jurisdiction of such matters and can obtain
jurisdiction of the parties.

The doctrine is well established that when the plaintiff
rests his right of action upon a foreign law he must be
held to all its ancillary provisions. This is illustrated

[31] 87 Fed. Rep. 752.
[32] 103 U. S. 11, 18 (26-439).

in the case of *Slater v. Mexican National Railroad Co.,*[33] decided in 1904 by the United States Supreme Court. In that case the court said:

When such a liability is enforced in a jurisdiction foreign to the place of the wrongful act, obviously that does not mean that the act in any degree is subject to the *lex fori,* with regard to either its quality or its consequences. On the other hand, it equally little means that the law of the place of the act is operative outside its own territory. The theory of the foreign suits is that, although the act complained of was subject to no law having force in the forum, it gave rise to an obligation, an *obligatio,* which, like other obligations, follows the person, and may be enforced wherever that person may be found. But as the only source of this obligation is the law of the place of the act, it follows that that law determines, not merely the existence of the obligation, but equally determines its extent. It seems to us unjust to allow a plaintiff to come here absolutely depending on the foreign law for the foundation of his case, and yet to deny the defendant the benefit of whatever limitations on his liability that law would impose.

This case was an action for damages brought in an American court by American citizens against an American company operating a railroad running from the United States to the City of Mexico, because of the death of the plaintiff's husband and father due to the negligence of the defendant. The main reliance of the plaintiffs for a cause of action was upon a provision of the Mexican Civil Code, and the question before the court was whether, this being so, the plaintiffs were to be bound by all the provisions of the Mexican law as to the kinds of relief that might be granted in the premises. The Supreme Court held, as may be inferred from the quotation that has been made from Justice Holmes' opinion, that they were so bound, and, as a result, they dismissed the action because the trial court had not had jurisdiction to make a decree of the kind required by the Mexican law.

[33] 194 U. S. 120.

This holding undoubtedly represents an extreme of comity towards the law of the foreign State, and was dissented to by three Justices. Chief Justice Fuller, speaking for these three, said: "It seems to me that the method of arriving at and distributing the damages [as fixed by the Mexican law] pertains to procedure and remedy,—that is to say, to the course of the court after parties are brought in, and the means of redressing the wrong,—and I think the general rule that procedure and remedy are regulated by the law of the forum is applicable."

In *Disconto Gesellschaft v. Terlinden,*[34] the question was presented whether a non-resident alien might sue another non-resident alien upon a cause of action accruing in a foreign country, and by means of garnishment or other remedy impound property of the defendant within the State, and obtain judgment to the detriment of a citizen of the court's own State who was also a creditor of the alien defendant. The State court said:

The plaintiff . . . is a non-resident; it has no property of any kind within the State; it has made no contract within the State or with any resident of the State. It has brought action against another non-resident alien, temporarily within the State, to redress a wrong committed without the State, and asks the courts of this State not only to give it judgment for that wrong, but also to lend the aid of its process to impound property within the State and satisfy such judgment therefrom to the prejudice of one of the State's own citizens who has a claim against the same debtor. It is true that the cause of action is transitory and the parties both within the jurisdiction of the court, and so the court has jurisdiction and may doubtless rightly entertain the cause. But is the court compelled to do so, because of an inherent right which the alien has to demand the action of the court; or does it do so upon the principles of comity, with the right to refuse relief when such relief prejudices the interests of resident citizens?

[34] 127 Wis. 651, 15 L. R. A. n. s. 1045, affirmed by the U. S. Supreme Court, *Disconto Gesellschaft v. Umbreit,* 208 U. S. 570.

To this question the court replied that the obligation to exercise its jurisdiction was based upon comity and that, therefore, it was within its discretion to grant or refuse relief, and that, in the instant case, it would refuse it.

In the Supreme Court of the United States this ruling was affirmed, the court, through Mr. Justice Day, saying:

Alien citizens, by the policy and practice of the courts of this country, are ordinarily permitted to resort to the courts for the redress of wrongs and the protection of their rights. But what property may be removed from a State and subjected to the claims of creditors of other States is a matter of comity between nations and States, and not a matter of absolute right in favor of creditors of another sovereignty, when citizens of the local State or country are asserting rights against property within the local jurisdiction.

As has been earlier said, and as opposed to the English doctrine, the American courts go so far in the matter of comity as to enforce obligations created by foreign law even though, under their own law, no obligation would have been created. Thus in *Huntington v. Attrill*,[35] the Supreme Court held that the courts of one of the States of the Union, under the Comity Clause of the Federal Constitution, was called upon to enforce a judgment rendered in a court of another State against officers of a corporation for making false statements regarding the amount of capital stock paid in, although the law of the State in which that judgment had been brought, did not provide for such a liability. Justice Gray, speaking for a majority of the court, said: "In order to maintain an action for an injury to the person or to movable property, some courts have held that the wrong must be one which would be actionable by the law where the redress is sought, as well as by the law of the place

[35] 146 U. S. 657.

where the wrong was done.[36]   But such is not the law of this court.   By our law, a private action may be maintained in one State, if not contrary to its own policy, for such a wrong done in another and actionable there, although a like wrong would not be actionable in the State where the suit is brought."[37]

This doctrine had been declared as early as 1810 by a State court in the case of *Greenwood v. Curtis*.[38]   In that case the court, speaking through Chief Justice Parsons, said: "A contract made in a foreign place, and to be there executed, if valid by the laws of that place, may be a legitimate ground of action in the courts of this State; although such contract may not be valid by our laws, or even may be prohibited to our citizens."[39]

[36] Citing *The Halley*, L. R. 2 P. C. 193, 204; *Phillips v. Eyre*, L. R. 6 Q. B. 1, 28, 29; *The Moxham*, L. R. 1 Prob. Div. 107, 111; *Wooden v. Western N. Y. & P. R. Co.*, 126 N. Y. 10; *Ash v. B. & O. R. Co.*, 72 Md. 144.

[37] Citing *Smith v. Condry*, 1 How. 28; *The China*, 7 Wall. 53; *The Scotland*, 105 U. S. 24; *Dennick v. Central R. Co.*, 103 U. S. 11; *Texas & P. R. Co. v. Cox*, 145 U. S. 593.

[38] 6 Mass. 358; 4 Am. Dec. 145.

[39] That this doctrine does not apply when to do so would be inconsistent with the public policy of the *lex fori*, as, for example, with reference to the enforcement of gaming contracts, see *Flagg v. Baldwin*, 48 Am. Rep. 308.

CHAPTER XXIII

CONFLICT OF LAWS

The exclusiveness of jurisdiction which every sovereign State asserts within its own territorial limits, and the rule that the courts of these States look exclusively to the legislative and political departments of their own governments for the laws which they are to apply in the causes coming before them for adjudication, are doctrines which are not contradicted by the force which they give to principles of international law or of admiralty and general commercial jurisprudence. And the same is true as to the effect which these courts give to the laws, judicial decrees and other public acts of foreign States. We have elsewhere had occasion to discuss the relation of international, admiralty and general commercial jurisprudential principles to municipal law, and to show that these principles are not applied by municipal courts except when, and to the extent that, they may be fairly said to have been received into the respective systems of municipal laws of the courts that apply them. We shall here be concerned only with the faith and credit given to the municipal laws, judicial decrees and other public acts of one State by the courts of other States,—a subject generally bearing the title "Conflict of Laws," or, "Private International Law."

The doctrine is undisputed that the laws, judicial decrees and other public acts of one State have no legal force, *ex proprio vigore,* in the judicial tribunals of another State. This doctrine, however, does not prevent the courts of one State from resorting to the laws, judicial decrees and other public acts of other States in order to determine what, as matters of fact, are the rights and obligations of the parties in the causes brought before them for adjudication. In other words, these foreign laws and decrees and other public acts are regarded not as, legally, the creative sources of the rights and obligations of the litigants, but as facts or circumstances in the case which determine, as do other facts and circumstances, the municipal laws of its own State which the court is to apply. This is what Professor Gray means when he says: "The laws of the other countries are simply facts which the court has to consider like other facts." [1]

Foreign Laws and Judicial Decrees as Facts. As descriptive of the manner in which laws of one jurisdiction are thus viewed as *facts* in another jurisdiction, we may quote the following from the opinion of Lord Justice Selwyn in the case of *The Halley* [2]: "It is true, he says, that in many cases the courts of England inquire into and act upon the law of foreign countries, as in the case of a contract entered into in a foreign country, where, by express reference, or by necessary implication, the foreign law is incorporated with the contract, and proof and consideration of the foreign law therefore became necessary to the construction of the contract itself. And as in the case of a collision on an ordinary road in a foreign country, where the rule of the road at the place of collision may be a necessary ingredient in the determination of the question by whose fault or negligence the alleged tort was committed. But

[1] *Nature and Sources of Law*, sec. 282.
[2] L. R. 2 P. C. 202.

in these and similar cases the English courts admit the
proof of the foreign law as part of the circumstances
attending the execution of the contract, or as one of the
facts upon which the existence of the tort, or the right
to damages, may depend, and it then applies and enforces
its own law so far as it is applicable to the case thus
established."

Lord Stowell, in the case of *Dalrymple v. Dalrymple*,[3] in an often quoted statement, speaking with
reference to the validity of a marriage celebrated in a
foreign country, said that the question "being entertained in an English court, it must be adjudicated according to the principles of English law, applicable to such
case. But the only principle applicable to such case by
the laws of England is, that the validity of Miss Gordon's
marriage rights must be tried by reference to the law of
the country where, if they exist at all, they had their
origin." He thus emphasized that, essentially speaking,
the law to be applied by the English court had necessarily
to be English law, and that this was not altered by the
fact that the domestic law looked to foreign law as one
of the substantive facts to be considered.

Comity. That it is a mere matter of complaisance or
"comity" that the courts of one country will resort to the
laws of another country for the adjudication of causes
coming before them, is admitted by all legal authorities.
The Supreme Court of the United States, defining
"comity" in a legal sense, says that it is "the recognition which one nation allows within its territory to
the legislative, executive or judicial acts of another
nation, having due regard both to international duty and
convenience, and to the rights of its own citizens or of

[3] 2 Hagg. 54.

other persons who are under the protection of its laws." [4] *Corpus Juris* [5] says: "The term signifies more than a mere manifestation of good will toward, or an extension of courtesy to, the foreign nation, but it carries with it no implication of relinquishment of sovereignty, the recognition of the foreign law being purely voluntary on the part of the nation in whose courts the occasion may arise."

The Court of Appeals of New York states the doctrine still more clearly when it says: "It is a principle of universal application, recognized in all civilized States, that the statutes of another State have, *ex proprio vigore,* no force or effect in another. The enforcement in our courts of some positive law or regulation of another State depends upon our own express or tacit consent. The consent is given only by virtue of the adoption of the doctrine of comity as part of our municipal law. That doctrine has many limitations and qualifications, and generally each sovereignty has the right to determine for itself their true scope and extent." [6]

Justice Story in his justly esteemed work on *Conflict of Laws,* says: "It has been thought by some jurists that the term 'comity' is not sufficiently expressive of the obligation of nations to give effect to foreign laws when they are not prejudicial to their own rights and interests. And it has been suggested that the doctrine rests on a deeper foundation: that it is not so much a matter of comity or courtesy, as a matter of predominant moral duty. Now, assuming that such a moral duty does exist, it is clearly one of imperfect obligation, like that of beneficence, humanity, and charity. Every nation must be the final judge for itself, not only of the nature and

---

[4] *Hilton v. Guyot,* 159 U. S. 113, 164.
[5] *Sub. nom. Conflict of Laws,* vol. XII, p. 432.
[6] *Marshall v. Sherman,* 148 N. Y. 9 (L. R. A. vol. XXXIV, p. 757.

extent of the duty, but of the occasions on which its exercise may be justly demanded." [7]

Limitations upon Credit to Be Given to Foreign Public Acts. If no other argument existed, the limitations under which the doctrine of comity operates would be sufficient to show that the laws and other public acts of one State are not conceded to have, *ex proprio vigore*, force in other States. It is not necessary to attempt an exhaustive statement of these limitations, but the more important of them may be indicated.

In the first place, the practice is universal that the courts of one State will not aid in the enforcement of the penal laws of another State. In the second place, the rules of comity are not applied when to do so would violate the positive law of the forum. Nor will enforcement of foreign laws or of judicial decrees be permitted in cases in which, by doing so, action contrary to the settled public policy or conceptions of morality of the local sovereignty will be authorized,—as, for example, with regard to such matters as gambling contracts, speculative enterprises, usurious rates of interest, marriages within certain degrees of blood relationship, etc. [8]

Nor does one State feel called upon, in all cases, to ascribe to an individual within its limits the status which the country of his domicile or primary citizenship has attached to him, as, for example, that he is a serf or a

[7] *Op. cit.*, sec. 33.

[8] "The public policy of a State is to be deduced from its constitution, laws, and judicial decisions." *Corpus Juris, sub. nom.* "Conflict of Laws."

In *Kaufman v. Gerson*, 20 Law T. R. 277 (1904), a British Court declined to enforce a contract entered into in France and legal there, on the ground that the inducement to it—to stifle a criminal prosecution against the defendant's husband—was an immoral one. So also, in *Hope v. Hope*, 8 De Gex. M. and G. 731 (1857), a case frequently quoted, it was declared that "A contract may be good by the law of another country, but if it be in breach, fraud, or evasion of the law of this country, or contrary to its policy, the courts of this country cannot, as I conceive, be called upon to enforce it."

slave, that he is fully *sui juris,* etc. As to the marital status, the general principle is that a marriage if valid where entered into is to be deemed valid in other jurisdictions. But this rule does not apply when, to do so, would do violence to the public policy of the foreign State, as, for instance, in case of polygamous or incestuous unions; and, in all cases, personal obligations arising out of the marriage relation are those of the law of the local forum and not of the place of domicile. Similar practice prevails in the matter of decrees of divorce with the added requirement that, to be entitled to foreign recognition, the courts rendering them must have had actual jurisdiction, based upon domicile, of at least one of the parties to the divorce proceedings.

Hilton v. Guyot [9] is American authority for the doctrine that judgments rendered in a foreign country, the laws of which permit their courts to re-examine foreign judgments upon their merits, need not be given more than a *prima facie* evidential force in American courts. In short, that the doctrine of reciprocity is to be applied.[10]

Finally, it is generally recognized that faith and credit will not be given to a foreign judgment when it is shown that a fraud has been perpetrated upon the foreign court such as to cause it to assert jurisdiction when, in fact, according to its own rules and municipal law, it properly had none, or such as to prevent the victim of it from presenting his full case to the court.[11]

As regards the evidential value to be ascribed by one court to the judgments and decrees of courts of foreign States, the early English rule, followed at first in America, was that these judgments and decrees had only a *prima*

[9] 139 U. S. 113.
[10] From this holding four justices dissented.
[11] Cf. *Moffat v. United States,* 112 U. S. 24.

facie value. But in both Great Britain and the United States the doctrine is now well established that they are to be conclusive of the merits of matter in controversy, provided—and this is an important proviso and one that has given rise to many difficult questions,—the courts rendering them had jurisdiction of the parties or of the *res*. Thus, in all cases in which rights are predicated upon a foreign final decree or judgment,[12] the plea in bar of *nul tiel record* is available to the defendant, and, under this plea, the courts of each State have been obliged to determine the facts which they will deem sufficient to give to foreign courts jurisdiction to render judgments either *in rem* or *in personam*.

When making this inquiry the courts of one country do not assume to differ with the foreign courts as to the construction by them of their own municipal law. If, in other words, those courts hold that their own municipal law gives them jurisdiction in the premises, the courts of other States will not dispute the correctness of this interpretation. However, as we have already seen, it is always open to the Government of a State, through its foreign office, to question whether another State has a system of judicial administration that affords a reasonable guarantee that justice according to law will be meted out to all, citizens and aliens alike, or whether, in particular instances, citizens or subjects of the first State have received what may be considered a fair hearing and adjudication of the legal rights which the local law promises to them. In the second place, it would seem that a State may protest if another State has sought to bring within its own legal control the persons or property of the citizens or subjects of the protesting State under circumstances

[12] The decree or judgment must have been a final one, conclusively settling, according to the rules of the foreign court, the matter in controversy.

which that State thinks do not bring the assertion of jurisdiction within the best or generally accepted principles of international comity.

Judgments in Personam. As to judgments *in personam,* that is, those which impose a personal liability upon the defendant, which follows him and may be enforced against him wherever he may be, or against property owned by him wherever it may be, it is a principle of Anglo-American Law that the courts must have obtained actual, and not merely constructive, service upon him. As regards the plaintiffs or petitioners in divorce or similar proceedings, it is usually necessary, in order to give the court jurisdiction, that they should have obtained a local domicil. As regards judgments *in rem,* it is universally deemed necessary that the *res* should be within the territorial jurisdiction of the local sovereignty.[12a] This last requirement often gives rise to perplexing problems as to the actual or presumptive *situs* of what is termed intangible personality, that is, of things which have no marketable value in themselves but are merely evidences of ownership of things of value, as, for example, promissory notes, certificates of stock, bonds, corporate franchises, etc. Especially difficult of settlement has been the determination of the legal *situs* of such forms of wealth for purposes of taxation. As to this something will presently be said in connection with the matter of taxation of incomes.

An examination of a few cases in American and British courts will serve to show the fundamental principles applied by them in determining this matter of jurisdiction.

[12a] However, courts of equity will sometimes require parties over whom they have obtained jurisdiction to execute conveyances or take other action with regard to property in other jurisdictions. In such cases the decrees do not directly affect the property, but operate upon the defendant. See *Wimer v. Wimer,* 82 Va. 890; and *Massie v. Watts,* 6 Cr. 148.

In *Pennoyer v. Neff*,[13] in the Supreme Court of the United States, the question was as to whether or not a court of one of the States of the American Union had obtained jurisdiction such as to enable it to render a decree *in personam* against the defendant. As will presently be pointed out, the jurisdictional power of the member States of such a Union as that of the United States is not always to be determined by the same rules as those which apply in determining the jurisdiction of a sovereign State. However, it happens that the principles laid down in this case are the same as those that apply in the case of sovereign bodies-politic.

In this action the plaintiff sought to recover possession of a tract of land situated in the State of Oregon which the defendant claimed to own by reason of a sale of the property on execution issued upon a judgment obtained against the plaintiff in one of the courts of the State, in which case the plaintiff (defendant in that case), at that time a non-resident of the State, had been served with only constructive notice of the suit. The Supreme Court of the United States declared that, not having been personally served, the Oregon court had not obtained a jurisdiction over Pennoyer such as would enable it to render against him a judgment *in personam*. The court said:

"It is in virtue of the State's jurisdiction over the property of the non-resident situated within its limits that its tribunals can inquire into that non-resident's obligations to its own citizens, and the inquiry can then be carried only to the extent necessary to control the disposition of the property. If the non-resident have no property in the State, there is nothing upon which the tribunal can adjudicate."

Constructive service, Justice Field went on to say,

[13] 95 U. S. 714.

may answer in all actions which are substantially proceedings *in rem*. "But where the entire object of the action is to determine the personal rights and obligations of the defendant, that is, where the suit is merely *in personam*, constructive service in this form upon a non-resident is ineffectual for any purpose. Process from the tribunals of one State cannot run into another State, and summon parties there domiciled to leave its territory and respond to proceedings against them. Publication of process or notice within the State where the tribunal sits cannot create any greater obligation upon the non-resident to appear. Process sent to him out of the State, and process published within it, are equally unavailing in proceedings to establish his personal liability."

In *Dewey v. Des Moines* [14], the Supreme Court held that a special assessment levied upon land within the State could not be made a personal liability of its non-resident owner, for the reason that the State had acquired no jurisdiction over him; and this was so even though the State by statute had asserted the right to impose such a personal liability. The court said: "We think that a statute authorizing an assessment to be levied upon property for a local improvement, and imposing upon the lot-owner, who is a non-resident of the State, a personal liability to pay such assessment, is a statute which the State has no power to enact, and which cannot, therefore, furnish any foundation for a personal claim against such non-resident. . . . To enforce an assessment of such a nature against a non-resident, so far as his personal liability is concerned, would amount to a taking of property without due process of law, and would be a violation of the Federal Constitution."

In *Schibsby v. Westenholz*, [15] a British court de-

[14] 173 U. S. 193.
[15] *English Ruling Cases*, V, p. 734.

clined to enforce a judgment obtained by default in a French court against a defendant domiciled in England who was not a subject of, and had not been a resident in, France, and who had no property there. Constructive service, as required by the French law, had been had upon the defendant, but this service the British court refused to recognize as sufficient to give to the French court that jurisdiction over him which would support a personal judgment against him which the English courts would feel themselves called upon to enforce. In the course of his opinion Justice Blackburn, after referring to the fact that by statute the English courts had been given jurisdiction in cases similar to the instant one in which the French court, under its municipal law, had asserted jurisdiction, nevertheless went on to say that whatever validity a judgment might thus have according to the law of the jurisdiction in which it was rendered, it was still proper for the courts of another jurisdiction to inquire, when reliance was had upon that judgment in suits brought before them, whether the original court had had a jurisdiction over the parties such as would support a judgment that might be availed of in foreign jurisdictions. Justice Blackburn said: "Should a foreigner be sued under the provisions of the [British] statute referred to, and then come to the courts of this country and desire to be discharged, the only question which our courts could entertain would be whether the acts of the British legislature, rightly construed, gave us jurisdiction over this foreigner, for we must obey them. But if, judgment being given against him in our courts, an action were brought upon it in the courts of the United States (where the law as to the enforcing of foreign judgments is the same as our own), a further question would be open, viz., not only whether the British legislature had given the English courts jurisdiction over the defendant, but whether he was under any obligation which the American courts could recognize to submit to the jurisdiction thus created. This is precisely the question which we have now to determine with regard to a jurisdiction assumed by the French jurisprudence over foreigners. . . . We think, and this is all that we need decide, that there existed nothing in the present case imposing on the defendants any duty to obey the judgment of a French tribunal."

From the foregoing it is seen that the British courts have declared substantially the same principle as that which the American courts apply; namely, that a foreign judgment will not be deemed to create a personal liability unless the court rendering the judgment has in some way obtained jurisdiction over the party against whom it is given, and that such jurisdiction cannot be obtained by merely constructive service upon a non-resident alien.

It is important to observe, as showing the mutual recognition by States of the right of each of them to extend its legal control over its own nations, wherever they may be, that it is conceded that its courts may obtain personal jurisdiction over non-resident subjects of its own sovereignty by constructive service, that is, by any sort of procedure which the State, by its municipal law, may declare to be sufficient.

In the course of his opinion Justice Blackburn said: "If the defendants had been at the time of the judgment subjects of the country whose judgment is sought to be enforced against them, we think that it would bind them. Again, if the defendants had been at the time when the suit was commenced resident in the country, so as to have the benefit of its laws protecting them, or, as it is sometimes expressed, owing temporary allegiance to that country, we think that its laws would have bound them. If at the time when the obligation was contracted

the defendants were within the foreign country, but left
it before the suit was instituted, we should be inclined
to think the laws of that country bound them; though,
before finally deciding this, we should like to hear the
question argued. . . . Again, we think it clear, upon
principle, that if a person selected as plaintiff the tribunal
of a foreign country as the one in which he would sue,
he could not afterwards say that the judgment of that
tribunal was not binding upon him."

An American court, commenting upon the doctrine of
Schibsby v. Westenholz, says: "If the obligation to enforce a foreign judgment is to be rested on the duty or
obligation of the defendant to pay the sum for which
the judgment was given, as Mr. Baron Parke and Mr.
Justice Blackburn suppose, then it is important to know
from what such duty or obligation springs. It is certain
that it cannot spring from the mere fact that some court
has assumed to render a judgment, but the proceedings
anterior to the judgment must have been such as fairly
imposed upon the party sued the obligation to appear and
make his defense to the demand set up, if any he had,
and if, under the circumstances, he was fairly entitled to
treat any notice of the suit which may have been given
him as unwarranted, and to disregard it, then it seems
plain that no obligation to recognize the conclusions of
the court in the suit could possibly arise." [16]

The American doctrine upon this point is summed up
in the *Cyclopedia of Law and Procedure,* as follows:
"Where the defendant was a citizen or subject of the
foreign country in which the judgment was recovered,
the court may have acquired jurisdiction over him in

[16] *McEwan v. Zimmer,* 36 Mich. 765; 31 American Reports, 332. For
affirmations of the doctrine of *Schibsby v. Westenholz,* especially as to
the binding force of judgments upon non-resident citizens or shareholders of national corporations, see *Rousillon v. Rousillon,* L. R. 14
Ch. Div. 351; *Vallee v. Dumerque,* 18 L. J. Exch. 398; *Douglas v.
Forrest,* 4 Bing. 686.

any mode or service or notice recognized as sufficient by the laws of that country." [17]

Doctrines of Civil Law Countries as to Comity and Conflict of Laws. The statements which have gone before have related almost exclusively to Anglo-American law. In a considerable number of respects the doctrines declared by the courts and legislatures of European and South American countries differ from those of the United States and Great Britain and her possessions, and the more important of these differences deserve mention.[18]

European and South American countries reject the Anglo-American doctrine that a judgment *in personam* can be rendered against a defendant if service of process is had upon him within the State, and without regard to his place of domicil, or as to where the cause of action accrued, or as to the location of the property to which it relates. "Service of process within the State is not a jurisdictional requirement in countries of the civil law for any cause of action. If jurisdiction exists, the defendant may be cited to appear and defend, although absent from the State." [19]

The doctrine that the powers of personal representatives appointed by the courts may not be exercised outside the borders of the State in which they are appointed, is peculiar to Anglo-American law.

In European and South American countries, execution may be had upon foreign judgments as such, provided they have been declared executory by a domestic court.

---

[17] *Op. cit.,* vol. XXIII, p. 1609, *sub nom.* "Judgments."
[18] These differences are pointed out by Professor Ernest Lorenzen in notes appended to his valuable collection of *Cases on the Conflict of Laws,* 2d ed., 1924. From these notes the statements that follow have been taken. See also Professor Lorenzen's article "Territoriality, Public Policy and the Conflict of Laws," in the *Yale Law Journal* for May, 1924.
[19] Lorenzen, *Cases,* p. 126.

"Judgments concerning capacity, status, and the like require no exequatur before being entitled to recognition." "Some countries decline to enforce foreign judgments in the absence of treaty (Holland, Japan). Others decline to do so except on the condition of reciprocity (Germany, Argentina). Others enforce them without any treaty or reciprocity, if certain statutory requirements have been satisfied. Some of these do so without re-examining the merits of the case (Italy, Brazil). Others only after a re-examination of the merits (Belgium, France)." "No foreign judgment will be given effect in Germany unless it was rendered by a court competent according to the rules governing the jurisdiction of German courts." [20]

[20] Lorenzen, *Cases,* p. 1055. See also Lorenzen, "The Enforcement of American Judgments Abroad," 29 *Yale Law Journal,* 188.

CHAPTER XXIV

OF the complete jurisdiction of a sovereign State over all property within its territorial limits, whether for purposes of taxation, of eminent domain, or the regulation of its use in private hands, there is no dispute. Controversies as to jurisdiction, therefore, seldom if ever arise with regard to corporeal things. It is only with reference to incorporeal hereditaments or intangible personality that questions as to *situs* for purpose of legal regulation or control occur.

Many of these questions are solved by applying the principle that *mobilia sequuntur personam*, but no State permits this general doctrine or fiction to defeat its jurisdiction if there are any substantial grounds for holding that the personalty or incorporeal hereditament has a *situs* within its borders independently of the place of residence or domicil of its owner. Thus, States have not hesitated, under certain circumstances, to exercise jurisdiction over intangible personalty, even when owned by non-resident aliens, when the evidences of ownership— the bonds, promissory writings, mortgage instruments, or other evidences of credits—are, in fact, situated within their respective limits. In other cases, as will presently be seen, States base their rights of legal control, especially for purposes of taxation, upon the fact that the credits taxed are in the form of profits arising out of corporate or other business undertakings carried on within its borders, or that the mortgages or other liens are upon

444

property similarly situated. An examination of some of the decisions of the Supreme Court of the United States with reference to the exercise of jurisdiction of this kind will disclose the general doctrines declared by American courts, and the reasoning upon which they have been based.

Special Considerations Applicable to States of the American Union. A considerable number of the cases which will be examined relate to the taxing powers of the individual States of the American Union. Because of the fact that these States have their powers curtailed by certain express or implied limitations in the Federal Constitution with reference, for example, to the impairing the obligation of contracts, to the taking of property without due process of law, to interference with interstate or foreign commerce, and to the denial to citizens of other States of the Union of privileges and immunities enjoyed by their own citizens, the validity of their tax laws as well as other laws comes before the Federal Supreme Court for final determination. These States, as between themselves, are foreign governments and their jurisdictions are strictly territorial in character, and, therefore, as between themselves, the Federal Supreme Court applies the same principles of public law that govern the relations of sovereign States to one another, and, for that reason we may quote the decisions of that eminent tribunal as to its conception of these general jurisprudential principles so far as concern the facts upon which municipal legal control may be predicated. In so far, however, as the decisions of the Supreme Court turn upon specific provisions of the American Constitution or arise out of any special constitutional characteristics of the American Union, they are, of course, without determining or interpretative force in the field of general public law.

Two further facts with regard to the jurisdictional

powers of the States of the American Union are to be observed. Because there exists above them the sovereign National Government and its supreme judicial tribunal, the Supreme Court of the United States, all questions of jurisdiction are judicially determined, and resort cannot be had to the political modes of protesting or redressing wrongs claimed to be suffered by one State because of a wrongful or oppressive exercise of jurisdiction by another State of the Union. In the second place, because of the non-sovereign status of these States, and the fact that they have no dealings, as independent political persons, with foreign States, they are wholly incapacitated from exercising jurisdiction over their own citizens who have obtained a foreign domicil. Thus, as is elsewhere pointed out, while it is a generally accepted principle of public law that a sovereign State may assert whatever jurisdiction it pleases over its own citizens wherever they may be, holding them responsible in its courts for breaches of its own laws both civilly and criminally, for acts committed by them while in foreign countries, the same is not true of the member States of the American Union. They can take no cognizance of acts committed outside their own territorial limits upon the ground that the accused or tort feasors are its own citizens. And, of course, these States have no jurisdiction upon the high seas such as sovereign States possess. Furthermore, as a matter of express provision of the Federal Constitution, each of them is compelled to give full faith and credit to the public acts, records and judicial proceedings of the other States of the Union,—an obligation which, as between sovereign States, is voluntary in character and discretionary in extent.

In the case of *United States v. Bennett*,[1] decided in 1914, the Supreme Court, dwelling upon the principles

[1] 232 U. S. 299.

to be applied in determining the jurisdictional powers of the individual States as distinct from those applicable in the case of the Union, pointed out that while the attempt of one of these States to tax property outside its territorial limits would be in violation of the provision of the Federal Constitution which prohibits it from taking property without due process of law, the same was not true of the United States itself. The court said: "The application to the States of the rule of due process relied upon [by counsel in the case] comes from the fact that their spheres of activity are enforced and protected by the Constitution and therefore it is impossible for one State [of the Union] to reach out and tax property in another without violating the Constitution, for where the power of the one ends the authority of the other begins. But this has no application to the Government of the United States so far as its admitted taxing power is concerned. It is coextensive with the limits of the United States; it knows no restriction except where one is expressed in or arises from the Constitution, and therefore embraces all the attributes which pertain to sovereignty in the fullest sense. . . . Because the limitations of the Constitution are barriers bordering the States and preventing them from transcending the limits of their authority, and thus destroying the rights of other States [of the Union], and at the same time saving their rights from destruction by the other States, in other words, of maintaining and preserving the rights of all the States, affords no ground for constructing an imaginary constitutional boundary around the exterior confines of the United States for the purpose of shutting that Government off from the exertion of powers which inherently belong to it by virtue of its sovereignty."

Territorial Jurisdiction of the British "Dominions." As regards the strictly territorial extent of their several jurisdictions, the British Dominions have a status similar to that of the individual States of the American Union. A discussion of the doctrines developed with reference to this matter of Dominion jurisdiction is the subject of a separate chapter in Keith's standard treatise on *Responsible Government in the Dominions.*[1a]

That the legislative or other jurisdictional powers vested by the British Parliament in the several colonies or Dominions of the British Empire, unless expressly otherwise provided by Act of Parliament, may be exercised by them only within their respective limits, or, at the most, with reference to violations of their respective municipal laws committed outside those limits by persons domiciled within them, has been repeatedly declared by the courts and by the Imperial Government. Thus, for example, special Acts of the British Parliament have been needed in order to provide for the extradition of fugitives from the justice of one colony or Dominion found in another possession of the British Crown. Some of the questions regarding the *situs* of personal property for purposes of taxation by the Dominions have resembled very much those which have arisen in the States of the American Union.

Taxation. The decision of the Supreme Court in the case known by the descriptive title "State Tax on Foreign-Held Bonds," [2] decided in 1873, has been one of the most discussed of the decisions of that court, and the doctrine therein declared, if not repudiated by later decisions, has at least been held down to practically the precise point then decided, namely, that bonds are property in the hands of their holders, and that, when these

---

[1a] Vol. I, part III, chap. II, "The Territorial Limitation on Dominion Legislation." See also Keith's *Imperial Unity and the Dominions* (pp. 132 *et seq.*), which is in a manner, a supplement to his earlier three-volume work.

[2] *Cleveland, etc., R. R. Co. v. Pennsylvania,* 15 Wall. 300.

holders are non-residents of the State in which the company issuing them is incorporated or doing business, they are beyond the jurisdiction of that State.

With regard to the general powers of taxation which a State possesses, Justice Field, rendering the opinion for a unanimous court, said:

"The power of taxation, however vast in its character and searching in its extent, is necessarily limited to subjects within the jurisdiction of the State. These subjects are persons, property and business which last is, of course, also a kind of property. Whatever form taxation may assume, whether as duties, imposts, excises or licenses, it must relate to one of these subjects. It is not possible to conceive of any other, though, as applied to them, the taxation may be exercised in a great variety of ways. It may touch property in every shape, in its natural condition, in its manufactured form, and in its various transmutations. And the amount of the taxation may be determined by the value of the property, or its use, or its capacity, or its productiveness. Unless restrained by provisions of the Federal Constitution, the power of the State as to the mode, form and extent of taxation is unlimited, where the subjects to which it applies are within her jurisdiction."

To this description of the State's taxing power may be added the statement, which has been earlier discussed, that sovereign States retain jurisdiction over their own citizens or subjects wherever they may be, whether for taxation or other purposes.[3]

---

[3] As to the situs of the property involved in this case, the court said: "Corporations may be taxed, like natural persons, upon their property and business. But debts owing by corporations, like debts owing by individuals, are not property of the debtors in any sense; they are obligations of the debtors, and only possess value in the hands of the creditors. With them they are property, and in their hands they may be taxed. To call debts property of the debtors is simply to misuse terms. All the property there can be, in the nature of things, in debts of corporations, belongs to the creditors, to whom they are payable,

In this Foreign-Held Bonds case the State law was held invalid because, as applied to the bonds, it was in violation of the provision of the Federal Constitution that no State of the Union shall pass a law impairing the obligation of contracts.[4] The obligation impaired was that between the corporations which were ordered to pay the tax and their non-resident bond-holders.

In *Hayes v. Pacific Steamship Co.*,[5] it was held that a State might not tax as property a ship of a foreign registry which was only temporarily in a port of the State,—which was, as it were, *in transitu*. Substantially the same was held in *Morgan v. Parham.*[6] So, also, in *St. Louis v. Wiggins Ferry Co.*,[7] it was held that the State of Missouri could not tax ferry-boats belonging to an Illinois company which boats were laid up on the Illinois shore when not in use. The Court said: "Where there is jurisdiction neither as to person nor property, the imposition of a tax would be *ultra vires* and void. If the legislature of a State should enact that the citizens or property of another State or country should be taxed in the same manner as the persons and property within its own limits and subject to its authority, or in any manner whatsoever, such a law would be as much a nullity as if in conflict with the most explicit constitutional inhibition. Jurisdiction is as necessary to valid legislative as to valid judicial action."

and follows their domicil, wherever that may be. Their debts can have no locality separate from the parties to whom they are due."

In other cases the Supreme Court of the United States has held that the right of a foreign corporation or non-resident to do business within a State may be subjected to what is in the nature of a license or excise tax. It has also been held that where foreign-held evidences of ownership or of credits are placed in the hands of resident agents for the purpose of collecting the interests, rents, etc., and of reinvesting the proceeds, they are to be deemed to have their situs within the State and therefore taxable by the State.

[4] Article I, section 10.
[5] 17 Howard 596.
[6] 16 Wallace 471.
[7] 11 Wallace 423.

In *Ogden v. Saunders*,[8] the Supreme Court held that a State of the Union could not give an extraterritorial effect to its insolvency laws.

Due Process of Law. In the immediately foregoing cases the Supreme Court of the United States held the State laws invalid simply as *ultra vires* from the standpoint of territorial jurisdiction, and without reference to any specific inhibition laid upon the States by the Federal Constitution. However, in the later cases of *Louisville, etc., Ferry Co. v. Kentucky*,[9] decided in 1903, and *Delaware, L. & W. R.R. Co. v. Pennsylvania*,[10] decided in 1905, the Federal Supreme Court declared that an attempt of a State to tax property which did not have its situs within the State was in violation of the express prohibition laid upon the States by the Federal Constitution that they should deprive no person of property without due process of law.[11]

In the first of these cases was invalidated the attempt of the State of Kentucky to include, for purposes of taxation, the value of a franchise granted by the State of Indiana to a Kentucky ferry company. "There is, in our judgment," said the court, "no escape from the conclusion that Kentucky thus asserts its authority to tax a property right, an incorporeal hereditament,[12] which has its situs in Indiana. . . . The taxation of that franchise or incorporeal hereditament by Kentucky is, in our opinion, a deprivation by that State of the property of the ferry company without due process of law in violation of the Fourteenth Amendment of the Constitution of the United

[8] 12 Wheaton 214.

[9] 188 U. S. 385.

[10] 198 U. S. 341.

[11] Fourteenth Amendment. As to this shifting of ground by the Federal Supreme Court, see the article by Dr. F. J. Goodnow, "Congressional Regulation of State Taxation," in the *Pol. Sci. Quar.*, vol. XXVIII (1913), p. 405.

[12] An incorporeal hereditament is ordinarily distinguished from intangible personalty by being a right attached to land.

States; as much so as if the State taxed the real-estate owned by that company in Indiana."

In *Delaware L. & W. R.R. Co. v. Pennsylvania,* the court, upon the same constitutional ground, held that a State of the Union could not, for purposes of taxation, include in the appraisement of the capital stock of a domestic corporation the value of coal mined by it within the State, but situated within other States, and there awaiting sale when the appraisement was made.

In *Union Refrigerator Transit Co. v. Kentucky,*[13] decided in 1905, the court similarly held that due process of law was denied a corporation of Kentucky by a tax of that State assessed upon its rolling stock permanently located in other States and there used for carrying on the company's business. The court said: "The arguments in favor of the taxation of intangible property at the domicil of the owner have no application to tangible property. The fact that such property is visible, easily found, and difficult to conceal, and the tax readily collectible, is so cogent an argument for its taxation at its situs, that of late there is general consensus of opinion that it is taxable in the State where it is permanently located and employed, and where it receives its entire protection, irrespective of the domicil of the owner." (Citing numerous cases.)

In *Maguire v. Trefry,*[14] decided in 1920, the court held valid the law of the State of Massachusetts taxing the income of a resident of the State from a trust, administered under the laws of another State, in securities in the possession of the trustee in such other State. "It is true," said the court, "that the legal title of the property is held by the trustees in Pennsylvania. But it is so held for the beneficiary of the trust, and such beneficiary has

[13] 199 U. S. 194.
[14] 253 U. S. 12

an equitable right, title, and interest distinct from its legal ownership. . . . It is this property right belonging to the beneficiary, realized in the shape of income, which is the subject matter of the tax under the statute of Massachusetts."

In *Savings and Loan Society v. Multnomah County*,[15] the court expressly overruled the dictum in the State Tax on Foreign-Held Bonds case that a non-resident mortgagee's equitable interest in land may not be taxed to him in the State where the land is situated.

In *Corry v. Baltimore*,[16] the court held that prior adjudications had conclusively settled the doctrine that the State could fix, for purposes of taxation, the situs of stock in a domestic corporation, whether held by residents or non-residents.

Inheritance Taxes. Some questions regarding the situs of property have been raised in connection with inheritance taxes. In general, however, with reference to the estates of non-resident decedents it has been held that, as to property within the State, the tax may be upheld as one upon the right of succession or as a transfer of title tax. Thus, in *Blackstone v. Miller*,[17] the court upheld a tax upon the transfer, under the will of a non-resident, of debts due the decedent by citizens of the taxing State. The court said: "No one doubts that succession to a tangible chattel may be taxed wherever the property is found, and none the less that the law of the situs accepts its rule of succession from the law of the domicil, or that by the law of the domicil the chattel is a part of a *universitas* and is taken into account again in the succession tax there. . . . The question, then, is narrowed to whether a distinction is to be taken be-

[15] 169 U. S. 421.
[16] 196 U. S. 466.
[17] 188 U. S. 189.

tween tangible chattels and the deposit in this case. . . .
If the transfer of the deposit necessarily depends upon
and involves the law of New York [the taxing State in
the instant case] for its exercise, or, in other words, if
the transfer is subject to the power of the State of New
York, then New York may subject the transfer to a
tax. . . . It is plain that the transfer does depend upon
the law of New York, not because of any theoretical
speculation concerning the whereabouts of the debt, but
because of the practical fact of its power over the person
of the debtor." [18]

**Taxation of Foreign Shareholders of Domestic Corpora-
tions.** In *Michigan Central R. R. Co. v. Slack*,[19] the Supreme Court, interpreting and applying a provision of
the Federal Internal Revenue Law as amended by the
law of 1886, upheld as an excise tax a percentum tax
on interest due by an American corporation, doing business in America, on its bonds issued before the revenue
law was enacted and held at the time by non-resident
foreigners. The law in question levied a general tax on
corporations, such as was the plaintiff company, to be
paid by them out of their earnings, income and profits,
and provided that the amounts payable should be deducted by the companies from their dividends, interest
or funded debt, etc., and paid over to the revenue agents
of the American Government.

In the course of its opinion the Court said: "Whether
Congress, having the power to enforce the law, has the
authority to levy such a tax on the interest due by a
citizen of the United States to one who is not domiciled
within our limits, and who owes the Government no
allegiance, is a question which we do not think necessary
to the decision of this case. The tax, in our opinion, is

[18] See also *Keeney v. New York*, 222 U. S. 525.
[19] 100 U. S. (10 Otto), 595.

essentially an excise on the business of the class of corporations mentioned in the statute." In other words, the tax was not, in truth, upon the non-resident holders of the bonds, although it was deducted from and paid out of the interest due them as such holders, but upon the corporations which paid the interest. However, the court went on to say: "It is true that the Act went further, and declared that, except when the company had contracted otherwise, it might deduct this tax from the amount due the bondholders. And where the bondholder was subject to congressional legislation by reason of citizenship, residence or situs of the property taxed, it was within the lawful power of Congress to do so. Whether, as a question of international law, this declaration would relieve the corporation from the obligation to pay its foreign bondholder the full sum for which it contracted, we need not discuss; for this court, on all such subjects is bound by the legislative and political departments of its own Government."

In *United States v. Erie R. R. Co.*,[20] decided in 1882, which was an action to recover taxes paid under protest, levied under the same revenue provision as that involved in the case just considered, Chief Justice Waite declared that the authority of that case should govern. Justices Bradley and Harland concurred in the judgment rendered, but not for the reasons stated in the earlier case. Justice Bradley, speaking for Justice Harlan as well as himself, said that he had always been of the opinion that the tax in question was on the incomes *pro tanto* of the holders of the bonds or stocks of the companies concerned. "The objection," he said, "that Congress had no power to tax non-resident aliens, is met by the fact that the tax was not assessed against them personally, but against the *rem*, the credit, the debt due *to* them.

[20] 106 U. S. (16 Otto), 327.

Congress has the right to tax all property within the jurisdiction of the United States with certain exceptions not necessary to be noted. The money due to non-resident bondholders in this case was in the United States,—in the hands of the company—before it could be transmitted to London, or other place where the bondholders resided. While here it was liable to taxation."

Continuing, Justice Bradley went on to define the general jurisdictional powers of a government in the following significant, even if *obiter,* words: "Whether taxation thus imposed would be respected by foreign Governments if the creditor could bring before their courts the debtor company or its property, does not concern us in considering the question now presented. There is nothing in the Constitution [nor, he might have added, in the nature of any sovereign State] which authorizes this court, or any other court, to disaffirm the power of Congress to lay the tax. Congress is its own judge of the propriety or expediency of laying it. Indeed, insofar as the power of Congress is concerned, regarded in reference to any power the courts have to limit or restrain it, I see no reason why Congress may not lay a tax upon any property on which the Government can lay its hands, whether within or without the jurisdiction of the United States. If, in imitation of the dues levied by Denmark upon vessels passing through the Cattegat Sound, Congress should levy a duty upon all vessels passing through the Strait of Florida, I do not know of any power which the courts possess to prevent it. It might create complications with foreign Governments, it is true, and involve the country in war, but Congress has the power, if it chooses to take the responsibility, of creating, or giving occasion to such complications. The responsibility rests upon it alone."

Justice Field, in a dissenting opinion rendered in this

case, took the position that the tax involved was upon
the income of non-resident aliens and nothing else. Upon
this point he was in agreement with Justices Bradley
and Harlan, but, differing from them, he declared that,
from the very nature of political authority, a sovereign
State is without legal right to tax the incomes of persons
over whom it has no jurisdiction either by way of citizenship or residence. "The foreign owner of these bonds,"
he said, quoting the language the lower court had used,
"was not in any respect subject to the jurisdiction of the
United States, neither was this portion of his income.
His debtor [the company] was, and so was the money
of his debtor, but the money of his debtor did not become
a part of his income until it was paid to him, and in this
case the payment was outside of the United States in
accordance with the obligations of the contract which he
held." "There are," continued Justice Field, "limitations
upon the powers of all governments, without any express
designation of them in their organic law; limitations
which inhere in their very nature and structure, and this
is one of them—that no rightful authority can be exercised by them over alien subjects, or citizens abroad or
over their property there situated."

Here it is clear that Justice Field fell back upon a
doctrine of what may be termed natural or inherent
limitations—limitations derived from no legal source, but
imposed by the very nature of things, and as a matter of
absolute ethical obligation.

It is, indeed, surprising that this Justice should have
been willing to give his support to a theory that, long
before his time, had been thoroughly discredited, and in
support of which he could adduce no judicial precedents.
He did, indeed, assert that the courts in England had considered the doctrine to be so obligatory upon them that,
where general terms used in Acts of Parliament seemed

to contravene it, they had narrowed the construction so as to avoid that result. But, admitting this to be true, this is far from a declaration by the English courts that, in cases where, because of the explicit language used, it was not possible to escape by means of construction from the force of parliamentary commands, they would in this or any other case, refuse to recognize the validity of such commands.[21]

Income Taxes. The question of the situs of property for the purposes of taxation is an especially acute one with reference to income taxes. Both in England and the United States such taxes have been imposed upon persons, whether citizens or not, and whether resident or not, with respect to profits derived from business enterprises carried on within their respective territories.

In the United States the Acts of 1861 and 1864 confined the tax to residents and to citizens residing abroad, but the Act of 1866 added the provision: "And a like tax shall be levied, collected, and paid annually upon the gains, profits, and income of every business trade, or profession carried on in the United States by persons residing without the United States, not citizens thereof"; and this same or a similar provision was embodied in the Acts of 1870, 1894, and 1913. Similar provisions are also to be found in the income tax laws of some of the States of the American Union, and, in the case of *Shaffer v. Carter*,[22] decided in 1920, the constitutionality of these acts was examined by the Supreme Court of the United States.

In the case of *Shaffer v. Carter* one of the questions involved was as to the constitutionality of a tax levied

[21] Justice Field also cites the case of *The Apollon* (9 Wheaton 362), which has been earlier discussed, and which, it has been shown, does not support, except possibly in an *obiter* manner, the doctrine in whose behalf Justice Field adduces it.

[22] 252 U. S. 37. See also *Travis v. Yale and Towne Manufacturing Co.*, 252 U. S. 60.

by the State of Oklahoma upon net incomes derived by non-residents from property owned by them within the State and from business or professions carried on by them within its borders. The law was upheld, the court saying:

"We deem it clear, upon principle as well as on authority, that just as a State may impose general income taxes upon its own citizens and residents whose persons are subject to its control, it may, as a necessary consequence, levy a duty of like character, and not more onerous in its effect, upon income accruing to non-residents from their property or business within the State, or their occupations carried on therein; enforcing payment, so far as it can, by the exercise of a just control over persons and property within its borders.[23] . . . The very fact that a citizen of one state has the right to hold property or carry on an occupation or business in another is a very reasonable ground for subjecting such non-resident, although not personally, yet to the extent of his property held or his occupation or business carried on therein, to a duty to pay taxes not more onerous in effect than those imposed under like circumstances upon citizens of the latter State."

This last qualification as to equality of treatment between residents and non-residents being one specially imposed upon the States of the American Union by the Federal Constitution, would not apply to the Federal Government in its dealings with non-residents in foreign States.

To the contention that the income tax in question was, in its very nature, a personal one, or a "subjective tax

---

[23] The court, in this statement, introduced the qualification that the tax upon non-residents should not be more onerous than upon residents, because of the express provision of the Federal Constitution that "the citizens of each State shall be entitled to all privileges and immunities of citizens in the several States" (Art. IV, Sec. 2).

imposing personal liability upon the recipient of the income," and, therefore, as to a non-resident, beyond the jurisdictional power of the State, the court replied that the essential point was as to its practical operation and effect,—"the personal element cannot, by any fiction, oust the jurisdiction of the State within which the income actually arises and whose authority over it operates *in rem*."

In the case of *De Ganay v. Lederer*,[24] decided in 1919, the Supreme Court of the United States upheld the federal income tax law as to the income from stocks and bonds of corporations organized under laws of the United States, and from bonds and mortgages secured upon property in the United States, owned by a non-resident alien, which income was collected and transmitted to such alien by an agent domiciled in the United States who had physical possession of the securities under a power of attorney which gave him authority to sell, assign or transfer any of them and to invest or reinvest the proceeds from such sales. These being the circumstances, the court declared that the securities constituted property which had its situs in the United States. To the contention of counsel that certificates of stock, bonds and mortgages are not themselves property but merely evidences of ownership of property, the court replied that, in general parlance and usage, they are so considered, and that the words of the Congressional statute are to be construed in the light of such usage. As to the situs of this property, the court said that the maxim *mobilia sequuntur personam* declares what, in many cases, is but a fiction which has to yield when the facts and circumstances of cases require it, and that there is abundant judicial authority (citing cases) that notes, bonds and mortgages may acquire a situs at a place other than the

[24] 250 U. S. 376.

domicil of their owners and be there reached by the taxing power.[25]

In *Buck v. Beach*,[26] the Supreme Court held that the mere presence of promissory notes within the State was not sufficient to create a situs, for purposes of taxation by that State, of the intangible personalty represented by such instruments, and that it was immaterial that these instruments had been sent into the State by their owner in order to avoid taxation upon them by the State of his residence. The court said: "The debts here in question were not property within the State of Indiana, nor were the promissory notes themselves, which were only evidence of such debts. The rule giving jurisdiction where the specialty may be found has no application to a promissory note."

Upon the other hand, in *Metropolitan Life Insurance Co. v. New Orleans*,[27] the court held that a company could not escape taxation by sending the evidences of credits outside of the State, when there were other reasons why the company should be taxed upon them. In this case the plaintiff, a foreign corporation, was doing business within the State and the court said: "The State undertook to tax the capital employed in the business precisely as it taxed the capital of its own citizens in like

[25] Quoting a decision of a state court (*Jefferson v. Smith*, 88 N. Y. 576), the Supreme Court said: "It is clear from the statutes referred to and the authorities cited and from the understanding of business men in commercial transactions, as well as of jurists and legislators, that mortgages, bonds, bills and notes have for many purposes come to be regarded as property, and not as the mere evidences of debts, and that they may thus have a situs at the place where they are found, like other visible tangible chattels."

As to the conformity of the doctrine of the instant case with that of the case of State Tax on Foreign Held Bonds (15 Wallace, 300), the court said: "The taxation in that case was on the interest on bonds held out of the State. Bonds and negotiable instruments are more than mere evidences of debt. The debt is inseparable from the paper which declares and constitutes it, by a tradition which comes down from more archaic conditions."

[26] 206 U. S. 392.

[27] 205 U. S. 395.

situation. For the purpose of arriving at the amount of capital actually employed it caused the credits arising out of the business to be assessed. We think the State had the power to do this, and that the foreigner doing business cannot escape taxation upon his capital by removing temporarily from the State evidences of credits in the form of notes. Under such circumstances they have a taxable situs in the State of their origin." [28]

A careful examination of the cases which have been reviewed shows that not yet has the Supreme Court of the United States found it necessary to pass squarely upon the jurisdictional power of the United States to tax non-resident aliens upon intangible personalty which cannot be construed to be actually or physically within the United States, or to be of the nature of a license or excise or franchise tax upon business carried on within, or special corporate rights granted by, the United States.[29]

The present federal income tax law requires the payment by non-resident aliens of a tax assessed upon incomes derived by them from all property owned or from any business or profession carried on in the United States. This tax, it is to be observed, is collected in many cases by the United States, not directly from the recipients of the income but from the corporations or concerns which earn it, and before it is paid over to those to whom it is due. It yet remains to be seen whether the Supreme Court will find itself able to hold that such income is property within the United States, even though the instruments evidencing the ownership of the property from which the income is derived are not physically within the United States, and the owners are non-resi-

---

[28] Justices Day and Brewer dissented.
[29] In *R. R. v. Jackson,* 7 Wallace 262, the court held that Congress had not intended, by its Income Tax Law of 1864, to tax incomes of non-resident aliens.

dent aliens and have no agents in the United States for the collection, or collection and reinvestment, of the incomes due them. If, however, one may judge by the general trend of the cases that have been reviewed, it is more than likely that the Supreme Court, when the question is presented to it, will uphold the federal law in this respect. If it should do so, it would of course be within the right of foreign Governments to hold that such income cannot properly be deemed to be property within the United States, and, therefore, to complain that the United States, taking advantage of the fact that it has within its actual control the property or businesses from which such income is derived, is improperly withholding property from the citizens of the complaining States, who are not residing and have no domicil in, and own no property located within, the United States. In other words, they might admit, as, of course, they would be compelled to admit, that the United States may tax business carried on or property located within its borders or the income derived therefrom, but that it cannot justly tax the income of non-resident aliens merely by reason of the fact that such income is derived from the earnings of such businesses or property: that the payments due to their own citizens remain the property of the concerns earning them until they are paid over to the persons to whom they are due, and that only when so paid to and received by these creditors do they become income, by which time, in the case of non-resident aliens, they will have passed beyond the jurisdiction of the United States.

Such an argument as this would of course be valid only as a matter of international right or as a rule sanctioned by generally accepted international law. It would have no force in municipal courts. For them, as has been so often reiterated, the only question would be as to what the municipal law provided. If, in bald terms, the statute should declare that a tax should be levied personally upon non-resident aliens, who owned no property within the State, who derived no income from property located or business carried on within the State, or that a tax should be levied upon alien-owned property located outside of the State, the courts of the enacting State would be bound to recognize the validity of such a law. The courts, when called upon to issue a decree in enforcement of such taxes might not be able to find any property within its jurisdicton against which a judgment *in rem* could be entered and enforced, but, if the municipal law so provided, it might enter a judgment *in personam* in default against the defendant, which might be satisfied out of property within the jurisdiction of the court which, at some later time, the defendant might come into possession of. It scarcely need be said that if the attempt were made to institute proceedings in a foreign jurisdiction to collect this judgment out of property there located and owned by the defendant, the courts of that State would be justified in refusing to give force to the judgment decrees, which, as to itself, would be foreign ones.[30]

A possible constitutional difficulty peculiar to the United States with reference to income taxation and not related to the implications of its sovereignty, is that raised by the powers of Congress under the Federal Constitution to levy direct taxes. Should it take the position which has been indicated, the court would have to hold that the tax thus collected was an income tax even though the jurisdiction to levy it was founded upon the proposi-

---

[30] For an interesting discussion of movements that have been made to obtain an international agreement and harmony of practice with regard to the taxation of intangible personal property, especially with reference to incomes, see the article by G. G. Cobaugh, "International Comity in Taxation" in the *Journal of Political Economy* for April, 1923, vol. XXXI, p. 262.

tion that the interest of the non-resident aliens in the earnings of the property or business represented by the stock, bonds or mortgages held by them, constituted property within the jurisdiction of the United States. For if the tax were not still regarded as upon incomes it would be a direct tax not covered by the Seventeenth Amendment to the Federal Constitution, and would therefore have to be apportioned among the States of the Union according to their respective populations.[31]

Addendum. Since the preceding pages were in type the Supreme Court of the United States, in the case of *Cook v. Tait*,[32] has decided that the United States might impose a tax on income received by an American citizen who, at the time the income was received, was permanently resident and domiciled in a foreign country; the income being derived from property located in that country. The scope and the power of a sovereign State to tax, it was declared, "is based on the presumption that government by its very nature benefits the citizen and his property wherever found." This doctrine, it was asserted, was implicit in the holding of the court in *United States v. Bennett*,[33] which, in effect, held that "the basis of the power to tax was not and cannot be made dependent upon the situs of the property in all cases, it being in or out of the United States nor was not and cannot be made dependent upon the domicil of the citizen, that being in or out of the United States, but upon the relation of the latter to him as citizen."

[31] Article I, section 9, paragraph 4, of the Federal Constitution provides: "No capitation, or other direct tax shall be laid, unless in proportion to the census or enumeration hereinbefore directed to be taken."

The Seventeenth Amendment provides: "The Congress shall have power to lay and collect taxes on incomes, from whatever sources derived, without apportionment among the several States, and without regard to any census or enumeration."

[32] 44 Supreme Court Reporter, 444.

[33] 232 U. S. 299.

CHAPTER XXV

CLOSELY connected with the sovereignty of the State are the matters of the amenability of the State itself or of its chief executive to judicial process, and the circumstances under which subordinate officers or private individuals may plead, in justification of otherwise illegal acts—tortious or contractual—executive authorization by the State. The first of these questions we shall consider under the title "The Suability of the Sovereign"; the second under the rubric "Acts of State."

As regards the suability of the Sovereign the distinction between the State, as the sovereign political person or entity, and its Government is to be kept steadily in mind, as is also the distinction between the chief executive of the State, often termed its "sovereign," and the State itself.

Non-Suability of the Chief Executive of the State. Historically, the conception of Sovereignty first attached itself to the ruling monarch rather than to the State, and it was not until the rise of modern republican governments with popularly elected chief executives that publicists began to draw a clear line of distinction between the status and powers of the ruler and those of the State he represented. Indeed, at the present time, according to the forms and phraseology of English law, sovereignty inheres in the King; he is the fountain, the original repository of all legal justice; it is his will, acting through Parliament, that creates law; and it is personal allegiance to him that British citizenship connotes.

466

As is well known, English public law rests, historically, upon feudal law, and it early became a principle of that law that a lord could be sued only by his own peers. Consequently, when the head of a Kingdom obtained a status superior to that of all the other feudal lords, there were no peers who might sue him, and, with the rise of monarchical absolutism this deduction from feudal law, became reinforced by doctrines of divine or patrimonial right.[1]

Blackstone, in his *Commentaries*, states the established rule, together with its reasons,—a rule which has not been since changed,—as follows:

"Our King is equally sovereign and independent within these his dominions, as any emperor is in his empire, and owes no kind of subjection to any other potentate upon earth. Hence it is, that no suit or action can be brought against the King, even in civil matters, because no court can have jurisdiction over him. For all jurisdiction implies superiority of power: authority to try would be vain and idle, without any redress, and the sentence of a court would be contemptible, unless that court had power to command the execution of it; but who, says Finch, shall command the King? Hence it is likewise, that by law the person of the King is sacred, even though the measures pursued in his reign be completely tyrannical and arbitrary: for no jurisdiction upon earth has power to try him in a criminal way; much less to condemn him to punishment. If any foreign jurisdiction had this power, as was formerly claimed by the Pope, the independence of the Kingdom would be no more: and, if such a power were vested in any domestic tribunal, there would be an end of the constitution, by destroying the free agency of

[1] There is some authority for the statement that the Saxon Kings were suable, and that this rule continued until the time of Edward I.

one of the constituent parts of the sovereign legislative power."

As is well known, this doctrine that "the King can do no wrong," that is, no legal wrong, is, and for many years has been supplemented by the constitutional practice that the King can exercise his governing powers only through some adviser or public official who thereby assumes political responsibility for the advice he gives and personal responsibility, civil and criminal, for the act, which responsibility may be enforced in the ordinary courts, and he cannot justify an act, otherwise illegal, by pleading the command of the Crown. Furthermore, in matters not of tort, the citizen legally aggrieved by the act of his State is permitted, even though not as a matter of strict legal right, that is, *ex debito justitiæ,* to obtain relief, in most cases, by petition of right or *monstrans de droit.*

Whether or not the Chief Executive of a popular or representative government has an immunity from judicial control with respect to his personal acts has not been certainly determined in the United States, but it appears to be reasonably certain that this is the case. Of course, in his case, such an immunity cannot be rested upon the premise that he has a divine or historical or patrimonial right of absolute rulership, nor upon any basis of feudal theory; rather, the doctrine, so far as it has been asserted, has been upon grounds of practical expediency or of necessity. This is shown by the reasoning of Chief Justice Chase in an opinion rendered in the case of *Mississippi v. Johnson,*[2] in which a motion for leave to file a bill of injunction had been sought by the State of Mississippi to restrain President Johnson from executing in the State certain acts of Congress asserted to be unconstitutional in character. The Chief Justice said: "The Congress

[2] 4 Wallace 475.

is the legislative department of the Government; the
President is the Executive Department. Neither can
be restrained in its action by the Judicial Department;
though the acts of both, when performed, are, in proper
cases, subject to its cognizance. The impropriety of such
interference will be clearly seen upon consideration of its
possible consequences. Suppose the bill filed and the
injunction prayed for allowed. If the President refuse
obedience, it is needless to observe that the court is without power to enforce its process. If, on the other hand,
the President complies with the order of the court and
refuses to execute the Acts of Congress, is it not clear
that a collision may occur between the Executive and
Legislative Departments of the Government? May
not the House of Representatives impeach the President for such refusal? And, in that case, could this
court interfere in behalf of the President, thus endan-
gered by compliance with its mandate, and restrain by
injunction the Senate of the United States from sitting
as a court of impeachment? Would not the strange
spectacle be offered to the world wonder of an attempt
by this court to arrest proceedings in that court?
These questions answer themselves. . . . We are fully
satisfied that this court has no jurisdiction of a bill
to enjoin the President in the performance of his
official duties; and that no such bill ought to be received by us.

"It has been suggested that the bill contains a prayer
that, if the relief sought cannot be had against Andrew
Johnson, as President, it may be granted against Andrew
Johnson as a citizen of Tennessee. But it is plain that
relief as against the execution of an Act of Congress by
Andrew Johnson is relief against its execution by the
President. A bill praying an injunction against the ex-
ecution of an Act of Congress by the incumbent of the

presidential office cannot be received, whether it describes him as President or as a citizen of a State."

In the trial of Aaron Burr for treason Chief Justice Marshall, who presided, is reported to have said: "I suppose it will not be alleged in this case that the President ought to be considered as having offered a contempt to the court in consequence of his not having attended, notwithstanding the subpoena was awarded agreeably to the demand of the defendant. The court would indeed not be asked to proceed as in the case of an ordinary individual." And again, in the same case, Marshall said: "In no case of this kind would the court be required to proceed against the President as against an ordinary individual. The objections to such a course are so strong and obvious that all must acknowledge them." [3]

---

[3] This immunity from judicial control thus predicated of the President has been ascribed in some of the States of the American Union to their respective Governors. In other States it has been denied. As to compelling the Governor by mandamus to perform a purely ministerial act the State courts are in conflict. See 6 L. R. A. n. s. 750, and 32 L. R. A. n. s. 355. And the same is true as to enjoining action upon his part. Cf. Burdick, *Law of the American Constitution*, p. 127, note 3.

Goodnow in his *Principles of the Administrative Law of the United States* (p. 108), says: "What has been said with regard to the remedies against the action of the President may be repeated with regard to the remedies against the action of the Governor. The Governor is held, for example, not to be subject to the process of the courts, but he may be personally liable after the expiration of his term of office for acts done in office. (*Druecker v. Salomon*, 21 Wis. 621.) The State Courts also are almost as careful not to come into personal conflict with the Governors as the United States courts are not to come into personal conflict with the President. The better rule is that they will not attempt to exercise a control over him personally. (*People v. Morton*, 156 N. Y. 136; *Darrett Petitioner*, 32 Maine 508.) The only exception to this rule is in the case of the *quo warranto*. There are several cases where the quo warranto has been issued to the Governor. (*Atty.-Gen. v. Barstow*, 4 Wis. 567; *Morris v. Bulkley*, 61 Conn. 287.) The courts have, however, very little hesitation about declaring an act of the Governor, in which it would appear that he exercises considerable discretion, null and void. (*People v. Curtis*, 50 N. Y. 321; *People v. Brady*, 56 N. Y. 182; *Dullam v. Wilson*, 53 Mich. 392; *People v. Platt*, 50 Hun. 454.) The courts will not, however, interfere with acts of the Governor which they regard as political in character."

That actions against the President personally for tort or crime, while he is in office, will not lie cannot be said to be certainly established; but at any rate, no such case is to be found in the American reports.[4]

However, the principle is well established that no public official or private individual can justify an act upon his part by a command of the President, or of the Governor of a State, which the President or Governor, by existing constitutional or statute law has not the authority to give. Thus in *Little v. Barreme*,[5] the United States Supreme Court, speaking through Chief Justice Marshall, held that a commander of an American ship of war, in obeying directions of the President acted at his peril, and was personally responsible for the consequences of his act, if the President was not legally authorized to issue the instructions.

Marshall said: "I confess the first bias of my mind was very strong in favor of the opinion that though the instructions of the executive could not give a right, they might excuse from damages. I was much inclined to think that a distinction ought to be taken between acts of civil and those of military officers; and between proceedings within the body of the country and those on the high seas. That implicit obedience which military men usually pay to the orders of their superiors,[6] which indeed is indispensably necessary to every military system, appeared to me strongly to imply the principle that those orders, if not to perform a prohibited act, ought to justify the person whose general duty it is to obey them, and who is placed by the laws of his country in a situation which in general requires that he should obey

[4] Mechem, *Law of Public Officers*, p. 395. See also Cooley *On Torts*, 1st ed., p. 377.

[5] 2 Cr. 170.

[6] The United States Constitution provides that the President of the United States shall be the Commander-in-Chief of the army and navy. Art. II, sec. 2.

them. . . . But I have been convinced that I was mistaken, and I have receded from this first opinion. I acquiesce in that of my brethren, which is, that the instructions cannot change the nature of the transaction, or legalize an act which, without those instructions, would have been a plain trespass."

Again, in *United States v. Lee*,[7] in which was sustained an action of trespass against certain military officers of the United States in possession of the Arlington estate, formerly belonging to Robert E. Lee, and claimed by the Federal Government as a result of certain confiscation proceedings, the court said: "This right [of the heirs of Lee to possession] being clearly established we are told that the court can proceed no further, because it appears that certain military officers, acting under orders of the President, have seized this estate, and converted one part of it into a military fort and another into a cemetery. It is not pretended, as the case now stands, that the President had any lawful authority to do this, nor that the legislative body could give him any such authority, except upon payment of just compensation. The defense stands here solely upon the absolute immunity from judicial inquiry of everyone who asserts authority from the executive branch of the Government, however clear it may be made that the executive possessed no such power. . . . No man in this country is so high that he is above the law. No officer of the law may set that law at defiance, with impunity. All the officers of the Government, from the highest to the lowest, are creatures of the law and are bound to obey it."

It scarcely need be said, however, that, in determining the legal validity of orders given by the President, the courts will not attempt to control the political or other discretionary powers that are constitutionally vested in

[7] 106 U. S. 196.

him. This is illustrated by the case of *Durand v Hollins*,[8] which was an action of trespass against an officer of the United States Navy for destroying by bombardment from a naval vessel certain property at Greytown in Nicaragua. In defense, the defendant urged that he was an officer of the United States Navy and acted under orders of the President of the United States and the Secretary of the Navy. Upon demurrer, the court, in the course of its opinion, said: "The principal ground of objection to the pleas . . . is that neither the President nor the Secretary of the Navy had authority to give the orders relied on to the defendant, and hence that they afford no ground of justification. . . . The interposition of the President abroad, for the protection of the citizen, must necessarily rest in his discretion; and it is quite clear that, in all cases where a public act or order rests in executive discretion, neither he nor his authorized agent is personally civilly responsible for the consequences [quoting *Marbury v. Madison*, 1 Cr. 165]. . . . The question whether it was the duty of the President to interpose for the protection of the citizens at Greytown against an irresponsible marauding community that had established itself there, was a public political question, in which the Government, as well as the citizens whose interests were involved, was concerned, and which belonged to the Executive to detemine; and his decision is final and conclusive and justified the orders given through the Secretary of the Navy."

Actes de Gouvernement in French Law. In the present treatise the writer has not sought to extend his inquiries for illustrations of general principles of public law beyond the jurisprudential systems of Great Britain and the United States. It is, however, worth while to make at least a reference to certain respects in which the French

[8] 4 Blatch. 451 (1860).

doctrine as to the suability of State functionaries is different from that of American and English law.[9]

First of all it is to be observed that the French law does not hold personally responsible, in civil damages, officials, who, while acting as officials, nevertheless act without legal right. The State, in such a case, may be held liable, but not the individual. Mr. Walton points out that this doctrine is based upon a juristic theory more subtile than that of the English doctrine of principal and agent or master and servant. "The State is not a master who gives instructions to his servants. It is a moral [corporate] person which, like other moral [corporate] persons, acts by its 'organes'. . . . When a physical person employs a servant there are two persons and two wills to be considered. But when the organs of a moral person act for it, and act within the range of the operations prescribed by law for the moral person, we may disregard altogether the personality of these organs. The will which they manifest is not their will, it is the will of the moral person."

When a French functionary is not acting officially he is personally responsible, civilly and criminally, for his acts, but it is often a difficult matter for the courts to determine what is, and what is not a *fait personnel*.

The French judicial tribunals exercise the right to refuse to impose penalties upon individuals for violations of administrative ordinances which are illegal because beyond the legal competence of the authorities issuing

[9] The observations which follow are largely based upon two excellent articles, by J. W. Garner, entitled "Judicial Control of Administrative and Legislative Acts in France," published in *The American Political Science Review*, November, 1915 (vol. IX, p. 637), and "French Administrative Law" in the *Yale Law Journal*, April, 1924; and an article by F. P. Walton, entitled "The French Administrative Courts and the Modern French Law as to the Responsibility of the State for the Faults of its Officials: A Comparison with the Common Law," which appeared in the *Illinois Law Review*, October-November, 1918. See also F. J. Goodnow, *Comparative Administrative Law*, vol. II, pp. 149-177.

them. The Council of State (*Conseil d'État*) also exercises the right to annul administrative orders if deemed *ultra vires*. Until recently, however, the Council of State made a distinction between simple ordinances emanating from the President, which did not, and "ordinances of public administration" (*règlements d'administration publique*) which did have to be submitted to the Council for its advice before promulgation. Only the first of these classes of ordinances, it held, might be annulled for excess of power. In 1907, however, this distinction was abandoned by the Council of State, and both classes of ordinance held subject to annulment if in excess of power. "The far-reaching effect of the decision can only be fully appreciated," says Garner, "when we remember that a very considerable and important part of French legislation today is being enacted not by the legislature but by the President in the form of ordinances of public administration, issued in pursuance of legislative delegation. In recent years there has been an increasing tendency on the part of the legislature to abdicate its functions and to delegate its powers of legislation to the executive. Almost every important act of parliament today concludes with the familiar clause: 'An ordinance of public administration shall determine the measures proper for assuring the execution of the present law.'"

The French courts still refuse to question the validity of Acts of Parliament upon the ground of their incompatibility with the provisions of the "Constitutional Laws," or for any other reason. And, as regards executive acts, there are still several classes which wholly escape from judicial control. Thus, as might be expected, and as is generally true in all constitutional States, the courts do not attempt to control such acts of the President as the summoning and closing of sessions of Parliament, the dissolution of the Chamber of Deputies (with the approval of the Senate), and his acts in respect to the conduct of foreign relations. Also, as yet, the Council has not claimed the right to annul ordinances of the President with regard to the colonies, though, as Garner points out, there is now, since the decision in 1907, no logical reason why it should not do so.

There still remains, however, immune from judicial control the class of acts termed by French publicists *Actes de Gouvernement*, which, in a general way, correspond to what in the United States are known as "Political Acts," but which, by some writers at least, include acts which become such by reason of the urgent public need which causes their commission, and which, therefore, would, according to American law, demand justification either under the "war powers" of the Government, or under what is known as the "Police Power" of the State, but which would not give them that immunity from judicial control which "Political Acts" enjoy.

As regards the definition of *Actes de Gouvernement* different writers have expressed different views. As quoted by Garner, Tessier says: "To *govern* is to oversee the functioning of the public authorities, to assure the execution of the laws, to carry on relations with foreign Powers; to *administer* is to assume the daily application of the laws and to watch over the relations of the citizens with the public authorities and the relations between the different administrative authorities." [10] Other writers, however, have defined the class so broadly as to make it possible to exclude from judicial control almost any abuse of official authority, and, specifically, governmental acts for protection against invasion, epidemics, floods, riots, insurrections, etc. "The whole theory," says Garner, "is an arbitrary one; it is hardly consistent with the liberal and enlightened jurisprudence of the Council of

[10] *La Résponsabilité de la Puissance Publique,* p. 42.

State and is condemned by some of the most distinguished jurists of France." This may be true as regards those acts which are sought to be removed from judicial control because of the conceived urgency of the public need for them, but it is not true of those acts which are "political" in the American sense of the word. These, it would seem, are by their very nature, and irrespective of the special circumstances under which they may happen to be exercised, such as to justify the courts in refusing to subject them to judicial control.[11]

Actes de Gestion (Fisc) in French Law. In French law, and, indeed, generally, in Continental law, a distinction is drawn between the acts of the State with reference to matters essentially political or public in character, and those in which the State appears as the owner of property, or the conductor of business enterprises. When acting in this latter capacity, the acts of the State are known in French law as *Actes de Gestion,* and these in turn are divided into two classes, acts of public *Gestion* and acts of private *Gestion*. As to both classes the State is held responsible in tort or contract, for unlawful acts, in the former class by means of administrative litigation; in the latter class in the ordinary courts. Acts of public *Gestion* relate to the operation by the State of public works. Acts of private *Gestion* are those that grow out of the state ownership or management of property or business enterprises of a character or in a manner similar to that of property or enterprises in the hands of private individuals.

In Germany these commercial or proprietary interests of the State are grouped under the term Fisc or Fiskus, a term inherited from the Roman Law. "In Germany," says Borchard, "the activity of the Fiskus, for which

[11] Of course the courts properly assert the right to determine for themselves whether or not a particular act is "political" in character.

liability is admitted in principle, includes what the French designate as acts of *Gestion,* both public and private. The German State, or, strictly speaking, its Treasury, is liable as a Fiskus, in its character as the owner of real property, of public works, domains, forests, roads, and provision magazines; when it emits loans or derives money from various sources of revenue, notably commerce in tobacco and salt, or establishes a lottery, operates a railroad or telegraph service (though here the officer rather than the State is made liable), or when through its officers it enters into contracts or other acts necessary to the administration or development of these various undertakings. In Germany, Austria and Switzerland the private law of obligations, including contractual and non-contractual liability, is applied to the State to a much greater extent than in France, although, as a matter of fact, while the French administrative courts firmly deny the applicability of the principles of the Civil Code, the doctrines of liability of private law are nevertheless generally applied." [12]

Suability of the State in Domestic Courts. From the question as to the suability of the Chief Executive or titular sovereign of a State we turn now to the amenability to judicial process of the sovereign State itself. Here, in Anglo-American law, we find no dispute as to the doctrine. Questions have often arisen, in specific instances, as to whether or not the judicial proceeding or writ is, in substance, against the State or personally against its officials,[13] but the former having been deter-

---

[12] *The Diplomatic Protection of Citizens Abroad,* p. 137. Cf. Sections 31 and 89 of the German Civil Code. See Borchard, *passim* for the principles of State liability recognized in other European States.

[13] See especially the study of Singewald, *The Doctrine of the Non-Suability of the State in the United States* (Johns Hopkins Univ. Studies in Historical and Political Science, vol. XXVIII, No. 3, 1910); and Willoughby, *The Constitutional Law of the United States,* vol. II, chap. LIV.

mined to be the case, American and English courts, without exception or hesitation, repudiate jurisdiction, unless the State has expressly or implicitly consented to be sued. Questions also arise as to whether certain bodies-politic, such as the member States of the American Union, or their municipal corporations, or the dependencies of a sovereign State, such, for example, as the Colonies and Dominions of Great Britain, the Indian Empire, or the Native States of India, or the so-called protectorates of international law, have a status such as to bring them within the operation of the doctrine of the non-suability of bodies-politic.[13a]

The carrying over of the doctrine of the non-suability of the ruling monarch or titular sovereign of a State to the State itself was effected without difficulty when the proposition was accepted that sovereignty is not an inherent personal or patrimonial right of the monarch. At first it was sought to locate sovereignty in the citizen body viewed as an organized unit. Later, however, the now prevailing conception was adopted which ascribes

[13a] As to the French doctrine of the suability of the State, Garner says: "Originally the doctrine of the non-liability of the State was the rule in France, but it has long since been abandoned, at least as far as its responsibility for the acts of administrative agents is concerned. The new principle of State responsibility was the result, in part, of the growth of the democratic conception that the State is a moral person possessing duties as well as rights; and, in part, of the enormous expansion of the activities of the State by which it came to be the largest employer of labor. . . . In response to this change of sentiment there has been developed in France an elaborate body of jurisprudence, mainly the work of the Council of State and the Tribunal of Conflicts, which definitely fixes the responsibility of the State and which assures to the injured individual reparation such as is entirely unknown in Anglo-Saxon countries. The basic principles of this jurisprudence is that the State is liable to the individual not only in contract but also in tort where the tortious act of the agent is not a purely personal act; that is, the State is liable where the injury is due to a fault of service (*faute de service*). The fault may be due to error, an omission, an act of negligence or even want of judgment on the part of the agent. On the other hand, if the injury is done by the agent in his personal and unofficial capacity, that is, if it results from a *fait personnel*, he and not the State is liable." *Yale Law Journal*, April, 1924, p. 616.

this supreme legal status to the State abstractly viewed as a political person. In other words, the State person, as regards the doctrine under consideration, takes the place occupied by the King or Emperor. Thus we find the English Court of Appeals in Chancery, in the case of *United States of America v. Wagner* [14] saying:

"It is contended that this foreign State, being a republic, cannot sue in its own name, and must either associate with it as plaintiff, or proceed in the name of the President of the Republic, or some other officer of state . . . . It was contended, then, that when a monarch sues in our courts, he sues as the representative of the State of which he is the sovereign; that the property claimed is looked upon as the property of the people or State and that he is permitted to sue, not as for his own property, but as the head of the executive government of the State to which the property belongs: and it was contended, in like manner, that when the property belongs to a republic, the head of the executive, or in other words the President, ought to sue for it. This argument, in my opinion, is founded on a fallacy. The sovereign, in a monarchical form of government, may, as between himself and his subjects, be a trustee for the latter, more or less limited in his powers over the property which he seeks to recover. But in the courts of Her Majesty, as in diplomatic intercourse with the Government of Her Majesty, it is the sovereign, and not the State, or the subjects of the sovereign, that is recognized. From him, and as representing him individually, and not his State or Kingdom, is an ambassador received. In him individually, and not in a representative capacity is the public property assumed by all other States, and by the courts of other States, to be vested. In a republic, on the other hand, the sovereign power, and with it the public property, is

[14] 1867, L. R. 2 Ch. App. 582.

held to remain and to reside in the State itself, and not in any officer of the State. It is from the State that an ambassador is accredited, and it is with the State that the diplomatic intercourse is conducted."

Grounds Upon Which the Doctrine of Non-Suability is Rested. It is often the case in law that a doctrine, originally deduced from certain premises, comes to be defended upon wholly different grounds. Thus we find the doctrine of the non-suability of the sovereign State supported by arguments, practical or dogmatic in character, which have little reference to its actual historical origin.

In the early American case of *Briggs v. Lightboats*,[15] Justice Gray made an extended inquiry into the history of the doctrine of the non-suability of the sovereign as developed in English and American law, but supplemented its historical basis by the following dictum as to its practical utility: "It would be inconsistent with the very idea of supreme executive power, and would endanger the performance of the public duties of the sovereign, to subject him to repeated suits as a matter of right, at the will of any citizen, and to submit to the judicial tribunals the control and disposition of his public property, his instruments and means of carrying on his government in war and peace, and the money in his treasury."

In the case of *United States v. Lee*,[16] which has been earlier referred to, Justice Miller declared of this doctrine: "It seems most probable that it has been adopted in our courts as a part of the general doctrine of publicists that the supreme power in every State, wherever it may reside, shall not be compelled, by process of courts of its own creation, to defend itself in those courts."

In a comparatively recent case [17] in the same court we

[15] 11 Allen 157.
[16] 106 U. S. 196.
[17] *Kawananakoa v. Polyblank*, 205 U. S. 349.

find Justice Holmes saying: "A sovereign is exempt from suit, not because of any formal conception or obsolete theory, but on the logical and practical ground that there can be no legal right as against the authority that makes the law on which the right depends." [18]

This proposition that a sovereign State cannot logically be conceived of as itself the "subject" of legal rights and duties, that is, as the entity in which they inhere, it will be remembered, was discussed in Chapter VIII. It will also be remembered that this is a proposition that is relevant only in national or municipal jurisprudence. In the field of International Law it is pre-eminently the States that are envisaged as the subjects as well as the objects of such rights and obligations as international jurisprudence is able to create or impose.

Suability of Sovereigns or of Sovereign States in Foreign Courts. Thus far we have been speaking of the non-suability of sovereign bodies-politic without their consent in their own courts. As a matter of universally observed international comity, municipal courts do not assert jurisdiction over foreign States or their chief executives.

A leading case as to sovereign rulers is *Da Haber v. Queen of Portugal*,[19] decided in 1851, in which the court, by Lord Chief Justice Campbell, said: "It is quite certain, upon general principles, and upon the authority of the case of *Duke of Brunswick v. King of Hanover*, recently decided in the House of Lords, that an action cannot be maintained in any English court against a foreign potentate, for anything done or omitted to be done by him in his public capacity as representative of the nation

[18] In this case the court held that the Territory of Hawaii partook sufficiently of the nature of a sovereign State, to render it immune from suit without its consent. It would seem, however, that a better ground for this holding would have been that the Territory, as to the matter in dispute, stood in the stead of the sovereign United States.

[19] 17 Q. B. 196.

of which he is the head; and that no English court has
jurisdiction to entertain any complaints against him in
that capacity. Redress for such complaints affecting a
British subject is only to be obtained by the laws and tribunals of the country which the sovereign rules, or by the
representations, remonstrances or acts of the British Government. To cite a foreign potentate in a municipal
court, for any complaint against him in his foreign capacity, is contrary to the law of nations, and an insult which
he is entitled to resent."

It will be observed that, in the quoted statement, the
court refers to suits based upon acts of a foreign sovereign in his public or official character. The rule, is, however, the same as to proceedings based upon the sovereign's private acts, and also as to proceedings against his
property.

In the *Parlement Belge*,[20] decided in 1878, the British
Court of Appeals declined jurisdiction in an action *in rem*
against a vessel which, it appeared, though operated, to
an extent at least, commercially, was the property of the
King of Belgium. The court said: "It is admitted that
neither the sovereign of Great Britain nor any friendly
sovereign can be adversely personally impleaded in any
court of this country. It is admitted that no armed ship
of war of the sovereign of Great Britain, or of a foreign
sovereign can be seized by any process whatever, exercised for any purpose by any court of this country. . . .
Having carefully considered the case of the *Charkieh*,[21]

[20] L. R. 5 Prov. Div. 197.
[21] L. R. 4 Adm. & Eccl. 59. This case was an action against the
ship *Charkieh* for damages arising out of a collision occurring in the
river Thames. In bar it was pleaded that the ship was the property
of Ismail Pasha, Khedive of Egypt. The court held that Egypt, at
that time, had not the sovereign or international status that would
entitle its Khedive to the immunity which was claimed. In fact the
court had received from the British Foreign Office the statement
"that the Khedive has not been and is not now recognized by Her
Majesty as reigning sovereign of the State of Egypt."

we are of opinion that the proposition deduced from the
earlier cases in an earlier part of this judgment is the correct exposition of the law of nations, viz., that as a consequence of the absolute independence of every sovereign
authority and of the international comity which induces
every sovereign State to respect the independence of
every other sovereign State, each and every one declines
to exercise by means of any of its courts any of its territorial jurisdiction over the person of any sovereign or
ambassador of any other State, or over the public property of any State which is destined to its public use, or
over the property of any ambassador, though such sovereign ambassador or property be within its territory, and
therefore, but for such common agreement, subject to its
jurisdiction."

This same doctrine was recognized by the United
States Supreme Court in the early case of *The Exchange*,[22] and has never since been questioned. Another
case in which the whole doctrine was exhaustively discussed was that of *Briggs v. Lightboats*,[23] earlier referred to.

Still another carefully considered American case is
that of *Mason v. Intercolonial Railway of Canada*,[24] decided in 1908. A fairly modern English case is that of
Mighell v. Sultan of Johore,[25] decided in 1893.

It has been seen that in the *Parlement Belge* the court
refused to entertain proceedings *in rem* against a vessel
owned by a foreign sovereign but devoted in part to ordinary commercial purposes. As to just how far the immunity from attachment or other judicial process will be applied in the case of property, especially ships, owned by a
State or its sovereign, and wholly devoted to commercial

[22] 7 Cranch 116.
[23] 11 Allen (Mass.) 157.
[24] 197 Mass. 349.
[25] L. R. (1849) 1 Q. B. 149.

purposes, the British and American courts are not in full agreement, nor can either of them be said to have established a hard and fast doctrine.

In *The Maipo* [26] it was held that a naval transport, owned by a foreign government and in its possession, through a naval captain and crew, although chartered to a private individual for commercial purposes, was not subject to seizure under a process of an admiralty court of the United States. The *Parlement Belge* was the chief authority relied upon in determining the general principle of public law. In a second case dealing with the same vessel,[27] in which the action was advanced by a stranger and based upon a tort, Justice Hough said: "Why was a war vessel exempt from seizure? Not because it was a war vessel, but because it was a part of the exercise or manifestation of sovereign power. Why is any other vessel exempt? Why may any other piece of property be exempt? For the same reason, just as the sovereign himself is exempt. . . . If the Republic of Chile considers it a governmental function to go into the carrying trade, as would appear to be the case here, that is the business of the Republic of Chile; and if we do not approve of it, if we do not like it, if we do not wish any longer to accord that respect to the property so engaged, which has hitherto been accorded to government property, then we must say so through diplomatic channels, and not through the judiciary."

This general subject has been recently examined in an able article by Mr. Charles H. Weston,[28] who summarizes as follows the results reached by him from an examination of the cases:

"In spite of some early criticism the law today gives

[26] 252 Fed. Rep. 627.
[27] *The Maipo,* 259 Fed. Rep. 367.
[28] "Actions against the Property of Sovereigns," *Harvard Law Review,* vol. XXXII (1918-1818), p. 266.

immunity to the property of a sovereign which is used for public purposes; and the wide functions of govern- ment are recognized in interpreting what is a public pur- pose. The distinction which in theory should be made between cases involving the domestic, and cases involving a foreign, sovereign has been so consistently glossed over that it can scarcely be said to exist as a living principle of law. The English courts have protected every inter- est which a sovereign may have in property. The Amer- ican courts have not as yet given immunity to private property employed by a sovereign. There is, further, in our [American] cases a limitation, the extent of which has not been settled, dependent upon the possession of the sovereign. The trend of recent decision, however, is probably toward a full recognition of the varied interests of government in property.

"With a large part of the world's shipping now owned or requisitioned by sovereign nations, many maritime claims cannot be liquidated except through the favor of government, through recourse to foreign courts, or through diplomatic exchanges. This situation is unsatis- factory and will probably require regulation by treaty." [29]

Sovereign States as Plaintiffs. It is a generally accepted

[29] For a careful discussion of recent English and American cases dealing with the immunity from judicial process of vessels and cargoes belonging to States, see E. T. Fell's *Recent Problems in Admiralty Jurisdiction* (Johns Hopkins Univ. Studies in Historical and Political Science, vol. XL, No. 3, 1922), chap. II, entitled "Jurisdictional Im- munity of Public Vessels and Goods." See also the article, "Admiralty Claims against the Government," by G. D. F. Lord in the *Columbia Law Review,* December, 1919. A. D. McNair in his article "Judicial Recognition of States and Governments, and Immunity of Public Ships" (*The British Year Book of International Law,* 1921-1922, p. 74), sums up the English doctrine as follows: "Ships which are not the property of a foreign State, but are chartered or requisitioned by it, or otherwise in its occupation, may not be arrested by process of the Admiralty Court while subject to such charter party, requisition or other means of occupation; but proceedings *in personam* against the owner of the ship, and (apart from arrest) proceedings *in rem* are unaffected, and a maritime lien or a judgment *in rem* may be enforced as soon as the occupation of the foreign State comes to an end."

doctrine that the immunity of a State or its sovereign ruler from suit, without its or his consent, whether in domestic or foreign courts, does not prevent the State or its ruler from instituting suits as a plaintiff and obtaining appropriate relief as against private individuals.

By the United States Constitution,[30] it is expressly provided that the Supreme Court shall have original jurisdiction to entertain "controversies to which the United States shall be a party; to controversies between two or more States [of the American Union]; between a State [of the Union] and citizens of another State [of the Union] . . . and between a State, or the citizens thereof, and foreign States." Jurisdiction is not here given in specific terms to entertain suits brought by the United States against one of the States of the Union, but the Supreme Court has held that this was intended to be given.[31] And, in a number of cases, both the State and Federal Courts have permitted foreign States to sue upon condition that they would hold themselves subject to any counterclaims or setoffs that might be advanced by their respective defendants. This also has been the practice of the British courts.[32]

Parens Patriæ. In all constitutionally organized States the State is permitted to sue in the courts not only with reference to its own proprietary or contractual interests, but also in behalf of the general interests of its citizen body. When appearing as plaintiff in the latter capacity

---

[30] Article III, sec. 2.
[31] *United States v. Texas,* 143 U. S. 621.
[32] The following citations are taken from a note by Professor Quincy Wright in the *American Journal of International Law,* vol. XVII, p. 742; *King of Spain v. Oliver,* 1 Pet. C. C. 217; *King of Prussia v. Kupper,* 22 Mo. 550; *Republic of Mexico v. Arrangoiz,* 11 How. Pract. 1, N. Y.; *Republic of Honduras,* 112 N. Y. 310; *State of Yucatan v. Argumedo,* 157 N. Y. Supp. 219; *Kingdom of Roumania v. Guaranty Trust Co.,* 250 Fed. 341, 344; *Kingdom of Norway v. Federal Sugar Refining Co. (The Gloria),* 286 Fed. 188; *King of Spain v. Machado,* 4 Russ. 560; *Emperor of Austria v. Day and Kossuth,* 3 De Gex, F. & J. 217; *United States of Am. v. Wagner,* L. R. 1867, 2 Ch. App. 582.

it is known as *Parens Patriæ*. This jurisprudential doctrine is stated in the *Cyclopedia of Law and Procedure* as follows: [33]

"A State, like any other party, cannot maintain a suit unless it appears that it has such an interest in the subject-matter thereof as to authorize the bringing of the suit by it. In this connection, however, a distinction should be noted between actions by the people or by the State in a sovereign capacity, and suits founded on some pecuniary interest or proprietary right. In its sovereign capacity the State, by its proper law officers and by appropriate proceedings, may establish and enforce the execution of trusts by public corporations, prevent the misappropriation or misapplication of public funds or property, and the abuse of power by public officers, and in general protect the interests of the people at large in matters in which they cannot act for themselves; and a suit by the State in its sovereign capacity, as the guardian of the rights of the people, may be maintained without any special injury to the State, and where a State claims property as sovereign, its bare assertion of title and averment thereof in general terms is sufficient; but suits by the State as an ordinary proprietor for the recovery or protection of money or property are governed by the ordinary rules applicable to suits between individuals, and cannot be maintained without proper averment and proof of title or ownership."

A reference to, and quotation from, two or three American cases will sufficiently illustrate the right of the State to sue as *Parens Patriæ*.

In *Missouri v. Illinois* [34] it was held by the United States Supreme Court that one State of the Union might properly sue to restrain another State from creating a

[33] Vol. XXXVI, p. 908, *sub. nom.* "States."
[34] 180 U. S. 208.

nuisance dangerous to the health of the inhabitants of the plaintiff State. In *Kansas v. Colorado* [35] it was held by the same court that, similarly, one State of the Union might sue to restrain another State from so diverting the waters of a river flowing through both States, as to deprive the inhabitants of the plaintiff State from an adequate supply of the waters in question.

In these cases the defendants were themselves States. They were held suable under the special provision of the United States Constitution which extends the federal judicial power over controversies between States. In the earlier case the court said:

It is true that no question of boundary is involved, nor of direct property rights belonging to the complainant State, but it must surely be conceded that if the health and comfort of the inhabitants of a State are threatened, the State is the proper party to represent and defend them. If Missouri were an independent and sovereign State, all must admit that she could seek a remedy by negotiation, and, that failing, by force. Diplomatic powers and the right to make war having been surrendered to the General Government, it was to be expected that upon the latter would be devolved the duty of providing a remedy, and that remedy, we think, is found in the constitutional provisions we are considering.

In *Oregon v. Metschan* [36] the Supreme Court of Oregon in sustaining a suit against the State Treasurer to prevent a misapplication of public funds, said:

This is a suit by the State in its sovereign capacity as the guardian of the rights of the people, instituted by its executive law officer, and can, in our opinion be maintained without showing any special injury to the State. . . . At common law the Attorney General of England could, by information in the name of the Crown, call upon the courts of justice to prevent the misapplication of funds or property raised or held for public use, and, in the absence of statutory regulation, the District Attorney in this State is vested with like powers. . . . Indeed the right of the State, through its proper

[35] 185 U. S. 125.
[36] 41 L. R. A., 692.

officer, to maintain such a proceeding, would seem to be one of the necessary incidents of sovereignty. Without it the rights of the citizen cannot be protected or enforced in cases where he is unable to act for himself. In a suit by an individual he is required to show some special injury to himself; and when, as in this case, the wrong complained of is public in character, affecting no one citizen more than another, it is impossible for him to do so, and for that reason he is without remedy, although he may be injured in common with the other members of the community.

Acts of State. It has been earlier pointed out that there are a variety of acts performed by a government which American courts termed "political", the committing of which will not be controlled by the courts and for the consequences of which, even when affecting private interests, these courts will not hold legally responsible those who command or perform them.[37] This immunity of political acts from judicial control results, in fact, from the general principle that courts will not attempt to control the exercise by legislative or executive organs or officials of discretionary powers vested in them by existing constitutional or statute law. However, the courts always assume and exercise the right to determine, in specific instances, whether the acts in question are or are not within the political or discretionary official authority that has been granted.

In England the term "Act of State" would not appear to have an exact or technical meaning. It is, in other words, not a term of "art," and is given different meanings by different writers.[38] It is generally used to include the matters which, in the United States, are termed "political." When employed in a more limited or special sense it indicates an act done with the authority

[37] Cf. Willoughby, *Constitutional Law of the United States*, vol. II, chap. LI.
[38] Cf. Halsbury's *The Laws of England*, vol. XXIII, p. 304.

of the Crown, outside British territory, and affecting aliens.[39]

As we have earlier had occasion to point out, it is of the essence of Anglo-American law that all public officials, with the possible exception of the titular sovereign or chief executive, should be held personally responsible by the ordinary or special administrative tribunals for their acts, official or private: that, in some cases they may be restrained from acts not warranted by their official powers; that, in other cases, affirmative action upon their part, in matters ministerial or non-discretionary in character may be compelled, and that, in all cases, they may be held responsible, criminally, or by way of civil damages, for acts in excess of their authority, or even for the arbitrary, malicious or otherwise wrongful use of their valid powers; and that, in all such cases, they cannot justify by appeal to orders given them by their political or administrative superiors, which those superiors did not have the legal right to give, or by appeal to statutes which the enacting legislature did not have the constitutional right to enact.

It would appear that, according to American jurisprudence this principle of official responsibility, and judicial

[39] Cobbett says: "The term 'Act of State' in English law strictly denotes a public act, or an act done by or under the authority of the Crown, outside the British territory, and affecting aliens" *Leading Cases on International Law*, 3d ed., vol. I, p. 18.

Stephen says: "I understand by an Act of State an act injurious to the person or property of some person who is not at the time of the act a subject of Her Majesty's authority, civil or military, and is either previously sanctioned or subsequently ratified by Her Majesty." *History of Criminal Law*, vol II, p. 61. A little further on (p. 64) Stephen says: "In order to avoid misconception it is necessary to observe that the doctrine as to Acts of State can apply only to acts which affect foreigners, and which are done by the orders or with the ratification of the sovereign. As between the sovereign and his subject there can be no such thing as an Act of State."

In *Johnstone v. Pedlar* (2 Ap. Cas. 262) the House of Lords in 1921 held that a friendly resident alien was in the same position as an ordinary subject and that, therefore, there could not be, as to him, an Act of State.

control, applies as well to acts by American public officials committed abroad and affecting aliens, and authorized by the political department of the American Government, as it does to officially sanctioned acts committed within American territory and not affecting aliens.[40]

The English doctrine of "Act of State" in its special sense would appear to be that an alien has no right to judicial relief in case he is injured by the act of a British official, ordered or approved by the British Government, if committed outside British territory, either upon the high seas or within the limits of a foreign State. The leading case upon this point is *Baron v. Denman*,[41] decided in 1840.

In that case, which was one of trespass against an alien and committed outside the British dominions, Justice

[40] It is, however, possible that an alien might not have an opportunity to bring an action against an American official, unless the alien could obtain entrance into the United States and thus furnish the American court with jurisdiction. Thus an alien illegally refused admission to the United States by an American official would not be able to bring the matter before the courts either for the purpose of securing admission or of obtaining damages against the official for his illegal act of exclusion, unless by statute he were given the right. It may be added that this is but an hypothetical case, for American statute law does provide means whereby aliens refused admission to the United States by administrative officials may have their right to enter determined, after a fair hearing, by the courts or by a superior administrative agency. It has been held that they are entitled, in this respect, to "due process of law," even though this may not mean a hearing in a court of law as distinguished from an administrative tribunal.
As regards English law upon this point we find the following declaration in *Musgrove v. Chun Teeong Toy* (L. R. Appeal Cases, 1891, p. 272) in which the Judicial Committee expressed what almost amounted to indignation that it should have been asked to pass upon certain very important imperial constitutional principles at the instance of an alien who had not, by reason of being within British territory, obtained a right to resort to the British courts. The Committee said: "No authority exists for the proposition that an alien has any such right. Circumstances may occur in which the refusal to permit an alien to land might be such an interference with international comity as would properly give rise to diplomatic remonstrance from the country of which he is a native, but it is quite another thing to assert that an alien excluded from any part of Her Majesty's dominions by the executive department there, can maintain an action in a British court."
[41] 2 Ex. Rep. 166.

Parke, charging the jury, said: "If the Crown ratifies an act, the character of the act becomes altered, for the ratification does not give the party injured the double option of bringing his action against the agent who committed the trespass or the principal who ratified it, but a remedy against the Crown only (such as it is), and actually exempts from all liability the person who commits the trespass."

In the much later case, *Musgrove v. Chun Teeong Toy,*[42] as we have already seen, the court held that an alien could not question in an English court the right of a British official to prevent his entrance into British territory.

W. Harrison Moore, in his volume *Act of State in English Law,* published in 1906, after a review of cases, says "the question whether the Crown has by the Constitution the power to carry out the executory provisions of a treaty of peace to the detriment of private rights is then an open one. The case resembles the interference and destruction to which private rights of property are subject by the actual operations of war. If this be in virtue of some prerogative of the Crown as lord of war which suspends and supersedes the ordinary law, it would be natural that the like permanent power should extend to the conditions on which peace is to be restored. If, on the other hand, it is no case of prerogative, but a mere power not confined to the Crown or to war, limited by the proved necessity of the case, there appears nothing to prevent the application of the ordinary doctrine of the law, that the Crown has no power without act of Parliament to confiscate and supersede existing rights in its dominions." [43]

[42] L. R. Appeal Cases, 1891, 272.
[43] *Op. cit.,* p. 91.

INDEX

Actes de gestion, 477
Actes de gouvernement, 473
Acts of State, 490 ff
Administrative unions of States, 186
Admission of States to family of nations, 308
Aerial jurisdiction, 351
Aliens, 356; rights of, 360
Allegiance. See Citizenship
American and German federations contrasted, 203
American Institute of International Law, declaration of, of rights of nations, 14
Annexation of territory, 331
Art of politics, 7
Association of States, 183
Austin, theory of, as to location of sovereignty, 116; definition of law, 129 ff; cited, 89; quoted, 76, 78, 109, 141, 146, 165, 196, 197
Aviation, 23

Belligerency, recognition of, 318
Belligerent status, 338
Bentham, cited, 156 n
Blackstone, quoted, 467
Bluntschli, quoted, 63, 106, 111 n; cited, 17
Bogert, cited, 352 n
Boghitchiwitch, cited, 326 n
Bonds, situs of, for taxation, 448 ff
Bornhak, cited, 326 n
Borchard, cited, 85, 363 n, 389, 478 n; quoted, 190, 384
Brie, views of, examined, 255, cited, 183
British Dominions, territorial jurisdiction of, 447
Brown, Jethro, cited, 77 n
Brownson, quoted, 169 n, 189
Bryce, quoted, 25, 180
Bundesstaat. See Federal State
Burgess, views of, criticized, 16, 55, 227; quoted, 269 n, 270

Calhoun, theories of, 255; quoted, 167
Carter, J. T., cited, 41 n
Castine, status of, 365
Church, the, as a person, 42
Citizenship, 69, 354 ff; in federal States, 205; double, 357
Citizen body, 68
Civil jurisdiction of acts committed abroad, 418 ff
Civil war, in United States of America, 252
Clan, political importance of, 153
Clark, quoted, 165
Cobbett, quoted, 296, 308, 325, 410 n; cited, 491
Cohen, quoted, 46
Comity, 431
Concept of State, 16
Confederations, juristic attributes of, 192 ff; status of, in international law, 316
Conflict of laws, 429 ff
Constitutions, 93
Constitutional law defined, 83 ff; limits governments, 84
Constitutional conventions in American law, 94 ff
Constitutional and juristic theory contrasted, 12
Conquered territory, status of, 375
Consent of the governed, 105
Cooley, quoted, 111n; cited, 86
Corporate person, 35
Corporations, taxation of, 449 n
Corpus Juris, quoted, 97
Courts and legislative power, 139
Crane, R. T., cited, 326, 354
Criminal jurisdiction of acts committed abroad, 409 ff
Custom and law, 136
Cutting case, 341, 413 ff

De facto and de jure governments, 178, 311, 370 ff, 377 ff, 384
De facto officers, 88

495

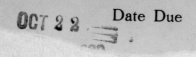